ASSOCIATION
P9-DTZ-989

Affairs of Honor

Affairs of Honor

National Politics in the New Republic

Joanne B. Freeman

Yale University Press New Haven and London

Published with assistance from the Annie Burr Lewis Fund and with the assistance of the Frederick W. Hilles Publication Fund of Yale University. Copyright ©2001 by Joanne B. Freeman. All rights reserved. This book may not be reproduced, in whole or in part, including illustrations, in any form (beyond that copying permitted by Sections 107 and 108 of the U.S. Copyright Law and except by reviewers for the public press), without written permission from the publishers.

Designed by Sonia Shannon and set in Galliard type by Achorn Graphic Services. Printed in the United States of America by R. R. Donnelley & Sons.

Library of Congress Cataloging-in-Publication Data

Freeman, Joanne B., 1962–
Affairs of honor : national politics in the New Republic / Joanne B. Freeman.
p. cm.
Includes bibliographical references and index.
ISBN 0-300-08877-9 (alk. paper)
1. United States—Politics and government—1789–1815. 2. Political culture—United States—History—18th century. 3. Politics and culture—United States—History—18th century. 4. United States—Social conditions—to 1865. 5. Elite (Social sciences)—United States—Political activity—History—18th century. 6. Honor—Political aspects—United States—History—18th century. I. Title.
E310.F85 2001
306.2′0973′09034—dc21 2001000915

A catalogue record for this book is available from the British Library.

The paper in this book meets the guidelines for permanence and durability of the Committee on Production Guidelines for Book Longevity of the Council on Library Resources.

10 9 8 7 6 5 4 3 2 1

To Mentor
From Mentee

Contents

Acknowledgments

I have been lucky enough to have a great deal of support from advisers, colleagues, and friends. First of all, I would like to thank "Mentor" Peter S. Onuf for his amazingly generous help over my years of graduate school and beyond. He guided me through a host of challenges, encouraged me to pursue the most improbable leads, introduced me into the scholarly community, spent many hours listening to me rant about dead white guys, offered invaluable insights that consistently sharpened my thinking, fed me meatloaf when times were bad, and, all in all, provided a model of mentorship and scholarship that I can only hope to live up to. To Mentor I shall be eternally grateful. In addition, Kristen Onuf and the entire Onuf clan made me feel like one of their own, a wonderful gift that was beyond the call of duty.

Other professors at the University of Virginia helped me invaluably in the development of the dissertation that led to this book. Stephen Innes, Joseph Kett, and Edward Ayers provided many hours of support and guidance, and Patricia Meyer Spacks's deep understanding of eighteenth-century British politics and culture profoundly shaped my thinking. By introducing me to the world of the Roman republic, Elizabeth Meyer enabled me to examine the American republic from an unusual and enlightening perspective. I owe a special debt of gratitude to J. E. Lendon; our weekly "honor teas" inspired some of my most provocative and original thinking about honor culture. Several graduate student colleagues also deserve thanks. Matthew Boesen, Andrew Burstein, Bruce Coffee, Bob Guffin, Kathy Jones, Albrecht Koschnik, Richard Samuelson, and Andrew Trees provided intellectual and emotional encouragement through many years of work. To Todd

Estes and Mark Smith, fellow members of the Fisher Ames Society and co-authors of "The Ames-iad," I owe an additional debt of gratitude for making me laugh.

Colleagues at Yale have been no less supportive. Several have been kind enough to read portions of the manuscript; Jennifer Baszile and Kariann Yokota, in particular, offered invaluable feedback, for which I thank them. Many others have offered encouragement, advice, and calming words at crucial moments. John Demos has been particularly enthusiastic about this project, for which I am deeply grateful. Nancy Godleski generously obtained some valuable primary materials for the Yale library, and just as generously supported me as a friend. Two Yale students have also been most helpful. Brian Neff checked footnotes and quotations (and was warped enough by my teaching to write a seminar paper on the Griswold-Lyon dispute); I thank him and look forward to seeing what he will accomplish in his promising future. The equally promising Luke Bronin was brave enough to read a draft of the epilogue, for which I thank him as well.

A number of outside scholars have also been extremely generous with their support, insight and scholarship. Lance Banning, Joseph Ellis, Richard John, Jan Lewis, Barbara Oberg, Paul Rahe, Herbert Sloan, Alan Taylor, Gordon Wood, and Bertram Wyatt-Brown represent the historical community at its finest. Michael McGiffert taught me invaluable lessons about the fine art of crafting an argument. Dickson Bruce, Robert Weir, and Chris Waldrep offered input on dueling and the honor ethic. Len Travers gave me the unexpected (and enlightening) chance to shoot a black-powder dueling pistol; his friend Victor Duphily gets special thanks for teaching me how to fire it.

Several friends have gone far above and beyond the call of duty. Meg Jacobs has supported me through many a writing crisis. Particular thanks go to Catherine Allgor and Jonathan Lipman, without whom I would never have survived my final year of writing; their friendship and love has enriched my life, and I thank them. My family—Allan, Barbara, Richard, and Marc Freeman—deserve special recognition for being endlessly receptive to my stories. The supportive Angelica Kaner deserves special recognition as well. Finally, for his moral support, intellectual stimulation, superb scholarship, and friendship, R. B. Bernstein has earned my eternal gratitude. Almost fifteen years ago, he ushered me into the world of history. He has been an adviser, a colleague, and a true friend ever since, reading endless drafts and offering invaluable criticism, for which I offer him my deepest and most abiding gratitude.

The fine scholars at a number of documentary editing projects and research centers have offered vital assistance. John Catanzariti at the Thomas Jefferson Papers offered invaluable insights into Jefferson's editorial alterations to his memoranda. Lucinda Stanton at Monticello was equally generous with her time and resources. Dorothy Twohig and the staff of the George Washington Papers gave me access to their holdings, and encouragement as well. John Stagg and the staff of the James Madison Papers helped me untangle some sticky questions. Ene Sirvet at the John Jay Papers not only offered assistance with my research but extended her hospitality during my research trips. Richard Ryerson and the folks at the Adams Family Papers not only opened their resources to me but, as important, fed me sugar and caffeine as well. Finally, the people at the First Federal Congress Project at George Washington University were kind enough to let me rummage through their files on several occasions. Chapter 1 would have been impossible to write without their generous help. Special thanks to Ken Bowling for feeding me large quantities of roast beef at lunch.

During my years of graduate study, a number of institutions provided financial and intellectual support. The International Center for Jefferson Studies, in league with the Thomas Jefferson Memorial Foundation, gave me a generous fellowship and an office just up the road from Monticello. More important, my ongoing conversations with Director Douglas Wilson not only were enjoyable, but they helped me work through some of the more challenging aspects of my project as well. The Intercollegiate Studies Institute was generous in its support. The financial aid offered by the University of Virginia History Department and the Graduate School of Arts and Sciences sustained me throughout my graduate career. Appropriately enough, considering the nature of my project, the Society of the Cincinnati also provided funding, as did Yale University, which contributed to the completion of this book with a Griswold grant.

A number of archives and libraries have been extremely supportive as well. The Massachusetts Historical Society funded a month of research, enabling me to unearth materials that were crucial for my project. David Fowler and the staff of the David Library of the American Revolution not only offered funding but extended their hospitality as well. The American Antiquarian Society and the Library Company of Philadelphia were kind enough to offer me research grants, though time constraints prevented me from accepting their generous gifts. John Riley at the Mount Vernon Library nobly donated time and resources. The staff of the Library of Congress has also been extremely supportive; in particular, Gerard Gawalt gave me advance access to his work on John Beckley.

Earlier versions of Chapters 2 and 4 have appeared in the *Journal of the Early Republic* (1995) and the *William and Mary Quarterly* (1996), respectively, and material in Chapter 5 has appeared in the *Yale Law Journal* (1999). My thanks to all three journals for their contributions.

In the final stages of manuscript preparation, my agent Jill Kneerim was supportive, enthusiastic, savvy, encouraging, and a calming presence when it was most needed. And my editor Lara Heimert at Yale University Press offered wonderfully effective advice on revising and tightening my manuscript, as did Susan Laity, my patient manuscript editor; indeed, Yale University Press, as a whole, has been very supportive of this project. I am extremely grateful to all.

Finally, I would like to give special thanks to friends who spent many a year insisting that I go to graduate school. During the years that I was employed by the Library of Congress, Diantha Schull, Selma Thomas, Ingrid Maar, and John Sellers never stopped encouraging me to pursue graduate studies in history. Like so many others, they went out of their way to encourage a beginning scholar. I can only hope to give back to the history karma what it has given me.

Introduction

On Saturday, July 18, 1795, an angry crowd stood gathered before Federal Hall in New York City, eager to protest the Jay Treaty, which eased ongoing tensions between Great Britain and the United States. Convinced that the treaty was too favorable to the British, leading Republicans had organized a rally, plastering the city with handbills and newspaper notices. Several Federalists were also present, thanks to the last-minute efforts of Alexander Hamilton and a few like-minded men. Meeting the night before the rally they had arranged to publish a city-wide appeal in newspapers and handbills urging people to attend the rally and listen to an orderly examination of the treaty.

The Republican meeting was to start at noon. At the stroke of twelve, Hamilton mounted a stoop and began to address the crowd, only to be silenced by "hissings, coughings, and hootings." Trying a different approach, he handed someone a resolution to read aloud. The crowd quieted in anticipation, but when they heard the resolution declaring it "*unnecessary to give an opinion on the treaty,*" they erupted in protest, someone throwing a rock that hit Hamilton in the head. Calling for the "friends of order" to follow him, Hamilton and a small body of Federalists stormed off, humiliated and defeated.[1]

They soon encountered a loud public argument between Republican James Nicholson and Federalist Josiah Ogden Hoffman. Fearing that the two would incite a riot, Hamilton tried to quiet them, only to be silenced by Nicholson, who denounced Hamilton as an "Abettor of Tories" who had no business interrupting them. When Hamilton urged the men to settle matters indoors, Nicholson snapped that he had no reason to heed Hamilton, who had once dodged a duel. "No man could affirm that with truth," Hamilton shot back, pledging "to convince Mr. Nicholson of his mistake" by challenging him to a duel. Stalking off, Hamilton and his friends soon encountered a group of Republicans, sparking a heated political discussion that quickly grew personal. Still seething from his first clash, Hamilton swore that if his opponents "were to contend in a personal way," he would fight the whole lot of them, one by one. Then, dramatically waving his fist in the air, he upped the ante, offering "to fight the Whole '*Detestable faction*' one by one," a dare that Republican Maturin Livingston could not ignore. As "one of the party," he accepted the challenge and offered to meet Hamilton with pistols "in half an hour where he pleased." Explaining that he already "had an affair on his Hands . . . with one of the party," Hamilton swore that when the first duel was settled, Livingston would get his due. Although Hamilton and Nicholson came within a day of dueling—Hamilton setting his finances in order in case of his death—both disputes were settled during negotiations.[2]

Hissings, coughings, hootings, strong words, clenched fists, and the threat of gunplay: this story displays America's founders as real people caught up in the heat of the moment on a summer afternoon, exposing with particular clarity the hot-headed, defensive streak that would cost Hamilton his career, and ultimately his life. But more than that, the events of July 18 offer insight into the personal reality of being a political leader in the early republic. Elevating himself above the crowd both literally and figuratively, Hamilton asserted his right to guide them as their superior—and the crowd responded with rocks rather than deference, adding injury to insult. The impact on Hamilton, both physical and spiritual, was profound and immediate, driving him to issue two duel challenges in a single afternoon. Clearly, far more than a treaty was under debate. The American political process was being hashed out on a New York City street. To men accustomed to power and leadership, this conflict had enormously personal implications.

This tug-of-war for political power was one of many unexpected consequences of America's founding. A new constitution had been written and a new government put into place, but there was no telling what kind of polity would emerge. The burgeoning political power of the American populace was one of many surprise developments. Increasingly, politicians needed to win power and prestige from popular audiences with unpredictable demands and desires. Political methods had to change, as did the stance of political leadership—and the transition was a rocky one. Hamilton was fighting a losing battle when he tried to rein in the masses at the Jay Treaty rally. However aggressively he asserted his authority, in a democratic republic the crowd had the ultimate say.

It was one thing to establish a polity grounded on public opinion and the popular will and quite another to feel the full impact of this will firsthand, as suggested by Hamilton's dramatic response. By literally hooting him off the stage, the crowd symbolically dismissed his rights of leadership, driving him into a defensive, fist-clenched rage. The precise meaning of political leadership was under debate in the early republic, and the practical business of politics compelled politicians to confront this unsettling assault on settled expectations on a continuing basis. Whether electioneering, running for office, or simply exercising the privileges of leadership, America's ruling elite was dependent on the whims of the democratic many, a state of affairs that contributed to the volatility of early national politics and the defensive spirit of political leadership.

The culture of honor was a source of stability in this contested political landscape. Democratic politicking shook the earth beneath the feet of those accustomed to leadership; the tradition-bound culture of honor provided solid ground, virtually defining genteel status. Gentlemen restrained their passions and controlled their words. Their manners were refined, and their carriage easy. They were men of integrity and honesty whose promises could be trusted; their word was their bond.[3] All these things were at the heart of the code of honor, which set standards of conduct and provided a controlled means of handling their violation. Its ethic limited and defined acceptable behavior; its rites and rituals displayed superiority of character through time-honored traditions recognized the world over. Far more than directives for negotiating a duel, the code of honor was a way of life. Particularly in a nation lacking an established aristocracy, this culture of honor was a crucial proving ground for the elite.

It would be hard to overstate the importance of personal honor to an eighteenth-century gentleman, let alone to a besieged leader whose status was under attack. Honor was the core of a man's identity, his sense of self, his manhood. A man without honor was no man at all. Honor was also entirely other-directed, determined before the eyes of the world; it did not exist unless bestowed by others. Indeed, a man of honor was defined by the respect that he received in public. Imagine, then, the impact of public disrespect. It struck at a man's honor and reduced him as a man. Hamilton's extreme actions are thus all the more comprehensible, for his very identity was up for grabs.

Central as the code of honor was to the political elite, it was not a codified rule book—at least, not entirely. Dueling rule books did exist, imported to America from Britain well into the nineteenth century. But although these books set out general rules and standards, they left much room for interpretation. Some things were common knowledge. A man of honor deserved respect, so signs of disrespect were dangerous. Certain slurs were off limits, tame as they are by modern standards. *Rascal, scoundrel, liar, coward,* and *puppy:* these were fighting words, and anyone who hurled them at an opponent was risking his life. The hushed anticipation at their mention is almost palpable in accounts of honor disputes. Faces blanch. People go still. Background noise stops. And all eyes turn to the accuser and his victim, waiting to see how the moment will play out. Hamilton needed no reminder of the implications of a charge of cowardice. Like any man of honor, he barely had to think before proffering his challenge.

Other aspects of the code were less predictable, for there could not help but be a vast gray area when dealing with things as subjective as honor and reputation. Not all insults demanded extreme action, for example. Perhaps a remark was unintentional or objectionable but within bounds; perhaps it was uttered in a drunken haze. Perhaps it was dropped on the floor of Congress, raising untold complications about the privilege of debate. Perhaps no one had witnessed the flashpoint of conflict. Perhaps there were extenuating circumstances; extreme youth, extreme age, or even a large family sometimes excused an offense or ruled out a challenge. There were regional variants of this code as well.[4] Southerners were quicker to duel than northerners, who withstood harsher insults but had their own breaking point. Such subtleties and subjectivities were the reason for "seconds"—friends who mediated between the principals and conducted negotiations in an affair of honor. There were many justifications for not "noticing" an offense, but a gentleman did so at his own peril, for as suggested by Nicholson's cutting remark, ignoring an insult could have serious consequences.

On the unstructured national political stage, this code assumed great importance, for politicking was about conflict and competition above all else. Whether they were debating legislation or campaigning for election, politicians were competing for limited rewards. This was no great surprise to the first national officeholders. What *did* surprise them was the intensity of the political game. Regional distrust, personal animosity, accusation, suspicion, implication, and denouncement—this was the tenor of national politics from the outset. The Union was fragile, and the Union makers were at odds. It was a recipe for disaster, disunion, and possibly civil war.[5]

In this maelstrom of discontent, at least one thing held true. Disagree as men might on the purpose, structure, or tenor of national governance—argue as they did about the meaning of concepts like federalism and republicanism—clash as they must about the future of the nation—they expected their opponents to behave like gentlemen. The penalty for acting otherwise was too severe. And as gentlemen, there was one accepted way to settle disputes. In essence, the code of honor was a remedy for the barely controlled chaos of national public life. There *was* a method to the madness of early national politics.

Think then of the impact of a democratized politics: when men of varied rank reached the national plateau, all standards would dissolve and chaos reign supreme—so it felt to many elite politicians, as revealed in their yelps of protest when their ranks were infiltrated. Thus the 1798 Sedition Act aimed at men who engaged in seditious libel against the government—but only certain men. The logic behind it is clear. War with France loomed on the horizon, making order a matter of national security. Attacks on national leaders upset this order and reduced the authority of government as well. The honor code channeled such confrontation between equals; offenses had a defined price and path of resolution. But what of one's inferiors? What of insulting newspaper editors and parvenu politicians? Before the Sedition Act the only recourse to an open insult in such cases was physical violence or a libel suit. The Sedition Act was an attempt to institutionalize and regulate an aspect of honor defense by providing leaders with a controlled way of defending themselves against inferiors at a time of crisis. Significantly, it was deployed almost exclusively against newspaper editors and men of questionable status. Restrictive, repressive, and wrong-headed as it was, its inherent logic was tied up with the culture of honor.[6]

The everyday impact of this culture is plain to see in the Nicholson-Hamilton clash. The two combatants needed no coaching on its dictates. In the blink of an eye, they converted a verbal shoving match into a regimented ritual of honor. A flash of outrage followed by a scripted stillness: it was a pattern that echoed throughout the lives of elite men in early national America. The threat of this moment governed their words and actions, compelling them to approach personal exchanges with care. Particularly in cockpits of political dissension like electoral campaigns and congressional debate, shared standards of honor kept passions in check and channeled those that flamed out of control. This was all the more necessary on the fragile national stage.

But the code of honor did more than channel and monitor political conflict; it formed the very infrastructure of national politics, providing a governing logic and weapons of war.[7] There were no organized parties in this unstructured new arena, no set teams of combat or institutionalized rules for battle. Political combat in the new national government was like a war without uniforms; it was almost impossible to distinguish friends from foes. National politics was personal, alliances were unpredictable, and victory went to those who trusted the right people at the right time in the right way. This was a politics of shifting coalitions and unknown loyalties, where an ally could become an opponent at the drop of a hat. There were any number of reasons to change course; regional interests, personal relationships, political principles and practicalities—all these and more guided a man's politics, and rare was the moment when they all agreed. Tempting as it is to see a two-party system in the clash of Federalists and Republicans, national politics had no such clarity to the men in the trenches.[8]

This is not to say that Federalism and Republicanism were indistinguishable. Certain types of men flocked to one ideological banner, others to the other. "Money-men" and merchants, New Englanders and city-dwellers tended to be attracted to the Federalist persuasion, which favored a strong national government and distrusted mass popular politicking outside of elections; southerners, farmers, and, eventually, ambitious members of the lower ranks tended to migrate toward Republicanism, which preferred a weaker national government and was friendlier to popular politicking. It was certainly possible to predict a man's politics, and amid so much ambiguity, politicians spent much time and energy doing just that. But absolute assurance and group discipline were rare commodities, and the most partisan man could occasionally leap a divide. Even Alexander Hamilton and Thomas Jefferson—the leading symbols of Federalism and Republicanism, respectively—sometimes seemed to drift into the opposite camp, or so their contemporaries assumed on several occasions. Underneath the ideological umbrellas of Federalism and Republicanism seethed a profusion of insecurities and unknowns, which this book seeks to understand. Count and graph votes, lump and split them as we might, our modern sense of team combat had no place on the early national political stage. Only in hindsight did political divisions become so clear. As these pages show, in many ways politicians looking back on the battles of their youth imposed much of the structure and order now taken for granted.

Reputation was at the heart of this personal form of politics. Men gained office on the basis of it, formed alliances when they trusted it, and assumed that they would earn it by accepting high office. Indeed, so predictable was the concern for reputation that many considered it a regulated force of government, the ultimate check in an intricate system of checks and balances. As Hamilton noted in *The Federalist* Nos. 69 and 70, only personal responsibility before the eyes of the public—the threat of dishonor before an ever-vigilant audience—could restrain self-serving, ambitious politicians.

There were many dimensions to the concept of reputation. Rank, credit, fame, character, name, and honor all played a role. Defining these terms for all civilizations and all times is impossible for they varied according to a particular society's culture and structure; defining them for a specific population is likewise no easy task, for their precise meanings overlapped and shifted depending on the people or circumstances under discussion. Still, ambiguous and abstract as they may appear, these words had clear meanings to those who lived by them.

Rank was a somewhat impersonal way of referring to a person's place within the social order. As in most societies, there were subtleties of rank in early America that are all but invisible now. *Credit* was a more personalized quality, encompassing a person's social and financial worth; people with good credit were trustworthy enough to merit financial risks. *Fame* embraced both the present and the future, referring to immediate celebrity as well as future renown; earned through great acts of public service, it carried a virtuous connotation that many related terms lacked. *Character* was personality with a moral dimension, referring to the mixture of traits, vices, and virtues that determined a person's social worth. Taken together, rank, credit, fame, and character formed a *name* or *reputation*—an identity as determined by others. Reputation was not unlike honor, and indeed, early Americans often used these words interchangeably. *Honor* was reputation with a moral dimension and an elite cast. A man of good reputation was respected and esteemed; a man of honor had an exalted reputation that encompassed qualities like bravery, self-command, and integrity—the core requirements for leadership.[9]

Political power and victory thus required close protection of one's reputation, as well as the savvy to assess the reputations of one's peers. It also required a talent for jabbing at the reputations of one's enemies, for a man dishonored or discredited lost his influence and lost the field. Forging, defending, and attacking reputations—this was the national political game, and different weapons accomplished these goals in different ways. Self-presentation was fundamental, for one's outward appearance affected one's reputation in the public eye and potentially broadcast one's politics as well. The political elite thought carefully about their clothing, manners, and lifestyles, costuming and conducting themselves to earn the right sort of reputation. More aggressive weapons centered on the deployment of words, the fodder for a politics of reputation. Whether spoken or written, words could stab at a man's character and destroy his influence. "Such a man is an apostate, says some impudent Quack. . . . The Calumny is believed and Character is lost," quipped one politician. Alexander Pope put matters even more concisely: "At ev'ry word a reputation dies."[10]

There were several ways to deploy this verbal ammunition. Political gossip was the easiest and most direct. "Collected" or "dropped" in "whisper campaigns," it was a deliberately deployed weapon governed by rules and standards. Broadsides, newspapers, pamphlets, and letters committed gossip to paper, addressing different audiences in different ways. Politicians opted for one medium over another depending on the nature of an insult or accusation; the subtleties of honor and reputation governed the logic of paper war. Dueling was a weapon of extremes, a threat hovering above the political playing field. Yet, dangerous as they were, duels too were deliberately deployed at moments of crisis as proof of character; contrary to popular belief, they were not the mere fallout of a slip of the tongue. Hamilton's humiliation at the Jay Treaty rally and his two challenges were cause and effect, a fact long overlooked by scholars unattuned to the political significance of dueling.

These weapons were not limited to the national stage, the American republic, or even the late eighteenth century. Politics, power, and character assassination go hand in hand in many times and cultures, and gossip still greases the wheels of governance. Neither is honor an American invention; it has assumed an endless variety of shapes across time. Indeed, this is precisely the point. In different places and at different times, honor culture has shaped politics in different ways, and because its vocabulary, rituals, and logic are not set in stone, close study of its impact in a given population offers invaluable information about a people's values, culture, and concepts of leadership and manhood. Thus the remarkable outpouring of honor studies since 1990.[11]

In the early American republic, the culture of honor met with a burgeoning democracy and an ambiguous egalitarian ethic of republicanism; the former questioned assumptions about political leadership, the latter renounced the trappings of aristocracy without offering a defined alternative. Threatened from below and above, the political elite turned to honor culture to prove themselves leaders, as did Hamilton when dismissed by an angry crowd. His claim to leadership directly challenged, he was all the more ready to prove it through a trial by fire; thus his remarkable two challenges in a single afternoon. Nicholson's quick thrust at Hamilton grew from similar insecurities, for he thought that Hamilton's public attempt to quiet him "implied censure."[12]

The problem with this logic was its inherent elitism, for honor culture was an aristocratic holdover premised on social distinctions. Only equals could duel; inferiors had to be beaten with a cane or publicly proclaimed (posted) as scoundrels. Only a privileged elite could do such things with impunity. This mindset hardly fit comfortably with an egalitarian regime. National politicians were not ethereal aristocrats competing for fine degrees of rank and distinction among a coterie of peers. Their personal and political careers relied on mass public opinion, as did the entire American political system. Obligated to be accountable to the body politic, political leaders performed before a vigilant and judgmental audience, so they adapted honor rituals to suit their purposes.

Nothing better shows this American difference than the newspaper appeals that often followed political duels. Rather than relying on word of mouth to transmit a duel's impact to a select few, politicians advertised their duels in newspapers, displaying their qualities of leadership before the voting public. They were aristocratic democrats, fighting battles of honor as part of the democratic process.

In early national America, honor, democracy, and republicanism joined to form a distinctive political culture, governed by a *grammar of political combat:* a shared understanding of the weapons at one's disposal—their power, use, and impact. This grammar was no defined rule book, no concrete tactical guide. It was a body of assumptions too familiar to record and thus almost invisible to modern eyes. National politicians had a remarkably precise understanding of this code, sifting through a defined spectrum of weapons in response to a corresponding spectrum of attacks. Publicly insulted by John Adams in 1798, James Monroe methodically considered these weapons when planning his response. Ignoring the offense was impossible, for "not to notice it may with many leave an unfavorable impression agnst me." Responding to Adams "personally" with a challenge to a duel was also impossible: "I cannot I presume, as he is an old man & the Presidt." A pamphlet might serve, but Monroe had tried that, and Adams continued to insult him.[13] Here is the application of an honor-bound grammar of combat.

This book is structured around this grammar, each chapter exploring a different weapon, its use, logic, and wider implications. Beginning with the fundamentals of reputation on the national stage, it proceeds from political gossip to the more specialized weapons of paper war and finally to the dramatic extreme and ultimate threat, the duel. The concluding chapter is a case study of these weapons in action during the presidential election of 1800. Finally, a brief epilogue looks back at these first years of national governance through the eyes of aged veterans who converted it into history in their memoirs, biographies, and autobiographies. To uncover this hidden world, each chapter focuses on a politician and a document, using his intentions, emotions, and language to expose the logic and impact of a specific weapon.

Within the time span broached by this book, the body politic learned to assert its power and influence, constructing local political institutions in the process. The political elite likewise learned the nuts and bolts of effective mobilization, and the meeting point of these learning processes represents the birth of a truly national politics. This complex dialogue between politicians and the public is studied most frequently from the perspective of the constituent rather than the congressman, detailing the birth of a political consciousness and public voice among the American people.[14] This work explores this interaction from another perspective, revealing how the nation's leaders struggled to find *their* public voice. Though elevated to their country's highest offices, they did not control this debate. Rather, they were caught in a difficult bind, torn between an unstoppable wave of democratic mass empowerment and their own assumptions about their status and role in the political process. This book examines the compromises they forged between the demands of the people and the demands of their own psyches. Rather than studying elite politics to the exclusion of all else, it reveals the enormous impact of the body politic on the self-perception and political practices of the ruling elite. Whether seen through the eyes of a national politician or an average citizen, this interaction between rulers and ruled holds the key to the birth of our political system.[15]

On a more general level, this book also demonstrates the importance of the link between politics and culture.[16] Any population has a code of conduct, a mutual understanding of constraints, fears, assumptions, and expectations that shaped decisions both personal and political; understanding this mental landscape frames these decisions in new and unexpected ways. There can be no better test of this theory than applying it to something as seemingly rigid as the conventional story of America's founding, a familiar tale peopled by Founders cast in stone. By applying the tool of culture, this book recasts this familiar story, restoring a neglected dimension of its logic; by acknowledging the link between honor and politics, it reveals a new political world.

Prologue
Walking on Untrodden Ground

THE CHALLENGES OF NATIONAL POLITICS

When the American republic sprang to life in the spring of 1789, many were disappointed. Compared with the members of the Continental Congress, the roughly one hundred men assembled in the national capital were none too impressive. "The appointments in general are not so good," thought Georgia Representative Abraham Baldwin; the members were less "heroic" than those in previous congresses, agreed Massachusetts Representative Fisher Ames.[1]

There was good reason for such concern, because the new Congress *was* different from congresses that had come before, representative in membership and mission in a way that no former interstate congress had been. The First and Second Continental Congresses (1774–81) had been focused on the heroic task at hand: organizing and winning a revolution. The Confederation Congress (1781–89) had been the administrative center of a league of independent states, its members appointed diplomats rather than representatives. But the new Congress was a permanent body devoted to the often tedious business of politics-as-usual, representative of the American people in an entirely different way. Aware that their congressmen would be the lone advocates of their interests in this new arena, voters and legislators throughout the states had selected true representatives: men of influence, to be sure, but not necessarily the patriot-heroes of the "old congress."

The result was a body of men who were solid and hard-working—up to the task at hand but a far cry from the Roman senators and "demi-gods" that many had expected. Middle-aged merchants, lawyers, and leisured gentlemen, some with wigs, some without, they were practical men of sober manners (with the exception of a few hotheaded southerners). More than half had shouldered arms during the Revolution. Nearly all had been legislators, in the Continental or Confederation Congress, the Federal Convention, or, most likely, their state assemblies. They were men of fine oratory and impressive appearance, accustomed to power and leadership, though on a different stage. Their portraits reveal a gallery of well-fed and watchful faces, keenly alert to their interests and standing.[2]

In lifestyle as well as talents and desires, the first Congress composed a sampling of the nation's ruling elite—to many, an alarming realization. The collective sigh of disappointment at the first Congress resulted from the discovery that the new American nation, assembled in representative form, was not as spectacular as expected. If, as Pennsylvania Senator William Maclay suggested, the new government was supposed to contain "the collected Wisdom and learning of the United States" ("We hear it ever in Our Ears," he complained), what were the implications of its mediocrity? Fisher Ames was philosophical in his disappointment. Having "reflected coolly" after his initial disillusionment, he decided that "the objects now before us require more information, though less of the heroic qualities, than those of the first Congress. . . . [I]f a few understand business, and have, as they will, the confidence of those who do not, it is better than for all to be such knowing ones; for they would contend for supremacy; there would not be a sufficient principle of cohesion."[3] Mediocrity was a virtue in a deliberative body, for an assemblage of demi-gods could never manage the mutual dependence that got day-to-day work done.

The spirit of the proceedings was no more encouraging. Although the government opened on March 4, 1789, it took almost a month to achieve a quorum of thirty in the House, and five days more to collect the requisite twelve senators. Many blamed bad traveling conditions, but there were also more substantial reasons. Some states had not set the gears of national governance in motion, and their congressional elections were still pending. Other states may have been acting according to past precedent, for during the Confederation Congress delegates had drifted in and out on a regular basis, some states going unrepresented for months and even years at a time. "I am inclined to believe that the languor of the old Confederation is transfused into members of the new Congress," bemoaned Ames. "This is a very mortifying situation. . . . We lose £1,000 a day revenue. We lose credit, spirit, every thing. The public will forget the government before it is born."[4]

Things were no more auspicious when Congress finally got under way (fig. 1). Personal ambitions and regional jealousies clogged the wheels of government, often reducing the national legislature to little more than a hotbed of name-calling and petty accusations. Illicit bargaining was the rule of the day rather than honest, open debate and compromise. The public good seemed all but forgotten. Observing the "yawning listlessness of many here . . . their state prejudices; their over-refining spirit in relation to trifles," Ames felt "chagrined" to see that the picture he "had drawn was so much bigger and fairer than the life." George Washington also considered the prevailing "stupor, or listlessness" a "matter of deep regret." Maclay agreed. "What must my feelings be on finding rough and rude manners[,] Glaring folly, and the basest selfishness, apparent in almost every public Transaction?" he wondered. Was it not "dreadful to find them in such a place"?[5]

To Maclay, as to other participants and onlookers, national politics was supposed to be something new, distinct from what had come before. Indeed, many considered America's experiment in republican governance an event of global significance. The fledgling nation would sweep away Old World corruption, initiating a worldwide conversion to an egalitarian, representative regime. But there was no precise model for this political experiment. There was no other such government in the modern world, and the Constitution was little more than a skeletal infrastructure. There were few absolutes and many questions, almost every rule, standard, and practice left open to debate; the most trivial decisions yanked fundamental principles into view.

The personal impact of this mindset was severe. Not only was the fate of the nation at stake, but the reputations of its first national officeholders were bound up with their experiment in government to an enormous degree. Convinced that the American people, and in-

Fig. 1. *Federal Hall, the Seat of Congress,* by Amos Doolittle, 1790. This is the only contemporary depiction of Washington's inauguration; he can be seen taking the oath of office in the center of the balcony.
(Courtesy of the Library of Congress)

deed, the entire civilized world, was watching, national politicians behaved like actors on a stage, hungry for the applause of their audience. Some strutted in fine clothes and paraded in carriages; some took to wearing ceremonial swords; some filled their hometown newspapers with impressive congressional speeches that had never been delivered.[6] Ambition ran high in the new national government, and given the history of past republics, this could have profound political implications. Julius Caesar, Catiline—history was weighty with examples of ambitious men who had thrust themselves into power through force or persuasion, destroying republics in their wake. Ambitious as they might be, national politicians were well-advised to mask their desires or risk losing the trust of their colleagues, as well as of the people at large.

Where there was opportunity for acclaim, there was also the chance of dishonor. As Maclay phrased it, the ultimate threat to a national politician was "disgrace in the public Eye."[7] Unlike members of a European court, America's politicians had no long-standing claims to elite status; in many cases, they sought just such authority in the national arena. The result was a population of self-absorbed, self-conscious strivers. Paradoxically, by creating an elevated stage where the nation's best men could consider the general welfare, America's new political system encouraged just the opposite, virtually compelling national politicians to be obsessively concerned with their reputations. Given that their political careers rested on their reputation in the public eye, to do otherwise would be self-immolation.

It was personal reputation that made national offices worth vying for. As John Adams put it, the "Titles and Pagentry" of high office would lure men to leave the comforts of home for the national stage. James Madison agreed. Debating the relative salaries of senators and representatives, he argued that senators should earn more because they couldn't display their talents from behind the Senate's closed doors. Without monetary compensation, he explained, "men of abilities . . . men of interprize and genius will naturally prefer a seat in the house, considering it to be a more conspicuous situation." Alexander Hamilton acknowledged such ambitions with characteristic bluntness: he "would not be fool enough to make pecuniary sacrifices and endure a life of extreme drudgery without opportunity either to do material good or to acquire reputation."[8] A limited number of men had been raised to the newly created top of the nation's political hierarchy. Clustered together in the national capital, some with their wives and families, their social lives centered around the nation's republican king George Washington, they constituted a "republican court."[9] In essence, election to national office promoted officeholders to the level of courtiers, a national elite performing in a political realm of high status and visibility.

Add the opportunity to walk in the shadow of such classical "founders" as Solon, Cato, Cicero, and Cincinnatus, and there was sufficient fodder for the most ambitious political appetites. Just as classical statesmen were exemplars for the political elite, this same elite hoped to impress future generations with their virtues and great deeds, and the surest path to this goal was through public service. The most glorious accomplishment of all, of course, was to found a nation. Understood in this context, national politics presented an unparalleled opportunity to earn reputation of the loftiest kind. As Benjamin Rush explained to John Adams, "We live in an important era and in a *new* country. Much good may be done by individuals, and that too in a *short* time."[10] A national politician could bolster his reputation to an unprecedented degree, perhaps garnering even world recognition. The prospect was dizzying, an undercurrent of possibilities that contributed to the nervous anxiety of national politics.

Finding one's footing on this new terrain would have been difficult among trusted friends, but national politicians lacked even this luxury. Surrounded by strangers of unknown politics from alien reaches of the republic, they did not know whom to trust. Cultural clashes were part of the problem, for men from different regions seemed to come from different countries with different customs, values, clothing, and manners. Many politicians were experiencing their first extended contact with people from other parts of the country, and not surprisingly, the result was often mutual dislike and distrust. Northerners tended to find southerners loud and showy, their clothes ostentatious, their oratory flamboyant, and their manners overblown; more than one New Englander complained about "southern blusterers." Southerners disliked the stiff formality and holier-than-thou austerity of the northerners and resented their apparent disdain. As onlooker Henry Lee confessed to fellow Virginian James Madison, "I had rather myself submit to all the hazards of war & risk the loss of every thing dear to me in life, than to live under the rule of a fixed insolent northern majority." What Pennsylvania Representative George Clymer said of New Yorkers could have been said by many men about delegates from other regions. "The New Yorkers and I are on an equal footing," he explained. "Mutual civility without a grain of good liking between us."[11] Clearly, a government that was national in name was not necessarily national in mind.

Given the undecided character of the new government, such cultural conflicts could have far-reaching consequences, for there was no telling how regional habits might warp the style of national governance. Whereas all could agree that the new nation would be republican in manner, there was little agreement on the precise nature of republicanism. As good republicans, Americans considered themselves everything that their corrupt European forebears were not—egalitarian, democratic, representative, straightforward, and virtuous in spirit, public-minded in practice. Republican leaders were supposedly exceptional as well, a natural elite of the talented and worthy who lived modestly, dressed practically, and behaved forthrightly in a spirit of accommodation. Yet though most people agreed on such generalities, concepts like simplicity, virtue, and public-mindedness were entirely relative, meaningful in comparison with European luxury and corruption but lacking an intrinsic meaning in and of themselves. Regional diversity added further complications, for southern simplicity might be garish extravagance to a New Englander; one man's virtuous republican restraint was another man's monarchical excess.

The looming presence of the European example only complicated matters. Whether defining themselves against it or striving to match it, national politicians had European precedent before their eyes. Given America's heritage, the example of Parliament had particular relevance. Faced with establishing a seemingly endless number of institutional routines and ceremonies, the first Congress looked to the British example time and time again. Worried about the new government's inherent weakness, some men favored royal customs like elaborate titles and formal court ceremony to lend national officeholders authority and power. Others condemned such efforts as a betrayal of Revolutionary principles, convinced that their opponents wanted to convert America's republican president into a king. All agreed that the easy path was to fall into old habits, so an American monarchy seemed like a distinct possibility. With the Revolution less than ten years past, even the most ardent Anglophiles wanted to avoid being branded monarchists—a powerful charge that was hurled with abandon.

Some opposed making New York City the national capital for such reasons, fearful that its high-toned manners would convert national politicians into aristocratic courtiers, thereby corrupting the entire nation. There is "an *Air loci,* which governs like the *lex loci* in all Countries," Pennsylvanian Benjamin Rush explained. "Contaminated" by the decadence and pomp of "a corrupted British army" during the Revolution, New York City would warp "the manners and morals of those men who are to form the character of our country." To Rush, the plain and sober "Quaker and German manners" of Philadelphia were far more republican, and thus Philadelphia was much better suited to be the national capital. Of course, many southerners disliked Philadelphia for just this reason, dreading its somber influence on the nation.[12]

It was hard to pierce the mystery of these strange men from the republic's far reaches, particularly given their unknown politics. For politicians did not arrive on the national scene bearing clear party affiliations. Some were nationalists who favored the Constitution and had dubbed themselves "Federalists" during the ratification debates; other men had opposed it, earning the name "Anti-Federalists" from their more mobilized opponents. But these affiliations were not predictors of votes. As politicians would discover within weeks of the government's launching, these labels were predictors of nothing at all.

With no established political parties—no public badge of political identity—it was difficult to determine a man's views and loyalties. As South Carolina Representative William Loughton Smith put it, commenting on a new crop of congressmen, "I can't judge of their Complexion." Their first vote augured well, but it was "impossible to predict what turn Members may take when they are tampered with."[13] Determining reputations on an ongoing basis in this war without uniforms, national officeholders filled their correspondence with their assessments. Faced with the undecided character of the new government and the unstructured nature of its politics, they shared a common set of concerns. What politics did their fellows have? What tone of governance did they envision for the new nation? Were they allied with other congressmen? Would they be a force to contend with? An institutionalized party system would have provided answers to such questions; without one, the political landscape remained a mystery, every man a potential enemy or friend.

Politicians used strikingly similar metaphors to describe this charged atmosphere. As Maclay expressed it in the midst of the contentious debate over the location of the national capital, "The Whole World is a shell and we tread on hollow ground every step." James Madison echoed these sentiments, lamenting that "we are in a wilderness without a single footstep to guide us." Washington, likewise unsettled by his weighty responsibilities, explained to English historian Catharine Macaulay Graham, "I walk on untrodden ground."[14] All three men felt that they were standing on unstable ground with no clear path to safety. Raised up to the eminence of national office, scrutinized on all sides by a widespread audience, the fate of the republic and their reputations hanging in the balance, national politicians lived a self-conscious existence.

With no enlightened assembly, no superior realm of government staffed by men devoted to the public good, there seemed to be nothing holding the nation together other than mutual goodwill; without the ability to achieve the general good, what was the new government but a tyrannical and bloated version of a state assembly, staffed by an overprivileged few? Indeed, the mediocrity of the government remained a lightning rod for controversy throughout its first difficult decades, an eternal seed of doubt in the republic's ability to beat the historical odds. Debate over the best way to handle this fundamental weakness—institutional bulwarks or a minimized role for the national government—was at the core of the period's ongoing war between Federalists and Republicans. And the alternatives—disunion, foreign dominance, or civil war — remained constant threats. The security of hindsight makes it difficult for us to recapture the contingency of this historical moment, leading many to deem the period's emotional extremes illogical or irrational, the product of empty rhetoric or the unfortunate result of a shared conspiracy mentality. But the politically minded had good reason to fear. They were constructing a machine already in motion, with few instructions and no precise model. The result was a politics of anxious extremes.

The Theater of National Politics

Few national politicians were as anxious as Pennsylvania's Senator William Maclay—or at least, few were as diligent about documenting it. For throughout the entirety of his two-year term of office, Maclay memorialized his anxieties on the pages of his diary in lavish detail. Judging from his entries, Maclay's fears were legion. He worried about his oratorical performances on the Senate floor. He worried about the counterthrusts and jabs of his peers. He worried about his comportment at social events, particularly in the presence of the great George Washington. He worried about Washington himself, fearful that the new president would allow corrupt friends and advisers to surround him with monarchical pomp and splendor. He worried about the political implications of almost everything; French lace, fancy carriages, and formal ceremonies all reeked of monarchical corruption, threatening the foundations of the new republic. Keenly observant, and anxious about almost everything he saw, Maclay suffered his way through his brief senatorial career (fig. 2).

It was not that he was unqualified for office. Like most of his colleagues, he had a long record of public service in his home state.

Fig. 2. *William Maclay* (1737–1804), by Nick Ruggieri, undated. This portrait captures Maclay's dour personality and watchful eye. (Courtesy of the Pennsylvania Bar Association)

Fifty-two years old, he boasted twenty-five years of experience in Pennsylvania politics, including membership in the State Assembly (1781–83) and Supreme Executive Council (1786–88), among other offices.[1] Trained in law and an experienced surveyor, he was an extensive landholder in the western backcountry, one of the largest in Northumberland County. He counted Pennsylvania proprietor Thomas Penn among his surveying clients and had twice traveled to London in Penn's interests. Wealthy, well-traveled, and well-connected, Maclay was an unquestioned member of the ruling elite, one of only six Pennsylvanians considered for a Senate seat. Intimidated by Maclay's bearing and importance, a contemporary confessed, "I was always half afraid of him; he seemed to awe me into insignificance."[2]

How can we reconcile this wealthy, self-assured landholder with the fretful grumbler of his diary? In part, the contrast reflects the difference between external appearance and internal reality: Maclay may have felt far less confident than he appeared. He was also dour and reserved by nature; "rather rigid and uncomplying" in temper by his own admission, he was a loner who tended to fear the worst rather than hope for the best. Though he attended the weekly dinners held by his state delegation, as well as other seemingly mandatory social events, he did not enjoy them. "We sat down to dinner half after 3," he noted after one Pennsylvania dinner. "Eating stopped our mouths Untill after about 4 & from that to near 9 I never heard such a Scene of Beastial Ba[w]dry kept up in my life." On another occasion, he "staid till the fumigation began. alias Smoking of Sigars. a thing I never could bear."[3] His wonderfully acid sense of humor remained largely restricted to his diary, where he vented his passions at the end of the day.

Clearly, Maclay was no hail-fellow-well-met, but the stream of anxieties that fill his diary, invading even his dreams, suggests that he was profoundly unsettled by national public life. In part, he was feeling the impact of the national stage, fretting about his reputation before a national audience. Dishonor and shame loom large in Maclay's diary. As he put it, his new office placed him "on an eminence," and a poor performance (or a venomous enemy) could easily pull him down. It was fear of disgrace that made Maclay so painfully self-conscious; this same fear was a driving force behind his diary, virtually leaping from its pages. Like his colleagues, Maclay also feared for the fate of the new republic, particularly given the disappointing mediocrity of its first Congress. "The New Government, instead of being a powerful Machine whose Authority would support any Measure, needs helps and props on all sides, and must be supported by the ablest names and the most shining Characters which we can select," he insisted toward the start of his tenure.[4] The reality was alarmingly far from the mark. But more than anything else, Maclay's fears stemmed from his political convictions, for he was part of a small minority of extreme republicans, distrustful of the slightest whiff of regal pageantry or aristocratic privilege.

Given his political predilections, Maclay had good reason to be disturbed. The opening of Congress raised a flood of questions about rules, regulations, and official ceremony, and to the rigidly republican Pennsylvanian the answers seemed unerringly geared toward converting the republic into a monarchy. The trouble began on April 23, 1789, the day George Washington was due to arrive in New York City, the new national capital. That morning, with the entire city "on tiptoe" in anticipation, as Maclay put it, the Senate began to plan Washington's inauguration. On "the great important day," both houses of Congress would receive the president-elect in the Senate chamber to administer the oath of office—a seemingly simple ceremony that raised a multitude of questions. When the president arrived in the Senate chamber, should the senators rise in respect to a superior or sit as before an equal? The answer risked casting the president as a monarch or the Senate as a House of Lords, prompting an extended debate. One senator testified that during the king's speech, the House of Lords sat and the House of Commons stood, an observation that seemed to have deep political significance until another senator made "this sagacious discovery, that the Commons stood because they had no seats to sit on . . . being arrived at the Bar of the House of lords." An interruption from the House clerk sparked yet another discussion; how should the clerk be received? Should he be admitted into the Senate chamber, or should the Sergeant at Arms (complete with ceremonial mace) receive his communication at the door? It was, Maclay sighed, "an Endless business."[5]

Ridiculous as such quibbling might appear (reducing even Maclay to laughter on at least one occasion), it had deeper implications. High-toned manners and high-flown ceremony could corrupt the fledgling government, pushing it ever closer to monarchy. They were the "fooleries fopperies finerries and pomp of Royal etiquette," Maclay charged; they were Old World corruption being foisted on the republic in its formative years, proof that Americans were already slipping back into their "old habits and intercourse."[6] Even worse, their foremost defender was presiding over the Senate. Vice President John Adams, a man of national renown whom Maclay himself had supported for office, seemed intent on creating a royal court and willing to manipulate Senate proceedings to achieve it. A large percentage of Maclay's fellow senators seemed similarly inclined. Supported by a majority, facilitated by legislative trickery, and secluded behind the Senate's closed doors, this monarchical agenda would almost certainly gain ground.

Secure in his republican virtue and fearing the fate of the nation, Maclay saw only one alternative. He would have to wage a war of resistance. His path would not be easy; the prudent Maclay saw this all too well. Unknown on the national stage, his talents yet unproven, he lacked the foremost weapons of political combat: reputation and personal influence. He had no trusted allies in this new arena, and no experience in interstate politicking. Alone and undefended, he would be pitting himself against powerful men of national repute, sacrificing all hope for reputation and influence in the process. As he concluded only days after Washington's arrival, by opposing pompous titles and "high handed Measures," he had "sacrificed every chance of being popular, and every grain of influence in the Senate."[7]

Nor could Maclay count on an enraged citizenry to bolster his cause. The Senate's proceedings were private, noted only in an official record that Maclay considered full of "the grossest Mistakes." The public had no knowledge of his campaign against corruption, no evidence of his self-sacrifice. His state legislators—the men with the power to reappoint him to office—likewise would see no sign of his struggle, a pressing concern given his brief term of office. One of the unfortunate few who drew a two-year term when the Senate divided its members into two-, four-, and six-year classes, Maclay would have to impress his state audience right from the start.[8] Underlying all these risks and challenges was Maclay's constant awareness that he was performing on an elevated stage, before a national, even international audience.

Within his first month in office, Maclay began to foresee his future. Unpopular and powerless on the national scene, he would earn powerful enemies, accomplish nothing, fail at reelection, and leave in disgrace. Desperate to avoid such a fate, he grasped at solutions. He corresponded with highly placed Pennsylvania friends, explaining his intentions and motives. He wrote newspaper essays to prod his home audience to action. He was obsessively attentive to the Senate record, insisting that it reflect his resistance with absolute accuracy, though

Senate secretary Samuel Otis remained uncooperative, his frequent errors seeming to favor Adams's preferences every time. ("The Minutes are totally under the direction of our President [Adams] or rather Otis is his Creature," Maclay charged.)[9] Ultimately, Maclay's entire national career would be little more than a series of "yeas" and "nays" in the Senate journal—and a poorly kept journal at that.

So in April 1789, Maclay began his own journal, taking cursory notes of each day's proceedings and fleshing them out in his diary each night (fig. 3). To expose his opponents and justify himself, he went one step further, noting his impressions, guessing at motives and intentions, and recording details of personal appearance and manner for insight into character and interests. His own contributions featured prominently, of course, including detailed accounts of his congressional oratory and voting record. But to reveal the depth of his commitment and sacrifice and the logic of his decisions, he had to record more than formal pronouncements from the Senate floor. He needed to document the full reality of politics, including the casual conversations and informal socializing that constituted the guts of political interaction. He thus described his social life in great detail, offering lengthy accounts of dinner parties and social calls, noting not only topics of discussion but also the demeanor of the guests, their gestures, and their tone of voice. To support his claims and accusations, he appended documentary evidence: newspaper clippings, correspondence, speaking notes, or suggested resolutions; twice, he solicited an affidavit from Otis attesting to his vote.

The end result was a massive three-volume diary, its published edition filling four hundred pages. Unflaggingly diligent, Maclay missed only twelve days in two years, his passionate and lengthy outpourings attesting to his diary's importance in his public life.[10] The only eyewitness account of proceedings in the first Senate (aside from the cursory official record), it offers an invaluable insider's view of the national government's first unsteady years, warts and all. Historians have long recognized the descriptive value of Maclay's observations. Rare is the study of the period's high politics that does not include some of his descriptive gems, and for good reason, given his eye for detail and his unabashed criticism of revered Founders like George

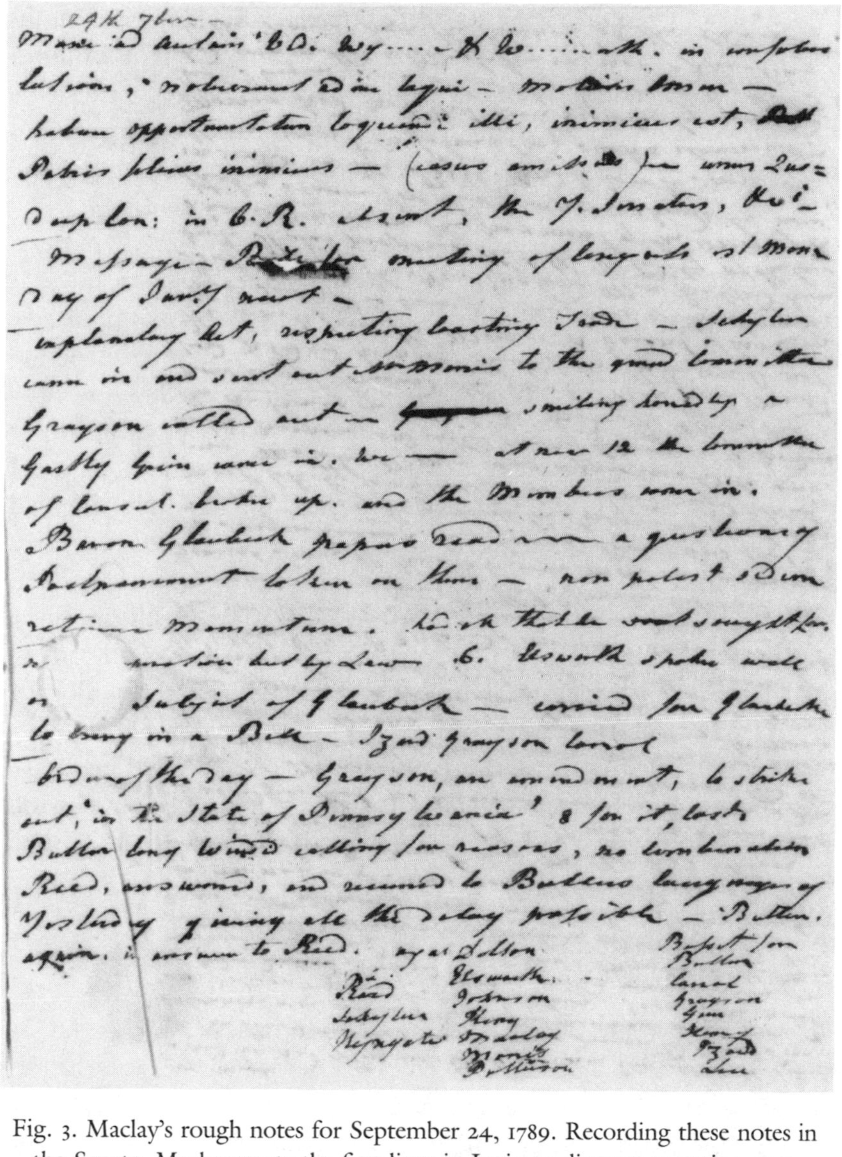

Fig. 3. Maclay's rough notes for September 24, 1789. Recording these notes in the Senate, Maclay wrote the first lines in Latin to discourage prying eyes, leaving unsaid the worst of his accusation. They read, "Stayed at the Hall Saw Wyngate and Wadsworth in conversation, they did not want to talk to me—Bad sign—Having opportunity to talk to them, they are my personal enemies, enemies of a happy country—(the reason for such being omitted)." This is the only known page of Maclay's rough notes to survive. (Courtesy of the Library of Congress)

Washington, John Adams, Thomas Jefferson, and Alexander Hamilton. But scholars have used the diary only as a sourcebook of anecdotes, never looking beneath the surface for Maclay's deeper message. He survives as little more than an acerbic quibbler, "one of those, to be met at almost any meeting, who are always rising to points of order."[11] His diary in its entirety receives no attention at all.

Yet only when viewed in its entirety is the diary's message clear. Maclay was alarmed by an evolving process, not distinct episodes. It was the larger pattern of events that he considered most important, and he self-consciously structured his diary to expose their terrifying implications. He assumed that his political diatribe would be seen by his state legislators; indeed, when he traveled to Philadelphia between sessions, his diary was in his saddlebag, ready for the asking.[12] Far more than a mere catalogue of detail, Maclay's diary is a narrative intended for people other than himself. A deliberately crafted political tool, it is a material artifact of an alien political world. It is also a rare testament to a national politician's mindset in the new republic. Full of hopes, fears, assumptions, and expectations, the diary presents one man's mental landscape at a critical moment in America's founding. Illogical or irrational as Maclay might seem, his diary contains immediate reactions to unfolding events, capturing the emotion and contingency of the moment as only a personal testimonial can. It offers a window on the realities of being a national politician on a shaky and unstructured stage.

"A Man Who Had Never Been Heard of Before"

Maclay's tribulations began almost upon his arrival in New York City (fig. 4). Well known and respected in Pennsylvania, he was entirely unknown on the national stage, a man without a reputation. As Abigail Adams expressed it, national politicians should be men "whose fame had resounded throughout the States." Maclay "might be a good man," but there were some who "did not like pensilvana's chusing a man who had never been heard of before."[13] Although friends with national connections like Benjamin Rush tried to bolster Maclay's standing with letters of praise to their high-placed friends, such efforts

Fig. 4. *A View of the Federal Hall of the City of New York . . . 1797,* by H. R. Robinson (after George Holland), 1847. The view is from upper Broad Street, looking toward Wall Street; Federal Hall is at center. Maclay saw this scene daily. He disliked New York City's narrow, winding streets, or "Alleys," as he called them, for "a Pennsylvanian can not call them Streets." (Courtesy of the Library of Congress)

did little more than invite people to be favorably disposed toward him. Maclay would have to prove himself in a new arena amid a multitude of strangers.

To Maclay, this sudden demotion was a nasty shock from which he never recovered. Elevated to the top of the political hierarchy, he had expected his reputation to benefit accordingly. Instead, he found himself struggling to make his name among inscrutable strangers of alien habits and conflicting interests. His disorientation justified his diary on a daily basis. Monitoring his colleagues might enable him to detect their motives, predict their actions, and plot a safe course. His diary was a personalized map of a foreign political landscape, every point within its compass significant in its relation to him alone.

This disorientation was distinctive to national politics, for in a state legislature, members largely were known quantities with familiar politics, histories, families, and friends. As John Adams put it in his early political career, "In a Provincial Assembly, where we know a Man's Pedigree and Biography, his Education, Profession and Connections, as well as his Fortune, it is easy to see what it is that governs a Man and determines him to this Party in Preference to that, to this System of Politicks rather than another, etc. . . . But here it is quite otherwise. We frequently see Phenomena which puzzles us. It requires Time to enquire and learn the Characters and Connections, the Interests and Views of a Multitude of Strangers." Conducting politics was almost impossible among a multitude of strangers, for how could one form alliances or predict attacks in an assembly of unknowns? Given the brief tenures of most national officeholders, extended time in office did little to help matters, for the cast of characters was ever changing.[14]

In addition, like many of his colleagues, Maclay was experiencing his first extended interaction with men from other regions—and he was not impressed. New Englanders seemed arrogant and disdainful, considering "Good humor[,] affability of ~~temper~~ conversation, and accomodation of temper and sentiment, as qualities too vulgar, for a Gentleman." New Yorkers were "Pompous People" with "high toned Manners," and the "Frothy Manners" of the southerners were entirely off-putting. Whom could Maclay trust in such an odd assemblage? As he confessed to his diary after a mere eight weeks in office, "I have been a bird alone. I have had to bear the Chilling cold of the North, and the intemperate Warmth of the South. Neither of which are favourable to the Middle State from which I come. . . . I could not find a confidant, in one of them, or say to my heart, here is the Man I can trust." Surrounded by colleagues with alien habits, Maclay grew to enjoy the "Company of Pennsylvanians" at the end of a trying day. Rather than broadening Maclay's perspective, the diversity of national public life reinforced his provincialism. Amid an array of clashing cultures from foreign nation-states, Maclay became more—not less—aware of his own.[15]

Yet much to his alarm, even fellow Pennsylvanians seemed strange and forbidding in this new arena. In part, they were mirroring Maclay's caution; unsure of themselves and their colleagues, they were wise to remain wary. As Maclay observed of representatives George Clymer and Thomas Fitzsimons, "I know not how it is, but I cannot get into these Men. There is a kind of guarded distance on their parts, that seems to preclude sociability. I believe I had best be guarded too."[16] Competition also inspired unfriendliness. Desperate to maintain their slightest advantage, his Pennsylvania colleagues were often deliberately difficult and standoffish. For example, Fitzsimons attacked Maclay for corresponding with Pennsylvania Comptroller General John Nicholson; to the competitive Fitzsimons, Maclay's letters were an ambitious attempt to garner information about state finances. Fitzsimons "would wish, that no man but himself should know any thing of the finances of Pennsylvania," Maclay griped. The status of high office was itself a reason for hostility, inspiring some delegates to assume airs. "What a Strange Peice of Pomposity this thing is grown," Maclay observed of Thomas Hartley after a year in office. Clymer's attitude was particularly grating. "The cold distant stiff and let me add stinking Manner of this Man . . . is really painful to be submitted to," Maclay fumed. "I really think out of respect to myself I ought to avoid his Company." Other Pennsylvania delegates remained detached out of a desire to avoid controversy, simply voting with the majority. As Maclay noted of Henry Wynkoop, "He never speaks never acts in Congress . . . but implicitly follows the Two City Members[.] he does not seem formed to act alone [in] even the most Triffling affair. well for him is it that he is not a Woman & handsome, or every fellow would debauch him."[17]

Whatever the reason, on the elevated stage of national public life, the wise politician remained a cautious observer, scrutinizing his peers in search of men to trust. What Maclay perceived as self-interested aloofness was in fact the mirror image of his own wary disorientation. Massachusetts Representative Elbridge Gerry declared himself "a spectator" until he could "form some adequate idea of *Men* and *Measures*." Fisher Ames felt similarly. "I am as silent as I can possibly be," he confessed to a friend in May 1789. "I am resolved to apply closely to the necessary means of knowledge, as I well know it is the only means of acquiring reputation." Even that "Strange Peice of Pomposity" Thomas Hartley felt overwhelmed, vowing to "study to understand my Duty and endeavour to practice it."[18] It was too easy to trust the wrong man or utter the wrong words, irreparably damaging one's reputation.

As revealed in Maclay's diary, close observation was a tool of survival in this uncharted political world. Each day Maclay scrutinized groups of congressmen whispering in corners or antechambers, seeking potential alliances. Sometimes, he hoped to manipulate these "friendships" for political advantage. The camaraderie between House Secretary John Beckley and Maclay's fellow Pennsylvanian, Speaker of the House Frederick Muhlenberg, for example, had potential significance. "Buckley is very intimate with the speaker on one hand and Madison on the other," Maclay noted. Given Maclay's familiarity with Muhlenberg, he could "thro this Channel communicate" what he pleased to Madison. Having already failed to exchange ideas with Madison, who would not condescend to hear Maclay's thoughts, Maclay had discovered a way to lead Madison without "letting him . . . see the String."[19]

Other congressional conclaves offered insight into political principles and intentions. When in July 1789 a few high-flown senators began to cluster regularly in conversation, Maclay suspected the formation of "a Court party" aimed at converting the president into a monarch. South Carolina Senator Ralph Izard confirmed Maclay's suspicions two weeks later, offering "a short History of the Court party" and its antipathy to the rigidly republican Maclay. Some months later, Maclay noted another brewing enclave during the 1790 debate over the assumption of state debts. The first phase of Secretary of the Treasury Alexander Hamilton's financial program, the Funding Act proposed that the national government pay off state debts remaining from the Revolution, making creditors beholden to the national government and thereby enhancing its power and prestige, one of Hamilton's core goals. Southerners, who had largely extinguished their debts through heavy taxes, resented this seeming reward to laggard northerners. Others, like Maclay, thought that the plan would benefit money-men and speculators. In fact, this was partly Hamilton's intention; he wanted to bolster the weak national government with the moral and financial support of the wealthy and powerful. Failure of this fundamental proposal meant the end of Hamilton's plan, his almost certain resignation, and to many, the collapse of the government, so debate was fierce and alliances soon emerged. "This the important Week & perhaps the important day, When the question will be put on the Assumption of the State debts," Maclay wrote on March 8, 1790. "I suspect this from the randevouzing of the Crew of the Hamilton Galley. it seems all hands are piped to Quarters." Working in lockstep with Hamilton, the "Secretary's Gladiators" seemed even more reprehensible than the "Court party," whose wrongheaded members were at least no man's tool. Maclay was not the only one searching for hidden alliances. When two new senators from North Carolina took their seats, Maclay heard it "whispered that means had been Used to attach them to the Secretary's System."[20]

Maclay was not alone in his vigilance. He himself was a frequent subject of observation, his colleagues unsure where his sympathies lay. On January 7, 1790, he noted that "uncommon pains were taken to draw from me some information as to the part I would act respecting the federal residence." The permanent location of the national capital was the other major controversy of that congressional session. Although Maclay held back, answering only, "I have mark'd out no ground for myself[.] my object shall be the Interest of Pennsylvania subordinate to the good of the Union," he was unsettled by the experience nonetheless.[21] Every word, every movement was grasped at for political meaning; he was constantly being questioned, prodded, pushed, and attacked, and his responses could affect his reputation and the republic, for better or worse. He could only marvel at the enormity of it.

Maclay's anxiety is a reminder of the underlying importance of such mutual observation. It was difficult enough to hold office in a government populated by strangers, for there was no telling what they might do, or how they might affect you. But more important, this unpredictable population was shaping the new republic during its earliest, most formative years. Their actions could have dire political consequences. The fate of Maclay's career and reputation was thus more than a personal matter. In his mind, the failure of a steadfast republican like himself meant the failure of the republic. If an honest and well-meaning man could not survive on the national stage, what sort of government was coming to life? By documenting his troubles in his diary, Maclay was displaying the instability of the government itself.

The Trials and Tribulations of Personal Reputation

Maclay could not hope to effect any change without power and influence, yet his staid personality and minority principles virtually ensured his powerless isolation. In his home state, where his reputation was well known, such virtuous independence had been an advantage, offending no one constituency and thus often pleasing them all. As fellow Pennsylvanian John Armstrong, Jr., put it, Maclay's appointment was due to "compromise" rather than talent.[22] On the national stage, however, he was beginning anew, and if he wished to make a difference, he had to bolster his suffering reputation. Much as Maclay might condemn his fellows for their selfish ambitions, personal reputation was the currency of national politics.

Congressional oratory was key to this mode of political warfare, each speaker attempting to shine brightest. Well aware of the importance of their performances, many politicians prepared them in advance, scribbling notes on bits of paper that could be hidden in their hat or the palm of their hand; they were actors who needed a script. This ruse often proved unsuccessful. Maclay spotted hidden notes on several occasions and denigrated the speaker accordingly, for in a contest of self-presentation, style often mattered more than content. Indeed, Maclay was frequently more interested in a speaker's manner than his words. South Carolinian Pierce Butler would explode in outrage at the slightest objection, his lack of "decorum" defeating the power of his arguments. George Read of Delaware ("the flexible Reed") was reliably unreliable, speaking at length but saying nothing at all. Through such observations, Maclay determined his colleagues' talents and evaluated their reputations. Nor did he neglect his own performance. As he explained in his diary, he often spoke in the Senate not because he had anything to say but because of "a kind of determination, that I have adopted of saying something every day."[23] What he said was secondary; Maclay hoped to impress his colleagues with his rhetorical style.

Given the competitive importance of oratory and the vulnerability of reputations, oratorical attacks had a peculiar power. Words could persuade, conceal, or delay. They could also tear a man to pieces, yanking him into the limelight only to mock his performance and damage his reputation. Indeed, among men so sensitive to their reputations, even inattention was a painful slap. "I never was treated with less respect," Maclay griped after one such instance. "Adams behaved with Studied inattention[.] He was snuffling up his Nose, kicking his heels or talking & Sniggering with Otis, the Whole time . . . I was up." Pierce Butler, though he bore such disregard with even "less temper" than Maclay, also engaged in "Earnest conversation" as Maclay spoke.[24]

Of course, galvanizing the attention of the Senate was virtually impossible, given the pandemonium of the Senate floor. Rarely were all members seated, their attention politely focused on the speaker at hand. Some wrote letters to family and friends; others conversed, read, or snacked on oranges and cakes. Members wandered into antechambers to propose bargains and formulate legislative strategies. They stood in small clusters in hallways and corners or around the stoves in winter, whispering and laughing. The secretary came and went, a rustle of papers accompanying his passage. The thump of boots on wooden floors or the rumble of passing carriages drowned out speakers. On one occasion the noise helped to drive Washington, seeking senatorial advice and consent on a treaty, into a presidential temper tantrum.[25]

Orators who bellowed to be heard above the din made matters worse. On different floors of the same building, the House and Senate were within earshot of each other, a loud speaker in one house compelling members of the other to shut their windows.[26] As Maclay attested on one chaotic day, "As well might I write . . . the Vagaries of a pantomine, as attempt to Minute the Business of this Morning. What with the Exits And the entrances of our [Secretary] Otis. The Announcings the Advancings Speechings drawings & Withdrawings of [House secretary] Buckley & [executive secretary] Lear And the comings & goings of our Committees of Enrollment &ca. And the consequent running of Doorkeepers opening and Slaming of doors the House . . . seemed in a continual ~~Tempest of Noise &~~ Hurricane. Speaking would have been Idle. for nobody would or could hear."[27]

Maclay considered the House even worse than the Senate. The representatives have "certainly greatly debased their dignity," he wrote after watching a debate. "Using base invective indecorous language 3 or 4 up at a time. manifest signs of passion. the most disorderly Wandering, in their Speeches, telling Stories, private anecdotes &ca. &ca." He knew for a fact that they enjoyed passing around riddles and rhymes lampooning their most renowned colleagues—men who deserved a strong dose of humility. John Adams, a favorite target, often watched from the visitor's gallery, unaware that he was being mocked in the notes passed below. Maclay guessed that the representatives must spend their nights devising such squibs "in Order to pop them on the Company to the greater advantage," though in fact, they often composed them in the midst of debate. "The rhyme-making does not interrupt our Attention to Business," swore Virginia Representative John Page, "for I arose between my 1st and 2nd stanza & rep[orted for the] committee."[28] It was difficult to perform in such confusion.

Direct attacks, however, were worst of all, and given their potential impact—immediate kudos for the attacker and disgrace for the victim—they flew fast and furious. Maclay felt their sting keenly, one attack of "the Most sarcastic Severity" literally driving him from the Senate chamber. "Alas! How shall I write it," he confessed to his diary that night. "I lost my Temper & finding no protection from the Chair left the Room." Of course, Maclay gave as good as he got, exulting at a "hard hit" received by his intended target. Within months of taking office, he was envisioning the Senate as a battleground "where all is Snip Snap, and Contradiction Short. Where it is a Source of Joy, to place the Speech of . . . a fellow Senator, in a distorted or ridiculous point of View." Unsettled by "buffitings" and "sentimental insults," he felt a guilty "Joy" when fellow Pennsylvania Senator Robert Morris fell victim, observing with pleasure Morris's "Nostrils Widen, and his nose flatten like the head of a Viper." Morris reacted similarly to an oratorical assault during debate over the location of the national capital, confessing to his wife that it had almost resulted in a "Serious quarrell"—a euphemism for an affair of honor.[29] Where political combat and personal reputation were so intertwined, duels were a constant threat.

Morris's emotional response reveals that Maclay was not alone in his anxiety. On the exposed national stage, even eminent men like the wealthy Morris bristled at disrespect. Indeed, Maclay's diary reveals a population of touchy men. Some bellowed and raged to silence their critics. Pierce Butler would erupt in wrathful resentment whenever Adams called him to order; given Butler's flaming oratory, this happened more than once. Others turned to the public record to literally erase their disgrace, as did Ralph Izard when one of his proposals went awry. When his suggestion for an overly ceremonious mode of communication between Congress's two houses reached the House, members of the Senate could hear the representatives "below laugh at it." Desperate to destroy all evidence of his embarrassment, Izard tried (unsuccessfully) to have his initial suggestion stricken from the minutes.[30] Like Maclay, Izard viewed the congressional record as a chronicle of reputation, often the only evidence of a senator's greatest victories or defeats.

In a population so sensitive to subtleties of reputation, men of national repute had a peculiar power. Maclay felt insulted by most such men, wounded by their arrogant disdain. He found James Madison particularly insulting. "Called on Madison. he made me wait long," Maclay complained in February 1790. When Maclay offered his ideas concerning the assumption of the national debt, Madison ignored them. "I do not think he attended to one Word," Maclay griped. "His pride seems of that kind which repels all communication. he appears as if he could not bear the Condescention of it." John Adams's vanity and self-importance offended Maclay on a daily basis. And the arrogance of Alexander Hamilton (dubbed "his Holiness" by Maclay) was beyond description.[31]

Nor was Maclay alone in his feelings. When he asked Pennsylvania Representative Thomas Scott to speak with Madison, Scott refused, explaining that "he was afraid of Madison's pride." It was Adams's arrogance that made him such a popular target for jokesters in the House. For example, on February 25, 1790, South Carolina Representative Thomas Tudor Tucker passed Virginian John Page a note containing the following riddle:

In Gravity clad,
He has nought in his Head,
But Visions of Nobles & Kings,
With Commons below,
Who respectfully bow,
And worship the Dignified *Things*.

Page solved Tucker's riddle "Impromptu" in the midst of debate on the House floor:

The Answer Impromptu by P[age:]
I'll tell in a Trice—
'Tis Old Daddy *Vice*
Who carries of Pride an Ass-load;
Who turns up his Nose
Wherever he goes
With Vanity swell'd like a Toad.

This lampoon—and a number of others—eventually circulated throughout Virginia. George Mason reportedly enjoyed them enough to make his own copies.[32]

Given the importance of reputation, an attack on a man's honor was the ultimate trump card. The power of such an attack is evident throughout Maclay's diary. When honor was at stake, all else fell by the wayside, for a man's sense of self and possibly his life were at risk. For example, Hamilton used his personal honor to withhold Treasury documents from Maclay. Confronted with Maclay's request for some papers concerning congressional business, Hamilton first tried a bureaucratic escape, barraging the Pennsylvanian with a smokescreen of evasive measures: he refused to deliver the papers, then agreed to surrender them if a committee voted for it, then promised Maclay a note on the subject (which never came), and finally declared that the papers were locked in the desk of treasurer Michael Hillegas—who was in

Philadelphia with the key. When the outraged Maclay "expressed great Surprize That Mr. Hillegas should lock puplic Papers belonging to the Treasury in his private desk," Hamilton resorted to his ultimate weapon: his honor. As Maclay expressed it, "Hamilton affected to believe I meant some censure on his Conduct"—he declared himself personally insulted, an ambiguous threat of an affair of honor that left Maclay unable to do anything other than sputter in disbelief and leave. "I need make no comment on all this," he fumed in his diary. "A School Boy should be Whipped for such pitiful Evasions."[33]

Congressmen were no less skilled at deploying assaults of honor. Indeed, carefully phrased honor attacks shaped and channeled congressional debate to an extraordinary degree. During a particularly fierce debate in the summer of 1789, for example, Izard attacked an opponent's honor in a last-ditch effort to forestall his foes. With the vote extremely close, Tristram Dalton of Massachusetts rose to his feet and "in the most hesitating, and embarrassed Manner" recanted his vote, claiming that the previous speaker had "altered his mind." Enraged, Izard "jumped up" and declared that nothing had been spoken "that possibly could convince any Man—that Man might pretend so, but the thing was impossible." Dalton was lying, Izard implied, his vote somehow bought—an attack on Dalton's private character that immediately shifted the terms of debate. Now the Senate was contesting a man's honor, the assault on Dalton's character and the debate intertwined. Those who agreed with him shared his disgrace, their motives and methods in doubt. Red-faced at such implications, Robert Morris "rose hastily" and "threw Censure on Mr. Izard[,] declared that the recanting Man behaved like a Man of honor."[34] Izard, not Dalton, was the man dishonored.

Neither Izard nor Dalton sustained permanent damage to his reputation, but not all combatants were so lucky. An insult to a man's honor was a dangerous weapon that could explode in one's face. Maclay witnessed one such disaster in March 1790, when South Carolina Representative Aedanus Burke made a "Violent personal Attack on Hamilton . . . which the Men of the blade say must produce a duel" (fig. 5). Burke had good reason for his assault. Accused of abandoning his principles to support Hamilton's proposed assumption of state

Fig. 5. *Aedanus Burke* (1743–1802), unidentified artist, undated. This portrait captures something of the fiery spirit that drove Burke to give Hamilton "the lie direct" from the floor of the House. (Courtesy of the Charleston Hibernian Society)

debts, Burke was desperate to defend his reputation. ("What poor supple things Men are," Maclay reflected upon hearing of Burke's vote.)[35] A public denunciation of Hamilton would prove that Burke was no man's tool.

With this goal in mind, Burke seized on a supposed insult against the southern militia that Hamilton had proffered eight months earlier during an Independence Day oration. Rising to his feet and turning toward the visitors' gallery, Burke hurled a ritualistic insult with high drama, declaring, "'In the face of this Assembly & in the presence of this gallery . . . I give the lie to Col. Hamilton.'" The attack seemed to have its desired impact, stunning congressmen and gallery onlookers alike, its shock waves crossing state lines. But Burke had misjudged his audience. His insult was too "Violent" and ultimately garnered him ridicule rather than respect. As fellow South Carolinian William Loughton Smith noted a few days later, Burke's "mode of speaking & his roughness only excite Laughter."[36]

Tone was everything in a politics of reputation. Too exaggerated an attack and you appeared crude and ungentlemanly; too feeble and you seemed cowardly and weak. Choice of an opponent was equally important, for an influential man could enlist his high-placed friends in his cause. Burke's attack on Hamilton was thus a great risk, inviting the scorn of Hamilton's powerful friends and colleagues in the executive branch. As Burke put it, "Falling out with one of that Sett I made the whole administration my enemies for drawing all together, like Mules in a Team they make a common cause of any dispute with others."[37]

Maclay's continued opposition to Adams was thus an enormous risk with a potentially dire impact on Maclay's reputation. More than a mere political disagreement, Maclay's campaign of resistance cast aspersions on a powerful and influential man. On several occasions, Maclay tried to calm the waters by urging a mutual friend to attest to Maclay's respect. His opposition "did not proceed from any motive of contempt" but rather from "a Sense of duty," he himself assured Adams, exposing the personal attack inherent in his opposition. Yet despite his best efforts, his campaign against Adams damaged his reputation, putting his motives and wisdom in doubt. As Maclay wrote to Benjamin Rush, by contesting Adams, he had "obtained the Character of being No Courtier, or to speak positively of being an indiscreet Man."[38] But if antagonizing Adams did no good for Maclay's reputation, neither did holding his tongue and betraying his principles. His diary was an alternate choice, aimed at protecting his reputation back home from the inevitable impact of his failed national career.

The Challenges of Maintaining a Federal Reputation

Maclay made every effort to appeal to his home audience, for regardless of his failure on the national scene, if Pennsylvanians appreciated his efforts, he would remain a respected man who could regain national office. He thus wrote countless letters to influential Pennsylvanians, penned newspaper essays to propagate his politics, and urged his friends to use their influence on his behalf. His diary was central to this campaign of self-promotion, displaying his steadfast republicanism in the face of constant opposition from a powerful majority. Yet still his reputation suffered. Pained at hearing "of the malignant Whispers Innuendoes and Malevolent Remarks Made respecting me," Maclay could not help but demand the specifics. What was the charge "made Against me?" he asked one nay-sayer. The response: "Nothing in particular, But every Body says *the People don't like You* the People Wont hear of Your Reelection."[39] Unsure of how to appeal to his home audience, Maclay discovered the complications of maintaining a federal reputation. Somehow he had to prove himself in two distinct arenas, each with its own demands. Appealing to Pennsylvania onlookers from a distant political stage would be one of the foremost challenges of Maclay's national career.

There were obvious political reasons to worry about one's home audience. After all, public accountability was at the heart of republican governance, particularly for national officeholders, who were far away and out of sight. But there were profoundly personal reasons for such fears as well, for accountability was ultimately about public opinion—and thus, about reputation. During the intertwined controversies over the assumption of state debts and the national capital, Pennsylvania's entire delegation feared a public shaming back home. Eager to pass the Funding Act (and possibly to benefit personally through speculation), many of Maclay's fellows were willing to situate the "federal city" in the South in exchange for southern assumption votes, thereby depriving Pennsylvania of the profits and prestige to be reaped as the seat of government. Thomas Fitzsimons worried "that Stones would be thrown at him in the Streets of Philada." because of his vote, and Robert Morris "looked as if he feared that his conduct . . . would be turned against him in . . . the public Eye." Had Maclay himself given such a vote, he "certainly dared not walk the Streets."[40]

Maclay had similar fears about his own performance, expecting to read his failure on the faces of his constituents. I feel "ashamed to meet the face of any Pennsylvania[n] Who shall put me to the Question What have You done for the publick Good," he confessed. Overwrought by the situation, Henry Wynkoop literally fled the scene. As Maclay recorded with some exasperation, Wynkoop, pressed by two Hamiltonians for his vote, "paused a little, got up rather hastily, said, God bless You. Went out of the chamber and actually took his Wife & proceeded home to Pennsylvania." Better to avoid the situation entirely than to make enemies with an unpopular vote. But even retreat afforded no escape, offending all parties and subjecting Wynkoop "to Ridicule." The way that "this good Man, can best serve his country is in superintending his farm," Maclay griped.[41]

The disgrace these men feared was palpable. Fitzsimons, Morris, Maclay, and Wynkoop dreaded public humiliation—sneers, snubs, ridicule, and even rocks. Some of the delegation's worst fears were realized on New York City streets when enraged New Yorkers, mourning the loss of the capital to Philadelphia (where it would rest for ten years), yelled out "dirty expressions" at Pennsylvania delegates as they passed; many of these slurs were pulled from abusive cartoons being sold in the street (fig. 6). Although other politicians were more central to the final deal, Morris—an eager negotiator—took much of the blame. The New Yorkers "lay all the blame of this measure on me, and abuse me most unmercifully both in the Public Prints private Conversations and even in the Streets," he complained to his wife.[42] He could only hope that Pennsylvanians would appreciate the sacrifice.

As the humiliated Wynkoop had discovered, silence was no protection from a watchful public. The habitual silence of Massachusetts Representative David Cobb likewise threatened his reputation before a home audience. "I have been spoken to by a number of your friends," Cobb's friend William Eustis wrote on December 4, 1794, as the congressional session drew to its end. "It is agreed on all hands you must make a speech, make one & print it, if it is about the black art, or cock fighting or Indian fighting or the age of reason, or the age of insanity[—]any thing but make a speech or I will forge one for you & hire some virtuous printer to make it yours." Eustis repeated his plea "in earnest" two days later, and again on December 18. "Make your speech or you never will have any character in Boston," he warned, for "this

Fig. 6. *Con-g-ss Embark'd on Board the Ship Constitution of America Bound to Conogocheque by way of Philadelphia,* unidentified artist, 1790. Typical of cartoons sold on the street, here the ship of state—its figurehead not an eagle but a goose—sails toward disaster at Philadelphia. "This way Bobby," the devil calls to Robert Morris as he directs Congress away from an easy passage to Conogocheque Creek (the Potomac). Following behind is a rowboat of northern congressmen, one calling to cut the tow rope (secede from the Union), a second man agreeing because the ship is "going to the devil." The "Controller" who cleared the ship's passage—mentioned by a third northerner—is President Washington, charged with agreeing to the deal out of "self gratification" because it holds no profit for "the owners" (the American people). The men in the boat at the base of the falls desire "the cargo" (the Treasury) but "never mind the Ship." (Courtesy of the Library of Congress)

thing is more spoken of than you would imagine, notwithstanding all your vanity."[43] Without at least one oratorical performance—contrived though it might be—Cobb would leave national public life without ever taking the stage, destroying his reputation in the process. Clearly, national politicians had reason to fear a public shaming: people were watching.

To avoid such a fate—and, as important, to defend the infant republic—politicians used a number of tools to communicate with the people back home. Maclay devoted much time and effort to one such tool, questionably useful as it was: his diary, a testament to his self-sacrifice. He also made frequent use of another, more commonly deployed mode of combat: the newspaper article. Indeed, Maclay was arguably the most prolific newspaper writer in the first Congress—not surprising, given his desire to thwart a dangerous majority. As he expressed it, he wrote "with a design to spirit up the State Legislatures, to attend to their own importance and instruct ~~the Stat~~ their Senators on all important questions."[44] To Maclay, this was the only way to quash the high-handed measures of men like Clymer and Morris; he himself might have little influence, but the people could not be denied.

Because of the power and importance of some of his targets, Maclay kept his efforts secret, asking Pennsylvania friends like Benjamin Rush and John Nicholson to arrange for the anonymous publication of his pieces. On the controversial issue of the assumption of state debts, he did not even write one of his newspaper contributions, instead sending his speaking notes to Rush for conversion into an article. Convinced that his speech was effective as it stood, he was furious when Rush edited (in Maclay's words, "mutilated") it.[45] As was his daily practice, Maclay had used these same notes to compose his diary entry. Through the medium of Rush, Maclay was reading his diary to a Pennsylvania audience.

Unfortunately, anonymous newspaper combat could not enhance Maclay's reputation and might even damage it. Although he struggled to mask his efforts—revealing himself only to Representatives Frederick and Peter Muhlenberg, and even then admitting authorship of only "two or Three pieces"—he worried that his efforts had "betr[a]y'd" him "in One Shape or other," antagonizing the president, his cabinet, the vice president, and their "Tools." Maclay even betrayed himself on one occasion, making one of his essays the basis of a speech; the competitive edge of his polished prose was simply too tempting to let pass by.[46] Not surprisingly, his newspaper campaign ultimately did his reputation little good. Grounded on the concealment of his identity and written in isolation, it earned him neither kudos nor allies, and occasionally exposed him to animosity instead.

Personal correspondence with influential Pennsylvanians was a different matter. A private letter was a powerful tool, enabling a politician to maintain strategic relationships, garner information, and monitor public opinion. Indeed, there was no better proof of local public opinion than personal letters; seemingly private, they had the credibility of a personal confession. As unrepresentative as such letters might be, they enabled national politicians to claim knowledge of the public voice. Maclay wielded his correspondence for political purpose on several occasions. To defeat Hamilton's financial system, he lobbied his state delegation with letters in hand. Did Thomas Scott have "any correspondence with Pennsylvania?" Maclay asked. When Scott "declared No," Maclay thrust a letter from Comptroller John Nicholson into his hand. A letter from state representative William Findley followed. "There were some People discontented in Pennsylvania," Maclay insisted, reading yet another letter "as a proof of it." When Scott resisted, Maclay offered still another letter, this time from Benjamin Rush. In the end, Maclay's campaign was only partially successful, convincing Scott on one or two minor points but failing to sway his vote—the product of Scott's sheer laziness, Maclay concluded.[47]

Maclay himself was swayed by a letter campaign during debate over the nature and form of the federal judiciary. Concerned that it would "Swallow by degrees all the State Judiciaries," he was persuaded otherwise by a barrage of correspondence. Informed that a number of noteworthy Pennsylvanians approved of the bill in their private letters, Maclay acknowledged that "the approbation of so many Men of Character for abilities has lessened my dislike of it." Given the authority of personal letters—and the difficulties of proving public opinion—it was for good reason that Maclay's Philadelphia colleagues usually withheld their correspondence, much to Maclay's chagrin.[48] The man with such proof of public opinion had power.

Of course, men with different correspondents might have entirely different conceptions of public opinion, and therein lay a problem. The "public" was a nebulous entity that could take many forms. Maclay confronted this issue on several occasions when he and Robert Morris held opposing views. Enraged by Morris's insistence that he alone understood the Pennsylvania public, Maclay claimed just the opposite.

He enjoyed "the Confidence of Pennsylvania in as unlimited a Manner" as Morris, he insisted, and thus "the General Sense of the State" was with him. Neither man could discredit the other, for public opinion was endlessly malleable, easily adapted to suit any cause. "It is thus that Ambitious Men obtain the Management of Republicks," Maclay observed; it was simply too easy to mask one's ambitions by claiming subservience to the public will.[49]

Maclay's comment strikes at a fundamental contradiction of republican politics. When both personal reputations and political careers rested on popular approval, what was the distinction between public-minded lawmaking and demagoguery? This problem hit home for Maclay during his reelection campaign, when a simple conversation with a state legislator resulted in charges of "begging of Votes." The personal letters of Massachusetts Representative George Thatcher attracted similar abuse. Accused of trying to gain people's favor, he insisted that he was no "people-pleaser." Indeed, his "sentiments upon almost every Subject is different from people in general"—a problematic attitude for a republican representative. Popular legislation raised similar concerns, as Maclay discovered during debate over congressional salaries. Convinced that he represented the public will, he proposed a minimal wage of $5 a day, a sum that brought Robert Morris roaring to his feet. Morris "cared not for the Arts people Used to ingratiate themselves with the public," he raged. He himself, on the other hand, paid "little respect . . . to the common Opinions of People," and thought that $8 a day was a more fitting sum.[50] The precise nature of national leadership was up for debate, and whether leaders should be superior men of merit or mere representatives of state interests had yet to be determined.

It was difficult to know how to relate to the public, particularly given its ambiguities. At different points in his diary, Maclay conceived of the public as his constituents, state assemblymen, state politicos, fellow senators, national officeholders, the national political community, and on occasion, the nation at large. All these groups populated Maclay's audience, no two with precisely the same expectations. Maintaining the right connection with these conflicting publics was the key to success in national politics. Maclay never managed it. Uncompromising, unpopular, and unknown, he remained a local politician on a national stage, devoid of power and influence.

The Politics of Self-Presentation

Yet Maclay was not entirely resistant to the demands of national politics. Even he felt compelled to compromise his principles on occasion. He found Washington's weekly levees distressingly monarchical, for example, and indeed, they precisely mirrored British royal tradition. Every Tuesday afternoon at three, guests entered the presidential mansion and formed a circle. After fifteen minutes the doors were closed, and Washington began his slow progress around the ring, acknowledging each man by name and engaging in a moment of small talk before moving on. As "a feature of Royalty," the levees were "certainly Anti-republican," Maclay noted. "This certainly escapes Nobody." Yet they persisted because true republicans were "borne down by fashion And a fear of being charged with a want of Respect to Genl. Washington." Thus, even the recalcitrant Maclay spent many a Tuesday afternoon in the presidential mansion, adorned in his finest clothing, grumbling all the while.[51]

It was this fear of "self-humiliating sensations" that gave monarchical precedents their peculiar power. Concern for reputation compelled more modest politicians to live up to the standards set by their more extravagant colleagues; the "frivolities" and "fopperies" of a few men could thus corrupt the government, and through emulation, the entire nation.[52]

Thus Maclay's obsessive interest in dinner parties, levees, table settings, and carriages. It is tempting to dismiss this preoccupation as the exaggerated fears of an insecure newcomer, but Maclay's diary suggests otherwise. For given the unformed character of the new national government, such seemingly trivial ceremonial matters could have an enormous influence. Republican leaders would ensure a republican people, a belief grounded on the assumption that the American people would naturally emulate their leaders in style, manner, and dress. As David Hume expressed it, considering the "sympathy or contagion of manners" within a nation-state, the influence of leaders "on the manners of the people, must, at all times, be very considerable."[53]

Whether or not it was true, national politicians assumed that they were walking exemplars for an impressionable, watchful public. Others agreed. Worried about the powerful influence of the national example, Virginian Walter Jones cautioned Madison to restrain "the ruinous adoption of European Fashions" and "pretensions to European Ranks" among public men. "There is a wide & secret inlet of mischief in our manners that if not controlled, will make legislative Forms of no avail."[54] Manners, not legislative forms, would determine the fate of the republic. Adopting a republican way of life was a public responsibility.

Cultural habits could shape the soul of the republic as pervasively as its constitutional framework did, an assumption that politicized the trappings of everyday life. As revealed by the meticulous detail of Maclay's diary, almost everything had political significance, intensifying the stilted self-consciousness of national politics. Foreign observers were quick to note the tone of sober circumspection that prevailed at even the most trifling social events. French minister Comte de Moustier thought that the nation's first characters appeared as tense as "a tight rope"; they were engaged in a "type of play" that seemed "neither agreeable nor useful." Moustier was witnessing the emotional impact of a central challenge of national public life: politicians were self-consciously crafting a political culture for a polity that was without precedent in the modern world.[55]

Personal habits were profoundly political, yet there was no single path to republican virtue. In general, republicanism encouraged a leveling of social distinctions as compared with the aristocratic Old World; the people reigned supreme. But this formulation raised troubling questions about the status of national representatives. Should they be superior men of wealth and standing, or should they mirror the body politic? What props of authority were appropriate for this new social rank?[56] Foreign relations complicated matters, presenting yet another judgmental audience with still different standards. Somehow, national leaders had to uphold their authority among foreign dignitaries without succumbing to monarchical excess. Understood within this context, Maclay's diary reveals that the period's seemingly theoretical debate over standards of government was also an inherently personal battle fought through differences of lifestyle and manner. In devising a national model of leadership, politicians were determining their standing and reputation as a ruling elite.

On occasion such issues exploded on the Senate floor. The debate over congressional salaries, for example, drove senators into "a Violent Chaff" about the proper lifestyle for a national representative. Would wealth and fine living dignify national politicians, or cast them as would-be aristocrats? The Senate could not agree. Izard argued that underpaid senators were forced into "boarding Houses[,] lodged in holes and Corners, associated with improper Company, and conversed improperly, so as to lower their dignity and Character." Pierce Butler added that senators "should not only have a handsome income but should spend it all," both men unabashedly claiming that fine living vested politicians with dignity of character, thereby establishing the authority of the government (fig. 7).[57]

The debate erupted in the newspapers with the congressional election of 1790. The nation's "high mightinesses" believe that lodgings of "five dollars per week, and travel on horseback . . . degrade the dignity of their character, and bring a stigma on our *wealthy* government," charged a writer in the *New-York Journal,* while lodgings at "ten dollars per week and travel in a carriage and four" inspire "respect and awe." Such unnecessary expense was an attempt to exclude from office "*low fellows* (a strange expression in a republic)." Other writers cited classical statesmen as proof that fine living was not essential to national leadership. "Was the simplicity of Cato, Cincinnatus, and Fabius . . . despised?" asked one essayist. Another noted that he had "read *Plutarch,* and can find no instance, where he praises the *tables* of his Grecian and Roman patriots."[58]

The Senate was no more agreed upon ceremonial titles, a topic that agitated Maclay to distraction. Verbal adornments that conferred instant status, titles seemed like an ideal way to clothe the new government in dignity and authority. For this same reason, others considered them anathema to republican governance: they were too blatantly Eu-

Fig. 7. *Mr. and Mrs. Ralph Izard (Alice DeLancey)*, by John Singleton Copley, 1775. Izard's high style is readily apparent in this portrait, painted during a stay in Italy. It is not surprising that he advocated large salaries for congressmen and considered his horse and carriage essential to his public persona. (Courtesy of the Museum of Fine Arts, Boston; Edward Ingersoll Brown Fund. Reproduced with permission. © 2000 Museum of Fine Arts, Boston. All rights reserved.)

ropean, too exclusive, too suggestive of an institutionalized breach between governors and governed.

This debate was more than a political abstraction, particularly to John Adams. As president of the Senate, what would become of his title when President Washington entered the Senate chamber? "What shall I be?" he asked in a panic, throwing himself back in his chair. Barely able to suppress a giggle ("God forgive me, for it was involuntary," Maclay confessed), Maclay watched as a "Solemn Silence" ensued while a senator thumbed through the Constitution and at length reported "with the most profound gravity" that "where the Senate is to be, then Sir you must be at the head of them. but further Sir, (here he looked agast, as if some tremendous Gulph had Ya[w]ned before him) I, shall, not, pretend, to, say." Adams's title was so central to his public identity that he feared he would be obliterated without it. Others mocked such pretensions by dispensing silly titles, dubbing the tall Maclay "Your highness of the Senate" and Adams "Your Rotundity."[59]

But Adams was not alone in his opinions. When a Senate bill styled some senators "the Honorable," the House voted to strike out the word—even before consideration of the bill itself. The Senate responded, Madison later recalled, with "an amendment to the amendt. by which the naming of the Senators was left out." The senators refused to have their names printed without the proper display of respect, charging the House, in turn, with the "Affectation of simplicity." The controversy was only "*apparently* of little moment," Madison cautioned, aware that it was part of a continuing debate over political leadership and national character.[60]

The problem was the lack of precise standards. Every politician assumed that he was a sound republican, straightforward and virtuous in spirit, public-minded in practice. It was people with different cultural standards who seemed to threaten national character. Maclay concluded as much within his first weeks in office. He had once thought that New Englanders were the most republican people in the nation, but a "full opportunity of observing the Gentlemen of New England" had convinced him otherwise. Northern men dwell on "trivial distinctions, and Matters of Mere form," he complained. They were not proper republicans. "We have really more republican plainess, and sincere openess of behaviour in Pennsylvania," he concluded, perplexed that "men born & educated Under republican forms of Government, should be so contrasted."[61]

Republicanism was thus far more than a disembodied philosophy of government; on the precedent-setting national stage, it was a way of life. Republican virtue was evident in a man's clothing and manner, the lace on his jacket or the ornaments on his table speaking volumes about his political character. Maclay well realized this, scrutinizing his colleagues' appearance as much as their votes. Whether engaged in debate or mingling at a levee, public men were reading each other's politics, decoding messages conveyed by demeanor and lifestyle. They were debating national character through self-presentation, each politician self-consciously crafting his own image of republican leadership.[62]

Defining themselves as a national elite, public figures variously avoided, adopted, and adapted past precedents, sometimes succumbing to habit, sometimes making deliberate republican modifications. Maclay's diary reveals a wide spectrum of interpretations, politicians employing different props of leadership according to their regions, fortunes, personalities, reputations, and politics. Not surprisingly, he reserved the most commentary for George Washington's performance. As America's republican monarch, Washington had an exceedingly difficult role: somehow he had to embody the new government's dignity and authority without rising to monarchical excess. It was an almost impossible task, for there was no clear definition of excess and, as suggested by Maclay's obsessive interest, a prevailing assumption about the overriding influence of Washington's example. In a sense, Washington was the new nation's political fault-line, and all eyes were watching for the first sign of slippage. As Maclay well recognized, "General Washington stood on as difficult Ground, as he ever had done in his life."[63]

Even the wary Maclay could perceive that the president was straining to hold a middle ground. As Washington himself explained, he aimed for "simplicity of dress, and every thing which can tend to support propriety of character without partaking of the follies of luxury and ostentation." His inaugural suit—made of plain brown American broadcloth and adorned with gilt buttons and diamond shoe buckles—was a particularly skillful compromise; its republican symbolism was clear, but the homespun was "so handsomely finished" that "it was universally mistaken for a foreign manufactured cloth."[64] His presidential uniform—a dignified blue or black suit, ceremonial sword, and hat—embodied a similar compromise (fig. 8). With it, he was *President* Washington. Without it, he was *General* Washington, a distinction that even the newspapers acknowledged.[65]

A family friend saw Washington "become" the president in the middle of an informal dinner. Informed that some men were waiting at the door to express their respect, Washington "disappeared, shortly thereafter making his appearance in full dress." After addressing his

Fig. 8. *George Washington* (1732–99), by Gilbert Stuart, 1796–97. Once owned by Alexander Hamilton, this portrait shows Washington wearing his presidential "uniform"—and reveals something of his imposing *gravitas* as well. (Collections of The New York Public Library, Astor, Lenox and Tilden Foundations)

visitors, he "again retired and came down to dinner in his usual costume."[66] Washington used his finery as a badge of office, hanging it—and the presidency—in his wardrobe when not in use.

Washington's costume change reveals the transformative power of fine clothing. Impressive attire enabled "great" men and women to appear great, literally enwrapping them in status. William Loughton Smith used this power to his advantage during a trip into the backcountry to determine public opinion of the new government. Dressed in plain clothes, he dined with a group of "respectable citizens" who "spoke their minds freely." After leaving "to dress" (as if he had been undressed in plain clothes), Smith stunned his companions upon his return. "We suppose, sir, from your acquaintance with the proceedings of Congress, that you probably are a member of that body," one man nervously asked. Smith identified himself. "Had we known who you were, we should have spoken with more reserve about Congress," came the response (though "they had said nothing offensive"). "It was on that account I had not discovered who I was," Smith responded. He wanted "to hear their opinions about Government with freedom."[67] Smith used plain clothes as a disguise, adopting formal dress and revealing his identity only upon completion of his mission.

Some men downplayed their apparel as much as possible—without straying *too* far from the more aristocratic standards set by some of their peers. For example, Secretary of State Thomas Jefferson wore relatively plain clothes. Visiting him upon Jefferson's return from Europe, Rush noted with satisfaction that he appeared "plain in his dress and unchanged in his manners." Maclay was less impressed. Jefferson's "cloaths seem too small for him," he noticed. "His Whole figure has a loose shackling Air . . . & nothing of that firm collected deportment which I expected would dignify the presence of a Secretary or Minister."[68]

To Maclay, Jefferson was too lax for a cabinet member (though, interestingly, not for a congressman); the hierarchy of public office demanded something more. Yet the perceptive senator detected Jefferson's way of compensating for his modest appearance. The secretary tended to ramble in his conversation, scattering "brilliant sentiments" and quaintly clever aphorisms—the witty style of a salonier that Maclay recognized as the "tone of European folly." To Jefferson, the ideal republican politician joined European cultural sophistication with an American disdain for luxury, a pose that struck many as deceptive. As one English observer put it, Jefferson "has a degree of finesse about him, which at first is not discernable."[69]

Washington's self-presentation had a different cast, vesting him with dignified authority. In manner, too, he self-consciously maintained a middle ground between authority and modesty,[70] most strikingly, perhaps, in his daily constitutional: at two o'clock each afternoon, he dispensed with his carriage and strolled around the block in the muck of the streets like anyone else—a seemingly trivial gesture with a powerful impact. Its graphic egalitarianism proved that Washington was *no* king. His afternoon walks won him high praise, particularly among Virginians, who considered a fine equipage the distinguishing mark of the planter gentry and thus appreciated the sacrifice. Given the grandeur of his cream-colored coach, drawn by six matching horses and manned by liveried coachmen, Washington's walks were politically savvy as well, for austere republicans viewed such display "with regret." Surrounded by such splendor, Washington identified himself as the nation's first character wherever he rode. To one senator, the executive branch was so weak that the president would only "have power as far as he would be seen in his Coach and Six."[71]

As demonstrated by Washington's daily walk, politicians were self-consciously promoting their republican virtue—and thus, their reputations as political leaders—by setting arbitrary limits on genteel display. Such deliberate compromises formed the language of America's republican court, in which national politicians struggled to prove their merit by displaying both their superiority *and* their republican sense of sacrifice. The problem was the lack of absolutes. One man's dispensable luxury was another man's essential prop of authority. Tristram Dalton left his carriage at home to avoid the appearance of "Parading," for example, but an unnamed senator—possibly Ralph Izard—considered his carriage so central to his public persona that he refused to leave the Senate without it, an early adjournment stranding him alone in the Senate chamber for hours at a time. "This is highly embarrassing," Maclay noted, "and some excuse must be formed for his staying for the Carriage. and he is now lame."[72]

Hamilton exercised a third option, occasionally dispensing with his carriage but remaining distant and unapproachable even among common folk in the streets. As newspaper essayist "Machiavel" quipped, anyone aspiring to be "first lord of the T[reasury]" should "appear in the streets but seldom, and then let him make care to look down on the pavement as if lost in thought profound."[73] By avoiding eye contact, Hamilton kept himself at a genteel distance, even when surrounded by people.

"Machiavel's" attack and the praise for Washington's afternoon strolls reveal that national politicians had reason to worry about their self-presentation: they really *were* being watched, as John Adams discovered on several occasions. Upbraided by an onlooker for using a carriage, he responded sarcastically that he "walked a league in the streets of Philadelphia everyday, which is more than any other member of Congress ever did. So that in this respect I am undoubtedly the man of the most merit, any where to be found." Adams may have made light of the charge, but others took it more seriously. In a letter to Washington, Virginian David Stuart censured Adams for never appearing "but in his carryage & six—As trivial as this may appear, it appears to be more captivating to the generality than matters of more importance." Attempting to mitigate Adams's sin, Washington admitted that the vice president was "high toned" but claimed that Adams had "never . . . appeared with more than *two* horses in his Carriage."[74] To Washington, the difference between two horses and six distinguished need from luxury.

Compelled to avoid ostentation, many politicians responded by glorying in female splendor, appraising social events according to the number of women present and the magnificence of their costumes. In his diary, Washington regularly recorded the number of "well dressed Ladies" at a function. During a 1791 trip to Charleston, South Carolina, he noted a concert attended by four hundred women, "the number and appearance of wch. exceeded any thing of the kind I had ever seen." Massachusetts Representative Theodore Sedgwick made similar observations in letters to his wife. On one occasion, he attended an assembly expressly hoping to "have found all the ladies of Philadelphia present." To his great disappointment, "there were not more (strange circumstance) than twenty single women & perhaps half that number of married ones." Even the austere Maclay took note of female splendor in his diary.[75] These men enjoyed such pageantry as they would a theater performance, for in the midst of so much anxious quibbling over male ostentation it confirmed their prestige as a governing class.

Yet even as they praised female splendor, politicians condemned it: women would corrupt the national political community—and thereby the public—with their natural love of luxury. "Aspiring men in power" would join with "players, Printers, Fops & fine Ladies" to corrupt the republic, warned Virginian Walter Jones. George Mason likewise thought that "those Damnd Monarchical fellows with the Vice President, & the Women" would destroy the nation.[76] Anxious about status and reputation but unable to indulge in ostentatious display, politicians were both attracted to and repelled by female display—a contradiction that reveals their ambivalence toward luxury and the pageantry of government.

Not surprisingly, John Adams was particularly sensitive to the pretense of republican sacrifice. To deny the need for honors and distinctions was "to practice a strange hypocrysy upon ourselves," he argued. Any government needed "signs and Ceremonies" as props of authority, and the American people were particularly responsive to such display. It was self-righteous republican politicians (like Maclay) who complicated matters. Given the state of affairs, Washington's secretary David Humphreys would "do well to lay aside" the "French embroidery" that adorned his jacket; among hyper-vigilant republicans, it was sure to cast doubt on Humphreys's politics. Adams's own clothes were French as well, he confessed, left over from his years in Europe and worn from necessity because his salary would "not admit . . . of my purchasing new ones, more cheap and plain."[77] Adams dressed like an aristocrat because he could not afford to dress like a republican—an excuse that reveals the contrived nature of republican simplicity.

Maclay's awkward self-consciousness was thus not a quirk of character or a literary guise adopted for self-defense. Nor were his detailed descriptions of personal manners and table settings born of a mere obsession. They were the natural result of the politics of self-presentation. National politicians were attempting to devise a style of national leadership amid conflicting and ambiguous standards, a cultural battle with profound personal and political implications.

The Politics of Indirection

Uncomfortable with Old World pageantry, national politicians were equally discomfited by the corruption and conspiracies of court politics. Intent on promoting their fortunes and reputations, traditional courtiers lived in a netherworld of political intrigue, a semi-institutionalized network of privilege with little if any interest in the common man. For Americans far removed from royal courts and only recently divorced from a corrupt ministry of their own, the image was powerful. Maclay feared that it was simply a matter of time before America fell back into its "old habits and intercourse."[78]

His worst fears came true during the debates over the assumption of state debts and the location of the national capital. As the gears of government ground to a halt, Maclay watched in horror as republican accountability gave way to a nefarious "under plot" of private bargains between champions of assumption and men who wanted the national capital in their home state. The process of government was unfolding in secret negotiations hidden from public view, and few men were more tangled in this web of intrigue than Maclay's fellow Pennsylvanian Robert Morris, whose "propensity for bargaining" was unrivaled (fig. 9). Informed of one of Morris's secret vote-trading schemes, Maclay responded with outrage. This was not the way of republican governance. "We must be able to declare upon honor that we have no bargain," he urged, and his plea hit home, for Morris appeared "a little hurt."[79]

Maclay felt that such "Jockeying and bargaining" set a dangerous precedent, and he was not alone. Oliver Ellsworth likewise complained of "a Secret Understanding a Bargaining, that ran thro' all our proceedings," as did William Loughton Smith, who regretted the "negotiations, cabals, meetings, plots & counterplots" that had "more influence on the public business than fair argument & an attention to the general good." Rufus King also railed against intrigue, venting his frustrations at the control center of political bargaining himself, Alexander Hamilton. Informed by Hamilton that he "*had made up his mind*" to sacrifice the national capital for his funding system, King protested that "great & good schemes ought to succeed not by intrigue or the establishment of bad measures." By removing the process of government from the public eye, such scheming circumvented open debate and compromise—the bedrock of republican governance. As a writer in the *Portland Gazette* wrote, "In republics there should be no secrets."[80] Condemning such behavior in their diaries and letters, national leaders bore witness to its pervasive influence.

Fig. 9. *Robert Morris* (1734–1806), by Robert Edge Pine, ca. 1785. The wealthy Philadelphia merchant earned national renown as superintendent of finance from 1781 to 1784. When America's credit ran alarmingly low during the difficult postwar years, Morris pledged his personal credit in its place. His financial luck ended in 1798 when his speculative empire collapsed and he was confined to debtor's prison. (Courtesy of the National Portrait Gallery, Smithsonian Institution)

All these men condemned political intrigue, yet none avoided it. Even as Smith complained about "plots & counterplots," he confessed to participating in a "meeting" of negotiation between "New England, New York & myself." King made a similar confession, telling an "astonished" Maclay that "he had engaged his Vote for the Assumption, if the Residence stayed in New York." And though Maclay never traded his vote, even he politicked covertly on occasion. Political practicalities demanded it. Sometimes only a counteroffer could compel a congressman to favor a national compromise over the interests of his home state. Private negotiations were immoral but alarmingly necessary. "All great Governments resolve themselve[s] into Cabal," Maclay reflected sadly. "Our's is a mere System of Jockeying Opinions. Vote this way for me, & i'll vote that way for you."[81]

In his diary, Maclay proudly resisted such intrigue; it would be the ultimate proof of his virtuous independence—and thus the ultimate explanation of his failure. Rather than resisting the demands of politics, more practical politicians chose a different course of action. Ever thinking of their judgmental audience, they devised ways to negotiate without violating republican sensibilities, creating an indirect means of politicking that is often illogical—even invisible—to the modern eye. Maclay recorded one such negotiation during the assumption and national capital crises. Eager to strike a deal with Hamilton, Morris took a peculiar course of action; rather than simply arranging a private meeting, he wrote a note to the New Yorker explaining that he "would be walking early in the Morning on the Battery, and if Col. Hamilton had anything to propose to him, he might meet him there as if by accident."[82] To avoid public censure and maintain the appearance of republican accountability, Morris arranged an elaborate charade, refitting casual socializing for political purpose.

Foreign ministers were perplexed by this distinctly American politics of indirection, unsure how to proceed without the ready convenience of back-room politicking. French minister Comte de Moustier was stunned when Washington refused to speak privately with him about Franco-American relations. Moustier had addressed himself "not to the President of the United States, but *to General Washington,*" the Frenchman explained. He was a "friend" who had not "the least idea of making the most remote overture for any negociation whatsoever." By requesting a meeting "*in conversation*" rather than in writing, he had "given proof" that he did not "mean to act officially with the President of the United States"—an explanation that revealed much about the subtleties of court etiquette. Moustier understood Washington's hesitance, acknowledging the importance of public ceremony, but back-room bargains were the stuff of politics. Close study of court etiquette the world over had taught him an important lesson: "Public forms are not to vary, but confidential measures are adapted to circumstances."[83] Moustier saw the need for a semi-institutionalized private channel of government. Washington did not agree.

If private negotiations were out of bounds, what was the proper stage for such informal politicking? Maclay's diary reveals the answer. As suggested by his close study of proceedings both on and off the floor of Congress, social events filled the gap. Dinner parties and receptions were ideal political stages, private enough for quiet asides yet public enough to avoid seeming secretive. Chatting informally at a dinner table, public figures could negotiate without compromising their principles or risking their reputations. Foreign observers well recognized the distinctive function of social events in American politics. As French minister Pierre Auguste Adet advised a countryman, "Your Minister could do nothing here did he not often have Congressmen at his table. . . . [I]t is after dinner that one relaxes, discusses matters, and it is during the toasts that confidence and persuasion can slip in."[84]

Given the significance of social events, no invitation seemed devoid of political purpose, no friendly aside without meaning. Maclay recognized Thomas Mifflin's dinner party as "an electioneering decision" intended to help Mifflin become governor of Pennsylvania. Seemingly innocuous social calls from the Reverend Doctor John Rodgers and Thomas Jefferson were attempts to influence Maclay's vote, as were invitations to dine with Washington. A visit from Izard was a "scrutinizing Errand" regarding the national capital. Even Maclay himself engaged in such social politicking, confessing with some embarrassment that a number of social calls were bids for support of his reelection. Several of his hosts said expressly that they "would support me at the ensuing Election," Maclay noted, "believing That to be the Object of my Visit. As it in some Measure was." In 1795 Secretary of State Timothy Pickering exposed the political purpose of social calls when he declined a dinner invitation from a private citizen, explaining that his limited finances restricted him to "*useful*" occasions. It was for this reason that Adams wanted a higher salary, for without it he could not entertain—and politick—in the proper manner.[85]

There was no shortage of social events to adapt to this purpose. In fact, there was a dinner, reception, theater performance, or levee almost every night of the week. There were Washington's formal levees every Tuesday afternoon and his public dinners every Thursday: attendance at the former was virtually de rigueur for national officials, the latter were by invitation only. A handful of political wives also held weekly levees, each claiming a different night of the week. Maclay also had a weekly dinner with his state delegation, featuring copious amounts of food, wine, cigars, and dirty jokes. These dinners (like most dinners at the time) lasted up to six hours—two hours longer than the average day at Congress.[86] Usually they featured several courses, a generous selection of wines, and, after the tablecloth had been removed, a lengthy period during which the ladies enjoyed tea in the parlor and the men drank port, smoked cigars, ate fruit and nuts, and talked politics in the dining room. The removal of the cloth (and the exit of the women) signaled the start of serious political talk. As Maclay noted during one particularly dull presidential dinner, after "the Cloath was taken away" and "Mrs. Washington at last withdrew with the Ladies," he "expected the Men would now begin." But Washington's solemn, unsmiling presence put a damper on the evening—even after Chief Justice John Jay told a dirty joke. Overcome by the endless stream of social events, Washington's fatigue and frustration were apparent, particularly in his absent-minded habit of banging his silverware against the table "like a drumstick."[87]

The politicization of socializing vested etiquette with extreme importance, for close adherence to its rules and rituals enabled public figures to avoid unintentional personal slights that might have political consequences. Among people so attuned to subtleties of reputation, a seemingly trivial faux pas could create an enemy for life. So John Adams discovered in the summer of 1789. Chatting with Washington at his levee, Adams saw someone bow to him, but he "could not whilst addressing the President return his bow with Propriety." Offended by this perceived snub, the wounded party launched a newspaper attack on Adams shortly thereafter, deriding Adams's pomposity and arrogance.[88] Printed in the *Massachusetts Centinel* the piece was an attempt to strike Adams where it would hurt: before his home audience.

Social calls were particularly rule bound, for visiting was a highly symbolic act; a visit made and returned was a deliberate expression of mutual respect, a vital display in a fragile political community of relative strangers. Neglecting to return a visit was a serious insult. Public figures thus carefully calculated visits owed and received, leaving a card to cancel their debt when someone was not at home. "Complimentary Visits . . . have kept me more engaged and fatigued me more than the closest attention to business," complained Virginia Representative Alexander White, as did Theodore Sedgwick of Massachusetts, who considered himself a "very great churl" because he owed more than fifty visits. Maclay thus had reason to be insulted when John Adams falsely claimed to have paid him a call, yet another seeming display of disrespect. Abigail Adams was more skilled at the art of the social call, deliberately visiting people when they were not at home, a strategy that enabled her to return as many as twenty visits in an afternoon.[89]

So serious were such obligations that when Moustier's sister-in-law Madame de Bréhan refused to call on congressional wives, she precipitated an international incident. Of course, Bréhan and Moustier were none too popular to begin with. Moustier had an annoying habit of bringing his own food to dinner parties to avoid having to eat American cooking, as he did at a dinner hosted by Hamilton. Even more distressing was the allegedly "illicit connection" between Bréhan and her brother-in-law Moustier—"her paramour" as Madison put it. Thus, when Bréhan declared herself too ill "to spend my life in paying visits," she was virtually ostracized, only "Two, or three Ladies" proving "indulgent" enough to visit, "sometimes without keeping accounts." The kerchief-tied hairstyle with which she received at least one visitor was the last straw, straining Franco-American relations enough to bestir John Jay and James Madison. Writing to Jefferson, America's minister to France, they obtained Moustier's recall. Bréhan departed at his side.[90]

Clearly, the symbolism of a visit mattered more than its content. Washington took full advantage of this fact during his first days in office, paying a call of respect on every congressman: the national executive paying homage to the people's branch. His visits were so symbolic, however, that he barely walked through each boarding-house door. As Maclay noted in his diary (without surprise), Washington rode up to his boarding house, dismounted, said good day, made two "complaisant Bows," mounted his horse, and departed.[91]

Interaction with the nation's republican king was the most politicized social intercourse of all, as suggested by Maclay's befuddlement around Washington. In part, Maclay's reaction was due to his near hero-worship of America's "first of men." But it was the political implications of such socializing that unnerved him more. Note, for example, his complex reaction to an August 1789 invitation to dine with the president—his first such invitation: "I really was surprized at the invitation. it will be my duty to go. however I will make no inferences Whatever. I am convinced all the dinners he can now give or ever could, will make no difference in my Conduct. perhaps he knew not of my being in Town. perhaps he has changed his mind of me. I was long enough in Town however before my going home. It is a thing of Course and of no Consequence. nor shall it have any with me."[92] Surprise instantly repressed to a sense of duty—suspicion about the dinner's political purpose—a flash of self-doubt—the hope that he may have mistaken Washington's disfavor—and a final pat on the back for his steadfast republicanism spill onto the pages of Maclay's diary in the space of a few sentences.

Maclay was no more poised around Washington at the end of his tenure. An invitation to sit beside the president at a January 1791 reception literally paralyzed Maclay with self-doubt; already moving toward an empty seat, he was brought to a standstill by Washington's friendly gesture. He longed to accept the honor, but would turning back imply monarchical deference? What was the republican thing to do? Priding himself on his principles, Maclay kept walking, though he marveled at Washington's attentions in his diary that night.[93]

There was at least one person who did not deign to mask his political intrigues: Alexander Hamilton. To Maclay, Hamilton was corruption incarnate, deliberately corrupting the legislature through illicit after-hours meetings behind closed doors. To a certain extent, Hamilton would have agreed. In his eyes, private agreements and political log-rolling were the essence of politics, and a politician was both foolish and impractical to think otherwise. Without the ability to bargain behind closed doors, the government would come to a grinding halt, its constitutional checks and balances producing a state of perpetual stalemate. It was this assumption that led foreign diplomats to single out Hamilton as the most cosmopolitan member of the new government. Unlike many of his peers, Hamilton was willing and eager to politick privately with diplomats and other functionaries, for it was in private conversation that alliances were forged and understandings reached. As British minister George Hammond said of him, "The S[ecretary] of the T[reasury] is more a man of the world than J[efferson] and I like his manners better, and can speak more freely to him. J[efferson] . . . prefers writing to conversing and thus it is that we are apart."[94] Hamilton's distinctly Old World style of politicking reinforced prevailing American suspicions about his politics, particularly for close witnesses like Thomas Jefferson.

In the public yet private realm of the social event, women became political actors as well. At a June 1789 dinner party, Robert Morris's wife Mary informed Maclay of an invaluable — and alarming — piece of news. Maclay had "ever been very attentive" to discover Washington's private views on monarchical pomp and ceremony. Mary Morris enlightened him. During a recent visit, Washington "had declared himself in the most pointed Manner for Generous Salaries, and added that without large Salaries proper Persons, never could be got to fill the offices of Government with propriety" — a statement that was distressing enough to merit underlining for emphasis. Considering Washington's notoriously icy demeanor, this was valuable information indeed. Isabella Bell, the daughter of a close friend, also passed on useful political news during an afternoon's walk, explaining that people thought Morris was playing a double game. Although Maclay reassured Bell of Morris's integrity, the accusation shook him.[95]

As political agents, women often had an advantage. Seemingly powerless and apolitical — a targeted audience for male display — they often gained access to privileged information. Sometimes flirtation led to political disclosures; Thomas Jefferson deemed his young secretary David Salisbury Franks politically unreliable because he had "too little guard over his lips . . . particularly in the company of women, where he loses all power over himself and becomes almost frenzied."[96] Sometimes social gallantry inspired political concessions. Abigail Adams assumed as much when she promised to put in a kind word for an office-seeking relative. Because the president was "always very civil polite and social with me," she might be able to "drop a word to him" at a dinner next week. Sometimes a woman's apolitical status invited men to let down their guard. For this reason, Tobias Lear thought that Martha Washington would be an ideal spy. "As the Ladies are very expert" at gathering information, she could collect public opinion of her husband's performance. Lear knew "no person better qualified—her very serious & benevolent countenance would not suffer a person to hide a thing from her." Lear was only half serious, joking that he "would give a great deal to be present" when his correspondent raised the matter with Martha Washington.[97] Nonetheless, his suggestion reveals that social events gave women access to pathways of political power.

The political significance of social events explains the contents and logic of Maclay's diary. Devoting equal attention to congressional debate and private socializing, he was attempting to chronicle the entirety of the political record. The indirection of national politicking made his account all the more important; Maclay would defend his reputation and reveal political corruption in one stroke. Unfortunately, his message went unheeded. Powerless on the national stage, he eventually left national office in a haze of obscurity, his diary ignored.

"The Pain & Mortification That I Experienced in My Honorable Station"

The irony of Maclay's national career did not escape him. His prestigious office had brought him nothing but humiliation, demonstrating his powerlessness on a highly exposed stage. He had achieved nothing: congressional salaries were higher than he had hoped, Hamilton's corrupt engine of aristocratic privilege was still in operation, and monarchical precedents seemed to multiply daily. He had been neglected, insulted, ignored, and dismissed. His unsuccessful bid for reelection was the final insult, a humiliating public rejection. Indeed, the dishonor of his lost election was so devastating that he devised an elaborate escape plan in anticipation of it: he would have his horse "in Readiness" and his "letter of Resignation . . . ready all to the filling [of] the Date," enabling him to make a hasty retreat, for "with so many Eyes Upon" him, there was no telling what he might do. Leaving Congress Hall on his last day in office, he "gave it a look, with that kind of Satisfaction which A Man feels on leaving a place Where he has been ill at Ease. being fully satisfyed that many A Culprit, has served Two Years at the Wheel-Barrow, without feeling half the pain & mortification, that I experienced, in my honorable Station"—his diary's closing words.[98] This was the ultimate legacy of his national career: the "pain & mortification" of a wounded reputation.

His only solace was his unflagging diligence. For two years, he had fought in debate, cajoled his friends, plied his correspondence, written newspaper essays, and compiled his diary in an attempt to stem the monarchical "torrent Which is pouring down Upon Us." Yet in the end, it was all for naught. "Nothing that I could do either by conversation or writing has been wanting to let ~~the People~~ Men see the danger which is before them," he insisted, his revision revealing much about his intended audience. He had focused his efforts primarily on one group of men—his state assemblymen, the men who could reelect him to office—yet they had shown no interest in either Maclay or his efforts, leaving his diary a closed book. As he reflected on December 31, 1790, looking back over the previous year, "This is the last day of the Year and I have faithfully noted every political transaction, that has happened to me in it. and of What avail has it been? I thought it probable, That I would be called on with respect to the part I had acted in [the] Senate by the Legislature of Pennsylvania, or at least by some of them. But is there a Man of them, who has thought it Worth while to ask me a single Question?" No one seemed "to care a farthing" about his efforts, and Maclay knew why. They were "straining, after Offices, Posts and preferments" in the new government, not simply uninterested in the government's problems but part of the problem themselves. Without their notice, his diary was of no use, he sadly concluded, "unless I wish gratification to myself."[99]

This rueful observation holds the key to Maclay's failure. Rather than forging a reputation among his peers, he focused his efforts on his home audience, a logical strategy that was poorly suited to the national stage. In an age before institutionalized parties, reputation was the currency of national politics, a personalized banner of character and standing that won or lost political contests. For strangers in a strange new arena, it was all the more important, for a man without a reliable reputation was untrustworthy, unknown, and destined for the sidelines, as Maclay learned over time. Obtaining, maintaining, and attacking reputations: this was the national political game, played out before a nebulous audience with conflicting demands. Ironically, Maclay's diary—his deliberately chosen path of resistance—was the worst possible strategy. The key to national politics lay in appealing to the proper audience, and despite Maclay's best intentions, his diary appealed to no audience at all.

It would be more than fifty years after his death before Maclay's diary received public notice, and even then the response was lukewarm at best. In the 1860s, after determining that there was no other detailed account of proceedings in the first Senate, Maclay's nephew George Washington Harris urged Congress to secure the diary's publication. In spite of Harris's best efforts, however, it continued to languish until 1880, when Harris published a highly censored edition at his own expense; even then, the government refused to purchase copies.[100] The diary was not professionally published until 1890, nearly a hundred years after the events that it chronicled had transpired. The government did not purchase Maclay's original three volumes until 1941, when it paid Maclay's descendants a whopping $750 for the privilege (fig. 10).[101]

The value and message of Maclay's diary went long unnoticed for good reason. Aside from its accounts of senatorial debates, it appeared to have little significance. Such is the price of an indirect politics of self-presentation and social events; the very camouflage that justified such politicking in the 1790s virtually guaranteed its invisibility to later generations. Yet this camouflage contains an essential truth about national politics in its earliest decades, revealing the overriding importance of appealing to an audience. National politicians were no isolated elite, politicking in a bubble of ideology and high ideals. For reasons both personal and political, they were accountable to a public with enormous power over their reputations and careers. They shaped

Fig. 10. *William Maclay's Diary*. (Courtesy of the Library of Congress)

their politicking and posturing around this nebulous audience, its ambiguities fueling the anxieties that so colored Maclay's world. Different national politicians may have attempted to suppress, stifle, or influence this public in different ways, but as a constant and judgmental audience in a culture of reputation, the public had a prevailing power of its own. This mutual push and pull is the dynamic of republican politics.

Reputation reigned supreme in such an environment, and Maclay's diary bears witness to its all-encompassing power. Though he occasionally fretted about his motives and desires, he was concerned primarily with his identity in the eyes of others. Even his diary was other-directed rather than confessional, a shielding device for his reputation. Maclay's aching desire to play the right part, joined with his uncertainty about which part to play, attests to the difficulties of politicking in a political culture yet in the making. With no defined model for national leadership, elite politicians were struggling to determine their political identities, a challenge that could not help but have a profound impact on their reputations and sense of self.

Maclay's diary thus tells a story that extends far beyond the Senate floor. By committing his mental landscape to paper, he exposed the assumptions that gave order to his world. Other national politicians did the same in their diaries, letters, and pamphlets. In years to come, still others documented their world in a more deliberate fashion, explaining their motives, intentions, and experiences in autobiographies, biographies, and memoirs penned in their old age; John Marshall's five-volume *Life of Washington,* published between 1804 and 1807, would launch this historical dialogue by infuriating those who disagreed with its Federalist worldview, Thomas Jefferson perhaps most of all. On the pages of these histories is preserved the politics of the founding era as its veterans understood it. Between the lines lurks the logic of politics on the national stage.

2

Slander, Poison, Whispers, and Fame

THE ART OF POLITICAL GOSSIP

Thomas Jefferson was angry. The first histories of the 1790s were appearing in print, filled with a pattern of Federalist lies. To Jefferson, the foremost offender was Chief Justice John Marshall's monumental five-volume biography of Washington, a history lauded as the most accurate to date, based on Washington's actual correspondence, the most authentic of evidence.[1] But Jefferson knew better. This history would tell the wrong story. He felt sure that it would be a Federalist diatribe, an intricate lie to dupe the people. To the aging president, such had been the Federalists' practice since they had first cast their shadow across the national stage.

Jefferson responded to this Federalist threat as he always had: he devised a way to circulate the "truth." In the past, he had relied on political weapons both printed and oral to expose partisan intrigue to the American people. True to Jefferson's hopes, in 1800 the people had chosen the right path, rejecting the Federalist regime in what he termed a "revolution of sentiment."[2] Now, a decade later, he felt confident that given a choice between Federalist lies and Republican truth, the people would choose correctly once again.

Jefferson's present battle differed from the political combat of the 1790s, but it was no less important a contest: he and Marshall were battling over the construction of history. To Jefferson, it was a critical fight, for Marshall's false history threatened to corrupt the future by misinterpreting the past. Jefferson's response was to create his own history. He would refute Marshall's lies by revealing the events and personalities of the early republic as Jefferson knew them to be.

Uncomfortable with direct confrontation, in 1809 he tried asking his friend Joel Barlow to write a history countering Marshall's, but Barlow refused. A few years later, Jefferson himself attempted a direct refutation of Marshall's work—a page-by-page revision of Marshall's fifth (and most offensive) volume, detailing the events of Washington's presidency. But by his third correction, Jefferson saw that this approach would be too limited. Marshall had written, "The continent was divided into two great political parties, the one of which contemplated America as a nation, and laboured incessantly to invest the federal head with powers competent to the preservation of the union. The other attached itself to the state authorities, viewed all the powers of congress with jealousy; and assented reluctantly to measures which would enable the head to act, in any respect, independently of the members. Men of enlarged and liberal minds . . . arranged themselves generally in the first party." Jefferson recognized this as the opening volley of an attack on the Republican party. "Here begins the artful complexion he has given to the two parties, federal and republican," he noted. "The real difference consisted in their different degrees of inclination to monarchy or republicanism."[3] With this, Jefferson laid down his pen, for in the face of such a fundamental bias, piecemeal corrections were useless.

Sometime between 1809 and 1818 Jefferson decided upon a new strategy: he would prepare a documentary collection of his papers as secretary of state, and let the manuscripts speak for themselves (fig. 11). The bulk would be official correspondence. But these could easily be misinterpreted, for Marshall's history relied on Washington's letters, but it was filled with distortions and lies. So to ensure the proper

Fig. 11. *Thomas Jefferson* (1743–1826), by Charles Willson Peale, 1791. Jefferson was forty-eight years old, in the midst of his tenure as secretary of state, when this portrait was painted. It was probably intended for Peale's museum of cultural and natural history, which featured a wall of portraits of Revolutionary War heroes and national leaders. (Courtesy of Independence National Historical Park)

interpretation of his letters, Jefferson included his private memoranda as well. For most of his public life, he had habitually recorded significant conversations on scraps of paper.[4] Supplemented by an explanatory introduction, these informal notes would be his strongest evidence against Marshall, providing a framing narrative of private anecdotes that would add meaning to the contents of his public papers.

Jefferson had long known that history unfolded in the spaces between official transactions. He lamented the impossibility of an accurate account of the American Revolution because the real history had taken place in "discussions . . . conducted by Congress with closed doors[;] and no member, as far as I know, having even made notes of them, these which are the life and soul of history must for ever be unknown."[5] The "life and soul" of political events occurred in private, removed from the formal realm of policy declarations, open debate, and polished legislation. Joined with his public papers, Jefferson's memoranda of private conversations would reveal the real history of Washington's administration.

In spite of Jefferson's meticulous ordering and reordering of his papers and memoranda, his history was never published as compiled. Confronted with three large volumes of documents, the first editor of Jefferson's papers, Thomas Jefferson Randolph, omitted the official documents to leave room for Jefferson's "conversations." Lumping them with memoranda not included in Jefferson's volumes and titling them *Ana*—Latin for a collection of table talk, anecdotes, or gossip—Randolph established a precedent followed by all succeeding editors of Jefferson's papers. From 1829 to the present, Jefferson's history has been dismissed as nothing more than a collection of conversations, a misperception that has led generations of historians to neglect and misunderstand the work. In 1992, however, the discovery of Jefferson's original table of contents for the volumes revealed the logic and message of what would come to be known as Jefferson's "Anas."[6]

Taken as a whole, Jefferson's recorded conversations speak with one voice. The groups of men engaged in private discussion all tell the same story—Jefferson's story—of a hidden Federalist plot of monarchical aspirations and corruption. Like Jefferson and Maclay, they saw important political plans unfolding beneath the surface of official transactions. Yet paradoxically, even as these Republicans exposed a subterranean Federalist network of whispered conversations, conspiracy, and secret agreements, they created a Republican version of their own. In doing so, they laid the groundwork for a national political alliance.

Thus, in ways that Jefferson never imagined, his history—the "Anas"—allows readers to see beneath official events to a deeper, more significant level of personal interaction and private discussion. From the vantage point of a participant, it demonstrates the logistics and organizational impact of a politics of reputation on the national stage. Maclay saw politics unfolding at dinner tables; Jefferson's memoranda offer us a seat, enabling us to hear conversations and witness their aftereffects. In essence, Jefferson's "Anas" reveals that beneath the political superstructure created by the Constitution, a subterranean politics of intrigue flourished, fueled by political gossip.[7]

A Politics of Gossip

Gossip was everywhere. New Yorker William Seton heard enough to offer Alexander Hamilton "the whisper of the day." Virginia governor Henry Lee condemned "that servile custom of re-echoing whatever is communicated without respect to fact." Jefferson fumed against Hamilton's slanders, Hamilton raged against Jefferson's whispers, and Washington pleaded for an end to the "wounding suspicions and irritating charges." To Representative Fisher Ames gossip was a sad fact of political life. "It is provoking," he sighed, "that a life of virtue and eminent usefulness should be embittered by calumny—but it is the ordinary event of the political drama."[8]

Political gossip—private discussion of revealing, immoral, or dangerous behavior learned and passed on through unofficial channels—was an "ordinary event of the political drama" in the early republic. It was a means of practicing politics. When politicians gossiped, they sized up their enemies, formed alliances, and agreed on common goals; they practiced partisan politics framed as conversation between friends. They were not merely conversing, for their discussions were urgent, disclosing hidden threats to the republic. They were not merely mud-slinging, for they substantiated accusations with proof. They did more than share news, for they attached judgments to their observations. Sure of their evidence and convinced of the corruption of their foes, purveyors of gossip believed that they were telling the truth, that their conversation was innocent, and that their aim was the public good.[9] Yet they denounced identical behavior in their adversaries as corrupt, dishonest, and self-interested. Condemning in others what they themselves practiced, politicians revealed the puzzling realities of inventing a polity envisioned as an exemplar to the world; high ideals did not always mesh with political practicalities, fueling the crisis mentality of the period's politics.

Words used to describe gossip reveal the dread and anger it provoked. Many referred to it as "slander" or "calumny," suggesting that their attackers were liars. In a culture of reputation this was no simple slap, for truthfulness was the foundation of genteel status. A truthful man could be trusted; a liar was weak, untrustworthy, and inferior—in sum, he was no gentleman. To give the "lie direct" was equivalent to striking a man: it became an immediate justification for a challenge to a duel, and indeed, many supposed liars settled their disputes with their accusers at gunpoint. "Slander" was thus no frivolous accusation, and those who hurled it were angry enough to risk violent repercussions.[10]

Some referred to gossip as "poison" and labeled their attempts to contradict it an "antidote." In a pamphlet written to defend himself against gossip, South Carolina Representative William Loughton Smith included an entire passage deprecating this form of character assassination. "*Slander* is in a moral what *poison* is in a physical sense: it is the resource of cowards. It is a species of attack against which it is impossible to defend ourselves. . . . It is at the convivial board, in the gay circles that the character of a virtuous man is blasted and delivered up to public execration. Not being present to defend himself (for were he present, these slanderers would be silent) . . . the most abominable falsehoods soon acquire the semblance of truth; the hearers don't take the trouble to enquire if the thing be true, they only remember to have heard it said." Gossip was poison, almost impossible to fight once it gained circulation. Sometimes the best strategy was to contradict a rumor before it started; Hamilton, concerned that a congressional investigation into his conduct as secretary of the treasury would provoke vicious rumors in Europe, sent a signed statement of innocence to an American diplomat overseas—"the antidote, to be employed or not as you may see occasion."[11]

Gossip was also maddeningly elusive, never occurring in its victim's presence. Many described it as "whispers," a discernible murmur that was frustratingly indistinct. A whisper campaign could destroy a political reputation quickly, quietly, and invisibly. As one of Hamilton's friends warned, "The throat of your political reputation is to be cut, *in Whispers*." Hamilton well understood the sting of such murmurings. In a phrase that captures the lurking but elusive threat of gossip, he called it "malicious intrigues to stab me in the dark."[12]

Gossip had to originate somewhere, and behind the scenes, industrious political "anecdote-hunters" stalked their victims, intently watching for a revealing moment. Presidential adviser Robert R. Livingston thought that Washington should hire "young men of gentle manners" specifically for this purpose; circulating at receptions and dinners, they would learn "many things which it will be not unimportant for" the president to know.[13] People described this process as "extracting" or "collecting" information, as though they were seizing a powerful substance against painful resistance. Indeed, gossip was potent enough to assume almost concrete form; it "fell" from people's lips or was "dropped" in conversation. Always, people stressed that what they had learned was privileged and therefore valuable, because someone did not want it known.

Given the political importance of social events, even a person's movements—his friends, enemies, and social engagements—were worth collecting. Republican politico John Beckley committed his spying technique to paper in the pivotal 1800 presidential contest, urging a friend to organize a secret "Committee of Observation" to guard against Federalist corruption. According to Beckley's careful instructions, committee members should "notice & report all Strangers" who came to town, "mark their persons, abodes, apparent business and intercourse," and pay particular attention to the comings and goings in "Senatorial *boarding houses*." Republicans were not the only ones focused on such comings and goings. In 1799 the infuriated Jefferson canceled a visit to Madison because of the vigilance of Albermarle County Clerk John Nicholas, alias "the little wretch in Charlottesville, who would make it a subject of some political slander, & perhaps of some political injury."[14]

The power of gossip was its ability to savage one's reputation now and forever, a double threat for the posterity-minded founding generation. Hamilton was thinking of both the present and the future when he tried to extricate himself from a 1791 blackmailing scheme, documenting his every action to ward off future allegations, for a "disastrous event might interest my fame." Indeed, gossip could so effectively destroy a reputation for all time that some men collapsed the entire process into one word, referring to gossip as "fame."[15]

As documented in Maclay's diary, such insecurities about honor and reputation made national politics particularly volatile. In a government lacking formal precedents and institutional routines, reputation was the glue that held the polity together. The fragile new republic was a government of character striving to become a government of rules within its new constitutional framework. In this highly personal political realm, an attack on a government measure was an attack on a politician, and an attack on a politician immediately questioned his honor and reputation. As one statesmen noted, "It is impossible to censure measures without condemning men." In this politics of personal reputation, gossip was the ultimate weapon. Focused on attacking and defending reputations, it was the language of national politics.[16]

The Etiquette of Gossip

To discourage unbridled conflict and deflect charges of slander, politicians observed an etiquette of gossip, a code of unwritten rules that made gossip seem like congenial socializing among friends. These rules transformed the true nature of gossip so effectively that two centuries later it remains elusive and difficult to define. Jefferson's "Anas" violated the foremost rule of gossip: *gossip should not be written*.[17] Personal correspondence was not always private in the eighteenth century. Letters miscarried or turned up in the hands of enemies who circulated or published them. An accusation in a signed letter could easily become public knowledge, transforming it into an open insult that dishonored the victim in the public eye. Tangible and durable, written gossip made its purveyors vulnerable to charges of slander or worse, if the victim felt compelled to challenge his offender to a duel. It was the newspaper publication of a letter describing Hamilton's dinner conversation, rather than the conversation itself, that invited Aaron Burr's challenge. In effect, written gossip converted one man's accusations into another man's weapon.

Careful political correspondents only hinted at gossip in their letters, promising full disclosure in later conversation. In 1792, for example, New Yorker Robert Troup warned Hamilton, "With regard to Burr's election I have a secret to tell you which I cannot communicate till I see you. . . . No good can result from any explanations at present; and therefore I shall be quiet. This hint is most confidentially communicated." Troup feared recording even this cryptic "hint." From Henry Lee, Hamilton received an even more urgent warning: "Was I with you I would talk an hour with doors bolted & windows shut, as my heart is much afflicted by some whispers which I have heard."[18]

Writers who did gossip in their correspondence usually took precautions, using nicknames, pseudonyms, initials, or ciphers to conceal the subject of their accusations. Maclay sometimes resorted to Latin when recording accusations about someone nearby. Even in his private memoranda, Jefferson resorted to cryptic concealment when recording something particularly inflammatory. For example, one memorandum reads,

> the affair of Reynolds & his wife.—Clingham Muhlenb's clerk.
> testibus F. A. Muhl. Monroe. Venable.—also Wolcott et <forsan> Wadsworth.
> known to J.M. E.R. Beckley & Webb.

Found among a collection of fully narrated anecdotes, this abbreviated entry stands out (fig. 12). Decoded, it refers to Hamilton's adulterous affair with Maria Reynolds, believed by some to be a fabrication concealing shady financial dealings between Hamilton and Maria's husband, James. "Clingham" was Jacob Clingman, whose arrest for financial misdealings along with Reynolds initiated the controversy. The second list of names includes those who investigated the affair (Frederick A. Muhlenberg, James Monroe, and Abraham Venable) and those who heard of it through Hamilton (Oliver Wolcott and Jeremiah Wadsworth); the third line notes those who learned of it through gossip: James Madison, Edmund Randolph, Clerk of the House John

[1792-3]

1792. Dec. 13. the President called on me to see the Model & drawings of some mills for sawing stone. after shewing them he in the course of subsequent conversation asked me if there were not some good manufactories of Porcelaine in Germany, that he was in want of table china & had been speaking to mr Shaw who was going to the East Indies to bring him a set, but he found that ~~befor~~ it would not come till he should be no longer in a situation to want it. he took occasion a second time to observe that Shaw said it would be 2. years at least before he ~~then~~ could have the china here, before which time he said he should be where he should not need it. — I think he asked the question about the manufactories in Germany merely ~~to have an~~ to have an indirect opportunity of telling me he meant to retire, and within the limits of two years.

Dec. 17. the affair of Reynolds & his wife. — Clingham Muhlenb's. clerk. testibus F. A. Muhl. Monroe. Venable. — also Wolcott at ~~forsan~~ Wadsworth.
~~known~~ to J. M. E. R. Beckley & Webb.
~~[illegible]~~

1793. Jan. 15. M. Blacon, member from Dauphiné, of the 1st. National assembly of France is now here. he was one of those who met at my house in Paris when the Monarchical patriots (afterwds called Feuillants) and the Republican patriots (afterwards called Jacobins) ~~[illegible]~~ about to form a schism, at a dinner at my Hammon[illegible]. today he recalls to my mind the names of all the members of both parties who met, to wit, La Fayette, Duport, Barnave, Alexr. La Meth, Blacon, Mounier, Maubourg, & Dagout. the result of that conference was that they made mutual sacrifices of opn. & prevented the schism. the Republicans gave up their opposition to a king, the Monocrats theirs to a single branch of legislature.

Jan. 16. at a meeting of the board for the sinking fund, in a conversation after business was over, mr Adams declared that 'men could never be governed but by force' that neither virtue prudence, wisdom nor any thing else sufficed to restrain their passions, that the first National convention of France had establ. a constn, had excluded themselves from it's admn for certain time, a new set of successors had come, had demolished their constitution, put to death all the leading characters concerned in making it, were now proceeding to make a new constn. & to exclude themselves for 6. years from it's admn. that their successors would in their turn demolish, hang them & make a new constn. & so on eternally, till a force would be brought into place to restrain them. — E. R. took notice of this declaration.

13890

Fig. 12. A memorandum from Jefferson's "Anas," December 17, 1792. This cryptic note discusses Hamilton's dalliance with Maria Reynolds. The crossed-out word *forsan,* "perhaps," suggests that Jefferson later learned that Wadsworth knew about the affair. The last paragraph, probably crossed out when Jefferson edited his memoranda in his old age, discusses the history of the affair and suggests that Jefferson thought more than a romantic liaison was at play: "Reynolds was speculating agent in the specul[ation]s of Govt. arrearages. He was furnished by Duer with a list of the claims of arrearages due to the Virga. & Carola. lines & bought them up, against which the Resolns of Congress of June 4 1790 were levelled. Hamilton advised the President to give his negative to those resolns." *Hamilton* is the most heavily canceled word of all. (Courtesy of the Library of Congress)

Beckley, and Beckley's clerk Bernard Webb—men included in Jefferson's gossip circle. So effective was this gossip ring that Jefferson knew of the affair a mere forty-eight hours after Hamilton confidentially confessed to it.[19]

As suggested by Jefferson's precautions, no matter where it was recorded, written gossip could threaten the writer's reputation. For similar reasons, politicians followed the second rule of gossip etiquette: *avoid gossiping without proof*. Unsubstantiated accusations degenerated into mere verbal abuse, but proof painted gossip as objective fact. The reputation of the gossiper counted for much: gossip gained credibility when it came from an informed and reputable insider and lost credibility when an insider contradicted it. Virginians believed reports that Aedanus Burke had killed Hamilton in a duel until a letter from another Virginian, Madison, set matters straight. Although Burke had only insulted Hamilton, the probable repercussions of his action were clear, and the farther the news traveled from its source, the more likely seemed such an outcome.[20] In a sense, chains of gossip were like modern games of "telephone," the message at one end often bearing little relation to the message at the other.

Wise politicians evaluated a rumor before passing it on, appraising its source and substantiating evidence, sometimes even researching its authenticity (and spreading the gossip in the process). Most valuable of all was eyewitness (or ear-witness) testimony, but any proof would do. Since many informants preferred to remain comfortably anonymous and thus uninvolved in another man's conflict, this research was often challenging and time-consuming. Jefferson's memoranda reveal that as he collected circulating gossip, he meticulously credited, questioned, or discarded tales depending on the result of his research; many memoranda include detailed genealogies of rumors and their documentation. Even when compiling his history a generation later, he continued to appraise each anecdote, assuring his readers in the introduction to his volumes that he had removed all gossip that was "incorrect or doubtful."[21]

More problematic were incidents that Jefferson himself had observed or anecdotes that he had "extracted" that had no proof other than Jefferson's word—which he promptly pledged when recording them. He introduced one anecdote by swearing "for the truth of which, I attest [before] the God who made me." On another occasion, after transcribing a conversation in which Hamilton discussed the benefits of monarchy, Jefferson wrote at its conclusion, "Th:J has committed it to writing in the moment of A. H's leaving the room."[22]

Many of the most calculated searches for proof focused on the authorship of anonymous newspaper essays and pamphlets. Everyone seemed to enjoy the game of "guess the author." Those who could prove a piece's authorship won respect for their political connections and gained a valuable piece of gossip to deploy against the writer. In one such instance, Clerk of the House Beckley told Jefferson that some newspaper essays attacking Washington had been written by Treasury official William Irvine, who had disguised himself as a Republican to win Washington to the Federalists' side. Beckley had learned this from John Swaine, the printer who received the pieces, but Swaine wanted his name withheld, so Jefferson was left without any proof. Anxious to expose Irvine, Jefferson asked Washington's secretary Tobias Lear to "get at some of Irving's acquaintances and inform himself"—to mingle with Irvine's friends and surreptitiously "collect" proof of authorship.[23]

In the case of the Irvine essays, Jefferson believed that the gossip was truthful, yet he honored the request of his source and sought other means of verification. By doing so, he obeyed a third rule of gossip etiquette: *never reveal your source without permission*. Unauthorized disclosure amounted to gossiping about a friend, a hostile act. Yet even the most substantiated accusation would not be believed if it fell from a man with personal motives. Effective purveyors of gossip obeyed a fourth rule: *show no malice when gossiping*. Conspicuous hostility was bad politics, making the accuser seem petty and indiscreet, and reducing the credibility of his claim. Ironically, a weapon grounded on personal relations and political enmity was most effective when there was no evidence of either. Purveyors of gossip maintained a pose of calm detachment. They were merely repeating what they heard from others. They were only discussing what others raised first.

Throughout the "Anas," Jefferson consistently referred to gossip in this manner, depicting himself as a passive conversationalist discussing topics raised by others. For example, on April 7, 1793, he recorded that "Mr. Lear called on me and introduced of himself a conversation of the affairs of the US"—a "conversation" full of proper Republican stories of Federalist intrigue. Even when Hamilton directly accused him of issuing "the most unkind whispers," Jefferson defended his conduct as "the mere enunciation of my sentiments in conversation, and chiefly among those who, expressing the same sentiments, drew mine from me."[24] Claiming that "they had heard" or "it is said," politicians who gossiped saw themselves as passive conduits for other people's aggression. It was a form of combat ideally suited to a population threatened by political conflict and discomfited by ambitious self-promotion.

A Community of Gossip

Those who gossiped shared an understanding of hidden meanings. They spoke of common enemies violating a recognized moral standard and exchanged hostile stories to expose the transgressors. This shared understanding was an unwritten code that enabled like-minded men to decipher gossip and appreciate its significance. Hamilton's praise of the British constitution, for example, was noteworthy only when one "knew" that Hamilton was a secret monarchist. Jefferson's "Anas" exemplifies the consistent worldview fostered by a community of gossip.

In the "Anas," anecdote after anecdote offers variations on the same theme. Monarchist, money-man, corruptor, and schemer: these allegations appear again and again, always attached to a Federalist and supplemented by a revealing anecdote. South Carolina Senator Pierce Butler described a dinner he attended during which Hamilton defended monarchy so vehemently that he broke up the party—proof of Hamilton's monarchism and the Republican loyalty of those who contested him. (Indeed, the dispute had been so violent that Butler himself suggested keeping it confidential, advice he clearly did not follow.) Washington's secretary Tobias Lear told Attorney General Edmund Randolph a story about Washington that Randolph in turn repeated to Jefferson and Madison. The story reported how Washington had resisted instituting levees for three weeks and how when he finally agreed to them, he was humiliated by an aide who formally trumpeted his entrance by loudly announcing, "The President of the United States." After the company had left, Washington reportedly growled to his aide, "Well, you have taken me in once, but by god you shall never take me in a second time." Not only did this story prove that the Federalists were trying to transform the president into a monarch, it showed Washington's virtuous resistance as well.[25]

These repeated accusations against the Federalists demonstrate one part of gossip's persuasive power. Frequent repetition transformed allegations into assumptions, giving the impression of universal agreement and potentially swaying the uncommitted. Repetition was what gossipers hoped for, for once a rumor was in circulation, the battle was near won. As one newspaper correspondent wrote, "Where so much was said there must be some foundation in fact."[26]

Politicians with opposing convictions—men entrenched firmly in conflicting worldviews—could not share gossip, for it was difficult to grasp the value of an anecdote when one disagreed with its code of allegations. Increasingly during the strife-ridden 1790s, national politicians seemed to speak different languages, making it difficult for friends to converse across partisan lines. The period was rife with fragile or broken friendships. Republican Henry Lee worried about his friendship with Hamilton; Virginian George Mason fretted about his friendship with Madison; Jefferson tried to patch up his relationship with John Adams. "Party animosities here have raised a wall . . . between those who differ in political sentiments," Jefferson observed in 1798. Clashing principles and clashing gossip had raised impenetrable barriers between political opponents. One man's truth was another man's slander.[27]

Washington and Jefferson experienced one such communication gap when Jefferson tried to pass on some damaging gossip in 1792. At a dinner a few months earlier, New York Federalist Philip Schuyler had argued within the hearing of Jefferson and Washington that hereditary government assured honesty and wisdom. To Jefferson, this could mean only one thing: Schuyler and his friends were monarchists intent on subverting the new republican regime. In a flash of clarity, this casual comment exposed a web of conspirators, a secret network of corrupt men. And because Schuyler was father-in-law to Hamilton, the monarchist ringleader, Schuyler's comment tainted Hamilton as well. It was gossip well-collected, as Jefferson told Madison a few days later, delighted that Washington had been listening, for it seemed impossible for him to miss the story's implications. At last the president would perceive the monarchical Federalist plot that Jefferson so wanted to reveal.[28]

The "Anas" includes Jefferson's conversation with Washington: "I recalled to his memory a dispute at his own table a little before we left Philada., between Genl. Schuyler on one side and Pinckney and myself on the other, wherein the former maintained the position that hereditary descent was as likely to produce good magistrates as election. I told him that tho' the people were sound, there was a numerous sect who had monarchy in contemplation. That the Secy. of the Treasury was one of these." To Jefferson's utter astonishment, the president remained unconvinced.[29] What was patently obvious to Jefferson was invisible to Washington. Jefferson's "proof" simultaneously revealed everything—and nothing.

This failed conversation between the two men, one of many in the "Anas," suggests one reason for Jefferson's increasing distance from the president. In his mind Washington was unwilling to face the truth. In frustration, Jefferson ultimately concluded that old age had impaired the president's memory, diminished his energy, and induced "a willingness to let others act and even think for him."[30] Washington's blindness to the Federalist threat was born of fatigue and corrupt ministers; it was surely *not* the result of simple disagreement, which would either depict Federalism as a viable alternative or place Washington among the politically damned.

Aside from Washington, the men seen gossiping with Jefferson in the "Anas" shared his worldview. John Beckley, George Mason, and Pierce Butler assumed that they were depositing valuable information with a trusted friend. These men also shared their gossip with others, forging an extensive national network. Indeed, the gossip in the "Anas" can be traced from friend to friend, reconstructing the formation of a national alliance. For example, in March 1793 Beckley gave Jefferson information about speculating congressmen; roughly six months earlier, Beckley had offered this same information to Philadelphia Republican Benjamin Rush. Rush obviously valued both the information and the informant, for a few weeks later he introduced Beckley to New Yorker Aaron Burr as a "fund of information about men & things."[31] Burr would ultimately funnel information about New York Federalists to Jefferson in the national capital.

Few women were included in Jefferson's gossip network, though women were as skilled as men at collecting and dropping strategic anecdotes. Abigail Adams, for example, recorded entire dinner conversations for the use of her husband and son, though she was somewhat ashamed of herself for doing so. "It is a little too much in the Tench Coxe stile to commit it to writing," she confessed on one occasion, referring to Coxe's penchant for publishing personal letters as political attacks. Abigail's transcribed conversations reveal that she actively politicked at the dinner table (and seems to have taken particular pleasure in prying information out of Jefferson). Jefferson, however, saw a divide between women and politics, and the "Anas" reveals the outcome. Although women were doubtless at many of the social events he described, they are almost entirely invisible in his memoranda. To Jefferson, women simply did not exist in the political realm. They were not political friends.[32]

Friendship spread gossip, and gossip spread friendship, reinforcing a network of friends — a community of gossip — people who shared the same worldview and trusted one another with valuable anecdotes about common foes. Friends who gossiped saw themselves engaged in important private conversations. But to the victims of these exchanges, these same friends constituted a political faction. It was for good reason that political alliances were often denoted as the "particular friends" of one or another leader ("the particular friends of Mr. Jefferson," "the particular friends of Mr. Hamilton"). Indeed, politicians often evaluated a politician's power and skill on the basis of his ability to attract and steer friends; thus the wary Maclay's ailing reputation. Clearly, *friend* was a charged word with a multitude of meanings, reflecting the bond between the personal and the political that characterized the period's politics.[33]

Thus the slippery divide between socializing and politicking. When Jefferson and Madison vacationed together in New York in 1791, they insisted that their trip was innocent of political purpose. But Federalists just as reasonably saw political intrigue behind the journey, which included a host of dinner parties with leading New York Republicans. Robert Troup spoke for most Federalists when he warned Hamilton, "There was every appearance of a pasionate courtship between the Chancellor, Burr, Jefferson & Madison when the two latter were in Town. Delenda est Carthago I suppose is the Maxim adopted with respect to you."[34] As innocently social as the trip might have seemed to Jefferson and Madison, by forging friendships over dinner, they were building a national alliance.

Other such meetings were more overtly political, particularly when orchestrated by the ever-direct Hamilton. For example, in August 1792 Hamilton arranged "several private interviews" with Virginia customs collector William Heth, during which they "spoke confidentially on several . . . subjects." Blatantly private meetings rather than seemingly innocuous social calls, they quickly attracted the attention of Beckley, who warned Madison. A strategic chat with Heth revealed one of their topics of conversation. As Beckley explained to Madison, Heth said "that Mr: H[amilton] unequivocally declares, that yo. are his *personal* and *political* enemy"—a declaration of open warfare that Hamilton had deliberately asked Heth to transmit to Madison.[35]

When politicians struggled to detect nascent friendships, they were charting the course of political activity; such was the purpose of Maclay's diary, a log of relationships suspected and proven. Politicians were forced to speculate about friendships and enmities because of the unpredictable nature of friendship itself. A government grounded on networks of friends was volatile and hard to manage, and gossiping politicians revealed their anxiety over their inability to predict or control its course. Yet even as they gossiped, politicians devised a solution: they formed and reinforced alliances and animosities, devised political strategies, and shared goals.[36] They created the very things they feared—communities of friends that were in reality political factions. Anxiety over gossip was anxiety over the alarming realities of national political life.

Channels of Gossip

National politicians were not the only men who gossiped. Local political leaders, eager to establish prestigious connections with national officeholders, sometimes offered gossip as an inducement to initiate a correspondence. Jefferson complained about this sort of behavior in the introduction to his history, charging that Marshall's history was full of such letters from ambitious men eager to establish a correspondence with Washington by offering valuable but (to Jefferson) erroneous information. As Jefferson explained, "We are not to suppose that everything found among Gen. Washington's papers is to be taken as gospel truth. . . . With him were deposited suspicions and certainties, rumors and realities, facts and falsehoods, by all those who were or who wished to be thought in correspondence with him."[37]

For national politicians, such "facts and falsehoods" were not entirely unwelcome. Isolated in the nation's capital, they were cut off from public opinion, and such letters, regardless of their accuracy, hinted at the prevailing attitude of the people toward their government.[38] Networks of local friends were thus an invaluable means of bridging the gap between leader and constituent. Mingling with the people and reporting their conversations, local correspondents were collectors of gossip.

Eavesdropping in taverns was a popular method of collection. "You know I am no grog drinker," swore a New Englander to Massachusetts Representative Theodore Sedgwick, "hence you will conclude that my motives for mingling upon the footing with those who profess liberty and equality are of an other sort." "Public opinion" was largely the transmission of local gossip to national leaders, the transmission itself forging valuable links between the national government and the nation.[39]

Jefferson's "Anas" contains numerous conversations in which Washington agonized about his inability to ascertain public sentiment. On occasion Washington would travel around the nation in person, observing and listening for signs of public acceptance or disapproval. More frequently, however, he dispatched agents who could mingle informally, as he could not. As surrogate ears for the president, these men collected useful information that circulated beyond his reach. One such agent, Arthur St. Clair, asked Maclay for his opinion of Washington's newly devised system of public access; overwhelmed by well-wishers, Washington had decided not to accept social invitations and would be seen publicly only during his Tuesday afternoon levees and Martha's Friday evening receptions. Aware that the policy was controversial (and probably egged on by Washington), St. Clair "wished to collect Men's Sentiments . . . to communicate them to the General." Tobias Lear served the same purpose when Washington was considering a second presidential term. As reported by Jefferson in a memorandum, Washington asked Lear "to find out from conversations, without appearing to make the enquiry, whether any other person would be desired by any body." He instructed Lear to pose as a disinterested conversationalist—to collect gossip. Lear accomplished his mission well, enabling Washington to inform Jefferson that "it was the universal desire he should continue."[40]

Of course, political accountability was only part of the story. There were less benign reasons for seeking local gossip. Often national politicians hoped to discover damaging truths about their foes, for the most useful information usually originated in a victim's home state, where he was best known. Hamilton, a New Yorker, was the primary Republican target, and the "Anas" reveals a continual stream of gossip flowing from New York to Philadelphia, the national political center (fig. 13). New Yorker Melancton Smith offered "proof" that Hamilton had written a refutation of Thomas Paine's patriotic pamphlet "Common Sense." John Beckley reported that a New Yorker had assured him that Hamilton's friend, the corrupt speculator William Duer, could "unfold such a scene of villainy as will astonish the world." Beckley traveled to New York himself and returned with an abundance of gossip: about Hamilton's hopes for a monarchy during the Federal Convention, about his secret service as a British agent, about the asylum secured for him in England if his attempt to institute an American monarchy failed.[41]

Republicans believed that they were searching for the truth about a dangerous enemy leading a corrupt squadron against the fragile republic. But Hamilton saw a secret plot to destroy him and his friends, topple those in power, and overthrow the government. The more pas-

Fig. 13. *Alexander Hamilton* (1755?–1804), by Charles Willson Peale, 1791. Painted in the same year as Peale's portrait of Jefferson, this was likewise intended for Peale's museum. Hamilton had been secretary of the treasury for roughly two years, and was either thirty-four or thirty-six years old (depending on his precise birth date, which is not known). (Courtesy of Independence National Historical Park)

sionately the Republicans tried to protect the nation, the more Hamilton and his friends discerned a plot against it. Men who considered themselves virtuous republicans were also devious, aggressive politicians deploying damaging information against constituted authorities.

The "Anas" displays this mix of political ideals and devious tactics in its account of Republican dealings with former Treasury employee Andrew Fraunces and Jacob Clingman (the same Clingman later implicated in the Reynolds affair). On June 12, 1793, Jefferson recorded valuable gossip implicating Hamilton in a corrupt speculating scheme; Fraunces had offered this information to Clingman, who had offered it to Beckley, who repeated it to Jefferson, the careful annotator of this chain of conversations. Fraunces was an invaluable informant for the Republicans. Having been fired by Hamilton and facing poor prospects for future employment, he was a man with a grudge who hungered for a useful alliance. According to Beckley, Fraunces had said that he "could, if he pleased, hang Hamilton"—a lead worth following, regardless of the methods required. The most likely things to grease this wheel would be alcohol or money, Beckley stated, for he knew that "Fraunces is fond of drink and very avaricious, and that a judicious appeal to either of those passions, would induce him to . . . tell all he knows."[42]

Not surprisingly, this search for evidence prompted Federalist suspicion—and gossip. As Beckley discovered, Hamilton soon learned of the Republican foray, sent for Clingman, "used every artifice to make a friend of him, and asked many leading questions about, who were his friends?" Beckley learned this from Clingman, who described the interview in detail. Beckley, in turn, reported the conversation with great precision to an unnamed friend. Hamilton asked,

> 1st Was he (Clingman) intimate with Mr. A. G. Fraunces of New York?
> Answer. He knew him.
> 2nd Did he ever board at his house?
> Answer. He never did.
> 3d. Did he not frequently dine and sup with him?
> Answer. He had once dined with him at a stranger's house.
> 4th. Did he not frequently visit Mr. Fraunces's Office?
> Answer. He had been there several times.
> 5th. Did he not visit Mr. Beckley sometimes?
> Answer. He knew Mr. Beckley, as he had seen him at Mr. Muhlenberg's.
> Mr. Hamilton then observed that Clingman did not put that confidence in him that he ought, as every thing that he (Clingman) said, was as secret as the grave.[43]

Anxious to track the flow of damaging information, Hamilton tried to win Clingman's trust and determine his friends — his gossip circle — hoping to collect information to deploy in his own defense.

Over the next two weeks, Republicans struggled to manage Fraunces, who swore that he had proof of Hamilton's corruption but revealed little concrete evidence, a serious problem for Republicans who wanted to spread truth, not lies; better to drop the entire affair than to risk the dishonor of circulating blatant falsehoods. No simple assurance would do; Beckley wanted affidavits, certificates, sworn oaths, and original documents. This search for evidence, in turn, alerted Hamilton's friends to the attack on his reputation. "Your enemies are at work upon Mr. Francis," William Willcocks warned. "They give out that he is to make affidavits, criminating you in the highest degree, as to some money matters." Eleven days later, he wrote a more urgent letter: "Slander is gratifying to the evil dis[position] of mankind and you may rest assured, [that as in] all other instances, so in this, nothing to your disadvantage is lost in the course of *circulation*. The Idea was, that Mr. Francis can substantiate some official criminallity against you, of a very serious nature. And yet no one pretends to any *precision*. Thus as you have written — The throat of your political reputation is to be cut, *in Whispers*."[44] Willcocks's evocative metaphor reveals the destructive power of a gossip campaign; whispers lurking just beyond Hamilton's reach would cut the "throat" of his reputation.

Hamilton responded as would any man of honor confronted by a base or cowardly foe: he "posted" Fraunces with a signed newspaper announcement, publicly defaming the former clerk and thereby discrediting his information.

> One Andrew G. Fraunces, lately a clerk in the treasury department, has been endeavoring to have it believed, that he is possessed of some facts, of a nature to criminate the official conduct of the Secretary of the Treasury; an idea to which, for obvious reasons, an extensive circulation has been given, by a certain description of persons. The Public may be assured, that the said Fraunces has been regularly and repeatedly called upon, to declare the grounds of his

> suggestion; that he has repeatedly evaded the enquiry; that he possesses no facts of the nature pretended; and that he is a dispicable calumniator.

Hamilton thus flung the lie direct at Fraunces, accusing him of circulating rumors without evidence—dramatic proof of the need to substantiate one's gossip. To stop the whisper campaign at its source, Hamilton strategically published his defense in a New York newspaper. Accusations from seeming intimates on his home ground were bound to be believed, and the worst damage to his reputation was being done in his absence. (Fraunces returned the favor by declaring in the next day's paper that Hamilton was a liar, but Hamilton didn't take the bait.)[45]

In the Fraunces campaign, Republicans strategically collected and deployed gossip to dishonor an enemy and destroy his career and cause. That same year Jefferson himself attempted a similar maneuver, as detailed in the "Anas." On March 23, 1793, he recorded a memorandum listing congressmen who owned stock in the Bank of the United States—an obvious conflict of interest, for their votes in Congress could affect the bank. To Jefferson this list would be the ultimate proof that a squadron of Federalists were manipulating government policy for their own greedy ends. As detailed in his memorandum, most of the names came from Beckley, who continued to feed Jefferson names as he discovered them. Jefferson recorded this process of transmission in dated and signed annotations to his list. In addition to Beckley's fodder, several men had "avowed" themselves stockholders "in the presence of T. J.," Jefferson's signed initials verifying his claim.[46]

Jefferson's friend Madison was in on this collecting mission as well; nine months before receiving Beckley's list of names, Jefferson had asked Madison for an earlier list in preparation for a meeting with Washington. As he explained to Madison, if "the P[resident] asks me for a list of particulars, I may enumerate names to him, without naming my authority, and shew him that I have not been speaking merely at random."[47] Jefferson would not gossip about congressmen without proof, but in accordance with gossip etiquette, he would not name his "authority," hoping that his ability to cite names would be enough to spark Washington's curiosity.

True to form, Jefferson described his meeting with Washington in a detailed memorandum. Setting the stage for his list, he warned the president that "there was a considerable squadron . . . whose votes were devoted to the paper and stock-jobbing interest, that the names of a weighty number were known and several others suspected on good grounds. That on examining the votes of these men they would be found uniformly for every treasury measure." The lure was cast, but Washington didn't take it, saying "not a word on the corruption of the legislature" but defending Hamilton's Funding Act instead. Finding Washington "really approving the treasury system," Jefferson had no cause to produce his evidence, and the conversation ended.[48] Because Washington did not share Jefferson's worldview, he did not even recognize the problem.

Jefferson the Politician

The three men at the heart of the Republican persuasion each had a specific role. John Beckley was the primary gatherer of gossip, as well as a skillful hands-on politico.[49] As clerk of the House of Representatives, he had easy access to files full of information about voting patterns and alliances. Present in the House but uninvolved in the debates, he could observe meetings and overhear conversations. Because he constantly shuffled congressional papers, he knew the handwriting of the representatives; joined with his familiarity with the printers who printed legislation and edited newspapers, this ideally positioned him to prove authorship of anonymous pamphlets and newspaper essays. Clearly, Beckley's office was the ideal platform for collecting gossip.

James Madison was the alliance's strategic coordinator as well as a national clearinghouse for information. In 1792 Madison was the man contacted when some New Yorkers wanted to run Aaron Burr for vice president. Prospective newspaper essayists and pamphleteers also consulted Madison, who filtered out the best efforts and passed them on to Jefferson for his approval.[50] With James Monroe's assistance, Madison guided a community of mobilized friends.

As suggested by Madison's filtering process, Jefferson was often comfortably detached from such paper-shuffling and negotiation, preferring to politick in different ways. In part, this stemmed from his notorious discomfort with conflict and confrontation. It also kept his hands (and reputation) clean from the dirty entanglements of routine politics, an ideal stance for the symbolic leader of a political persuasion. But Jefferson's detachment was deceptive, for he was a master of dinner-table politicking—a vital skill for national political success, as demonstrated by the failure of the standoffish Maclay.[51] The political intentions of Jefferson's dinner parties reveal that the seemingly aloof Virginian was a skilled politician.

Jefferson subtly set his dinner table as a political stage, inviting the proper mix of persuaded and persuadable guests, plying them with fine wines and deploying conversational props to direct the conversation. At an 1804 dinner during Jefferson's presidency, for example, New Hampshire Senator William Plumer (a Federalist with wavering sympathies) observed that among the eight types of wine and the "great variety of pies, fruit & nuts" were two bottles of water from the Mississippi River and a piece of the "Mammoth Cheese"—an enormous, 1,200-pound wheel of cheese, four feet in diameter, that had been presented to Jefferson during his 1801 inauguration. (Forcing down some of this cheese three years after Jefferson received it, Plumer declared it "very far from being good.") The stage was literally set to woo guests with an evening of stimulating conversation, focused around topics of interest—the Mississippi River, the Mammoth Cheese—that, by chance, showed Jefferson in a particularly good light. "Dominating the situation but never the conversation," Jefferson masterfully drew information from his guests and deposited information of his own.[52]

Even his dumbwaiter played a role in Jefferson's Epicurean stage management. By discouraging interruptions, it encouraged free conversation, capitalizing on the potential for guests to drop bits of useful information. As one guest observed, the dumbwaiter kept conversation uninterrupted and prevented "officious tattling domestics" from divulging topics of conversation to others. As suggested by Plumer's experience, Jefferson used dinner parties to good effect during his presidency to instruct and direct a cadre of congressional agents.[53] For reasons personal, political, and organizational, Jefferson's method was ideally adapted to the early national political world.

Ironically, this technique is best revealed in memoranda intended to incriminate Jefferson's enemies. On page after page, Jefferson encourages people to talk—soaks up information—records it in detail—passes on what seems important—and urges others to collect gossip in service of the Republican cause. In essence, his notes reveal Jefferson the politician at work. On January 2, 1792, for example, he invited Representatives Thomas Fitzsimons of Pennsylvania, Amassa Learned of Connecticut, and Elbridge Gerry of Massachusetts to dinner, along with several other guests. After everyone but the three congressmen had left, the conversation magically "turned" to "the subject of References by the legislature to the heads of departments"—to what Jefferson considered the key to Hamilton's power. The secretary of the treasury was the only cabinet position that had an explicit connection with Congress. As set out in the Treasury Act, the secretary was to respond to congressional requests for information and prepare reports on the revenue, opportunities that Hamilton used to full advantage, successfully proposing legislation on more than one occasion.[54] The four men discussed the "mischief" inherent in this practice, leading Jefferson to note in a memorandum at evening's end that Gerry and Fitzsimons were "clearly opposed" to it. Two days later, when the House referred a question to Hamilton, Jefferson noted on the same memorandum with satisfaction, "Gerry and FitzSimmons opposed it." Two weeks later, Fitzsimons again opposed a reference to Hamilton, and Jefferson again took careful note of it on that same page. Finally, six weeks later, on March 7, Republicans in Congress broached the issue in earnest, arguing that the House was capable of doing its own business. After an animated debate, Hamilton's supporters prevailed. "Gerry changed sides" in favor of Hamilton, Jefferson observed, concluding, "On the whole it shewed that treasury influence was tottering."[55] His innocent dinner party had in truth been a deliberate attempt to test and reinforce the sympathies of potential supporters in the House, the start of a campaign against Hamilton's congressional influence that was documented in Jefferson's detailed memorandum.

In contrast to Jefferson's politics of persuasion, Federalist strategy and spirit revolved around the industrious Hamilton. Bold, energetic, and organized, with a passion for military command, Hamilton was skilled at organizing, directing, and manipulating campaigns on a huge scale. He was ever the commander-in-chief, sizing up the enemy, devising campaign tactics, marshaling his troops, issuing them orders, and spurring them into battle. At his disposal was a national network of Treasury employees (customs collectors and revenue officers) built into the infrastructure of the government. (An "Organized System of Espionage thro' the medium of Revenue Officers," Beckley called it.) The organized, hierarchical, quasi-military style of Hamilton's leadership was, in fact, what most disturbed his opponents. It was no coincidence that Jefferson frequently resorted to military terminology when complaining about Hamilton's methods: Hamilton headed a "squadron," a "corps," a "campaign."[56]

Yet despite its usefulness in marshaling and deploying political forces, Hamilton's political style restricted the scope of national Federalist activity to the limits of his energies and interests. Commanded rather than persuaded, some supporters felt disconnected, unimportant, or unappreciated, leading them to ignore his advice and act independently, making it difficult for Federalists to spread a unified message. Equally problematic, Hamilton's national network was inner directed, focused on collecting and relaying information but rarely addressing the body politic—a strategic error that Hamilton would come to see over time. Ironically, Hamilton the devoted nationalist was often ineffective at coordinating national campaigns.[57]

The limits of Hamilton's method—and the effectiveness of Jefferson's—are apparent in the 1790 controversy over the assumption of state debts. As Jefferson relates it in his 1818 introduction to the "Anas," on his way to visit Washington one day, he met Hamilton in the street:

> He walked me backwards and forwards before the President's door for half an hour. He painted pathetically the temper into which the legislature had been wrought; the danger of the *secession* of their members, and the separation of the States. He observed that the members of the adminis-

> tration ought to act in concert; that though this question was not of my department, yet a common duty should make it a common concern . . . and that the question having been lost by a small majority only, it was probable that an appeal from me to the judgment and discretion of some of my friends, might effect a change in the vote, and the machine of government, now suspended, might be again set into motion.

True to character, Hamilton issued instructions, asking Jefferson to speak with his southern friends. Jefferson was equally true to form, proposing a dinner party: "I told him that I was really a stranger to the whole subject. . . . I proposed to him, however, to dine with me the next day, and I would invite another friend or two, bring them into conference together, and I thought it impossible that reasonable men, consulting together coolly, could fail, by some mutual sacrifices of opinion, to form a compromise which was to save the Union."[58]

At the ensuing dinner, Madison and Hamilton forged a compromise, Madison agreeing to moderate his opposition, and Hamilton agreeing not to block the relocation of the capital to the banks of the Potomac. Looking back on this dinner in later years, Jefferson declared it the single greatest regret of his life, insisting that he had been duped by Hamilton. He had taken no part in the deal "but an exhortatory one," he insisted, claiming the deniability of a mere host. But given that such dinner parties were Jefferson's political modus operandi, such protestations become suspect, at best. Nothing better attests to his appreciation of the political importance of such gatherings than his lifelong habit of describing them on scraps of paper.

Jefferson was, indeed, simply talking with friends. Yet he was also engaged in political discussions criticizing Hamilton's influence and policies. Thus, in the same way that Jefferson was justified in attacking Hamilton's command of a squadron of supporters, Hamilton had every right to accuse Jefferson of orchestrating a whisper campaign devoted to Hamilton's subversion. To Hamilton, Jefferson's clandestine politicking was dishonest, self-serving, and opposed to the principles of honest government. It was Jefferson's denial of his active politicking that so enraged Hamilton, leading him to brand Jefferson a hypocrite. As Hamilton wrote in the *Gazette of the United States* in September 1792, "Mr. Jefferson has hitherto been distinguished as the quiet modest, retiring philosopher—as the plain simple unambitious republican. He shall not now for the first time be regarded as . . . the aspiring turbulent competitor."[59]

In the same way that Jefferson could boast of his unwillingness to influence congressmen, Hamilton could pride himself on his candor and honesty in acknowledging that his political strategy sessions were just that. Unlike Jefferson, when Hamilton wanted to engage in a political discussion, he said so. Compare Jefferson's masterfully indirect dinner with a similar dinner orchestrated by Hamilton. "I wish to have the advantage of a conversation with you," he wrote to Robert Morris in November 1790. "If you will name a day for taking a family dinner with me, I shall think it the best arrangement. . . . The chief subjects will be additional *funds* for public Debt and the *Bank*. Would you have any objection that Mr. Fitsimmons should be of the party?"[60]

In the end, the Republican network of mobilized friends was better adapted to joining people in shared cause and spreading the word, and many Federalists perceived its wide-reaching power. Charles Carroll suspected that "a communication of Sentiments is maintained by the leaders of this party throughout the United States." Fisher Ames wrote that the Republicans "make up by union what they lack in numbers and by zeal and clamor what is wanting in proof till a little knot of conspirators of a thousand or two thousand persons shall lead the satisfied and unapprehensive million to the brink of ruin." Federalists never created such a network of passionate believers; they saw no need to. They were too confidently situated in office, too sure of their success. As Ames warned, "Success is poison to party zeal. . . . The opposers are industrious, watchful, united."[61]

Ultimately, it was their staggering loss in the election of 1800 that taught Federalists their error. The Federalists had "neglected the cultivation of popular favour," Hamilton ruefully admitted. James McHenry put matters more bluntly. "Have our party shown that they possess the necessary skill and courage to deserve to be continued to govern?" he asked. "What have they done? . . . They write private letters to each other, but do nothing to give a proper direction to the public mind. They observe even in their conversations generally, a discreet circumspection, illy calculated to diffuse information or prepare the mass of the people for the result they meditate in private."[62] Federalists had been too "discreet" in their conversations, limiting their sphere of influence in the process.

The Citizen Genet Affair

The 1793 "Citizen Genet" affair was a significant exception to standard Federalist practice. Under normal circumstances, Federalists discouraged popular rabble-rousing. They believed that the people should allow their elected rulers to rule; if they were dissatisfied, they could vote for new leaders at the next election. But the gaffes of the impulsive French minister Edmond Genet were too tempting an opportunity to let slip by. So Federalists orchestrated a strategic leak of confidential information to the general public, attempting to destroy Genet and the French-loving Republicans in the process. Effective as their public gossip campaign would prove to be, Federalists considered it the exception that proved the rule—an emergency measure born of a crisis.

"Citizen" Genet stirred up trouble almost immediately upon his arrival on American shores. Viewing him as a spokesman for the French Revolution, many Americans showered him with their love for the French cause, seemingly a noble offspring of the American Revolution; through France—and Genet—America's spark of liberty would spread over the earth (fig. 14). Democratic-Republican societies were one product of this revolutionary fervor. Clubs that met regularly to coordinate displays of enthusiasm and support for France, they communicated with one another, state to state, in what the Federalists came to see as an extraconstitutional effort to steer foreign affairs, control the political process, and overthrow the government. Although it is easy to dismiss these anxieties as paranoid delusions born of a siege mentality, Federalists had good reason to fear, for "self-created" committees of correspondence, communicating state to state, had fueled the American Revolution and overthrown the British government less than twenty years past.[63]

Fig. 14. *Edmond Charles "Citizen" Genet* (1763–1834), by Gilles-Louis Fouquet Chrétien, 1793. Dating to the height of Genet's popularity in America, this profile is encircled by Genet's official title. After the scandal, Genet married Cornelia Clinton, daughter of the powerful New York Republican George Clinton, and took up residence in the United States. (Collection of the Albany Institute of History and Art, Bequest of Augusta Georgia Kirtland [Mrs. George Clinton] Genet)

Thus, when Genet tried to capitalize on the popular uproar by stirring up support for France, Federalists were quick to detect an impending crisis. As New Yorker Rufus King protested, "But this is altogether wrong. We have with great Trouble established a Constitution which vests competent powers in the hands of the Executive. . . . It was never expected that the executive should sit with folded Arms, and that the Government should be carried on by Town Meetings, and those irregular measures, which disorganize the Society, destroy the salutary influence of regular Government, and render the Magistracy a mere pageant."[64]

Such disorder was bad enough, but when Genet went one step further and crossed the line of diplomatic relations, Federalists leaped into action. Genet made his mistake on July 6, 1793; confronted by the national government's insistent neutrality in the conflict between France and England, he threatened to go above Washington's head to the American people, asking them to help outfit French privateers in American ports (fig. 15). Genet supposedly voiced his threat to Alexander Dallas, an emissary of Pennsylvania governor Thomas Mifflin. Dallas repeated the story to Mifflin and later to Secretary of State Thomas Jefferson, who went to Genet to investigate matters. Mifflin, meanwhile, spread the story to Secretary of the Treasury Alexander Hamilton and Secretary of War Henry Knox. The entire cabinet then told President Washington.

Regardless of their feelings toward France, Washington's advisers agreed that this was an ill-advised attack on American sovereignty, an attempt by one nation to override the government of another. But publicizing the issue could precipitate an international incident, so until they decided on a course of action, the president and his cabinet decided to keep the affair quiet. Hamilton, however, was quick to see the advantages of Genet's insult. Properly communicated to the American public, this rude dismissal of the government—and even worse, of the great Washington—could sway public opinion against Genet, France, and the French Revolution, and guide foreign policy in the process. This would do more than distance America from the revolution's social chaos: it could potentially inspire goodwill toward Great Britain, discrediting French-loving Republicans in the process. Skillfully manipulated, the Genet affair could convert the nation to the Federalist point of view.

Even without encouragement, news of Genet's actions was spreading. On July 16, New Yorker Aaron Burr asked John Nicholson in Philadelphia whether he, too, had heard "a rumor . . . that Genet has come to an open rupture with the President—That he has publickly threatened to appeal to the people." Three days later, William Smith in Baltimore asked his son-in-law Otho Williams if he could confirm

765
(154)

Philadelphia, Auguſt, 1793.

ALL able bodied ſeamen who are willing to engage in the cauſe of Liberty, and in the ſervice of the French Republic, will pleaſe to apply to the French Conſul, at No. 132, North Second-ſtreet.

Particular attention will be paid to the generous and intrepid natives of Ireland, who, it is preſumed, will act like thoſe warlike troops from that oppreſſed country, who took refuge in France about a century ago, and performed prodigies of valor under the old government of that country.

Theſe, and volunteers from any other country, will be received into preſent pay, and comfortable accommodations.

N. B. The Republic has, at this preſent time, in her ſervice, officers and ſoldiers from every civilized country in Europe, and natives of America, who, in imitation of the heroes from France in the American revolutic[illegible] are a glory to themſelves, and an honour to the country which gave them birth.

Fig. 15. Broadside, August 1793. Part of Genet's campaign to recruit Americans to support France in its war against England, this broadside openly defies American neutrality—precisely the sort of gesture that panicked Federalists and ultimately destroyed Genet's diplomatic career. It was printed at the height of the controversy, at least three weeks *after* his threat to go directly to the American people. (Courtesy of the Library of Congress)

the tale. Everyone had heard the story, but no one could ascertain its truth, for the handful of men with proof were maintaining an official silence. And the farther the gossip traveled from its source, the less accurate it became. By the time the news reached New Hampshire, the report was that Genet had assassinated the president.[65] Without direct knowledge of events or reputations, gossip was difficult to evaluate.

Encouraged by the piecemeal public discovery of Genet's actions, Hamilton urged Washington to explain the entire affair to the American people in a published statement—a distinctly un-Hamiltonian suggestion. As Jefferson explained to Madison, "Hamilton & Knox have pressed an appeal to the people with an eagerness I never before saw in them." Afraid of the complications inherent in a public statement, Washington maintained his official silence, but Federalists soon filled the void. Unable to communicate Genet's actions through official channels, they turned to less formal means. Hamilton opened the campaign on July 31 in a Philadelphia newspaper, writing as "No Jacobin" that it "is publicly rumoured in this City that the Minister of the French Republic *has threatened to appeal from The President of the United States to the People*."[66] But his report of a public rumor had no substantiation, for almost anything Hamilton added would reveal that "No Jacobin" was a cabinet member going above Washington's head, thereby discrediting himself and damaging the Federalist cause by association. Gossip about Genet would have to spread through less official channels.

Aware of the demands of the moment, Senator Rufus King and Chief Justice John Jay took action, revealing Genet's indiscretion in a signed statement that appeared in the New York *Diary:* "Certain late publications render it proper for us to authorize you to inform the public, that a Report having reached this City from Philadelphia, that Mr. Genet, the french minister, had said he would appeal to the People from certain Decisions of the President; we were asked on our return from that place whether he had made such a declaration, we answered that he had, and we also mentioned it to others, authorising them to say that we had so informed them."[67] Jay and King were validating a piece of gossip in writing with the authority of their names and reputations. In doing so, they committed its transmission to paper: a rumor from Philadelphia had reached New York; to substantiate it, people had consulted with two men recently returned from Philadelphia; the two witnesses had confirmed the rumor; they had then passed it on under the sanction of their name, encouraging people to spread the word.

Jay and King claimed responsibility for their gossip, but by printing it in a newspaper under the authority of their names, they intimated that it was something more. Secret information made public and attributed to public figures did not sound like gossip; it sounded official. Robert R. Livingston thought that the two Federalists spoke for Washington: "I am certainly surprized at Jay & King's certificate—They certainly would not have taken this step without having been well aprized of the president's approbation & yet it appears to me that it lessens the dignity of government to resent an affront in this indirect way."[68] Jay and King could not have chosen a more efficient way to disseminate their information.

During the next few months, the gossip spread. People talked of both Genet's threat and the equally shocking *Diary* gossip certificate, eventually driving Genet to defend himself publicly. Predictably, he and his supporters attacked Jay and King where they were most vulnerable, accusing them of gossiping without proof. As one anonymous author wrote, "Any school-boy knows hearsay testimony to be inadmissable even before a Justice of the Peace when not five Shillings is at stake and yet a Chief Justice & Senator when prosecuting or rather persecuting the French minister before the awful tribunal of the public—and when his & their characters are at stake—bring forward nothing but hearsay declarations & those are third or fourth hand."[69] Gossip could be a powerful political tool, but in this case it was proving to be problematic.

Ultimate proof rested with Republicans Dallas and Jefferson, the only men who had spoken with Genet—the only eyewitnesses. Cornered by the Federalist campaign and concerned by its apparent success, both men felt pressed to publish statements of their own. On December 9, 1793, Dallas published an ambiguous account in the *Daily Advertiser* admitting that he had spoken with Genet but implying that

Genet had not threatened to appeal to the people. Dallas's statement offered evidence, however weak, that the Federalists might be lying. His publication thus proved useful to Jefferson, who had been preparing a public statement of his own.[70]

Jefferson was caught in an uncomfortable situation. He knew that Genet had indeed threatened to appeal to the people. "You will see much said & gainsaid about G[enet]'s threat to appeal to the people," he wrote to Madison. "I can assure you it is a fact." Trying to quash Federalist rumors without lying outright, Jefferson side-stepped the issue by manipulating Genet's words: Genet's appeal to the "people" was actually an attempt to appeal to Congress, he argued. The "Anas" includes Jefferson's carefully worded 1793 memorandum explaining that Genet's dim understanding of the American Constitution, joined with his volatile temper, had garbled an intended congressional appeal. Evidence suggests that Genet was, indeed, confused by constitutional law, for in the midst of the melée, he bought a copy of "the Laws of the United States" from Republican editor Philip Freneau.[71] Still, Jefferson's explanation was not entirely convincing, and Dallas's ambiguous statement allowed him to withhold it from publication. As Monroe informed Jefferson, in a valiant attempt to untangle a chain of conversations, "I find the establishment of the charge agnst Mr. Genet will depend principally upon what you heard Mr. Dallas say. This latter will deny that he ever said anything like what the certificate states. Jay & King heard it from Hamilton & Knox, these latter from Mifflin & I am told that there is a difference between those gentn. & Mifflin, & likewise between him & Dallas as to what they respectively stated." Jefferson could hide behind Dallas's ambiguity, for Federalist charges were too difficult to substantiate.[72] Monroe's letter reveals the problem with using gossip as a political tool. Powerful because it was as natural as conversation, like conversation gossip altered from person to person. When needed for official purposes, rumor and gossip could be frustratingly imprecise.

Jefferson's silence damned him in the eyes of the Federalists, just as publication damned Jay and King in the eyes of the Republicans. (Genet had called Jay and King "Lyars" and had "proved that they were so," cheered his future wife, Cornelia Clinton.) But nothing could save

Genet. Even if he had meant to appeal to Congress rather than the general public, he had slighted Washington and set off a national chorus of support for the president and his administration. As Hamilton intended, gossip was helping to destroy both Genet and popular support of France. The usually pessimistic Fisher Ames rejoiced, "The town is less frenchified than it was. Citizen Genet is out of credit. . . . I like the horizon better than I did; there are less clouds." The more effusive Robert Troup wrote, "No measure was ever better timed—and none has ever been attended with more powerful & happy effects. If you were now with us you would suppose the millennium had arrived or was near at hand."[73]

Alarmed at the Federalist "millennium," Madison planned a counterattack. Unable to save the impulsive French minister, he set out to separate the Republicans from Genet, and Genet from France. He first scripted a statement explaining that Republicans did not support Genet, nor did the minister properly represent France. He then assigned Monroe the task of carrying the message throughout Virginia, offering it to reputable men to be read at district courts as a means of swaying public opinion. In addition, the two men sent letters to reputable Republicans, attacking Federalist motives along familiar lines: the Federalists were publicizing Genet's indiscretion to create "an unnatural connection with Great Britain."[74] Good Republicans should counter this offense by offering the people the "truth"—the Republican view.

Madison undertook his dissemination campaign so that the "genuine sense of the people could be collected"—a word choice that reveals much about the dynamics of conversation. Politicians who claimed to be dispassionate "collectors" of public opinion were describing the process as they envisioned it. In reality, no conversation purposefully aimed at leading an audience to discuss political events was a mere collection of public sentiment: it was the proper seeding of public opinion and the reaping of the desired response. In fact, on at least one occasion, Madison prepared scripted statements of "public opinion" to be disseminated and then "collected" back. People who gathered public opinion in taverns attempted a similar maneuver when they tried to "make bar-room converts," as did William Loughton Smith when he collected public opinion by observing what newspapers were being read—and gave Federalist papers to those reading the "wrong" one. When audience members did not respond properly, they were the "wrong" public. To national politicians, public opinion represented the response to strategic conversations orchestrated by political leaders. As Republicans eventually understood more fully than Federalists, the game of government could be won by the party that best orchestrated these conversations.[75]

The Defense Pamphlet

During the Genet affair, Jefferson, Genet, Jay, King, and Dallas had considered publishing statements to counter rumors that threatened their reputations. Each man saw that the most effective defense against gossip was a signed, printed refutation, an official but personal statement. Aside from Jefferson's memoranda, this type of written defense constitutes the most telling evidence of a largely oral political weapon.

Print was effective for many reasons. A controlled means of presenting an argument, printed refutations displayed substantiating evidence in a manner not possible by word of mouth. In written statements, individual politicians virtually stood before the reader in person, contradicting rumors with evidence and the weight of their reputations. There could hardly be a more direct way to silence whispers. Gossip left tone, insinuation, and accuracy in the hands of the speaker; print allowed writers to present their case as they wished it understood.

Aware of the power of print, politicians crafted their defenses with care, selecting the best medium for their message. Broadsides, newspaper essays, pamphlets, and public-minded personal letters had different tones and readerships, forming an arsenal of paper weapons that were each adapted to a different purpose. Hamilton, for example, first refuted Andrew Fraunces with a posting in a newspaper, dismissing both Fraunces and his charges as too base for further action. When Fraunces received more credence (and Republican support) than Hamilton expected, he began work on a pamphlet, collecting affidavits, certificates, and correspondence to prove his point.[76] Such choices constitute the shared logic of paper war.

As suggested by Hamilton's actions, pamphlets were the ideal medium for refuting rumors substantiated by impressive evidence or stellar reputations. Long-lived, dignified, and typically aimed at a small circle of "men of influence," they easily encompassed lengthy legalistic arguments, and writers could assume a certain degree of insider's knowledge. "Defense pamphlets" were a public means of silencing private conversation; they removed gossip from the shadows and exposed it as malicious lies.[77]

Many early national political pamphlets, long misinterpreted as petty personal diatribes, become logical methods of defense when recognized as defense pamphlets. They conform to a genre: they are signed public statements that begin with an explanation of the "truth" and an attack on the accuser's motives, followed by documentary evidence. When Jefferson threatened to defend himself in print at the height of his opposition to Hamilton, he had in mind a defense pamphlet. In a long letter of outrage to Washington, he reserved the right to appeal to his "country, subscribing my name to whatever I write, & using with freedom & truth the facts & names necessary to place the cause in it's just form"—the precise definition of a defense pamphlet.[78]

Understood in this context, the "Anas" is a logical response to Marshall's "five volumed libel."[79] It was Jefferson's defense pamphlet, and like any author of such a tract, Jefferson signed his name to his work. He began with an introductory statement, explaining the truth and maligning the motives of Marshall and his Federalist friends, and appended documentary evidence—his public papers and private memoranda—as corroboration. By adopting the conventions of the defense pamphlet, Jefferson betrayed his true purpose in compiling his history. His seemingly objective collection of documents was actually a highly personal attempt to defend his reputation and the Republican worldview.

Jefferson's public papers were appropriate fodder for a defense pamphlet: they were signed public statements. But his private memoranda—formerly seen by no one but himself—were unusual pieces of evidence with little proof of authenticity. For this reason, he attested to their physical existence in his introduction, depicting them as "ragged, rubbed, and scribbled" scraps of aged paper that had been bound into his three volumes while he watched. To confirm their accuracy, he added, "After the lapse of twenty-five years, or more, from their dates, I have given to the whole a calm revisal, when the passions of the time are passed away, and the reasons of the transactions act alone on the judgment. Some of the informations I had recorded are now cut out from the rest, because I have seen that they were incorrect or doubtful, or merely personal or private, with which we have nothing to do."[80] Jefferson thus implied that all of the anecdotes in the "Anas" were authentic and accurate. By offering them to his readers, he believed that he was practicing good politics, defeating corrupt and deceitful foes by revealing the historical truth to the American public. To Jefferson, gossip was indeed "the life and soul" of history. It was his strongest evidence—the reality of political event.

The reality Jefferson presented was a Republican view of the 1790s: the Federalists were corrupt monarchists, the Republicans saviors of the republic. Yet sincere as his professions might be, Jefferson understood the difficulties of persuading his audience. As with all gossip, certain rules governed authenticity. Most important was the question of Jefferson's motives. If he seemed too obviously partisan, his charges would be dismissed as the ranting of an ambitious politician with a personal grudge. Jefferson knew that he could never pass as an unbiased observer of the events of the 1790s, but he could moderate his tone and control his evidence to obscure his personal involvement. The more impartial he seemed, the more believable his account would appear.

Thus, throughout his history, Jefferson took care to remove all evidence of his involvement in political intrigue. Though he himself drafted the "Giles Resolutions" (congressional resolutions calling for an investigation of Hamilton's activities as secretary of the treasury), he did not include the draft in his three volumes. Instead, he inserted an ambiguous memorandum that stated, "See in the papers of this date, Mr. Giles's resolutions." He similarly excluded three letters to Washington chock full of accusations against Hamilton, for they would defeat the pose of impartiality he was struggling to achieve.[81]

Jefferson's biggest problem in preparing his history was Alexander Hamilton. Although the work was intended to discredit the New Yorker, Jefferson's evidence would not be convincing if he showed personal animosity. Somehow he had to indict Hamilton without allowing his emotions to leak into his argument. In part, he achieved this through the selective inclusion of evidence. His carefully moderated introduction served the same purpose. There he allowed Hamilton to indict himself in an anecdote describing how he praised the "corruption" of the British monarchy while seated at Jefferson's dinner table. Aware of the animosity underlying this story, Jefferson then reestablished the proper tone by praising Hamilton as "a singular character" of "acute understanding, disinterested, honest, and honorable in all private transactions, amiable in society, and duly valuing virtue in private life."[82]

To veil his animosity, Jefferson also annotated his memoranda of more than twenty years past—part of the "calm revisal" that he touted in his introduction. In the memorandum reporting the story that Hamilton had secured asylum in England, for example, Jefferson added in the margin, "Impossible as to Hamilton; he was far above that." Under Beckley's story about Hamilton's supposed attempt to institute a monarchy in the 1780s, Jefferson added, "Beckley is a man of perfect truth as to what he affirms of his own knowledge, but too credulous as to what he hears from others." Jefferson considered these memoranda dangerously hostile toward his longtime foe, but important enough to include, so he edited them. Memoranda that were too nasty to edit were withheld altogether.[83]

Like others who gossiped, Jefferson protected his friends and sources by excluding them from his accusations. Madison is barely mentioned in the "Anas," despite his pivotal importance to the Republicans and his close friendship with Jefferson. Discussing the 1790 dinner deal concerning the Funding Act and the national capital, Jefferson's history mentions only a dinner attended by Jefferson, Hamilton, and "a friend or two," although Jefferson's original 1792 account of the negotiation reveals Madison's central role in the process.[84] Ironically, such attempts at impartiality made Jefferson's history intensely personal by centering it entirely around his enemies and friends.

Despite his meticulous attention to detail, Jefferson never published his history, a seeming paradox that was actually a final attempt to appear impartial. By leaving his three bound volumes to be discovered among his papers, Jefferson implied that they were little more than a compendium of raw materials, carefully arranged by the writer, but authentic nonetheless. If Jefferson himself had brought his history into public view, readers would have recognized it for what it was—a personal defense. As its self-proclaimed "author," Jefferson would have thrust himself into the political arena as a partisan combatant, damaging his reputation as a bystander to political intrigue and destroying his history's credibility in the process. By aggressively taking aim at his opponents, he also would have bolstered the Federalist worldview by acknowledging it as a threat. In essence, personally publishing his history would have undermined his purpose for creating it. Leaving his work among his papers like a ticking time bomb, Jefferson remained comfortably detached from political conflict, a passive conversationalist, like all purveyors of gossip. Ultimately, he distanced himself from his work by capitalizing on the detachment of death.[85]

Jefferson's alterations may seem overtly manipulative, but he never would have conceded this charge. He was so firmly convinced of the truth of his vision that he saw no conflict in editing documentary evidence.[86] He well knew that surface events often clouded the "truth" of political contests. In his eyes he was merely making this truth clear for posterity, pushing aside "false facts" of Federalist duplicity in service of the true facts of Republicanism. For Jefferson, as for so many others in the founding generation, the construction of history continued the party battles of the 1790s. He and his opponents were appealing to posterity, attempting to win future political battles with carefully crafted presentations of the past.

Posterity did not always receive Jefferson's message. As with all gossip, credibility depends on the perspective of one's audience. For those who disliked Jefferson or disagreed with his convictions, the

"Anas" was damning evidence of an ambitious, cunning politician—a pack of lies from a self-serving partisan. In fact, condemnation of Jefferson's "Anas" would reverberate well into the nineteenth century. Critics echoed the sentiments of Theodore Dwight, author of *The Character of Thomas Jefferson* (1839). "No frank, open-hearted, sincere man, ever made a practice of noting down private conversations between himself and those with whom he was accustomed to associate. . . . Whoever does it, must be actuated by some secret, sinister, and insidious design," Dwight argued, and in many ways, he was right.[87] Jefferson's history *was* a personal attack with an ulterior motive, filled with surreptitiously recorded private conversations. But these very human characteristics give the work its value. The "Anas" reveals how Republican politicians understood the period's politics, allowing us to view the world through Republican eyes.

Thus, in ways that Jefferson never understood or intended, gossip is indeed history. Properly deciphered, it offers a window into the heart of national politics in the early republic. Rather than impartially relating historical fact, it reveals a hidden level of government—an undercurrent of personal interaction that forged political alliances and enmities—a world that politicians recognized as the grounding of national politics in the unstructured new nation.

The Art of Paper War

John Adams lacked Jefferson's political finesse. He was too prone to emotional outbursts, too trusting, too honest, too passionate by half about friends and enemies. As his secretary of war James McHenry explained, whether Adams was "sportful, playful, witty, kind, cold, drunk, sober, angry, easy, stiff, jealous, careless, cautious, confident, close, open, it is almost always in the *wrong place* or to the *wrong persons*" (fig. 16). McHenry knew firsthand about Adams's emotional eruptions; near the close of Adams's presidency, in 1800, the secretary resigned his office during a presidential temper tantrum over Alexander Hamilton. As McHenry recorded it, Adams ranted that "Hamilton is an intriguant—the greatest intriguant in the World—a man devoid of every moral principle" and "a Bastard."[1] Clearly, unlike Jefferson, Adams was not careful with words, a fatal flaw in a politics of reputation; in 1800 this failing subjected Adams to the most venomous attack of his public career—written by none other than Hamilton himself.

To Adams, few tormentors of the pen were as aggravating as

Fig. 16. *John Adams* (1735–1826), by Gilbert Stuart, ca. 1800–1815. Begun after Adams stepped down from the presidency and never finished, this portrait was commissioned by the Massachusetts Legislature to be hung in the House of Representatives. Adams appears somewhat wary, but humor plays over his features as well. He enjoyed sitting for Stuart, who kept him "constantly amused by his conversation." (Gift of Mrs. Robert Homans, Photograph © Board of Trustees, National Gallery of Art, Washington, D.C.)

Hamilton—on this, he and Jefferson agreed. Unlike Jefferson, however, the irascible Adams unleashed his abuse against the New Yorker in his diary, his letters, and even his autobiography. "The bastard brat of a Scotch pedlar," Adams called Hamilton on more than one occasion, an "insolent coxcomb who rarely dined in good company, where there was good wine, without getting silly and vaporing about his administration like a young girl about her brilliants and trinkets." Some of this animosity stemmed from a simple clash of personalities. Adams was stubbornly independent, and Hamilton tried to steer him. Adams had a strict sense of virtue concerning women; Hamilton did not. There were practical political reasons for Adams's dislike as well: he resented Hamilton's persistent meddling in elections, cabinet meetings, foreign policy, and in fact, much of the doings of Adams's administration. A private citizen, Hamilton nonetheless received regular dispatches from Adams's cabinet for much of his presidency, for most of the cabinet members were holdovers from Washington's administration. But there was one thing above all others that Adams could never forgive, and it grew from his eruption against Hamilton in 1800.[2]

That year Adams had discovered the extent of Hamilton's influence over his cabinet and had dismissed or forced the resignation of most of the members in a rage. Shutting Hamilton out of national politics was bad enough, but the enraged president went a step further, attacking Hamilton in private conversation as the head of "a British faction" more devoted to England than America—as good as a charge of traitor to this generation of Revolutionary War veterans. "Mr. Adam's personal friends seconded by the Jacobins will completely *run us down in the public opinion,*" Hamilton fretted when he learned of Adams's charge, well aware of the power and reach of gossip. Hamilton's friend McHenry added fuel to the fire by giving Hamilton a transcription of his last, explosive meeting with the president. Fearful for his reputation, furious at Adams, and thinking ahead to the pending presidential election of 1800, Hamilton lashed back.[3]

Hamilton's "Letter . . . Concerning the Public Conduct and Character of John Adams" served a double purpose. A vindication of Hamilton and his supporters, it was also an attempt to destroy Adams's hopes for the presidency in the next campaign. As suggested by its title, it not only criticized Adams's political career, but it maligned his character as well—the egotism, vanity, and ungovernable temper that deprived Adams of "self command," the central pillar of manhood.[4]

To Adams, this egregious attack demanded a response. Not only was Hamilton stabbing at Adams's reputation in the here and now, but he was stabbing at his immortal fame as well, the lodestar of Adams's public life. Uncomfortable with his ambitions yet ambitious nonetheless, Adams channeled his desires into that greatest of goals, recognition as the founder of a nation.[5]

Given Adams's discomfort with self-promotion, an open defense of the sort waged by Hamilton was out of the question. So Adams chose a more roundabout form of defense, devoting his energies to tending the historical record. He deposited public documents with the

Massachusetts Historical Society and published them in newspapers to inscribe his accomplishments in the public record. He aggressively corrected inaccurate works of history that came his way, including the efforts of former family friend Mercy Otis Warren, whose *History of the Rise, Progress, and Termination of the American Revolution* (1805) he lambasted with particular fervor. (The perceptive Warren told Adams that had he not "been suffering suspicions that his fame had not been sufficiently attended to, he would not have put such a perverse construction on [my] every passage.") He began an autobiography so that "Posterity" might see in his "own hand Writing a proof of the falsehood of that Mass of odious Abuse of my Character, with which News Papers, private Letters and public Pamphlets and Histories have been disgraced for thirty Years." In private letters, Adams railed along the same lines. He even drafted a page-by-page refutation of Hamilton's pamphlet, though he consigned it to his private papers without publishing it, possibly intending it to enlighten future generations in the manner of Jefferson's "history." Hamilton's death did nothing to arrest this campaign. As Adams himself put it, he would not permit his "Character to lie under infamous Calumnies, because the Author of them, with a Pistol Bullet through his Spinal Marrow, died a Penitent."[6]

Much as Adams's efforts might have vented some spleen, they did little for his reputation after decades of abuse. Increasingly, he feared that posterity might never glance his way at all. Great acts did not always garner great rewards; the deserving man was not always credited for his accomplishments and their legacy. The passage of time had revealed an alarming truth to Adams: a leader in the fight for American independence, a diplomat who had sacrificed his domestic happiness to the national cause, a vice president during the nation's precarious first years, a president who saved his country from the ravages of war, he might still die an obscure man.

Hungry for recognition yet unable and unwilling to court it, Adams bitterly watched himself fade into obscurity—until 1809, when the seventy-four-year-old found himself in the political arena once again. With hostilities brewing between America, France, and England, two Massachusetts countrymen, Erastus Lyman and Daniel

Wright, sought Adams's counsel. "Venerable father of New-England!" they pleaded, "O save your native state from ruin and destruction!" Adams's advice would be "commanding still," they insisted. "Thousands will hear your voice."[7] At this moment of crisis, people were turning to Adams for guidance. To Adams, *not* responding to such a plea would be a sacrilege, violating the pledge to public service that had fueled his career. And who could offer better counsel than a former president, who had taken the nation through a similar crisis?

In fact, foreign affairs had dominated Adams's presidency. Throughout the 1790s, the fledgling nation had been caught up in a longstanding conflict between two warring powers, England and France. A friendly gesture toward one of these nations unavoidably soured relations with the other. And Americans were themselves divided about the British and the French. Federalists favored England for its stable system of government and sound commerce; Republicans favored France for its republican revolt against the aristocratic standing order. During Washington's presidency, the balance had tipped toward England with the 1795 Jay Treaty, and the French had retaliated by ordering the seizure of American ships carrying cargo to British ports. To avoid war, Adams had sent peace commissioners to France, where the French minister refused to meet them unless they paid a massive bribe. The affair roused a wave of patriotic fury in America, and the nation's armed forces were readied for war. The resulting "Quasi-War" was a boon to the Federalists, who gloried in the opportunity to war against France, discredit the French-loving Republicans, and build up America's military in one fell swoop, enjoying enormous public support all the while (fig. 17).

But Adams burst this bubble in 1799 by sending a diplomatic mission to France when the French seemed willing to seek peace. Not surprisingly, this peace mission enraged most Federalists, including Hamilton, whose active meddling in this affair sparked Adams's anger—and Hamilton's response. In the end, Adams avoided war but sacrificed his reputation (and thus the presidential election) in the process. Given the importance of self-sacrifice to his sense of self, it is no wonder that he considered the 1799 peace mission the crowning achievement of his public career. In his eyes, the mission should "be

Fig. 17. *A New Display of the United States*, by Amos Doolittle, August 14, 1799. Created during the Quasi-War with France, this engraving shows popular approval of the president in a time of crisis—the type of tribute that Adams received all too rarely. (Courtesy of the Library of Congress)

transmitted to posterity as the most glorious period in American History, and as the most disinterested, prudent, and successful conduct in my whole life. For I was obliged to give peace and unexampled prosperity to my country for eight years . . . against the advice, intreaties, and intrigues of all my Ministers, and all the leading Federalists in both houses of Congress." Since that time, the Federalists had pursued Adams "with the most unrelenting hatred," joining with the Republicans "to conceal from the people all the services of my life." To Adams they had "succeeded to a degree, that I should scarcely have believed it possible for a union of both parties to effect."[8]

Now, with another foreign conflict brewing, Adams was being called out of obscurity with a direct reference to the very act that had cast him into the shadows, and his answer would serve the public during a time of crisis. The appeal was irresistible. So on March 24, 1809, Adams responded to Lyman and Wright by pleading for neutrality—and recognition as well. He had always considered "the whole Nation as my Children," he confessed at the conclusion of his letter, but "they have almost all been undutiful to me. . . . You two Gentlemen are almost the only ones out of my own house, who have for a long time, and I thank you for it, expressed a filial affection." Although Lyman and Wright had said nothing about publication, their appeal to Adams to address "thousands" made it difficult to assume otherwise. And indeed, his response appeared in newspapers and broadsides within weeks, provoking a mixed reaction.[9]

At least one acquaintance felt sympathy for the forgotten founder. "I know not when my sensibilities have been more exquisitely touched, than they were by . . . the concluding sentence of your letter," wrote William Cunningham, an ardent Federalist and distant relation.[10] Those panting for war with either England or France were less kind, decrying Adams's letter in newspapers and goading the former president to reply in turn. For the first time in his life, Adams found himself defending his reputation in print before a national audience.

The unexpected turn of events was a windfall for a man who had been stewing over his reputation for decades. Adams was "all at once and very unexpectedly, a man of . . . much importance in the world," he observed wryly. Called into the public eye, he decided to seize the moment to redeem his name. "I will either throw off that intolerable load of obloquy and insolence that they [his enemies] have thrown upon me, or I will perish in the struggle," he declared to Cunningham. Noting a recently founded newspaper called the *Boston Patriot,* Adams addressed a letter to its editors, requesting "a little room" to explain his French mission, the first in a series of almost three hundred letters published twice a week, every week, for three years. "My pen shall go as long as my fingers can hold it," he swore to Cunningham. "I will not die for nothing."[11]

Adams's *Boston Patriot* letters were a remarkable phenomenon. After years of silence, a former president was pleading his case in that most public forum: a newspaper. Unprecedented in America, the action was also uncharacteristic for Adams, and his heartfelt confessions and accusations, signed and claimed by their author, were unusual newspaper fodder as well. Cunningham immediately recognized the novelty of Adams's actions, and his ensuing questions and comments opened an active correspondence with the author. With typical candor, Adams explained himself in detail during the course of the exchange. The result would be one of many controversies in Adams's life sparked by his carelessness with words. In the end, Adams's *Boston Patriot* letters would affect his reputation in ways he had never hoped for or imagined.

Adams's sufferings reveal the risks in committing one's thoughts to paper. Not only did a writer endanger his own reputation, but he entangled other reputations as well. Such would be the outcome of Adams's *Boston Patriot* essays, one link in a long paper chain of personal defenses. Seen outside this larger context, Adams's newspaper campaign seems like little more than an illogical temper tantrum, and so it is typically treated—as is Hamilton's "Letter."[12] However, framed in a culture of honor and reputation, and tied in with the other voices in this dialogue, these works become much more. Given the severity of Hamilton's attack, Adams had every reason to rant. By the rules of paper combat, he also had every reason to stage a counterattack. This contemporaries expected. Hamilton likewise had ample reasons for writing his pamphlet, as a chorus of supporters well understood. The real question is why the two campaigns failed, and to understand that, we must wrestle with the logic of paper war.

The Weapons of Paper War

Most politicians in Adams's situation would have chosen a different course of action. A defense pamphlet would have been the usual medium for combating Hamilton's publication; the best forum for an extended argument advanced with documentary evidence, it was the customary vehicle for a lengthy character defense and the medium that Hamilton himself had used to wage his attack. Indeed, many Federalists expected such a publication. "I have reason to suspect that the President will, like some other great men, write a vindication of his official conduct," wrote Adams's secretary of the treasury Oliver Wolcott, who began stockpiling documents in case he needed to respond. Others expected pamphlets from McHenry and Timothy Pickering, both dishonorably dismissed from Adams's cabinet. One man even expected some such response to Adams's *Boston Patriot* essays. Such expectations—and the prevailing surprise that Adams chose a newspaper—reveal the shared assumptions underlying paper war. Strategically written "private" letters, pamphlets, broadsides, and newspapers each had a different power and reach, and politicians chose the medium best adapted to their purposes.[13] It is an idea worth repeating: when politicians chose a medium for their writings, they declared their intended purpose and audience—a useful fact for scholars trying to interpret those writings today.

At the core of such decisions was a fundamental question: How much of his reputation should a writer invest? A signed attack bore the clout of its writer's reputation but risked it by thrusting him into the public eye.[14] Unsigned publications offered the safety of anonymity, but without the authority of a name they had less power. A poor choice of medium could backfire, as Adams would learn all too well. Hence the ongoing stream of letters from men seeking advice on paper war. Although the stubbornly independent Adams consulted no one before launching his *Boston Patriot* campaign, most politicians were more cautious. For example, Virginian John Taylor of Caroline sought

James Madison's advice concerning a 1793 manuscript attacking the National Bank. "Ought it to appear in a pamp[h]let or in the newspapers?" he asked. "The latter are meer ephemere, and tho' containing merit, read & forgotten. The best political essays being often supposed to proceed from the printers in a course of trade." The abundance of such letters suggests the importance of selecting the right weapon—and the risks involved with choosing the wrong one.[15]

Public-Minded Personal Letters

Personal letters were the most private paper weapon, though they became public all too easily. Letters fell out of mailbags, were misplaced by postmasters, and could be published in newspapers if they fell into the wrong hands. Private correspondence was none too private in an age of difficult and erratic communication, yet it was fundamental to national politics, linking representative to constituent when the government was in session, and ally to ally when it was not. There was a good reason why correspondents catalogued letters sent and received at the opening of their own letters, or scrawled "Confidential" on the wrapper or in the heading.[16]

Some private letters were simply that: personal communications between allies or friends, although even such simple exchanges had risks. Note the fate of Philadelphia visitor Count Paolo Andriani, who ridiculed America's new government in a letter to friends overseas. When an American abroad heard tell of it, he sent the letter to President Washington, who had it "handed about" in Philadelphia so that Andriani "might be treated in the way that he ought"—evidence of Washington's oft-overlooked political savvy. As one of Andriani's friends noted, the count became so "detested" that he soon found it necessary to "decamp."[17]

Some letters had more complex purposes. Framed as a private address from one gentleman to another, these public-minded personal letters were in fact intended to be circulated among small numbers of elite readers; endorsed with "the authority of a name," a public-minded letter was a sworn statement of fact, the writer staking his honor on its veracity. Seeking to prove circulating charges about Republicans, one Massachusetts Federalist insisted that it "ought to be mentioned in private letters that the Rascals may be known upon good authority." In essence, signed letters were a written form of face-to-face communication, the signature standing in for the writer's physical presence and identity.[18] Adams's letters were rarely this contrived, which was part of his problem. He was not self-conscious enough about what he committed to paper.

Politicians typically used such letters to defend themselves before small circles of intimates or to sway fence-sitters in preparation for battle. For example, to refute accusations of financial malfeasance in 1792, Hamilton wrote to a supporter in the state where the charges originated, giving the lie to his accuser by denouncing the assertion as "a gross and wicked slander." Considering its extreme language, he intended to restrict the letter to a small circle of men but not to publish it in a newspaper, and he so instructed his correspondent. Jefferson wrote a similar letter in 1803 responding to charges that he had trifled with the wife of his (now former) friend John Walker as a young man. Instigated by Walker's demand for "satisfaction" and negotiated through seconds, this was a formal affair of honor. To redeem his wife's reputation, Walker demanded—and received—a written statement from Jefferson confessing to his dalliance, to be shown to a select group of Walker's friends, but the Federalist Walker circulated the precious document more widely than Jefferson expected. Ultimately, it reached a large enough audience that Jefferson felt compelled to write yet another letter, this time to defend his reputation among "particular friends."[19] In the presidential election of 1800, such public-minded letters held together the northern and southern components of both the Federalist and the Republican persuasion.

Sometimes beleaguered politicians solicited such letters to use as affidavits. Incredibly, at the height of their opposition in 1793, Hamilton asked Jefferson for such a letter to refute charges that he had mismanaged foreign loans, counting on Jefferson's honor as a gentleman to attest to the truth. As Jefferson explained to Madison, Hamilton told him that "his object was perhaps to shew it to some friends whom he wished to satisfy." Although Jefferson complied with Hamilton's wishes (running his draft by Madison before delivering it), he made sure that Hamilton would "not find my letter to answer his purpose."[20]

Public-minded letters had particular importance in the print-deprived South. In New England, newspapers broadcast national political news on a wide scale; in the South, circular letters filled this role. A genre used by southern Federalists and Republicans alike, circular letters were printed progress reports from national congressmen, issued in batches of several hundred and sent to local men of influence who could disseminate their news. Framed like personal letters, complete with a conventional opening, closing, and signature, they yoked the personal authority and man-to-man intimacy of private correspondence to a public cause. For national politicians far from home, these public letters maintained the pose of personal accountability to individual constituents. John Adams deemed the practice "correct and REPUBLICAN."[21]

These letters declared their intended audience. Others were more deceptive. Reputedly private but written for display, they capitalized on the power of private information; the more private a piece of writing, the more truthful it appeared to be. Such letters, signed by a national politician, had added value as inside knowledge. When Republican John Taylor of Caroline feared that a supporter was swaying in his convictions, he told Madison that "the most likely thing to fix him, would be a letter from you. Some thing in a kind of friendly stile. And having three or four pointed sentences against the bank law, and expressing a necessity for its repeal." Even if the letter did not "fix" its target, Taylor was confident that the man would show it to others, inspiring them "to take up the idea, and gore" him upon the subject.[22] Grounded on the status and reputation of the letter writer, this form of persuasion masked political wrangling as casual communication between friends.

Pamphlets

Political pamphlets aimed at wider circles of elite readers—"the thinking part of the nation" who could "set the people to rights," as Jefferson put it or, as Hamilton phrased it, men of the "first" and "second class." Usually dignified in tone and lengthy, they were ideal platforms for presenting a detailed argument. Indeed, they virtually required such detail. So Washington assumed when he read Hamilton's draft of his farewell address. Far too long to appear in a newspaper, it would have to dilate "*more* on the present state of matters" if it appeared in a pamphlet.[23]

Printed in mass quantities during presidential elections—witness Republican John Beckley's distribution of roughly 1,200 pro-Jefferson tracts in 1796 and 5,000 such tracts in 1800—pamphlets were more commonly printed in batches of several hundred and distributed to men of influence. Thus, pamphlet writers who addressed themselves to "the people" did so more for effect than for accuracy. As one Massachusetts Federalist fumed in 1796, Republican Edmund Randolph might claim to be addressing the people in a recent pamphlet, "but the PEOPLE will never read it, and—he knew it! *Knew*—it would be impossible to have it scarce read at all, in a Pamphlet, except in the large Seaports."[24]

The truth of this statement is particularly evident in the South, where scattered settlement patterns made it difficult to circulate publications on a wide scale. Note, for example, the pamphleteering efforts of Virginian John Preston from Montgomery County, in the far southwest portion of the state. A candidate in an upcoming election, in January 1796 Preston asked a friend to deliver a pamphlet manuscript to a printer in Richmond, who may have been the closest one, though he was almost an entire state away. The printer received it on February 2 with a request for five hundred copies. A second friend, Richmond resident Robert Gamble, informed Preston a week later that the printer would finish the job in roughly two weeks, a longer delay than Preston had hoped. The logistics became even more difficult when Gamble tried to send Preston the completed pamphlets. Unable to "hear of any waggon from your part of the Country or *to your part*," Gamble pressed pamphlets on anyone headed in Preston's direction: over the course of five weeks, a William King took ninety copies, one Gordon Cloyd fifty (and ultimately agreed to "struggle" with a hundred); David Kean and "a Mr. Jno. George" (a complete stranger) took thirty; Patrick Boyd took only fifteen or twenty, but Captain Caperton took fifty, promising to distribute them in "Different parts of the County [where] he thinks the . . . influential people live"; John Glen took as many as he could hold; and Mr. A. Smith refused to carry any. By

March 26—roughly two months after the printer had received Preston's manuscript—Gamble still had 240 copies in hand. In the end, it took two and a half months for Preston to print and receive his pamphlets, yet even so, he declared himself pleased.[25]

Because of their limited range and impact, pamphlets were best published and circulated with precision, coordinated with the political calendar, and given to "gentlemen of wieght [*sic*] and influence" who could "make proper use of them," as one Massachusetts Federalist put it. Note, for example, the precise plans for the publication of Taylor's 1793 pamphlet. It would have maximum impact if it appeared just before the opening of Congress, Jefferson calculated, making it "a new thing" that congressmen could "get into their hands while yet unoccupied." These carefully laid plans were almost spoiled when Republican editor Philip Freneau printed extracts in the *National Gazette* before the pamphlet's publication. Because pamphlets derived much of their power and impact from their relative exclusivity, such piecemeal publication in a newspaper could prove disastrous. Freneau's actions were "both unwise and indelicate," Taylor told Madison. "Unwise, as mutilated anticipations, will weaken its effect, if it should appear in a pamphlet. Indelicate, as in that event, the performance will exhibit the ludicrous aspect, of a compilation from his newspapers."[26] Taylor's ideas would seem far less weighty if culled from newspapers.

There were various reasons to publish a pamphlet. Sometimes writers hoped to instigate a public discussion—or more precisely, to instigate an elite discussion that could be strategically transmitted to the masses. Most such pamphlets were stripped of all regional and personal ties to appear unbiased and thus more convincing. Some, however, relied on just such evidence for their impact; Albert Gallatin, Tench Coxe, DeWitt Clinton, John Beckley, Alexander Hamilton, William Loughton Smith, and James Madison all wrote anonymous pamphlets sprinkled with details that revealed their authors to have inside connections.

Other pamphlets were spawned by heated newspaper debates, an argument shifting to higher ground when it became serious enough to merit an extended discussion. Such was the case when a newspaper debate about the Burr-Hamilton duel suddenly vanished from newsprint. Some Boston printers attempted to do the same with Adams's *Patriot* letters, though Adams wanted "nothing to do with it." He was seeking a much wider audience.[27]

Most personal of all were defense pamphlets. Signed, structured character defenses brimming with hard evidence, they were legal briefs argued before a tribunal of one's peers, the writer personally vouching for their veracity. As one reader remarked concerning Hamilton's attack on Adams, "the assertions of ye pamphlet, I take it for granted, are true."[28] They demanded the greatest risk, the authority of the author's name and reputation, but to the victim of a serious attack, this was a risk worth taking. Of course, personal as they were, defense pamphlets were political publications aimed at attacking foes as much as defending friends, but their defensive tone masked their intentions; like gossip and dinner-table politicking, pamphlets justified and channeled aggression by framing it as something else.

Such was the logic behind Hamilton's pamphlet (fig. 18). Enraged by Adams's insults and eager to promote Charles Cotesworth Pinckney for the presidency in his place, Hamilton thought that he could accomplish both purposes in "the shape of a *defence of my self*"—a delicate balance that required a more restrained pen than his proved to be. In the end, his "Letter" sounded more like a vindictive personal assault than a rational self-defense, suggesting that Hamilton, not Adams, had the flawed character. In contrast to the dignified tone of most pamphlets, Hamilton's ranting seemed all the more excessive. A weapon of paper war misused, Hamilton's "Letter" backfired, destroying his reputation. "Some very worthy & sensible men say you have exhibited the same *vanity* in your book which you charge as a dangerous quality & great weakness in Mr. Adams," wrote one Federalist. Another was harsher. "I do not believe it has altered a single vote in the late election," wrote Hamilton's friend Robert Troup. "The influence however of this letter upon Hamilton's character is extremely unfortunate. An opinion has grown out of it, which at present obtains almost universally, that his character *is radically deficient in discretion*. . . . Hence he is considered as an unfit head of the party."[29] Discretion—caution with words—was essential to political leadership. Here was the price for poor choices in print.

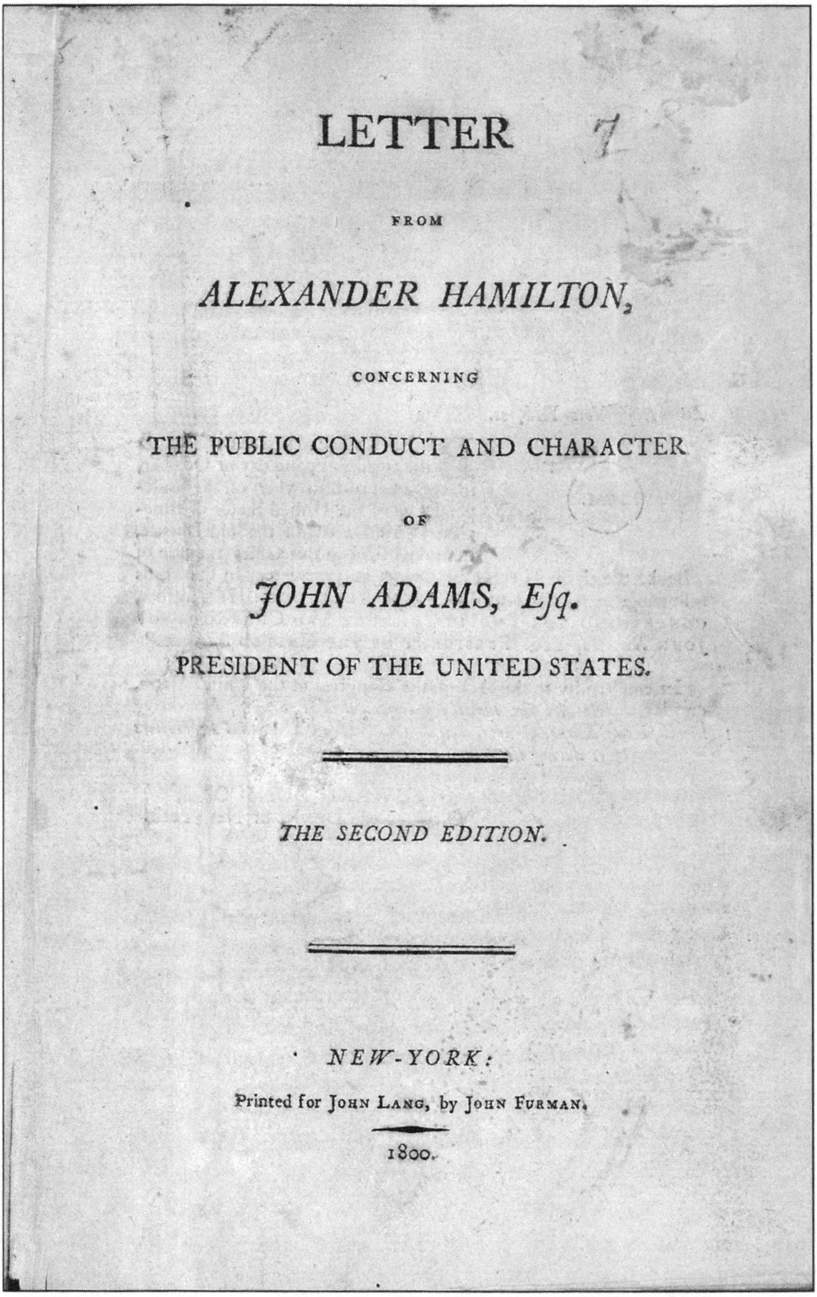

LETTER

FROM

ALEXANDER HAMILTON,

CONCERNING

THE PUBLIC CONDUCT AND CHARACTER

OF

JOHN ADAMS, Esq.

PRESIDENT OF THE UNITED STATES.

THE SECOND EDITION.

NEW-YORK:

Printed for JOHN LANG, by JOHN FURMAN.

1800.

Fig. 18. *"Letter . . . Concerning the Public Conduct and Character of John Adams,"* by Alexander Hamilton, 1800. Adams's rage over the accusations in this defense pamphlet fueled his self-defense in the *Boston Patriot* nine years later. Although Hamilton initially intended it for a small circle of elite readers, unauthorized newspaper excerpts ultimately compelled him to publish it in newspapers in its entirety. (From the author's collection)

Broadsides

High emotion was better suited to less personal media like broadsides and handbills, which were mainly intended to rouse public passions. Hastily printed, usually anonymous sheets tacked onto buildings, signposts, and trees or distributed hand-to-hand, they were low-risk publications that appealed to a mass audience. As Jefferson put it, they should be "short, simple, and levelled to every capacity." Their broad local impact made them particularly useful during elections. In the presidential contests of 1796 and 1800, politicians sent packets of broadsides to men of influence around the nation with instructions to distribute them widely; in 1796, John Beckley distributed a thousand such postings throughout Pennsylvania. And incredibly, in preparation for the election of 1800, Jefferson planned to print ten to twenty thousand handbills and distribute them "through all the U.S." enclosed in private letters from Republican congressmen.[30] Such mass mailings helped nationalize partisan battles at the seat of government. When Adams's two public supplicants converted his letter into a broadside in 1809, they were hoping for an immediate local impact, probably with a view toward the state elections a few weeks away.

Aimed at a general audience, broadside attacks were usually considered beneath the notice of elite politicians. So Burr assumed in 1800 when confronted with one of the period's most infamous electioneering broadsides—"Aaron Burr!"—a catalogue of the supposed sins of "this accomplished and but too successful debauchee" (fig. 19).[31] Despite (or because of) the broadside's extreme claims, Burr forbade his friends to respond "either by recrimination or by any printed denial," deeming it too low to merit a counterattack.

Such an undignified medium was no place for the personal politicking of a high-ranking politician. Plus, a signed personal attack printed on a broadside came perilously close to being a ritualistic posting, the prescribed way to obtain satisfaction from an offender who was too low or cowardly to duel: with no other way to redeem his reputation, the wounded party was entitled to "post" his offender with broadsides tacked up in public spaces, declaring him a liar, rascal, scoundrel, and coward—ritualistic honor insults all. On the same page

THE following hand-bill was circulated in the year 1801, by the Federal party. It is now re-published for the *gratification* of those Federal gentlemen who are now supporting "this Cataline." The original may be seen at the office of the Citizen.

Aaron Burr !

At length this Cataline stands CONFESSED in all his VILLAINY—His INVETERATE HATRED of the Constitution of the United States has long been displayed in one steady, undeviating course of HOSTILITY to every measure which the solid interests of the Union demand—His POLITICAL PERFIDIOUSNESS AND INTRIGUES are also now pretty generally known, and even his own party have avowed their jealousy and fear of a character, which, to great talents adds the deepest dissimulation and an entire devotion to self-interest, and self-aggrandizement—But there is a NEW TRAIT in this man's character, to be unfolded to the view of an INDIGNANT PUBLIC!—His ABANDONED PROFLIGACY, and the NUMEROUS UNHAPPY WRETCHES who have fallen VICTIMS to this accomplished and but too successful DEBAUCHEE, have indeed been long known to those whom similar habits of vice, or the amiable offices of humanity have led to the wretched haunts of female prostitution—But it is time to draw aside the curtain in which he has thus far been permitted to conceal himself by the forbearance of his enemies, by the anxious interference of his friends, and much more by his own crafty contrivances and unbounded prodigality.

It is time to tear away the veil that hides this monster, and lay open a scene of misery, at which every heart must shudder. Fellow Citizens, read a tale of truth, which must harrow up your sensibility, and excite your keenest resentment. It is, indeed, a tale of truth! and, but for wounding, too deeply, the already lacerated feelings of a parental heart, it could be authenticated by all the formalities of an oath.

I do not mean to tell you of the late celebrated courtezan N———, nor U———, nor S———, nor of half a dozen more whom first his INTRIGUES have RUINED, and his SATIATED BRUTALITY has afterwards thrown on the town, the prey of disease, of infamy, and wretchedness—It is to a more recent act, that I call your attention, and I hope it will create in every heart, the same abhorrence with which mine is filled.

☞ When Mr. Burr last went to the city of Washington about 2 months ago, to take the oath of office, and his seat in the August senate of the U. States, he SEDUCED the daughter of a respectable tradesman there, & had the cruelty to persuade her to forsake her native town, her friends and family, and to follow him to New-York. She did so—and she is now IN KEEPING in Partition-st. Vice, however, sooner or later, meets its merited punishment. Justice, though sometimes SLOW, is SURE. The villain has not long enjoyed this triumph over female weakness. The father of the girl has at length after a laborious and painful search, found out the author of his child's RUIN, and his family's DISHONOR.—HE IS NOW IN THIS CITY, and VENGEANCE will soon light on the guilty head——Fellow-citizens, I leave you to make your own comments on this complicated scene of misery and vice.—I will conclude with a single observation.—Is that party at whose head is this monster, who directs all their motions and originates all their nefarious schemes worthy of your SUPPORT?

Fig. 19. *Aaron Burr!* 1804. This notorious broadside was reprinted for the heated New York gubernatorial campaign of 1804—the contest that would eventually lead to the Burr-Hamilton duel. Posted as handbills and printed in a newspaper, it was the most explicit attack on Burr's morals yet in print, accusing him of seducing countless young women. Burr forbade friends from responding, declaring that he presumed friends would "treat as false, every thing, said of me, which ought not to be true." (© Collection of the New-York Historical Society)

as one of Adams's *Patriot* essays, the newspaper reported one such incident in Virginia, where a man posted a signed broadside "at the corners of public streets" declaring his offender "'to be a slanderous lying rascal.'"[32]

Thus, the consequences were potentially fatal when Hamilton's 1792 defense against charges of financial wrongdoing appeared in a broadside during a congressional campaign. Given his letter's extreme language—he had given the lie direct to his accuser, Republican candidate John Francis Mercer—he intended to restrict its circulation. But his Federalist correspondent served his own electoral purposes by publishing Hamilton's letter in a broadside—effectively posting Mercer as a liar. Mercer was outraged. "Decorum of situation" was not "in the least regarded, in committing your name, with the harsh expressions you have used in regard to me, to be publickly handed about and pasted upon Sign Posts to influence the weak and uninform'd during a contested Election," he fumed. Hamilton responded that he had authorized only "a free personal communication" of the letter, which could be "inferred from my prohibition of its insertion in a News Paper which became possible by its circulation in a hand bill"—a striking reference to the hierarchy of print. Addressing select men of influence, Hamilton had been more abusive than he would have dared in a more public attack. It was one thing to malign someone among a few friends, another to dishonor him before the world. The incident almost resulted in a duel.[33]

Newspapers

Most wide-reaching of all was the newspaper. Printed in a single newspaper, an essay or news item easily migrated into others, forming a national bridge of communication beyond any one man's control. By linking regions together with bonds of political consciousness, interconnected partisan newspapers were a nationalizing influence, a literal arm of government connecting the extended republic through chains of information. In a new polity that was exploring its political and regional bounds, newspapers were a vital part of the growing process. Foreign observers were quick to note the distinctive role that newspapers played in the infant republic. "All, from the Congressman to the work-man, read one or other of the thousands of newspapers which appear," wrote one French observer. French traveler Brissot de Warville agreed, declaring newspapers "the channel of information in America." Many Federalists blamed their loss of the presidency in 1800 on Republican skill with this powerful weapon.[34]

There were indeed thousands of newspapers in early national America, but they bore little resemblance to the newspapers of today. Usually consisting of a single folded sheet, these four-page publications typically had international news on the first page or two, national and local news on the second and third pages, and advertisements and poetry on the fourth. The format varied during international or national controversies, and different types of papers (mercantile gazettes, for example) had slight modifications. The size of their readership varied greatly. Whereas the nation's largest newspaper, the Boston *Columbian Centinel,* printed roughly four thousand copies twice a week, most newspapers were much smaller, the average daily paper claiming a circulation of roughly five hundred copies. Still, multiplied out, in 1790 the United States postal system delivered approximately five hundred thousand newspapers in a country with a population of 3.8 million; add to that the people reached by newspaper sharing or group readings in public spaces—both common practices—and newspapers reached an impressive percentage of the population.[35]

A blend of political propaganda, local gossip, domestic news, and foreign reports, some documented, some hearsay, newspapers made it difficult to evaluate news. For such reasons, in 1797 *Gazette of the United States* editor John Ward Fenno refused to print an article by Secretary of State Timothy Pickering because its insider details would suggest that it was "an *official* publication, tho' anonymous."[36] Hence the countless letters to national politicians and their families seeking validation of newspaper reports.

John Adams's son Thomas sought such reassurance in 1800 after the publication of one of his father's letters filled with accusations against Thomas Pinckney. The Philadelphia *Aurora* had reported that Pinckney and a friend had called on the president to demand an "explanation" for the charges in the letter—the first step in an affair of honor.

Thomas knew that the report must be a lie, he wrote his mother, but a written denial "from good authority would have a good effect," enabling him to deny the charge to others. The rumor was not true, Abigail responded, but was written "with a design to tempt the Pr[esiden]t to say something which they could catch hold of and by misrepresentation use and pervert to the vilest purposes."[37] Counting on Adams to make an unguarded comment, the newspaper writer knew his target.

Clearly newspaper writers had to watch their words, for poor judgment could have dire consequences. In this sense, a newspaper's wide reach was both its power and its threat. Particularly for a politician, whose reputation was his livelihood, newspaper exposure could do as much damage as good. Witness the many affairs of honor that erupted over newspaper squibs. This was why Jefferson considered newspapers "a curb on our functionaries." For reasons both professional and personal, the threat of dishonor before a wide audience was a powerful restraining influence. Newspapers were thus far more than mere partisan rags. In essence, they were a vehicle of government, enforcing the accountability of public representatives to a vigilant public; they were public opinion incarnate, their potential impact on elite reputations giving them enormous power over national actors and affairs. This was the reason Maclay objected to the Senate's closed doors. "I am now more fully convinced than ever I have been at the propriety of Opening our doors," he wrote after a 1791 debate concerning the National Bank. "I am confident some Gentlemen would have been ashamed to have seen their Speeches of this day, reflected in a News paper of tomorrow."[38]

Subtleties of audience, influence, tone, and reputation had to be taken into account when planning a print attack. Hamilton, for example, followed a careful (if flawed) process of reasoning before publishing his 1800 "Letter." Adams's accusations were serious enough to merit a written response, Hamilton reasoned. A newspaper would have the widest possible impact, but decorum precluded using it; a refutation of the president of the United States required a more select and dignified forum. Far better to attack Adams with a defense pamphlet that would bear the force of Hamilton's reputation and could be "addressed to so many respectable men of influence as may give its contents general circulation."[39]

Directing himself to this audience, Hamilton gave his venom free rein, confident that those familiar with his character would grasp his meaning. But he overshot his mark, drawing disapproval and disbelief down on his head. Matters were made worse when the *Aurora* and the New London *Bee* published juicy snippets from the pamphlet, the result of an advance copy obtained surreptitiously. The news that his pamphlet was being broadcast in a newspaper left Hamilton speechless (a rare occurrence), but "soon afterwards he recollected himself."[40] His unplanned newspaper appearance in effect placed him before the public screaming epithets at the top of his lungs, hardly the actions of a wise or discreet man. "We must soon search for common sense exclusively among the old women of our nation!" wrote William Vans Murray to John Quincy Adams. No "correct & temperate man" could approve of Hamilton's pamphlet, agreed Hamilton's friend Rufus King. "May every Enemy of the President write a Pamphlet," toasted Adams's friend William Tudor shortly after Hamilton's fiasco.[41]

Adams went through the same process of reasoning when he decided to refute Hamilton's pamphlet in the *Boston Patriot*. In his mind, only a newspaper could reach the broad public that Hamilton had poisoned; and unlike a pamphlet, a newspaper could circulate widely enough to prove Adams "Father of the Nation" rather than simply New England. Adams's reasoning was sound, but he characteristically underestimated the power of his words. Raging against Hamilton in the public press, he seemed cruel, hysterical, and unbalanced—just as Hamilton had pronounced him to be. Such excess would have been damaging enough in a pamphlet circulating among Adams's peers. But broadcast from a newspaper, it became a tantrum on paper, an explosive "breaking out of a stifled resentment in print," as Cunningham put it.[42] Whatever good Adams did his suffering ego, he achieved little for his reputation, exposing his vulnerabilities rather than vindicating his name, and sparking a string of angry retorts that would extend over decades.

The Authority of a Name

Part of what differentiated weapons of paper war was the presence or absence of a signature. A man who gave information "with his own signature" staked his reputation on the veracity of his words, thereby giving them weight and power. Hamilton banked on this fact when he signed his name to his attack on Adams. As he put it, given the source of the attack and the severe damage to his reputation, "facts must be stated with some authentic stamp. . . . Anonymous publications can now affect nothing." Adams followed the same logic when he signed his name to his *Boston Patriot* letters. In his mind, only such extreme measures could counter the "vile slanders" that obscured his true worth.[43]

It was the power of a signature that made politicians so wary of the mails, inducing them to use ciphers or cryptic comments in letters rather than risk exposing sworn statements to their enemies. In a culture where gentlemen cultivated a distinctive hand, even an unsigned letter could bear the reputation of its penman. John Beckley, for example, attributed an essay to Hamilton because it was "in the handwriting of one of his Clerks." And according to Adams, Jefferson's handwriting was "more universally known" than his face. So powerful was such personal authority that correspondents sending implausible or important news sometimes enclosed torn fragments of letters from men of known reputation to display an assertion in the writer's own hand. Some writers included detachable pages in their private letters for the same reason.[44]

As Adams well knew, readers evaluated information by considering the character of its source. During the 1800 election, his son Thomas had dismissed some charges against his father because they came from men of low character. "The reputation of these people is literally so bad, especially for veracity, that they are obliged to take their oaths to everything they lay before the public," Thomas assured his mother; their words were thus no threat. As with gossip, unaccredited news was thus problematic. In January 1801, when diplomat William Vans Murray heard that letters from America were declaring Jefferson the new president, he did not know whether to believe them, for he was "ignorant of the credit of their writers."[45]

Hence the careful attribution of many unsigned newspaper reports. Note, for example, the contents of one page of the *Boston Patriot*. Rhode Island election news came from "a gentleman from Providence last evening." A description of a "shocking" murder at sea came from "a letter politely handed us, (dated *Gottenburg,* June 28th)." News of Franco-Russian relations was learned "verbally from a gentleman passenger in a vessel arrived off Sandy-Hook, from a port in Ireland, whence she sailed about the 22d of July." In all three cases, editors David Everett and Isaac Munroe authenticated their news by explaining exactly how they got it (in a conversation the previous night, from a letter passed from person to person) and specifying the genteel status of their informant (a "gentleman passenger," a letter "politely handed us"). A gentleman was always true to his word; such was the very definition of *gentleman.*[46] It was the central importance of truth-telling to genteel status that made "giving the lie" an insult grievous enough to demand a duel.

Thus, even the most outrageous assertions seemed credible coming from a man of character and influence. During the presidential election of 1800, thousands of handbills were printed in Maryland, claiming that Jefferson had told Republican Peregrine Fitzhugh that John Adams was at heart a sound republican. "Fitzhugh is a man of known honour and integrity; his veracity is not questioned by anyone," worried Maryland Republican Gabriel Duvall. "Is it possible that Mr. Jefferson, after reading Mr. Adams's volumes . . . should be of opinion that he is a republican?" His own confidence in Jefferson shaken by the authority of Fitzhugh's name, Duvall had good reason to fear that the handbill would "influence many."[47]

The trick to effective print warfare lay in manipulating the authority of one's name without implicating it. A skilled politician knew how to invest just enough of his reputation to have an impact, and no more. Thus the power of pseudonyms. Anonymous print attacks enabled politicians to malign their foes without owning their comments. Often the sting of such attacks lay not in their anonymity but in just the opposite: in the insular world of high politics, elite readers often had little difficulty guessing the authors of such pieces, giving them the authority of a reputation without the liability of blame. Anonymous attacks were not without risk—witness the many duels they provoked—but they provided deniability for both their authors and their victims. An unaccredited insult could be dismissed as low abuse from a low source; given the option of ignoring an attack, many politicians chose not to notice.

Printers suffered the downside of this ambiguity. If they surrendered the name of an offending writer, they destroyed their reputation for confidentiality and lost work as a result. If they refused to reveal a writer's name, they risked taking the blame for his offenses, and a caning or libel suit would be the likely consequence. In 1804, the printers of a pamphlet by Burrite William Van Ness were threatened with a libel suit unless they gave up the author, but if they did, the printers complained, "All hopes of succour from the Burrites would . . . have been at an End." Although Burr and his friends had promised to defend the printers in case of legal action, the Burr-Hamilton duel had intervened, and Van Ness and Burr had fled town, leaving the printers in the lurch.[48]

Because it enabled men of honor to behave dishonorably, anonymous print warfare had equivocal status. Many considered it a cowardly means of attacking one's foes without fear of retribution. And responding to such attacks was particularly challenging, for answering them—with or without using one's name—might give them a weight they did not deserve, while ignoring them could harm one's reputation. Hamilton's anonymous newspaper campaign against Jefferson at the height of their opposition was thus infuriatingly difficult to counter. Without the investment of his name, Hamilton could not be held responsible, yet everyone knew him to be the author, giving his essays the authority of his name. It was a win-win situation for Hamilton; either he would compel Jefferson or his defenders to oppose the government in print, or he would reign victorious through Jefferson's silence. Jefferson's desire to cut Hamilton "to pieces" was a visceral response to the pain of such public exposure.[49]

The ever prickly James Monroe was well versed in such matters. "Good men" often choose to "avoid dissipating scandal by newspaper discussion lest possibly doubts may thereby be created where none existed before," Monroe explained. "But this modest timidity . . . is often carried too far, & to the injury of the soundest reputations, for it often happens that the slanders wh[ich] are thus circulated in whispers, poison where the antidote never extends." Far better for the "injured person" or his friends to provoke a public discussion through print.[50] Newspaper defenses could repair wounded reputations, but given a newspaper's wide reach, this cure required a bold hand.

Jefferson overcame this risk by defending his name through champions of the pen like Madison, Monroe, or Beckley, who wrote on his behalf. Fiercely independent and distrustful of political ties of convenience, Adams usually allowed scandal and accusation to circulate unopposed, savaging his reputation in the process. A master of opportune alliances, Aaron Burr chose the same strategy for different reasons; convinced that political muckraking was beneath notice, he forbade his followers to respond, with grim results. As Burr's loyal lieutenant Matthew Davis hyperbolized, Burr's enemies took advantage of his "sullen silence" to topple him "from the proud eminence he once enjoyed to a condition more mortifying and more prostrate than any distinguished man has ever experienced in the United States."[51] As Monroe suggested, it was often better to initiate a public discussion, particularly if friends were willing to defend your name. A supporter who championed his "chief" in the public papers defended his leader's reputation with both his words and his loyalty. It was stubbornly independent men like Burr, Hamilton, and Adams whose reputations were most damaged in print.

Indeed, Adams's distrust of allowing anyone but himself to champion his cause was what pushed him into his *Patriot* campaign in the first place. As he explained to Cunningham, "No human being but myself, can do me justice," and even he himself would not be believed. "All I can say will be imputed to vanity and self love," he predicted (accurately). His only hope for redeeming his name was to invest it fully—no holds barred. As Monroe had suggested, Adams could salvage his reputation by making it a topic of debate in the public realm. He might also dishonor himself, but to Adams this was a risk worth taking. Assailants could not "sink me lower than the bottom," he told Cunningham, "and I have been safely landed there these eight years."[52] By requesting the authority of Adams's name, Lyman and Wright had called it into the public realm, but this time it would be on Adams's terms, for better or worse.

The "Scorching Flames" of Dishonor

Grounded on personal reputation and character, paper war struck at the core of a politician's career and identity, inflicting an almost palpable wound. Adams exposed the near-physical pain of such dishonor in one of his *Boston Patriot* letters. Looking back on the "opposition and embarrassments" of his public career, he sometimes compared himself in his "jocular moments" to "an animal I have seen, take hold of the end of a cord with his teeth and be drawn slowly up by pullies, through a storm of squibs, crackers, and rockets, flashing and blazing round him every moment: and though the scorching flames made him groan, and mourn, and roar, he would not let go his hold till he had reached the ceiling of a lofty theatre, where he hung sometime, still suffering a flight of rockets, and at last descended through another storm of burning powder, and never let go, till his four feet were safely landed on the floor."[53] Underlying Adams's "jocular" metaphor is the agony of a wounded reputation.

The written word would be the medium of his salvation. Yet this very medium had inflicted his wound. It was the "eternal revilings" of newspapers and pamphlets—both Republican and Federalist—that most disturbed him. "The causes of my retirement are to be found in the writings of Freneau, Markoe, Ned Church, Andrew Brown, Paine, Callender, Hamilton, Cobbett, and John Ward Fenno," he claimed in March 1809, citing a long list of printers and pamphleteering foes as his main tormentors.[54] It was for good reason that some referred to a newspaper attack as an "assassination," a "character inquisition," or a "beating." Jefferson's desire to destroy Hamilton in the press is surprisingly savage when viewed in this light. "For god's sake, my dear Sir, take up your pen, select the most striking heresies, and cut him to peices [*sic*] in the face of the public," he begged Madison in 1793, unwilling to inflict the blows himself but glorying in the prospect.[55]

Adams likewise could be a fierce print assailant in thought, if not in deed. Attacked in the newspapers by his former secretary of state Timothy Pickering, Adams longed to "whip the rogue . . . till the blood come," but friends advised him to remain silent. Pickering, in turn, responded to Adams's *Patriot* essays by reveling in the thought of the Federalist counterattacks that were sure to follow. Adams "will be scourged," Pickering wrote, "& his vanity won't let him see it, but it will *torture* him as tho' skinning him alive."[56] Such blood-lust reveals the rage beneath the surface of paper war. Where reputations had such importance, a print attack was more vicious—and painful—than we might imagine. Clearly, newspapers and pamphlets were vital outlets for the stifled aggressions of self-controlled public men. A politician might not be able to strike his opponents at will, but he could wield the club of print as effectively.

Pitting man against man in the public eye, print warfare was a bloodless duel that could affect reputations as profoundly as an "interview" on the field of honor (fig. 20). In fact, print combatants often adopted the language of the duel; Massachusetts Federalist Joseph Ward was typical of many when he offered to "challenge opposers to meet us in the field of argument before the tribunal of the public." Even the retiring Thomas Jefferson was a self-declared paper duelist. As he explained during one battle, by defending himself in letters to be circulated among his friends, he fought in "such a way as shall not be derogatory either to the public liberty or my own personal honor." In this epistolary mode of combat, Jefferson was willing to "meet every one." Adams, on the other hand, usually preferred not to fight at all. As he himself put it, "I never hired scribblers to defame my rivals. I never wrote a line of slander against my bitterest enemy, nor encouraged it in any other."[57] Rather than malice, it was his habitual candor on paper that provoked controversy time and time again.

If print attacks were the equivalent of a public beating, then women, children, and the dead were inappropriate targets. Assailing such defenseless people in print was like dueling unarmed opponents; there was no honor in an unfair fight. As Fisher Ames put it when his wife was attacked in the public papers, "The newspapering [of] a woman is an outrage I had hoped Hottentots would not commit."

For Orville Carpenter of Maryland, the sacred status of women proved a convenient shield. Eager to defend the ladies of Baltimore from a newspaper attack on their "dress and manners," Carpenter wrote his refutation in the guise of a woman to avoid provoking an honor dispute. As he explained to his sister, the disguise had "the desired effect—The beaus left their walking sticks at home," unable and unwilling to defend their names by caning a woman.[58]

Adams's relentless *Patriot* attack on Hamilton—killed five years past—thus earned Adams criticism. Such abuse was "coarse and unmanly," charged Hamilton's friend James McHenry. Cunningham was equally alarmed, urging Adams to restrain his venom. Such bitterness might not be "the method of treating Hamilton, the best adapted to the satisfaction of the public of your own vast superiority," Cunningham suggested diplomatically.[59]

As with political gossip, rules were central to a mode of combat with such high stakes. Without them, political conflict would be a deadly free-for-all; with them, there could be at least a modicum of control. Given the risk entailed in exchanging words, even personal correspondence conformed to such strictures. Of course, rules could be manipulated, like the fellow who was instructed not to make a copy of a letter—so he recited it from memory. But as much as he violated the spirit of the law, the man hadn't broken the "law" itself. As Adams wrote to Cunningham after revealing his innermost feelings in dozens of letters, misuse of correspondence was "a breach of honour and of plighted faith."[60] Adams had committed his feelings to paper out of trust; betraying that trust was dishonorable in the extreme, potentially destroying the betrayer's reputation.

How, then, can we explain the multitude of private letters that were leaked to the press or the many pamphlets that were shown to the very people from whom they were intended to remain hidden? The fervor of partisanship holds part of the answer. To a politician in the throes of a political crisis, exposing a threat could be an honorable act—in fact, if publishing a private document served the public good, then *withholding* it was the dishonorable course. Given the crisis mentality of the period's politics, such logic prevailed increasingly throughout the turbulent 1790s, a trend that contemporaries noticed.[61]

[185]

It follows of courſe that authors of great vigour, ſhould be charged higher than meek writers for printing a work of the ſame length, on account of the extraordinary ſpace their performances muſt neceſſarily occupy; for theſe gigantic, wrathful types, like ranters on a ſtage, or Burgoyne at Saratoga, will demand ſufficient elbow room.

For example—ſuppoſe a newſpaper quarrel to happen between M and L*

M begins the attack pretty ſmartly in

Long primer.

L replies in

Pica Roman.

M advances to

Great Primer.

L retorts in

Double Pica;

and

* Leſt ſome ill diſpoſed perſon ſhould maliciouſly miſapply theſe initials I think proper to declare that M ſignifies *merchant*, and L Lawyer.

Fig. 20. Pages from "A Plan for the Improvement of the Art of Paper War," by Francis Hopkinson, 1792. Hopkinson humorously suggests a system for committing anger to print using a sample "newspaper quarrel" between M[erchant] and L[awyer], showing through typeface the slow buildup of steam

[186]

and at laſt the conteſt ſwells up to

Raſcal, Villain, Coward,

in five line pica; which indeed is as far as the art of printing or a modern quarrel can conveniently go.

A philoſophical reaſon might be given to prove that large types will more forcibly affect the optic nerve than thoſe of a ſmaller ſize, and therefore become mechanically expreſſive of energy and vigour; but I leave this diſcuſſion for the amuſement of the gentlemen lately elected into our philoſophical ſociety. It will ſatisfy me if my ſcheme ſhould be adopted and found uſeful.

I recol-

that could lead to ritualistic insults—and worse. From this point, "M" and "L" would have transferred their argument from the page to the field of honor. (Courtesy Beinecke Rare Book and Manuscript Library, Yale University)

Even Cunningham succumbed to such partisan fervor. "No man is more deeply penetrated with a sense of the inviolability of confidential trusts," he wrote to Adams in 1810, but "a promise nor an oath of secrecy, is not to be constructed to extend to the transgression of the duty we are under from the instant of our birth"—the duty of patriotism. A "sense of public duty" might require him to publicize Adams's letters. Cunningham voiced this threat as his friendship with Adams drew to a close, for friends did not expose friends. Publishing a friend's letter against his will was the moral equivalent of gossiping about him—a hostile act.[62]

Former friends, however, had little reason to withhold letters, and given the high emotion and shifting loyalties of politics, there were many broken friendships—and many private letters published in newspapers against the writer's will. As Abigail Adams ruefully advised her husband,

> Say no more unto your Friend
> than you would to your Foe
> For he that is your friend today
> May be your foe tomorrow
> and then [reveal] what you have said
> Unto your grief and Sorrow.[63]

A second explanation for such betrayal lies in the other-mindedness of honor. Leaking a private document to the press was not sinful in itself; what mattered was whether you were caught: "The man of honor does not care if he stinks, but he does care that someone has accused him of stinking." Dishonor required an audience. With the vulnerabilities of the mails and the carelessness of printer's boys, there were any number of covert ways to bring private documents before public eyes. For example, depending on whom one believes, it could have been Aaron Burr, John Beckley, a disloyal clerk, or some combination of the above who surreptitiously obtained the advance copy of Hamilton's "Letter" that was leaked to the press.[64]

Such treachery was not uncommon, but neither was it the rule. In fact, considering the intimacy of the early national political community, a striking number of private documents remained private. In 1800

Adams could not even get a glimpse of many of the handbills and pamphlets that attacked him.[65] He did not see one such pamphlet until 1812, when a friend mailed him a reprinted edition; claiming to be amused by its excesses, Adams nonetheless wrote a six-page letter of correction to the printer. Adams assumed that Hamilton's "Letter" had remained private as well, declaring that Cunningham had never read it in its entirety but seen only the newspaper excerpts. Cunningham's response—that a friend who had received a copy from Hamilton had shown it to him—reveals the relative control maintained over such publications.[66] Even a controversial pamphlet by a well-known author had not been readily available, tendered to Cunningham by a single friend. Without an understanding of the overriding importance of honor, it is impossible to understand how politicians could have assumed that some of their inflammatory writings could remain limited in circulation.

This is not to say that politicians were too honorable to violate the rules of print combat; rather, they feared the consequences. Dishonorably exposing another gentleman could endanger one's standing among the elite. During the presidential election of 1800, Virginia Republicans were outraged when someone proved "so ungentlemanly as to give up" an electioneering letter to the press. Cunningham similarly rebuked someone who apparently released one of Adams's private letters to the press, though he himself would commit the same crime years later. And Adams could scarcely contain his rage at Timothy Pickering for providing Hamilton with many of the documents and cabinet secrets that pepper his "Letter." As Adams put it, such a betrayal was "Treachery and Perfidy" of the worst kind.[67]

A personal correspondence was thus a mark of trust, each writer trusting the other to protect his reputation; the more confidential information contained in a letter, the more faith the writer placed in the recipient. Violating this trust was a personal betrayal, as suggested by the howls of protest from correspondents who were thus exposed, however inadvertently. William Eustis of Massachusetts was "d----d mad . . . to be sure," when Massachusetts Representative David Cobb—relaying news from home—showed one of Eustis's letters to Vice President Adams in 1794. "Never shew to the Vice [President] or any other creature any nonsense of mine for I have *some little pride,*" Eustis warned. "The next time you expose me to any living creature, I will give to Wm. Cooper some of your heresies to be made public in the Chronicle."[68] By revealing private letters, friends exposed friends to the world without their full public armor.

Given the risks inherent in transcribing one's intimate thoughts and feelings, an expressive, confessional correspondent had to be trusting indeed, as was John Adams, whose letters reveal his emotions in full force, even at the distance of two centuries. Far from unrealistic as a politician, Adams nonetheless bestowed his trust freely—and was stunned by betrayal again and again. His well-known correspondence with Thomas Jefferson in their final years shows his habitual candor at its best. Adams's letters are a jumble of feelings, confessions, and observations, as he questioned, chided, lectured, and praised his old friend into a wide-ranging discussion of their lives, careers, and intellectual pursuits, all with characteristic self-deprecating humor. ("In the 89 year of his age still too fat to last much longer," he quipped in the closing of one letter).[69] Jefferson's letters, though framed with obvious affection and respect, are stiff and guarded by comparison. He considered his every word. Adams did not.

It was this quality that Hamilton attacked with his pamphlet and that Benjamin Franklin memorialized by describing Adams as "always an honest Man, often a wise one, but sometimes, and in some things, absolutely out of his senses." Adams himself admitted as much in his better moments, confessing that there had "been very many times in my life when I have been so agitated in my own mind as to have no consideration at all of the light in which my words, actions, and even writings would be considered by others."[70] Combined with his fist-clenched independence, Adams's impulsive self-disclosure could not help but hurt his public image. Not only did he often say things that he later regretted, but he had few allies to champion his cause and redeem his name.

And yet his emotional outbursts were honest reactions to malicious abuse—particularly the outbursts during his presidency, the fodder for Hamilton's "Letter." So Adams explained in a public address on his birthday given two years after the publication of the pamphlet:

"Under the Continual provocations breaking and pouring in upon me from unexpected as well as expected quarters, during the two last years of my Administration, he must have been more of a modern Epicurean Phylosopher, than I ever was or ever will be, to have born [*sic*] them all, without some incautious expressions at times of an inutterable Indignation." Any man would have done the same, he suggested, and he had "no other Apology to make to Individuals or the Public."[71]

Adams did not, however, surrender total control of his emotions. Though he denounced Hamilton heartily in his *Patriot* essays, he still exercised some restraint, slight though it was. When Cunningham suggested that Adams's attack on Hamilton was too harsh, Adams spilled his real feelings into a letter so filled with bile that he demanded the original back with no copy taken. He did the same when Cunningham defended Hamilton's character by citing Hamilton's final statement, written the night before his duel. Surely a man who had spoken with such "moving tenderness of his 'Wife and Children'" was not as depraved as Adams imagined, Cunningham wrote. Adams responded with a stream of venom intense enough to shock Cunningham and once again requested his letter back uncopied.[72]

Here was the undiluted agony of a wounded reputation, the emotional fuel guiding Adams's pen. Yet trusting as he was, even Adams knew better than to release control of these acid letters. Though Cunningham possessed Adams's "sacred confidence"—as had Cunningham's grandfather, grandmother, and father before him—there was no telling who might see the letters by mistake.[73] Adams's caution was well taken, for in years to come he would discover that personal honor and partisan fervor were uncomfortable bedfellows, making one man's public duty another man's personal betrayal.

"The Arena of Political Controversy"

Adams expected some negative response to his newspaper essays. Cunningham expected it as well. "I cannot conceal from you my apprehension, that in throwing yourself into the troubled element of dispute, you will meet with many angry surges," he fretted in May 1809. A month later, he gave Adams a full report on this swelling tide. William

Coleman, editor of Hamilton's journalistic mouthpiece the *New-York Evening Post,* was going to respond to Adams's essays, Cunningham noted. Smaller local papers, "mere puppies of the pack," were also daring "to bark" at some of Adams's essays. The Boston *Repertory,* "the highest note on the Federal gamut," was making similar accusations. Even the clergy were gossiping. One minister "made a pass" at Adams in an election sermon. Another "elderly and respectable Clergyman" reported that Adams's minister had said that Adams's family disapproved of his campaign but that the former president was "inexorable to their entreaties to desist"—an idea that afforded Adams and his family "a delicious laugh" around the dinner table.[74] Adams seemed to be deliberately placing himself in the "*arena* of political controversy." Of course, to Adams, this was precisely the point. He was using a political crisis to bolster his reputation, a campaign that relied on public notice.

Regardless of what medium they chose, national politicians thrust their reputations into public view when they picked up their pens, sending a written representation of themselves out into the world. The response to these writings hints at the impact of national politics and politicians on a wider public. For example, the insatiable hunger for letters from national politicians is a reminder of how difficult it was to get reliable news outside of the capital. Newspapers were some help, but it was difficult to separate rumor from reality. News issued under the authority of a name, however, was as good as fact. Hence the onslaught of questioning letters to national officeholders. "Is Randolph really in discredit, as the gazettes allege?" asked former Representative Fisher Ames of Representative Josiah Quincy in 1806, the first in a string of inquiries about newspaper claims. Apologizing for his barrage of questions, Ames reminded Quincy of the value of such information: "While you are seeing the play, I, who have no ticket, should like to know the *dramatis personae* a little better." Massachusetts Republican Henry Langdon put matters more concisely, thanking fellow Republican William Eustis for sending "all the political information that you Congress folks think is proper for us to have."[75]

It was Cunningham's hunger for reliable political information that had first led him to Adams, years before the *Boston Patriot* controversy. Eager to write a pamphlet attacking Jefferson before the 1804 presidential election, he had asked Adams to aid his "patriotic purposes" by providing "interesting incidents" in Jefferson's career; Cunningham was an anecdote hunter seeking useful political gossip. Aware of the risk in transcribing such information, he offered to visit Adams if he would rather disclose himself "in conversation than in writing"—an offer that Adams accepted on at least one occasion.[76]

Sometimes the *contents* of a letter from a high-ranking politician were all but irrelevant, for the simple receipt of a letter from a man of national repute aggrandized the recipient by association. Republican Hugh Henry Brackenridge was particularly blunt in making such a request of Jefferson in January 1801, as the nation anxiously awaited the outcome of the presidential election. "Address a letter to me, should it contain but a News paper," Brackenridge wrote to Jefferson. "It will have the effect of giving me consequence and power to support myself and my friends in this country." John Ogden sought a correspondence with Jefferson for less elevated purposes; he was hoping to impress his mother-in-law.[77] A correspondence was a mutual exchange of respect and trust, so a letter from a national politician displayed respect of the highest kind.

Not all such letters were welcome. Because correspondence linked reputations, a letter from the wrong national figure could have dire consequences. In 1798, for example, several Connecticut Federalists were discredited for receiving letters from Vermont Representative Matthew Lyon, a rabid Republican. Hearing a rumor that Lyon and some southern Republicans had cultivated correspondents throughout Connecticut (it is worth noting that this was considered news), Massachusetts Federalist Peter Van Schaack "wrote immediately" to an "utter stranger" of reputation in Connecticut for confirmation. The man proved remarkably well informed about mail throughout his entire state. Virginian William Branch Giles had "not written letters nor franked news papers to any Citizen" of Connecticut, the informant reported, but Lyon had forwarded letters and copies of the Republican Philadelphia *Aurora* to one person in each of the towns of Sharon, Salisbury, Cornwall, and Canaan. The writer had even *seen* one of Lyon's letters, "filled with *beastly* invectives against the Executive and the Connecticut representation in Congress." To Van Schaack, any Federalist who received such a letter was "both a hypocrite & a Jacobin." Franked mail from a congressman was particularly revealing of one's politics, for the writer's name was inscribed on the wrapper as postage, leading one Republican congressman to ask a more moderate colleague to frank his letters to New Englanders.[78]

If reputation was the currency of politics, correspondence with a national politician was a windfall. Indeed, some national politicians took advantage of this fact to forge channels of communication throughout their districts, writing regularly to local individuals and empowering them as politicos in the process; in return, they received invaluable information about local affairs and public opinion in their home state. Thus were national webs of political influence and alliance formed. For example, Representative Theodore Sedgwick was a primary news source in parts of his own Massachusetts as well as in upstate New York. Though he wrote every few days to Peter and Henry Van Schaack, his main conduits, he could not write fast enough. "Give us something from Congress that we may have something to talk about," wrote Henry in 1798. "At present we are gazing and gaping as if [we] were stupified." Roughly two weeks later, he again urged Sedgwick for a letter, hinting, "I wait impatiently for tomorrow's mail." More desperate a month later, he implored Sedgwick, "For God's sake give me a letter by every mail.—You know I am one of the under labourers in the federal vineyard—without information from the fountain head—what can I do?" Pennsylvanian Joseph Chambers wanted to serve the same role in Wade County, begging Albert Gallatin to correspond with him as a means of informing the "respectable proportion of staunch persevering Republicans."[79]

Following the path of Sedgwick's news reveals much about the dissemination of national political influence and information. Sedgwick regularly forwarded national newspapers, privileged news, and copies of his congressional speeches to friends like the Van Schaacks back home; they spread this Federalist fodder among their friends and neighbors by word of mouth, letter, and hand-to-hand passage, ultimately proffering it to Loring Andrews, the editor of the Albany *Centi-*

nel. Sedgwick also sold subscriptions to Andrew's paper and, equally important, occasionally convinced national newspaper editors like William Cobbett of *Porcupine's Gazette* or John Ward Fenno of the *Gazette of the United States* to reprint excerpts from the *Centinel* in the hope of giving Andrews "some consequence."[80]

As suggested by this one network among many, the mails were a central vehicle of national governance. Yet this political system, grounded on personal relationships and the written word, was tenuous at best. The primitive state of the mails only complicated matters. There was no telling how long it might take mail to travel between two points; a lame horse or a sick post rider could delay it for days. In 1797 the absence of "the Young man who keeps the P[ost] Office" prevented people in Charlottesville, Virginia, from receiving their mail for almost a week.[81]

Equally problematic was the sporadic closure of the government between congressional sessions, for without a central clearinghouse of information, it was almost impossible to get a national perspective. As William Vans Murray of Maryland put it, he knew nothing of politics to the north or south, because "no one hears of such things except at Philad.," and without letters from the national capital, he was "in the dark."[82] In 1807, Massachusetts Republican James Sullivan tried to surmount this problem by creating a second information center. What was needed was "a central point of communication and influence, to which the leading characters in the States can repair, as to a centre of union and information," he wrote to Jefferson. "You sir ought to assume the trouble of being that centre." South Carolina Representative Robert Goodloe Harper made a similar suggestion to Hamilton.[83]

Given the personal and political value of national correspondence, "men of influence" who didn't receive any had reason to take offense. Asked how he avoided offending such men, Matthew Lyon revealed that he took advantage of the poor state of the mails: "When I am canvassing my district, and I come across a man who looks distantly and coldly at me, I go up cordially to him and say, 'My dear friend, you got my printed letter last session, of course?' 'No, Sir,' replies the man with offended dignity, 'I got no such thing.' 'No!' I cry out in a passion. 'No! *Damn that post-office!*' Then I make a memorandum of the man's name and address, and when I get back to Washington I write him an autograph letter, and all is put to rights." In 1800, Massachusetts Federalist George Cabot poked fun at this same phenomenon, writing to Hamilton that he expected a copy of his "Letter . . . Concerning the Public Conduct and Character of John Adams" despite the fact that he was "not '*an influential man*.'"[84]

Given the prestige and information they channeled from the national center, letters from national politicians were often treated like public commodities by constituents. Nowhere is this better seen than in post offices, where national political letters often became public property. A letter from Republican Representative Edward Livingston, for example, attracted "a curious crowd . . . at the NY post office, where the letter was handed around from one person to another." As reported by Republican newspaper editor John Daly Burk, the Federalists in attendance handled the letter "with evident marks of inquietude and alarm, lest the sedition or treason should *ooze* out and convert them to the cause of democracy." During the closely contested election of 1800, a letter from Representative Theodore Sedgwick caused a similar sensation, as explained by his son, who was studying law in Kinderhook, New York. As he wrote to his father, "The morning that I received your letter I was summoned at sunrise by two young men of this place to go to the Post Office and open a letter from you which was the only one for this town. . . . [W]hen I arrived there was a Troop headed by my [School] Master all waiting with staring eyes, and open mouths, to hear the news. When lo it contained nothing but what we *had heard*, you may Judge what was the disappointment of such a clan of Newsmongers." The arrival of Sedgwick's letter had an immediate impact, attracting a crowd at sunrise that had no qualms about demanding to hear the contents of the town's only letter. It is no wonder that politicians often asked if their letters had arrived properly sealed. When Secretary of War James McHenry sent President Washington a letter with a faulty seal, he was reprimanded.[85]

Close surveillance of the mails made post offices politically treacherous spaces, enabling eagle-eyed observers to spy letters from national politicians and scrutinize people's faces as they read their mail.[86] Surrounded by friends and neighbors in a post office, a man who refused to read aloud his mail from a national politician could seriously implicate his character and politics, as did Samuel Canfield of Connecticut, a supposed Federalist who received a letter from Matthew Lyon. Canfield "utterly refused to share his mail," Peter Van Schaack informed Theodore Sedgwick, proving Canfield "both a Jacobin & a liar." Aware that he might need to "perform" his correspondence, Federalist Harrison Gray Otis asked his wife to discuss confidential matters at the end of her letters, so he could avoid the awkwardness of skipping a line when reading them aloud.[87] Rather than spontaneous expressions of thought and feeling, letters were artfully contrived performances.

Local postmasters had inordinate power in this system of postal espionage, for they could screen mail from political allies or expose mail from foes to reveal alliances in the making. The two Van Schaacks were particularly concerned about their local postmaster, repeatedly pleading with Sedgwick to "purify the Post Offices" by purging them of Republicans. With a "Jacobin" postmaster, "a thousand disorganizing papers and letters may come and go without it being known," complained Peter. Even worse was the postmaster's access to Federalist mail, particularly since he lodged with the town's two Republican newspaper editors. "Now Mr Sedgwick," wrote Van Schaack with high sarcasm, "our Post Master is the Landlord of these Editors, and they his tenants, have the care of this self same Office in the absence of the principal, and which by the bye is not seldom — What conclusion will you draw from this, methinks, I hear you ask? To one less penetrating and less cal[l]ous to the public good, I would say that all the Post Masters, and all those attending in Post Offices, ought to be federal men."[88]

To Van Schaack, disloyal postmasters were a serious political liability. Only "sound Federalists in the different Post Offices" could choke off the Republican fount of disorder, for from "the subscription on Letters and papers corrupted channels may be discerned." And if these links between local men and national politicians were severed, the Republican cause would wither and die. Not surprisingly, when the Federalist *Porcupine's Gazette* did not reach Kinderhook for several weeks, Van Schaack immediately blamed Republican postmasters. If

Cobbett was sending his papers on schedule, then there was "something rotten somewhere" that Van Schaack vowed to expose.[89]

Some of Van Schaack's worst fears came true when his local postmaster began peddling newspapers for the editors housed in his post office. "[A] few days ago I was at the Post Office here, and was introduced by [Postmaster] Danforth to the Editor Merrill," he wrote to Sedgwick in 1798. "I was asked by the former—will you subscribe to the Berkshire Gazette? Not until I know the political sentiments of the Editors—'They will print nothing ag[ains]t the government.' Upon which two of the papers were put in my hands."[90] This very personal process of persuasion reveals another way the mails spread national political influence: newspaper subscriptions. Not only did newspapers disseminate national news throughout the nation, but they carried national reputations as well. Subscriptions traveled along lines of friendship—the central organizing force of national politics—calling forth the faithful, exposing the faithless, and forcing fence-straddlers to take a stand.

The mechanics of this process offers a fascinating glimpse at the power of personal reputation. Madison, for example, took full advantage of his public standing to gain subscriptions for the *National Gazette,* making subscribing a matter of honor and loyalty. As he explained in letters to potential subscribers, he sought their patronage not only to promote a valuable "vehicle of information" but also "from a desire of testifying my esteem & friendship to Mr. Freneau by contributing to render his profits as commensurate as possible to his merits." Withholding aid not only betrayed Madison, it dishonored him in Freneau's eyes, and by reducing Freneau's profits, it dishonored the editor as well. To further emphasize the personal nature of his appeal, Madison delivered his letters through Francis Childs, who handed them to the recipients in person.[91] Equally persuasive was the practice of some elite politicians who subscribed friends to national newspapers—unbeknownst to them—and then demanded repayment. To preserve their friendship with a man of influence, these involuntary subscribers were well advised to pay. Such efforts reinforced and extended networks of friends, helping to stretch loyalties across state bounds.

Thus, even as they helped shape public opinion on a massive scale, newspapers were also profoundly personal documents, linking subscribers in a shared cause. Indeed, subscribing to a newspaper—and thereby contributing the authority of one's name—was as good as a pledge of faith to its political bias, inspiring some national politicians to avoid subscription lists entirely. By 1813, with the Republicans well in power and his political career at an end, Jefferson felt far easier about giving the authority of his name to a partisan paper, subscribing to New Yorker Tunis Wortman's *Standard of the Union* as a stab at the opposing press.[92] As Jefferson well knew, becoming a subscriber would be as good as an advertisement for the paper; the prestige of his reputation would attract other subscribers eager to gain status by association. Hence the efforts of editors to solicit from the political elite the "sanction of your name."[93]

Given the intertwining of their personal reputations with the press, men of influence faced serious consequences if a national newspaper failed to deliver, literally or otherwise. Henry Van Schaack willingly plied subscriptions to Cobbett's *Gazette* until he discovered that the papers were arriving embarrassingly late or not at all. Cobbett was dishonoring him, Van Schaack complained to Sedgwick; having convinced his friends to subscribe, Van Schaack was personally "pledged for punctuality." When little had changed six months later, he swore that he would never again seek subscribers for Cobbett, whose inattention had cost him at least twenty subscriptions. But two weeks later, Van Schaack changed his mind when a Williams College student asked for the paper. The student body was "poisoned with antifederal trash," which Van Schaack hoped to counteract through this one subscription.[94]

Although far removed from Massachusetts in the national capital, Sedgwick was a vital link in this subscription chain. While Van Schaack drummed up new patrons for the *Gazette,* Sedgwick often ended up footing the bill. When subscriptions came due in March 1798, at least five friends in Massachusetts asked him to pay their debt, promising to reimburse him later.[95] Thomas Jefferson and South Carolina Federalist John Rutledge did the same for their local friends. At times, the financial outlay for such a service was substantial. Virginia Representative

John Page bluntly noted the demands on his purse in a circular letter, remarking that if a district relied solely on its national representatives for news of "the proceedings in Congress, it must depend in no small degree on the length of his purse. . . . However dexterous he may be in writing and making up letters, if he cannot afford to buy newspapers, and pay for the printing of copies of his letters, he can send but little information to his District."[96] As Page's complaint suggests, newspapers were vital purveyors of national news, but their passage relied on personal relationships. An impersonal print medium in many ways—disseminated to a widespread audience and filled with anonymous essays—newspapers were also a highly personal form of communication, grounded on reputation, status, and friendship as much as on devotion to a cause. Through a web of solicitors and subscribers, politicians used this fact to get national newspapers sold.

It was the power of a national reputation that prompted Lyman and Wright's letter to Adams. By yoking the authority of Adams's name to their cause, they could attract state and even national attention. This same power was what troubled Cunningham. Battered as Adams's reputation was, it would still lend enormous weight to his words; as Cunningham explained to Adams, regardless of the accuracy of his *Boston Patriot* essays, "the profound respect which has been imbibed for your name" would undoubtedly sway a credulous public.[97] This power would be no threat if Adams intended merely to defend his name. But increasingly, he seemed more interested in defaming Hamilton, condemning the cause of Federalism in his wake. Such behavior was dangerous during a time of crisis, Cunningham thought, for there was no telling what unwise alliances the French-loving Republicans might forge if left to their own devices. For the sake of Federalism and national security, something had to be done.

"Your Letters, if They Are Not History, They Are Nearly Allied to History"

At first Cunningham tried persuasion. Adams had asked for his opinion of his essays, so Cunningham complied. His comments centered around Adams's primary target: Alexander Hamilton. To Cunningham, Adams's attack on the New Yorker was far too personal—as indeed it was (fig. 21). Hamilton was not native born, Adams reminded his readers; he knew nothing of the American character, had no respect for the *real* Revolutionary patriots, was guilty of countless debaucheries and "indelicate pleasures," put his personal ambitions above all else, lacked the military knowledge of a drill sergeant, was more juvenile than an awkward schoolboy, maligned any man who seemed superior in the public eye, and spent his time writing "ambitious reports" while his underlings conducted the actual business of the Treasury. Adams even mocked Hamilton's virility, sneering that he was feeble-framed and short—an insult that the small-statured Cunningham found particularly harsh.[98] By striking at Hamilton, Adams had struck at Federalism, and as a fervent Federalist, Cunningham felt the blow.

Did Adams have to be so bitterly personal? Cunningham asked. Did he have to destroy Hamilton to vindicate the Adams name? And in striking so cruelly at Hamilton, had he not struck at Hamilton's friends and followers as well? If the New Yorker was deluded and ignorant, what did this say about his supporters? If he was as awkward as a schoolboy, did this not reflect on anyone who had trusted his talents? On the universities that had bestowed him with honors? On the historians who had praised his accomplishments?[99] A blast at one reputation left a host of others wounded in its wake.

In fact, according to Cunningham's logic Adams need not have replied to Hamilton's pamphlet at all, for it violated the rules of honor. Hamilton had laid the groundwork for his publication by demanding to know whether Adams had accused him of leading a British faction; ritualistic in form and content, Hamilton's letter to Adams was the opening of an affair of honor, as contemporaries well recognized. When Adams (predictably) responded with a chilling silence, the code of honor entitled Hamilton to post the president, condemning his character before the world. Hamilton's "Letter" had been just that—a ritualistic public posting with a political purpose. In his eagerness to provoke a fight, however, Hamilton had never specified a precise moment of offense—ironically, the very charge that he would hurl at Burr during their duel negotiations four years later. "The demands made by Hamilton were very indefinite, and unauthorised by the laws

BOSTON PATRIOT.

NUMBER 27. SATURDAY, JUNE 3, 1809. VOLUME I.

Fig. 21. *Boston Patriot,* June 3, 1809. Adams's self-defense appears on the front page of this issue, as it did for much of his three-year campaign. Here he begins by refuting Hamilton's pamphlet but quickly moves on to denounce Hamilton as a foreigner who spent his time indulging his "pleasures." (Courtesy of the American Antiquarian Society)

of honour," Cunningham explained, so Adams was not compelled to respond.[100]

Cunningham had put his finger on a central reason for Adams's newspaper campaign. His *Patriot* essays were more than an emotional eruption. They were a return volley in an affair of honor begun nine years past. Prevented by the dignity of his office from responding, and unwilling to fight Hamilton head to head in the press, the outraged Adams had held his tongue (and pen) for almost a decade. But when fate called him into the public eye, he seized the chance to clear his name, well aware that his primary target could not respond from the silence of the grave.

Enemies yet living were spared. Most notably, Timothy Pickering's name is missing from the *Patriot* essays, despite Adams's towering hatred of the man. His silence was not due to lack of evidence, for Adams filled several letters to Cunningham with harsh criticism of Pickering, accusing the former secretary of being the main conduit of Hamilton's influence over his cabinet. But though Pickering had done his part to destroy Adams's reputation, Adams did not wish to address him in the press. "I have no disposition to enter into newspaper controversies with Pickering, or his friends or Editors," Adams explained.[101]

His silence was telling to at least one man. In the Hudson, N.Y., *Northern Whig*, a "gentleman in Massachusetts" noted, "There is a person of unspotted and incorruptible integrity, who was connected with the old man in his highest state of elevation, who can, and I PRESUME will in proper time, shew documents, to prove the fallacy and turpitude of his recent statements. . . . In all the elaborate pieces that dotage has produced and sent out to the world, not once has the writer mentioned this man's name! no—and because the man is living and can *too* ably defend himself and too ably expose his antagonist." Although unnamed, the "person of unspotted and incorruptible integrity" connected with Adams's presidency was undoubtedly Pickering, spared by Adams because he would "ably defend himself." And indeed, Pickering began planning a response after the appearance of only a handful of Adams's essays. The former president was "giving a history of his administration, *in his own way*," he wrote to McHenry, a fellow sufferer at Adams's hand. "Doubtless it may become proper that this history be reviewed."[102]

Adams's cautions show that his *Patriot* essays were not an unbridled three-year rant. Indeed, compared with his initial 1801 draft response to Hamilton's pamphlet, the 1809 essays were relatively tame. Adams's 1801 draft, for example, described Hamilton's "exuberant Vanity and insatiable Egotism," which prompted him to be "ever restless, and busy and meddling, with Things far above his Capacity and inflame[d] him with an absolute rage to arrogate to himself the Honor of Suggesting every measure of Government"—Adams's words spilling over themselves in anger. In a later draft, he entirely omitted this passage. The *Patriot* follows the edited version almost exactly, with one additional swipe at Hamilton's ignorance and egotism.[103] Adams's *Patriot* essays were more tightly focused on Hamilton than his final 1801 draft, but they were not as enraged as his initial outpourings.

It is in the differences between the 1801 and 1809 tracts that Adams's ulterior motives peek through. The final version of the 1801 draft was an embryonic defense pamphlet, refuting the charges in Hamilton's "Letter" page by page. The 1809 campaign was aimed at defaming Hamilton as much as at vindicating Adams's name, using passages from Hamilton's pamphlet as entry points into a larger critique of the New Yorker's character and accomplishments.[104] By mocking Hamilton's virility, intelligence, morality, and political insight, Adams was attacking his heroic reputation and all that he stood for, and in so doing, discrediting the Federalists of 1809 as well.

This in itself would have been unsettling to an ardent Federalist like Cunningham, but Adams's timing was even more alarming. At a time when America needed to protect itself against Napoleonic France, Adams was ridiculing the man who had best understood the French threat. Perhaps Adams's emotions were running away with him, Cunningham suggested hopefully. But increasingly, Adams's private letters implied otherwise. When Cunningham worried that Adams was antagonizing the Federalists, Adams was defiant. Let them "spit their venom and hiss like serpents," he declared. He expected no mercy "from British Bears and Tory Tigers," whose system would "lead this country to misery"—a stray comment that put Cunningham on the alert. Surely Adams did not mean to condemn all Federalists indiscriminately?[105]

All of his past contact with Cunningham suggested otherwise. In 1803 and 1804 Adams had been all too willing to provide Cunningham with anecdotes to deploy against Jefferson. Adams had likewise been far more charitable toward Hamilton in the past. As Cunningham related in a letter, during one conversation, Adams had professed his respect for Hamilton and, turning his eyes toward heaven, "breathed a desire for his forgiveness." Cunningham could cite Adams's conversations of years past because he had recorded them; like any effective partisan, he had documented table talk and gossip for future use, never expecting to employ them against Adams himself.[106]

Suspicious of Adams's motives, Cunningham harped on the same theme in letter after letter, seeking reassurance that Adams was doing nothing more than defending his name. Finally, on August 13, Adams confessed his intentions outright. "I should have gone to my grave without writing a word, if the very system of Hamilton, a war with France, had not been revived, and apparently adopted by a majority of New-England. The British faction, and the old tories, appeared to have disciplined the Federalists to a system which appeared to me fundamentally wrong, and I determined to oppose it." This was no personal defense. It was a political attack. As Cunningham bluntly put it, "Under the semblance of a personal vindication," Adams was waging political war. His "personal complaints" about his wounded reputation were nothing more than "a convenient apology" for his public appearance.[107]

And indeed, for months before his first essay, Adams *had* been increasingly alarmed at foreign developments, as relations between England, France, and America grew ever shakier, and Federalists began to murmur about war with France. It was an echo of the crowning events of Adams's presidency, and he felt uniquely prepared to offer advice. Yet he knew that no one would listen if he simply stepped forward. "To what purpose, my friend, is it for me to give my opinion when every appearance indicates that it will not be followed now any more than it was in 1800?" he asked a friend shortly before the *Patriot* campaign.[108]

Lyman and Wright had provided the answer. By requesting the authority of Adams's name for political purposes, they had pushed a willing victim into the political arena, enabling him to redeem his reputation and promote his politics by offering selfless advice at a time of crisis. It was the Adams equation of public life. This same public-minded patriotism fueled Cunningham's response to Adams's campaign. If Adams continued to denounce Hamilton and his cause under the "authority" of his "august name," Cunningham felt sure that he would either drive the nation into war with Britain or split it in two.[109]

So on December 29, 1809, Cunningham took action. "I wish myself enlarged from your injunctions" of secrecy, he told Adams; given the seriousness of the pending foreign crisis, Cunningham wanted permission to publish Adams's past and present letters to display his flip-flopping politics and weaken the authority of his name. So concerned was Cunningham about Adams's evil influence that he was even prepared to publish Adams's letters without his permission. "I can hardly persuade myself, that my obligations to you are paramount to those which I owe my country," he declared. Regardless of "the inviolability of confidential trusts," he would obey the demands of patriotism.[110] The honorable path would be to violate Adams's trust.

Though he would have been loath to admit it, there was also a personal dimension to Cunningham's actions, for in abandoning his former politics, Adams had abandoned Cunningham as well. "I do not know that I have an opinion on any political subject unsupported by your authority," Cunningham explained toward the end of their correspondence. "It would be an endless labour to recite the sentiments, written and oral, of yours, upon which most of my political speculations have been founded." For years, Cunningham had used his friendship with Adams as a claim to political authority. Adams's conversion cut off this font of prestige and influence, thereby slapping at Cunningham's reputation.[111] For Cunningham, publishing Adams's letters was thus more than a political gesture. By exposing Adams's inconstancy to the world, Cunningham would be defending himself.

Despite Cunningham's threats, he ultimately published only a few fragments, and he sent these to Adams for approval before publication, so strong was his conviction in the sacred trust of private correspondence between friends—even former friends. "I shall be scrupulously cautious against bringing myself under reproaches of my conscience," he swore to Adams, who reminded him that publishing their letters would be "a breach of honour and of plighted faith." After Cunningham died, however, his son had no such qualms. Ardently opposed to John Quincy Adams's bid for the presidency, he published the Adams-Cunningham correspondence in 1823, attacking the son by dishonoring his father. Readers should take from the letters an important lesson: "whether it be safe to engraft a Scion of this old Stock in our tree of Liberty."[112] In a manner unanticipated by the elder Cunningham, Adams's self-defense would be yoked to the cause of Federalism.

The strength of young Cunningham's publication was the privacy of its evidence. Nothing could be more revealing than personal letters, he explained in his pamphlet's introduction: "It is well observed, that the truest delineations and traits of human character, are found in private intercourse and in familiar correspondence. Here, the mind discharges its sentinels—the heart is liberated from the restraints of policy and affectation—and the whole man unbends and displays the ingredients of his composition, and speaks the language of his real feelings and sentiments."[113] To Cunningham, Adams's letters revealed his true nature: his envy, resentment, disloyalty, indiscretion, and distemper—Hamilton's charges brought back to life.

Cunningham hoped that the power of private letters would condemn the Adamses, father and son, but like many a public attack on a politician's honor, his pamphlet cut a wider swath than intended. Within months, Jefferson knew about it. "I had for some time observed, in the public papers, dark hints and mysterious innuendoes of a correspondence of yours with a friend, to whom you had opened your bosom without reserve," he wrote to Adams in October 1823, and it was now "said to be actually published." Based on extracts leaked to the newspapers, Jefferson saw all too clearly that Adams had virulently attacked him in many letters. But Jefferson would not allow this "outrage on private confidence" to destroy their friendship, he wrote in an eloquent letter professing support to their dying days. "'How generous! how noble! how magnanimous!'" went the cry around the

Adams table when the letter was read aloud, followed by "a universal cry that the letter ought to be printed." "Not without Mr. Jefferson's express leave," Adams shot back, well aware of the problems of betrayed correspondence. A few weeks later, Jefferson allowed a John Quincy Adams supporter to publish his letter in the *Boston Patriot,* once again a center of controversy.[114]

Timothy Pickering was less genteel. As Adams suspected, he was only too eager to defend his name. As early as June 1809 he had begun to prepare a response to Adams's *Patriot* essays, reporting his activities to McHenry, who was less than thrilled by the idea. Would Adams's writings "become history?" McHenry asked. "Who pronounces the name of this calumniator of the dead with veneration? Who celebrates his acts? Who is emulous to tread in his footsteps? In a few years his name and his fame, if not borne up by other pinions than his own, will sink in that gulph destined to swallow up all memorials of merit and demerit like his."[115] To McHenry, Adams's newspaper diatribe was no part of the historical record. But where politics—and thus history—were so personal, it was hard to say what ultimately would gain sanction as historical truth.

So Pickering thought, unpersuaded by McHenry's pleas. Hamilton's name, the cause of Federalism, and thereby Pickering's life's work and reputation required defending. For a few years he responded to Adams's essays in a series of notebooks, answering charge by charge, letter by letter, much as Adams had responded to Hamilton's pamphlet in 1801. Like Adams, he then withheld his work until accusations in the published Adams-Cunningham correspondence called him into the public eye. "In all of my life I have never met with such a mass of calumny," he fumed upon reading the pamphlet. "The whole noble family of Adams will regret this act of the ex-president, alike imprudent and malevolent." Pickering's response, titled "A Review of the Correspondence Between the Hon. John Adams . . . and the Late Wm. Cunningham, Esq.," was published the next year, becoming yet another link in a paper chain of reputations.[116]

Far more than a response to Cunningham's pamphlet, Pickering's "formal vindication" was a history of the 1790s. His expanded aims were prompted by Jefferson's letter of friendship to Adams, which had been reprinted in the *Boston Patriot*. The letter seemed "calculated to lead the readers into a misconception" about the integrity of the two men's characters, and thereby into a misunderstanding of historical truth, Pickering charged.[117] To Pickering, as to his contemporaries, history was a tale of character and reputation, and only by showing characters in their true light could historical truth be known. In this context, defense pamphlets were more than political fodder; attempting to straighten the historical record by attacking and defending reputations, they were history itself.

Although a few Adams supporters published newspaper defenses, there was relatively little response to Pickering's publication. To many, the sight of the seventy-eight-year-old Pickering attacking the eighty-nine-year-old Adams was more pathetic than anything else. Martin Van Buren noticed the pamphlet, bringing it to Jefferson's attention during a visit to Monticello and sending him a copy shortly thereafter. According to Van Buren's autobiography, Jefferson was stunned at the intensity of Pickering's hatred, claiming that he had never harbored any ill feelings toward the arch Federalist.[118] For Van Buren the pamphlet demonstrated Jefferson's fairness of character—a conclusion that would have made Pickering shudder.

Thus, far from an irrational outburst of spleen, Adams's *Boston Patriot* essays were part of a broader public appeal that was itself enmeshed in an even larger battle of reputations fought with weapons of print. Hamilton's pamphlet, Adams's string of responses (his draft essay, his letters to Cunningham, his *Boston Patriot* essays), Cunningham's newspaper extracts from Adams's letters, his son's pamphlet, Jefferson's published letter, Pickering's pamphlet, and Van Buren's autobiography were all part of the same argument. Partisanship, personal reputation, and the historical record were bound together in a volatile brew that would simmer for decades. As late as 1846, descendants of Oliver Wolcott (yet *another* embittered veteran of Adams's cabinet) were slashing at Adams's *Patriot* essays. In *Memoirs of the Administrations of Washington and Adams*—a biography of Wolcott framed as a history of the 1790s—Wolcott's grandson George Gibbs quoted extensively from Adams's essays as proof of his vanity and obstinacy, validating Hamilton's claims with Adams's own words. "Though of no other historical importance," Gibbs wrote, the "unguarded confidences" of Adams's essays offered inside information about personal opinions and private conversations—the world captured in Jefferson's "Anas" as the *real* history of Washington's administration.[119]

For self-declared Founders engaged in history-making events, history was about reputation above all else. Dishonor in print thus did more than inflict pain in the present; it damned a man's reputation for all time. Dread fear of this outcome fueled Adams's defense campaign for three years; this same fear inspired Jefferson's three-volume history and an outpouring of similar memoirs, histories, biographies, and autobiographies besides. As the next chapter reveals, Hamilton's thoughts turned the same way the night before his duel with Burr. By tending to the historical record, these national political veterans were safeguarding their reputations as well. Like gossip and defense pamphlets, their addresses to posterity had to appear passive and detached to be effective; only then might these personal pleas seem like objective historical fact. Thus the failure of Adams's *Patriot* essays and Hamilton's "Letter." The pain, anger, and hatred running through their pages destroyed any appearance of objectivity. Adams and Hamilton had deployed conventional weapons in unconventional ways, letting their resentment run rampant—with the authority of their names—in the precise manner that the honor code was designed to prevent. Tearing away the mask of restraint that framed political combat, they revealed the raw emotion lurking beneath the surface of a politics of honor and reputation.

Dueling as Politics

On the evening of July 10, 1804, Alexander Hamilton was a man tormented. At dawn he would duel Aaron Burr. Hamilton considered himself "strongly opposed to the practice of Duelling," yet the following morning he would stand opposite Burr on the heights of Weehawken, New Jersey, pistol in hand, awaiting the command to fire.[1]

This day of reckoning had been long approaching, for Hamilton had bitterly opposed Burr's political career for fifteen years. Charismatic men of great talent and ambition, the two had been thrust into competition with the opening of the national government and the sudden availability of new power, positions, and acclaim. Socially and professionally they had remained friendly and cooperative throughout that time, mingling in the same social circles, eating at the same dinner tables, sometimes serving together on the same legal cases. Personally they remained collegial as well.

But Hamilton and Burr were very different men. Burr was the grandson of the great divine Jonathan Edwards, making him the equiv-

Fig. 22. *Aaron Burr* (1756–1836), by John Vanderlyn, 1802. Painted two years before the duel with Hamilton, this portrait hints at Burr's commanding carriage and piercing dark eyes — his most remarked-upon feature. Burr helped fund Vanderlyn's studies, ultimately sending him to Paris to complete his training. (Courtesy of Yale University Art Gallery, Bequest of Oliver Burr Jennings, B.A. 1917, in memory of Miss Annie Burr Jennings)

alent of New England royalty. He viewed politics as a game and enjoyed playing it. More of an opportunist than an ideologue, he was seemingly dedicated to nothing other than the advancement of his political career. Many considered him oblivious even to the restraints of honor and reputation, a man bemused rather than outraged by disapproval of his lifestyle and appetites (fig. 22). There seemed to be nothing holding Burr back from doing precisely as he chose.

Hamilton was a different sort of politician with a very different

Fig. 23. *Alexander Hamilton* (1755?–1804), by Ezra Ames, ca. 1802. Painted shortly after the death of Hamilton's oldest son, Philip, who was killed in a duel defending his father's name, this portrait shows the tinge of sadness in Hamilton's countenance that friends marked thereafter. Hamilton's wife, Elizabeth, considered it an excellent likeness. (Courtesy of Sotheby's)

heritage. Born poor and illegitimate in the West Indies, he had raised himself to power by his wits, talents, energies, and charm. He was a born fighter, walking a high-wire of self-creation, and the founding of the republic was his ticket to fame and glory (fig. 23). A threat to the nation was a threat to his hard-won status and reputation, and in Hamilton's eyes the talented, power-hungry Burr—virtually bred to a position of leadership—was the greatest threat of all. Add to this Hamilton's unshakable political views, his impulsiveness, extreme candor, and brash confidence—even arrogance—and we can begin to understand the fire and fury of the Burr-Hamilton rivalry, and the reason why they cut such wide paths through the imaginations of their peers.[2]

By 1804 both men had been cast off the national stage and were competing in the more limited circle of New York state politics. Burr, however, seemed to have larger ambitions, courting Federalists throughout New England to unite behind him and march toward secession—or so Hamilton thought—and Burr's first step on that path appeared to be his gubernatorial ambitions in the 1804 election. Horrified that Burr could become New York's chief Federalist, corrupt the Federalist party, sabotage Hamilton's influence, and possibly destroy the republic, Hamilton stepped up his opposition. Anxious to discredit Burr, Hamilton attacked his private character, calling him a "profligate" and a "voluptuary in the extreme," a man whose flawed character would drag his followers to ruin.[3]

Burr was keenly aware of Hamilton's opposition and no longer willing to overlook it, for the 1804 election was his last hope for political power. From the reports of his friends and the pages of the *American Citizen,* he knew that Hamilton was whispering about him. He assumed (wrongly) that Hamilton had written several of the venomous pamphlets published against him in the past few years, and reportedly swore to "call out the first man of any respectability concerned in the infamous publications." By January 1804, *Citizen* editor James Cheetham was publicly daring Burr to challenge Hamilton to a duel.[4]

Burr was thus quick to respond when he discovered concrete evidence of Hamilton's antagonism in a letter published in the Republican *Albany Register*. After noting Hamilton's opposition to Burr, the writer, Charles D. Cooper, assured his correspondent that he "could detail . . . a still more despicable opinion which General Hamilton has expressed of Mr. Burr." Though Cooper only hinted at an offensive personal insult, Burr seized on this remark as provocation for an affair of honor and demanded an explanation from Hamilton.[5] After roughly ten days of negotiation, Burr issued Hamilton a challenge, and Hamilton accepted.

The logic behind both men's actions has largely eluded historians. What prevented Hamilton from ending the affair with an apology or an explanation? And why did Burr instigate a duel on such dubious grounds? Many have attributed these self-destructive decisions to emotional excess, suggesting that Hamilton was suicidal and Burr malicious and murderous. Admittedly, Hamilton and Burr were haunted by private demons. Though born at opposite ends of the social spectrum, each spent his adult life challenging the confines of his ancestry—for Hamilton, his illegitimacy, and for Burr, the saintly mantle of his famed grandfather. Self-created men of high ambition, they were insecure and touchy, ever ready to prove their worth. Yet though personal insecurities may have made Hamilton and Burr likely duelists, they do not explain how the men justified the duel to themselves.[6] One strategy among many for redeeming one's name—though undoubtedly the most extreme weapon in the political arsenal—dueling was part of a larger grammar of political combat.

Of the two decisions, Hamilton's was the more conflicted. Unlike Burr, Hamilton was not prepared to duel upon commencing negotiations. He was the unsuspecting recipient of a challenge, morally and theologically opposed to dueling yet profoundly protective of his honor and "religiously" committed to opposing Burr's political career. Unsure how to proceed upon receiving Burr's initial demand, he consulted with "a very moderate and judicious friend," Rufus King, to discuss the propriety of Burr's demand for an explanation, ultimately deeming it too "general and undefined" to merit a response. Aware that this decision could provoke Burr, Hamilton also told King that he would accept a challenge if offered—but would not necessarily fire at his challenger. King was stunned. A duelist was justified in preserving his life, he insisted; Hamilton would be shooting in self-defense. Nathaniel Pendleton, Hamilton's second, made the same argument a few days later, finally eliciting a promise from Hamilton that "he would not decide lightly, but take time to deliberate fully."[7]

On the evening of July 10, the night before the duel, Hamilton made his choice. In the midst of a final planning session, he told Pendleton that he had decided "not to fire at Col. Burr the first time, but to receive his fire, and fire in the air." Pendleton vehemently protested, but Hamilton would not be swayed. His decision, he explained, was "the effect of a religious scruple, and does not admit of reasoning." Pendleton did not understand. Neither had King. Aware that even his most intimate friends disapproved of his actions, about to risk his life for his reputation, Hamilton felt driven to explain himself. Alone in his study after Pendleton's departure, he took up his pen.[8]

"On my expected interview with Col. Burr, I think it proper to make some remarks explanatory of my conduct, motives, and views," began Hamilton (fig. 24).[9] He then set down his apologia, a four-page series of lawyerly assertions penned in an uncharacteristically constrained hand. The attorney Hamilton was defending his reputation before the tribunal of posterity, explaining his decision to duel.

Hamilton first solicited his putative jury's sympathy by presenting himself as a law-abiding husband and father. He was "certainly desirous of avoiding this interview," he explained, substantiating his claim with an enumerated list of reasons: the duel violated his religious and moral principles and defied the law, threatened the welfare of his family, put his creditors at risk, and ultimately compelled him to "hazard much, and . . . possibly gain nothing." Given these considerations, refusing Burr's challenge seemed the logical choice.

Yet, he continued, the duel was "impossible . . . to avoid." There were "*intrinsick* difficulties in the thing," because Hamilton had, indeed, made "extremely severe" attacks on Burr's political and private character. Because he had uttered these remarks "with sincerity . . . and for purposes, which might appear to me commendable," he could not apologize for them. More complicating were the "*artificial* embarrassments" caused by Burr's behavior throughout their negotiations. Hamilton's supposed offense was too "general and indefinite" to explain, "if it had really been proper . . . to submit to be so questionned."

Burr's manner was also insulting. In his first letter to Hamilton, Burr had assumed "a tone unnecessarily peremptory and menacing" and in his second, "positively offensive." Such treatment almost compelled Hamilton to accept Burr's challenge, yet even in the face of such an affront, he had "wished, as far as might be practicable, to leave a door open to accommodation." He had struggled so diligently to avoid a confrontation that he was unsure whether he "did not go further in the attempt to accommodate, than a pun[c]tilious delicacy will justify." If so, he hoped that his motives would deflect any charges of cowardice.

No 12

On my expected interview with Col
Burr, I think it proper to make some remarks
explanatory of my conduct, motives and views—
I was certainly desirous of avoiding
this interview, for the most cogent reasons—
1 My religious and moral principles
are strongly opposed to the practice of Duelling, and
it would ever give me pain to be obliged to shed the blood
of [a fellow creature] in a private combat forbidden by the laws.
2 My wife and Children are extremely
dear to me, and my life is of the utmost importance
to them, in various views—
3 I feel a sense of obligation towards
my creditors; who in case of accident to me, by the
forced sale of my property, may be in some degree
sufferers. I did not think myself at liberty, as
a man of probity, lightly to expose them to this
hazard.
4 I am conscious of no
ill-will to Col Burr, distinct from political
opposition, which, as I trust, has proceeded
from pure and upright motives.
Lastly, I shall hazard much,
and can possibly gain nothing by the issue of
the interview.
But it was, as I conceive,
impossible for me to avoid it. There were
intrinsick difficulties in the thing, and artificial embarrassments, from the manner of proceeding
on the part of Col Burr.
Intrinsick—because it is not
to be denied, that my animadversions on the
political principles character and views of Col
Burr have been extremely severe, and on
different [occasions] I, in common with many others, have

Fig. 24. Front page of Hamilton's apologia, written between June 28 and July 10, 1804. Hamilton's handwriting is unusually constrained in this final statement, probably written the night before his duel with Burr. The revised sentence suggests that Hamilton had some trouble finding the words to discuss bloodshed. (© Collection of The New-York Historical Society)

Hamilton now approached the crux of his defense: his attempt to accommodate the mandates of honor and politics with those of morality, religion, and the law.[10] He had satisfied the code of honor by accepting Burr's challenge, violating civil law only under duress. He had maintained his political integrity by refusing to apologize for sincere political convictions. Now he would uphold his moral and religious principles by withholding his fire. Because of "my general principles and temper in relation to similar affairs," Hamilton explained, "I have resolved, if our interview is conducted in the usual manner, and it pleases God to give me the opportunity, to *reserve* and *throw away* my first fire." Hamilton's seemingly illogical plan thus comprised four reasoned decisions, each prompted by a separate code of conduct.

Hamilton had ruled out many options, but one remained. Why not simply refuse to participate? Addressing himself to "those, who with me abhorring the practice of Duelling may think that I ought on no account to have added to the number of bad examples," he explained his fundamental reason: "All the considerations which constitute what men of the world denominate honor, impressed on me (as I thought) a peculiar necessity not to decline the call. The ability to be in future useful, whether in resisting mischief or effecting good, in those crises of our public affairs, which seem likely to happen, would probably be inseparable from a conformity with public prejudice in this particular."

Hamilton had accepted Burr's challenge to preserve his "ability to be in future useful" in political crises. In his mind, the duel was a praiseworthy attempt to serve the common good: a public, political act. Yet it was also an intensely personal attempt to preserve his public career and private sense of self—to prove to the world, and to himself, that he was a man of his word, a man of courage and principle, a leader. And in less sympathetic eyes, the duel could appear to be a politically motivated effort to prevent a rival from bolstering his reputation at Hamilton's expense.[11] In his final hours before the duel, compelled to transcribe the conflicted logic of a life-threatening decision, Hamilton gave voice to the complex blend of cultural and political influences that led politicians to duel.

"What Men of the World Denominate Honor"

Perhaps the most common misunderstanding about the American political duel concerns its purpose. For twentieth-century onlookers far removed from the culture of honor, the duel was a ritual of violence whose purpose was to maim or kill an adversary. But to early national politicians, duels were demonstrations of manner, not marksmanship; they were intricate games of dare and counterdare, ritualized displays of bravery, military prowess, and—above all—willingness to sacrifice one's life for one's honor. A man's response to the *threat* of gunplay bore far more meaning than the exchange of fire itself. Politicians considered themselves engaged in an affair of honor from the first "notice" of an insult to the final acknowledgment of "satisfaction," a process that sometimes took weeks or even months. Regardless of whether shots were fired, these ritualized negotiations constituted an integral part of a duel.[12]

This more precise understanding of the duel reveals that there were more honor disputes in the early republic than previously recognized; for example, Hamilton was involved in ten such affairs before his duel with Burr.[13] As a partisan leader (and a particularly controversial one at that), Hamilton doubtless attracted more than his share of abuse. Yet his level of involvement in honor disputes was not unique. In New York City, Hamilton's adopted home, there were at least sixteen affairs of honor between 1795 and 1807, most of them heretofore unrecognized because they did not result in a challenge or the exchange of fire. Most of these duels did not result from a sudden flare of temper; politicians timed them strategically, sometimes provoked them deliberately. Often, the two seconds published conflicting newspaper accounts of a duel, each man boasting of his principal's bravery and mocking his opponent's cowardice. Fought to influence a broad public, synchronized with the events of the political timetable, political duels conveyed carefully scripted political messages.[14]

Politicians manipulated the affair of honor to serve their immediate political needs, but they also shared a profound respect for its personal dimension, its impact on their sense of self. The duel was a subtle blend of the strategic and the sincere, the self-interested and the selfless, the political and the personal, the public and the private. Political duelists were not rapacious predators deliberately masking their evil intentions under the guise of honor. They were men of public duty and private ambition who identified so closely with their public roles that they often could not distinguish between their identity as gentlemen and their status as political leaders. Longtime political opponents almost expected duels, for there was no way that constant opposition to a man's political career could leave his personal identity unaffected. As Hamilton confessed on his deathbed, "I have found, for some time past, that my life *must* be exposed to that man."[15] By opposing Burr's political career, Hamilton had wounded him as a gentleman, making himself vulnerable to a challenge. Nowhere do we witness this ambiguity more affectingly than in Hamilton's apologia, his testament to the complexities of political leadership among men of honor.

Personal honor was a concern of politicians throughout the nation. North and South, they recognized the need to remain alert to tone, intent, and implications to preserve their status. Dependent on the community at large for both personal honor and public career, they had to be acutely sensitive to public opinion, the prevailing tone of a community's conversation. The character of politics in the early republic—the prevailing distrust of political parties, the small-scale, localized political realm—magnified this obsession with reputation. Political combat readily degenerated into battles of "asperities and personalities."[16] Many of these skirmishes were settled in ritualistic affairs of honor.

Northerners were as well versed in this code as southerners; it was in their utilization of violence that they differed most noticeably. A northerner might cane a man or post him as a liar in a newspaper or on a broadside rather than challenge him to a duel, but in densely populated, print-saturated New England, a print attack on a man's honor inflicted a severe wound. It was dueling that proved problematic for New Englanders. A duelist took revenge "in cool blood." Willing to kill or be killed, he calmly and deliberately violated the laws of God and man.[17] In a sense northerners and southerners spoke different dialects of the language of honor, balancing the conflicting value systems of honor, religion, and the law in regionally distinct ways.

Yet even New Englanders who disapproved of dueling often found it difficult to turn their backs on an affair of honor. It was one thing to condemn dueling generally and quite another to ignore a personal insult or challenge, driving many northerners to condemn dueling in one breath and justify it in the next. Massachusetts Federalist Christopher Gore was typical of many when he declared that he could not duel without feeling "disgraced & debased," even as he agreed to accept a challenge. Harvard student John Farnham drew a similar conclusion in 1810 after hearing about a friend's duel. He was "heartily sorry & grieved" at the news, for it would hurt the reputation of any "young man who depends on the estimation of the publick for a living." Yet, he continued, "I must confess that considering . . . the greatness of the insult . . . that he is not guilty of a great moral sin. . . . [T]hough perhaps the opinion of the most respectable part of the community in N. England is abhorrent to the practice of duelling—it is in vain to expect or presume that . . . the decisions of a court will wipe off the stain on a mans reputation—or that [a] man will ever obtain any consequence & respect who suffers himself to be trodden under foot."[18] Hamilton would struggle with this same ambivalence during his negotiations with Burr.

Northerners found insults to their honor even more difficult to ignore on the elevated national stage, particularly when offered by a southerner. Because of the ambiguous link between regional ties and partisan loyalties, battles between Federalists and Republicans were largely battles between northerners and southerners, placing new demands on New Englanders accustomed to a less belligerent dialect of honor culture. Protective of their comparative status as northerners and Federalists and worried about southern domination of the Union, New England congressmen were thus quick to note insults and often urged personal vindication. They had good reason to feel belligerent, for southern congressmen often "crowded" New Englanders—bullied and taunted them—because they knew that northerners would resist gunplay. So notorious was southern crowding that one newspaper editor satirically branded it a plot by southerners to "thin off the northern members [of Congress] so as to secure to themselves a decided majority."[19] In essence, the nationalization of politics led to a backlash of defensive regionalism, played out most dramatically in honor disputes on the floor of Congress.

Charges against rivals, ranging from accusations of official misconduct to character slurs, usually shared one underlying theme: politicians accused one another of behaving like politicians. They charged one another with the sins of self-interest and private ambition.[20] They cried out against corrupt dependencies grounded on the distribution of favors. All around them they saw what they most feared, the selfish motives and hidden intrigues of faction. Yet in struggling against these enemies of the republic, these same politicians created factions of their own. When a politician defended his honor, he was defending his ability to claim power, promoting himself and his "particular friends" in public-minded contests with political opponents. In essence, he was conducting partisan politics.

For politicians of the early republic, honor was thus much more than a vague sense of self-worth; it represented the ability to prove oneself a deserving political leader.[21] Hamilton was trying to do as much in his final statement. Burr was compelled by the same logic when he challenged Hamilton. Politicians were simultaneously asserting their concern for the common good and their partisan biases, their selflessness and their private ambitions. These conflicting urges joined to produce an ambiguous form of politics, fueled by public-minded personal disputes couched in the language of honor.

The strictures of honor controlled, channeled, and masked political combat by providing a shared code of conduct that enforced gentlemanly standards of behavior. Men who did not abide by these rules were neither gentlemen nor leaders. As Burr warned Hamilton during their negotiations, "Political opposition can never absolve Gentlemen from the necessity of a rigid adherence to the laws of honor and the rules of decorum." A true gentleman avoided crossing lines but knew how to behave if lines were crossed. As a congressional onlooker to a 1798 honor dispute commented, "In well-bred Society, when a man receives an affront, does he knock down the person giving it? No.

He represses his feelings; and takes another time and place to obtain justice."[22]

The laws of honor also indicated when insults could not be ignored, branding a man a coward if he let a serious affront go unanswered. Hamilton experienced this during the 1795 Jay Treaty melée, when James Nicholson dismissed him as a man of no importance because he had once shirked a duel. In 1803, Postmaster General Gideon Granger of Connecticut went into hiding when confronted with similar charges, condemned by even his allies as "a base coward." And in 1804, when the eccentric John Randolph of Roanoke threw a glass of wine in the face of Willis Alston, Jr., broke the glass over his head and threw the bottle at him, "Men of honor of both Federalists & Democrats" had but "one opinion on this subject—& say that they must fight—That Alston will be disgraced if he do not." Hoping to avoid such an outcome, President Jefferson was "anxious for a compromise"; even the president himself abided by the strictures of the honor code.[23]

For all these men, the "laws of honor" constituted a standard of conduct by which a man could gauge himself and his rivals. They enabled him, his peers, and the public at large to "judge of the correctness of the conduct of their representatives" and so distinguish those who were worthy of leadership from those who were not.[24] A means of empowering oneself while deposing one's foes, of asserting one's merit while remaining self-righteously defensive, the code of honor was a powerful political tool. But it was a curiously indirect form of combat, functionally adapted for a society that feared and condemned open ambition and factional politics.

"If Our Interview Is Conducted in the Usual Manner"

In planning his course of action on the dueling ground, Hamilton relied on the universal recognition of the language of honor. Like other politicians, he had a keen understanding of the honor code, enabling him to pick and choose strategies from a clearly defined spectrum of options, in response to a corresponding spectrum of insults. Duels represented one extreme in this grammar of combat. Most political weapons were designed to refute or substantiate charges of official misconduct. They pitted words against words. Affronts that hit at a politician's "private character" demanded something more. They required a demonstration of honor, bravery, and self-sacrifice that would vindicate his character and justify his claim to leadership. In the same way that a pamphlet discredited accusations with signed correspondence and legal depositions, a duel enabled an aggrieved politician to refute character slurs by acting in accordance with the most exacting standards of behavior. A true gentleman was always gracious and calm, even in the face of imminent death.[25] Attitude was the key to proving oneself a man of honor.

Northerners and southerners, frequent duelists and those who never dueled, all understood the strictures and rituals of the code of honor. For example, everyone understood the implicit meaning of a caning—a sound beating about the head and shoulders with a cane. Because only equals were supposed to duel, canings displayed the victim's inferior status. A caning was no symbolic smack; gentlemen often purchased "stout hickory" walking sticks deliberately for this purpose. Busily writing a letter in the House in 1798, George Thatcher lurched in his seat at the heavy thwack of a cane making contact with a head.[26] Not surprisingly, many canings inflicted permanent damage. William Coleman, editor of the *New-York Evening Post,* ended his days paralyzed from the waist down because of a caning. As suggested by Coleman's fate, newspaper editors were frequent caning victims, for politicians considered them too low to merit a challenge.

A "nose-tweaking" was another slap at a man's status that sent a powerful message. Grabbing and twisting a man's nose was a grave insult that demanded a challenge. When Republican Brockholst Livingston insulted Federalist James Jones, Jones responded by first caning Livingston and then trying to "wring his nose"—so serious an affront that it prompted a discussion about precisely how much of Livingston's nose had been grabbed.[27] The tussle resulted in a challenge, a duel, and Jones's death. The implied insult of both canings and nose-tweakings was the same; not only were they profoundly humiliating public assaults, they were badges of inferiority as well.

Postings were yet another shared ritual of the honor code. When someone proffered an insult but refused a challenge, the offended party was entitled to "post" his attacker in a broadside or newspaper denouncing him as a coward, a liar, a rascal, and a scoundrel. By slashing at his offender's reputation and discrediting his charges, the wounded party cleared his name. When Virginia Representative John Randolph refused a challenge from General James Wilkinson, for example—declaring that "*he would not reduce himself to his level*"—Wilkinson posted Randolph "in the newspapers in very opprobrious language."[28] Many such postings appear in early nineteenth-century newspapers under the heading "A Card."

Verbal assaults were equally obvious. Politicians were well aware of the key words and phrases that signaled the commencement of an honor dispute, and attuned to the subtleties of meaning in the wording and timing of a response. *Coward, liar, rascal, scoundrel,* and *puppy* all demanded an immediate challenge, for they struck at the core elements of manliness and gentility. Any man who uttered them in a dispute was declaring his intention to engage in an affair of honor. And onlookers who witnessed such affronts watched for the appropriate response. When Matthew Lyon and Roger Griswold exchanged harsh words on the House floor, a host of onlookers scrutinized each man's face as the other delivered his insult, watching for the proper expression of repressed outrage; several were surprised and concerned when Lyon appeared not to notice one barb. Aedanus Burke knew what he intended when he threw "the lie" at Hamilton on the floor of the House. As Maclay noted, "Men of the blade" said that this "Violent personal Attack" must produce a duel. And Hamilton responded as expected, saying that he would "at all times disregard any observations applied to his public station . . . but that *this* was not to be passed over."[29]

Such an attack could set off a wave of reaction that rippled throughout the political community. Often, transmitters of such news attached a clear judgment to their accounts, evaluating the participants' behavior and measuring them against shared standards of honor. James Madison never fought a duel, but when Lyon and Griswold broke into an open brawl on the floor of the House, he nonetheless had strong opinions about its etiquette.

The dispute was certainly noteworthy. In 1798, Matthew Lyon of Vermont insulted Connecticut's representatives in a private conversation off to the side of the House floor. Overhearing the remark, Roger Griswold of Connecticut responded by hinting at charges of cowardice that had haunted Lyon from Revolutionary War days; when Lyon didn't react to the insult, Griswold walked up to him, set his hand on Lyon's arm, and repeated the remark. Lyon responded by spitting in Griswold's face. When a House committee voted not to expel "Spitting Matt," Griswold took action.

Purchasing a strong hickory walking stick, he strode up to Lyon on the House floor and struck him full force more than twenty times, denouncing him as a "scoundrel," while Lyon tried in vain to extricate himself from his desk. Once free, Lyon ran behind the Speaker's chair and grabbed a set of fireplace tongs to defend himself, Griswold beating him all the while (fig. 25). Though several men yelled to the Speaker to call the House to order, he refused, allowing Griswold to clear his name until onlookers intervened and pulled the two apart; the same thing happened minutes later, when the two men again took arms, some crying out, "Part them, part them," others shouting, "Don't." To Madison, Griswold had dishonored himself by opening the affair to a congressional investigation; in his view, Griswold should have immediately responded to Lyon's affront with a beating or a challenge: "If Griswold be a man of the sword, he shd. not have permitted the step [of a congressional investigation] to be taken; if not he does not deserve to be avenged by the House. No man ought to reproach another with cowardice, who is not ready to give proof of his own courage"—a byword of the honor code.[30] Only a "man of the sword" could engage in such name-calling, for an insult offered by someone unwilling to fight was an insult without risk—a cowardly act. A confrontational man had to be willing to take responsibility for his words and thus had to be consistently ready to duel. Madison's comment implies what Lord Chesterfield asserted as an irrefutable truth: "There are but two alternatives for a gentleman; extreme politeness, or the sword."[31]

Alexander Hamilton and James Monroe were undeniably men of the sword. An eyewitness account of a dispute between them captures the precise moment when the two men—both clearly prepared

Fig. 25. *Congressional Pugilists,* unidentified artist, 1798. This is one of several cartoons satirizing the fracas between Roger Griswold and "Spitting Matt" Lyon on the House floor. Griswold waves a cane on the right; Lyon waves fireplace tongs on the left. An audience of congressmen whoops in the background—and in truth, many discouraged interference so Griswold could cane Lyon and clear his name. Smiling down from the chair is Jonathan Dayton, Speaker of the House, who resisted calling the House to order; Dayton initiated his own honor dispute on the Senate floor five years later. (Courtesy of the Library of Congress)

to fight—shifted abruptly from angry quarreling to the rigid and distinctive language of the duel. When newspaper editor James Callender charged Hamilton with misusing Treasury funds, Hamilton was sure that Monroe had provided Callender with incriminating information. On July 11, 1797, he paid Monroe a visit with his brother-in-law John Barker Church in tow. When Monroe denied involvement, Hamilton told him, "This as your representation is totally false," suggesting that Monroe was a liar. The insult brought both men to their feet. Monroe replied, "You say I represented falsely, you are a Scoundrel," topping

Hamilton's indirect charge with an explicit dare to fight. Hamilton responded as would any man of honor, declaring, "I will meet you like a Gentleman." Monroe's reply was also predictable. Declaring that he was ready to fight, he asked Hamilton to get his pistols. At this point Church and David Gelston, Monroe's friend, shoved between the two men and separated them, pleading for moderation.[32]

Although Monroe and Hamilton skipped a few steps in the heat of the moment, the rules for negotiating an affair of honor were relatively clear. Once an insult had been proffered, the insulted party was supposed to request an explanation from his offender, giving him the chance to clear up any misunderstanding or misrepresentation. Someone who omitted this vital step in a rush of emotion was usually scolded soundly. As Hamilton told a man who precipitously accused him of not behaving like a gentleman, "To take it for granted that you had received an injury from me, without first giving me an opportunity of an explanation, and to couch your sense of it in terms so offensive as some of those used in your letter, is an additional instance of precipitation and rudeness." Angry at his correspondent's presumption, Hamilton concluded by indirectly indicating his willingness to duel: "It will depend on yourself how far I shall be indifferent, or not, to your future sentiments of my character," he challenged.[33]

Hamilton himself received a scolding after his 1795 confrontation with Nicholson. Outraged at being called a coward, Hamilton demanded to duel Nicholson, naming the place and time. Nicholson accepted the invitation, expressing his own desire to duel the next morning, but reprimanded Hamilton for the "peremptory tenor" of his letter. Hamilton, in turn, used this as an opening to backpedal and allow Nicholson room for an explanation.[34] He had not requested one earlier, he explained, because of what Nicholson said "on a certain very delicate point." Accused of being a coward, Hamilton had felt unable to do anything other than extend a challenge.

Initial letters of inquiry were warnings that a line had been crossed. Following a set form and phrased in ritualistic words of cool formality, they were easily recognizable and unmistakably threatening. A typical letter began by repeating an offending remark—a means of discouraging unnecessary challenges by ensuring common agreement on the meaning and form of an offense. The writer next demanded that the recipient "avow or disavow" the insult, ensuring the propriety of his challenge by allowing his recipient an opportunity to explain himself. Letters usually ended with a demand for an immediate response. Typically, the writer justified his demand by claiming the respect owed a gentleman. Any mention of a man's honor was a clear sign that his honor had been offended. If the letter mentioned a friend—as the bearer of the message or the recipient of a response—a correspondent could be sure that this friend was a second, the principal's sole representative throughout all negotiations and his assistant on the field of honor.

These key phrases reveal references to honor disputes that are invisible to modern eyes. To the uninitiated, Hamilton's three-sentence note to Monroe might seem like a simple courteous request for a meeting: "Mr. Hamilton requests an interview with Mr. Monroe at any hour tomorrow forenoon which may be convenient to him. Particular reasons will induce him to bring with him a friend to be present at what may pass. Mr. Monroe, if he pleases, may have another."[35] An understanding of the language of the duel reveals the letter's implicit threat. The note is a demand for a meeting of inquiry about an affair of honor; Hamilton is bringing a second and has alerted Monroe to bring one as well.

As implied by the code of honor's precautionary rituals, few men began an affair of honor with the explicit purpose of exchanging fire. Most conflicts waned during negotiations and concluded when each principal felt that his honor had been vindicated. Such was the role of a principal's second, who acted as a sort of legal representative, attempting to defend his client's honor without necessitating a duel. When his son Philip was involved in a duel in 1801, Hamilton assumed that the matter would end without gunplay; by that time, he himself had been involved in eight affairs of honor without fighting a single duel. Learning to his horror that negotiations had ended, he rushed to the home of their family doctor, David Hosack, knowing that Philip would choose Hosack as his attending physician. Philip had indeed requested the doctor's services, and the two had departed together early that morning; hearing the news, Hamilton fainted dead away at the Hosacks' door. Awaking to discover that Philip had been fatally wounded, he rushed to his son's side and remained with him until Philip died the next day, in great agony.[36]

A skillful duelist could demonstrate his readiness to fight without touching a pistol. A fair duel was a game of chance that displayed the willingness of both principals to die for their honor, not their skill at inflicting pain or death. As one pamphleteer noted, the "polite" duelist fought "without any design to injure his adversary." Hamilton's dueling consultant Rufus King agreed. Duels motivated by "the thirst for blood or the malignant purpose of destroying the life of another" were "ferocious, barbarous and savage" and "repugnant to any code of honor," reducing "private combat to assassination."[37]

By provoking a duel, Burr was thus not necessarily proposing to kill Hamilton; he could redeem his honor without felling his rival. Indeed, fatalities in political duels were uncommon, for killing one's opponent was more of a liability than an advantage, leaving a duelist open to charges of bloodthirstiness and personal ambition.[38] By law, a politician who slew his opponent was also guilty of murder, though ironically these lawyers and lawgivers were seldom charged. Sometimes police officers simply refused to tangle with men of influence; on those rare occasions when legal authorities made the law known, politicians often persisted in their duel negotiations regardless. Remarkably, when Burr faced murder charges after killing Hamilton, eleven sympathetic Republican senators signed a petition to New Jersey governor Joseph Bloomfield, reminding him that political duels were *not* usually prosecuted. Pleading for Burr's prosecution to be discontinued, they argued that "most civilized nations" did not consider dueling fatalities "common murders" and reminded Bloomfield that previous political duelists at Weehawken had not only been spared judicial proceedings but had later received judicial appointments.[39]

Dueling fatalities were unfortunate facts of public life, acceptable if the duel had been fair and the duelists strict adherents to the honor code. What James Nicholson said of duelist Brockholst Livingston was true of any politician unfortunate enough to kill his adversary: after killing James Jones, Livingston seemed "conscious of having done nothing but what he was compel[l]ed to do & at the same time sorry for the Necessity." Most duels that involved gunplay ended with minor injuries, suggesting a desire to avoid anything more serious. Leg injuries were frequent enough to cast doubt on the power and meaning of the practice; hinting that affairs of honor entailed more pretense than peril, a newspaper editor jeered that one combatant "was said to have received a wound in that fashionable part, *the leg*."[40]

Because a man of the sword was presumably always ready to fight, any principal who attempted to negotiate his way out of a duel dishonored himself. Combatants had to rely on their seconds—their "particular friends"—to settle an affair of honor. During Hamilton's 1797 dispute with Monroe, Monroe's second, David Gelston, made a serious mistake when he turned to Hamilton and suggested a means of settling matters. Gelston noted that Hamilton responded with only "a word or two which I understood as not disapproving the mode I proposed," a grunt of approval that was followed by a long, awkward silence. Realizing with a shock that he should not have attempted to negotiate with a principal, Gelston turned to John Barker Church, Hamilton's second, and observed that "perhaps my proposition . . . would have been made with more propriety to him than to Colo. H." He then repeated his suggestion to Church, start to finish, and the process of negotiation resumed.[41]

Highly offended principals sometimes insisted on dueling. In these cases, to draw negotiations to a quick but courteous close the offended party usually demanded an apology that was too humiliating for the offender to accept. Such was Hamilton's charge against Burr. As he stated in his apologia, "The disavowal required of me by Col Burr . . . was out of my power, if it had really been proper for me to submit to be so questionned." New York Senator DeWitt Clinton also felt compelled to reject a deliberately humiliating demand for a written apology. Forced to duel against his will, he exclaimed on the dueling ground, "I am compelled to shoot at one whom I do not wish to hurt, but I will sign no paper—I will not dishonor myself."[42]

A duel became inevitable when a challenge was accepted. From that point on, seconds and principals concentrated on orchestrating their "interview": a date had to be set, a location selected, and rules devised. The duel between Hamilton and Burr followed the conventional script. In a heretofore overlooked account of the trial of Burr's second, William P. Van Ness, for his involvement in the duel, participants described the proceedings in great detail, including practices intended to evade laws against dueling.[43] For example, the guns were hidden in a "Portmanteau," enabling the boatmen who rowed the participants to the dueling ground to testify that they "saw no pistols."

Many rituals prevented participants from witnessing the actual moment of gunfire—the moment when both principals became guilty of fighting a duel. Under oath, the two boatmen stated at Van Ness's trial that they had stood with their backs to the duelists, enabling them to testify that they "did not see the firing." Likewise, attending physician David Hosack could attest only that he saw the two seconds and Hamilton disappear "into the wood" and "heard the report of 2 firearms soon after." Hearing his name called, he rushed onto the dueling ground and "saw Genl. H . . . and supposed him wounded by a ball through the body." Having rowed across with Hamilton, the doctor could also testify that he had never seen Burr on the field. When Hosack climbed up the embankment to tend to Hamilton's wounds, Van Ness skillfully whisked Burr off the dueling ground before he could be seen. Hosack testified that he "did not see Col. Burr" and did not learn "that Col. Burr was the other party" until a conversation with Burr's second after the duel.

The rituals of dueling reveal its paradoxical nature. As displayed in Van Ness's trial, politicians who engaged in mortal combat to defend their public reputations at the same time protected one another through a shared oath of secrecy. Of course, concealing a duel served everyone's interest, for indictment of one participant could implicate all. Yet these rituals did more than discourage legal prosecution. By enforcing a uniform code of behavior, ensuring equitable competition, and preventing social inferiors from fighting, the code of honor made all participants equal. When a failing politician provoked a duel, he salvaged his reputation by placing himself in an environment of mutual respect, a brotherhood of honor and fair competition—the exact opposite of a competitive political realm that encouraged conflict and rewarded aggressive self-promotion.

"Political Opposition, Which . . . Has Proceeded From Pure and Upright Motives"

When Hamilton received Burr's initial letter of inquiry, he sought the advice of Rufus King. Upset by Hamilton's intention to withhold his fire, King did as Hamilton had done. He turned to a friend, Matthew Clarkson, hoping to find a way to prevent the duel. Because Hamilton, by this point, had accepted Burr's challenge, Clarkson regretfully concluded that he and King were powerless to intercede. During the next two weeks, the distraught King mentioned the duel to two more friends, Egbert Benson and John Jay. Burr, likewise, discussed the imminent duel with close friends, consulting with Matthew Davis and John Swartwout.[44]

As it passed from friend to friend, news of the impending duel revealed and reinforced a network of political friendships and enmities. Hamilton, King, Clarkson, Benson, and Jay were Federalists. Burr, Davis, and Swartwout were Burrite Republicans. These two chains of friendship were part of a larger network of partisan alliances, made manifest by the selective secrecy of the code of honor; in a sense, news about an impending duel was the most socially bonding gossip of all. At one time or another, Republicans James Monroe, DeWitt Clinton, Aedanus Burke, and James Nicholson supported each other in an interrelated series of honor disputes. Through Monroe's involvement, even Thomas Jefferson and James Madison were duel consultants on occasion.[45] Federalist duelists had a similar network of political support, reinforced by a decade of duels. An individual duel had its own dynamic, but it was only one battle in an ongoing war of honor and makes sense only when examined in the context of a larger pattern of encounters.

Between 1795 and 1800, New York City Federalists fought Republicans on the field of honor. The latter had no single leader who served as a lightning rod; the Federalists had Hamilton, his party's "political thermometer," who was involved in four affairs.[46] With Jefferson's election as president, a new world of political opportunity opened for Republicans, who turned against one another in their scramble for prestige and power. From 1800 until 1804, Clintonian Republicans competed against Burrite Republicans at the ballot box, in print, and on the dueling ground. The few disputes between Federalists and Republicans all involved Hamilton and were fought to preserve whatever slim chance his political fortunes had for revival. After his death and Burr's consequent fall in 1804, duels once again pitted Republicans against Federalists.

Hamilton, Burr, and DeWitt Clinton were leaders with widespread political connections, high ambition, and great promise. All three were political "chiefs"—men who could lead their followers to power, position, and prestige. All were supported by groups of "intimate friends." In exchange for the patronage of their chief, friends defended him in person, in print, and, when necessary, on the field of honor. For a group of supporters, a chief was a political "rallying point"—he was "the cause."[47]

Newspapers issued the call to arms. By 1802, each chief had a newspaper and an editor under his command, pledged to defend his name and "write down" his foes: William Coleman at the Federalist *New-York Evening Post,* James Cheetham at the Clintonian *American Citizen,* and Peter Irving at the Burrite *Morning Chronicle*. Newspapers were imperative in a "war of words." Burr learned this lesson when attempting to refute a Clintonian pamphlet without the support of a sympathetic newspaper. Frustrated that "there seems at present to be no medium of communication," he launched the *Morning Chronicle* three months later.[48]

Newspapers also demonstrated the strength and loyalty of a leader's following. When the *Chronicle* seemed ready to "expire" in 1805, Matthew Davis believed that "the instant the Chronicle ceased to exist, the Burrites would become 'uninfluential atoms,' there would be no rallying point; and they would certainly have been considered as abandoning their Chief; as incapable any longer of supporting a press, that could be supposed friendly to him; and of course that their attachment for their leader or their influence with the community had diminished."[49] Combat between these political fighting units consisted of attempts to dishonor an opposing chief, his intimate friends, or his editor. Damage to any one of these three essential elements hurt chief and follower alike. Discredited followers or a failed newspaper dishonored a chief; and a dishonored leader could offer his followers neither influence nor status, making him an unfit rallying point.

Politicians considered their *own* fighting unit a band of friends, men of honor who promoted the common good. Their opponents saw them as a vicious, self-seeking political faction that threatened the republic. In the *Chronicle,* Burrites depicted Clintonians as greedy knights serving a feudal lord who ordered his defenders to "lie, fawn, flatter, promise, and betray." The *Citizen,* in turn, portrayed the Burrites as a "sect of new Lights," separated from the Republican fold, with a blind religious devotion to their leader and a formal "creed." In many ways, these satirical attacks were accurate. Clintonians and Burrites *were* groups of loyal followers supporting ambitious leaders. These followers *were* interested in reaping benefit from their support. New York City politicians were engaged in a battle of self-deception. They could not—or would not—recognize in themselves what they condemned in their rivals, the self-serving motives of the factional politician.[50]

The political duelist envisioned himself as striking a blow at factional politics in the person of his adversary. In 1803, when Senator Jonathan Dayton of New Jersey rose to his feet in the Senate and accused DeWitt Clinton of "impeaching in debate the motives of Members," he believed that he was reprimanding a reprehensible partisan politician. When Clinton responded by declaring "that Mr. Dayton's assertion was unfounded and untrue," he thought that he was defending his reputation and, like Dayton, assumed that he was assailing a dishonorable politician. Yet Dayton's attack was neither selfless nor indiscriminate. Clinton and Aaron Burr were locked in a bitter power struggle in New York City, and Dayton was a Burrite. He insulted Clinton on the day before Clinton left the Senate to become mayor of New York. Dayton's attack was thus a strategically timed political strike against Clinton's political standing and personal reputation. Clinton had won an important election, and the Burrites bolstered their ailing status and denounced their foe by instigating an affair of honor.[51]

Taken together, New York City's affairs of honor reveal distinct patterns of conflict. Most such disputes occurred in the weeks following an election or a political controversy. Usually a member of the losing faction—the group dishonored by defeat—provoked a duel with a member of the winning faction. Always, the political community understood that when a supporter dueled, he represented both his faction and his chief. After exchanging five shots with John Swartwout in 1802, Clinton declared him a meager substitute for Burr, stating with an almost palpable sneer, "I dont want to hurt him [Swartwout], but I wish I had the *principal* here—I will meet him when he pleases" (fig. 26).[52] Most of New York City's political duels were not the result of an angry politician's slip of the tongue. They were intentionally provoked partisan battles, couched in the gentility of the code of honor.

To accommodate partisan goals, politicians modified the traditional affair of honor, most strikingly in their use of newspapers as publicity tools. When a duel was particularly controversial—when a duelist died or a chief was involved—politicians capitalized on widespread public interest with contending newspaper accounts, both sides attempting to win public approval while dishonoring their foes. Regardless of his behavior on the field, a duelist's reputation depended on the success or failure of these publicity campaigns. Political duels were won by the faction that best controlled public opinion.

Such publicity campaigns exposed the political motives for dueling. As a writer for the *Post* recognized, "When men take the liberty of appealing to the public about their private quarrels, it can be done with no other view than to influence public opinion in favor of themselves." A writer for *The Balance* attributed the duel's popularity to such appeals: "Among the further incentives to dueling *peculiar* to this country, I am constrained to mention with pointed disapprobation the recent practice of publishing, in news-papers, the various particulars of such bloody affrays. . . . There is not another country in christendom—probably not in the world—where the *seconds* in a duel . . . have the presumption, immediately after the contest, to publish with the signature of their names, a detailed relation of its commencement, progress and catastrophe, together with encomiums on the gallant behavior of their respective *principals*. Europeans must read such publications with astonishment."[53] These newspaper advertisements reveal the profound

Fig. 26. *A Genuine View of the Parties in an Affair of Honor After the Fifth Shot, at Hobuken, 31st July, 1802,* unidentified artist, 1802. This cartoon satirizes the duel between Republican DeWitt Clinton and Burrite John Swartwout at Hoboken, New Jersey. The two seconds had made peculiar arrangements, directing the principals to spin and fire; in most duels, the principals simply stood face to face. After exchanging fire five times—Swartwout repeatedly asserting that he had not received "satisfaction"—Clinton declared the matter settled, ended the duel, and was thereafter denounced as a coward by Burrites. This cartoon clearly favors Swartwout. "O my bowels! my bowels! they melt, they melt!" Clinton howls while defecating in the wig of his second, Richard Riker, who states, "Dear Sir, I am the depository of your honor. . . . Damn this liquid honor—my wig is full of it!" (© Collection of The New-York Historical Society)

influence of a democratic politics. Proving their "gallant behavior" and strength of character on the field of honor, political duelists were proving their worth as leaders before people who could depose them with their votes. By parading their bravery in newspapers rather than pamphlets, they signaled their desire to reach a mass audience—not simply to appeal to a small group of equals.

To deny self-serving intentions to themselves and to the wider populace, politicians boasted of their nonpartisanship in these written duel accounts. They avoided declaring themselves victors; to do so would be to display self-interest and violate the people's right to draw their own conclusions. Instead, they began their reports by professing devotion to the public interest: the people demanded a complete and accurate account of all proceedings.[54] They augmented these professions of duty with angry attacks on their reprehensible, politically driven foes. Clinton's duel with Swartwout provoked an onslaught of these reproaches. In the *Citizen,* "An Old Soldier" wrote the following:

> MODERN BRAVERY. Write a bombastic account of a duel . . . threaten your antagonists with death if they [presume] to lisp any thing different from what your might[iness] has written. MODERN VIRTUE. When a citizen opposes your schemes of aggrandizement . . . when you find your defects too palpable to attempt vindic[ation], rid yourself of such an opposer and such a cit[izen by] pushing forward an humble tool.

In the *Post,* "A Young Soldier" responded by describing "Modern Humanity":

> If your friend differs from you in any political point, take an opportunity in his absence to call him lyar, rascal, villain, &c and should he hear of it and justly ask an acknowledgment of your error . . . refuse it in any way but that which you point out yourself, especially if you contemplate being a candidate for a high office. Should your mode of apologizing not prove acceptable, meet him with a pair of good pistols, at ten paces distance.

Clintonians claimed that the ambitious Burr had instigated and orchestrated the entire affair. Burrite William S. Smith, Swartwout's second, replied that "the infamy of attempting to attach to the sacred uphold of private honor, the mean spirit of party rancour, I flatter my self *my* breast will always be a stranger to."[55] His clever retort accused politicians who hurled charges of "party rancour" of committing that very crime.

Partisan politics in the early republic transformed the traditional affair of honor into something distinctly American. Political duelists were not isolated aristocrats competing for glory and preferment at court. Instead, they constituted a novel hybrid: they were aristocratic democrats, popular politicians who used the traditional etiquette of honor to influence public opinion and win political power. Political duels testified to the blend of deference and equality, courtliness and sincerity that characterized politics in the early republic.

"I Shall Hazard Much, and Can Possibly Gain Nothing"

On June 18, 1804, roughly six weeks after he lost the gubernatorial election, Burr wrote to Hamilton regarding a letter that had appeared in the Republican *Albany Register* in the heat of the campaign several months earlier; a friend had just put it in Burr's hand. The writer, Charles D. Cooper, was responding to a broadside that contradicted one of Cooper's private letters; ironically, the person doing the contradicting in the broadside was none other than Hamilton's father-in-law, Philip Schuyler. Outraged at being posted as a liar *and* at the public knowledge of a personal letter ("that was EMBEZZLED and BROKEN OPEN," he complained), Cooper wrote to Schuyler insisting on the truth of his claims. Yes, Hamilton had denounced Burr as "a dangerous man . . . who ought not to be trusted with the reins of government." Cooper and many others had heard these words for themselves. In fact, Hamilton had offered "a still more despicable opinion" of Burr, but Cooper knew better than to commit it to paper.[56]

Cooper's letter is a study in the period's distinctive grammar of political combat. Outraged that one of his private letters was the subject of a broadside — a violation that almost landed Hamilton in a duel on one occasion — Cooper responded with a carefully worded letter of defense that touched on the honor and reputations of all involved. Yet though Cooper deliberately omitted Hamilton's most sensational accusations, even this mere reference to such gossip was a vulnerability when committed to paper, let alone published in a newspaper. Indeed, the entire controversy was centered completely on hearsay and political gossip, the product of prevailing confusion about shifting political loyalties. No one knew whether Hamilton and some of his Federalist followers would support Burr or Republican Morgan Lewis for governor. Debating the issue in broadsides, letters, and newspapers, they sparked the most extreme honor ritual—a duel.

Vague as it was, Cooper's letter was Burr's first "authentic" evidence of Hamilton's attacks on his private character. Until this point, Burr had heard only secondhand accounts of ambiguous insults—gossip without proof.[57] In 1804, however, he gained Federalist support, which probably gave him access to Federalist gossip circles full of Hamilton's accusations. After years of such abuse, concrete evidence of an insult made it "impossible that I could consistently with respect again forbear," Burr later explained—particularly given that the slur had been broadcast in a newspaper. As William P. Van Ness, Burr's second, explained after the duel, Hamilton's abuse was "patiently borne, until resistance became a duty, and silence a crime."[58]

Burr was a man with a wounded reputation, a leader who had suffered personal abuse and the public humiliation of a lost election. A duel with Hamilton would redeem his honor and possibly dishonor Hamilton. Twice before, Hamilton's remarks about Burr had merited a challenge, and both times Hamilton had anticipated Burr by "coming forward voluntarily and making apologies and concessions." If Hamilton attempted a similar maneuver a third time, Burr could declare him a coward who "woud not fight." More important, if Burr did not receive some sign of respect from Hamilton—either an apology or the satisfaction of a duel—he would lose the support of his followers. As Van Ness explained, if Burr "tamely sat down in silence, and dropped the affair; what must have been the feelings of his friends?—they must have considered him as a man, not possessing sufficient firmness to defend his own character, and consequently unworthy of their support.—While his enemies, with malicious triumph, would, to all the other slanders propagated concerning him, have added the ignominious epithet of coward."[59] To remain a political chief, Burr had to defend his honor.

As with the other duels in New York City, the timing of Burr's challenge was more important than the offense that prompted it. Because Cooper's letter contained no specific insult, Burr later received criticism for challenging a man for an unspecified affront. Hamilton himself objected that Burr's inquiry was too vague for "a direct avowal or disavowal"; as Hamilton would later explain, Burr was objecting to comments dropped during a dinner at least six months back. But Burr felt such a compelling need to prove himself a man of honor and a political leader that he responded to Hamilton's protests by broadening his demands: he demanded an apology for *any* "rumours derogatory to Col: Burr's honour . . . inferred from any thing he [Hamilton] has said."[60] In essence, he called on Hamilton to apologize for any personal abuse that Burr had suffered from throughout their fifteen-year political rivalry. Burr demanded this humiliating apology in order to force Hamilton to fight.

Modern writers love to speculate about Hamilton's "real" insult, the most popular suggestion being that Hamilton accused Burr of sleeping with his own daughter, Theodosia. Appealingly sensational as that claim might be, it is grounded on twentieth-century assumptions that only an insult of such severity could drive a man to duel. But if we understand duels as political weapons deliberately deployed by countless politicians, such theories make no sense—particularly given that this was not Burr's first duel but rather the *fourth* time he had engaged in an honor dispute and the second time he had taken the field. Five years earlier, he had dueled with Hamilton's brother-in-law John Barker Church, and twice before by Burr's count he had almost dueled with Hamilton. There is no deep, dark, mysterious insult at the heart of the Burr-Hamilton duel. Like any other politician, Burr was manipulating the code of honor to redeem his reputation after the humiliation of a lost election, seizing on this insult above others because it was in writing, vague as it might be.

Hamilton did not want to duel. His reluctance is apparent in his ambivalent and conflicted response to Burr's initial letter of inquiry—a response reflecting Hamilton's struggle to accommodate clashing values. To appease his moral and religious reservations about dueling, he attempted to placate Burr with an elaborate discussion of the "infinite shades" of meaning of the word *despicable*—a grammar lesson that Burr found evasive, manipulative, and offensive. To defend his personal honor and political power, he countered Burr's insultingly vague inquiry by pronouncing it "inadmissible" and declaring himself willing to "abide the consequences" should Burr persist in his present course—a statement that Burr found insufferably arrogant. Ultimately, it was outrage at Hamilton's seeming lack of respect that drove Burr to broaden his demands and thereby force Hamilton to accept his challenge.[61]

With his acceptance, Hamilton gave the code of honor priority. Burr's second noted that "Gen. Hamilton, subsequent to his acceptance of the challenge, behaved in a proper and becoming manner." Confident that he had saved his reputation, Hamilton could now satisfy his religious and moral "scruples" with a compromise. He decided that he would observe all the expected dueling rituals on the field, but to avoid shedding Burr's blood, he would withhold his fire. As he explained to his wife, "the Scruples of a Christian have determined me to expose my own life . . . rather than subject my self to the guilt of taking the life of another. . . . But you had rather I should die innocent than live guilty." Hamilton's apologia, so often taken as evidence of a death wish, was an attempt to explain this decision. Burr, too, wrote a final statement the night before the duel, bidding farewell to his daughter and son-in-law.[62]

On the morning of July 11, Hamilton and Burr fought their duel (fig. 27). Critically wounded, Hamilton died the following afternoon. The only duel between two political chiefs fought in New York City between 1795 and 1807, the Burr-Hamilton "interview" would have been assured public notice by this singularity alone. But when one chief killed another, a duel became a subject of heated public controversy. The Burr-Hamilton duel was common knowledge just hours after it took place. Hamilton had been rowed back to New York and carried to a friend's house by 9:00 A.M.; by 10:00, "the rumour of the General's injury had created an alarm in the city."[63]

People stood on street corners discussing the affair. A bulletin was posted at the Tontine Coffee House, informing the public that "General Hamilton was shot by Colonel Burr this morning in a duel. The General is said to be mortally wounded." By the time Gouverneur

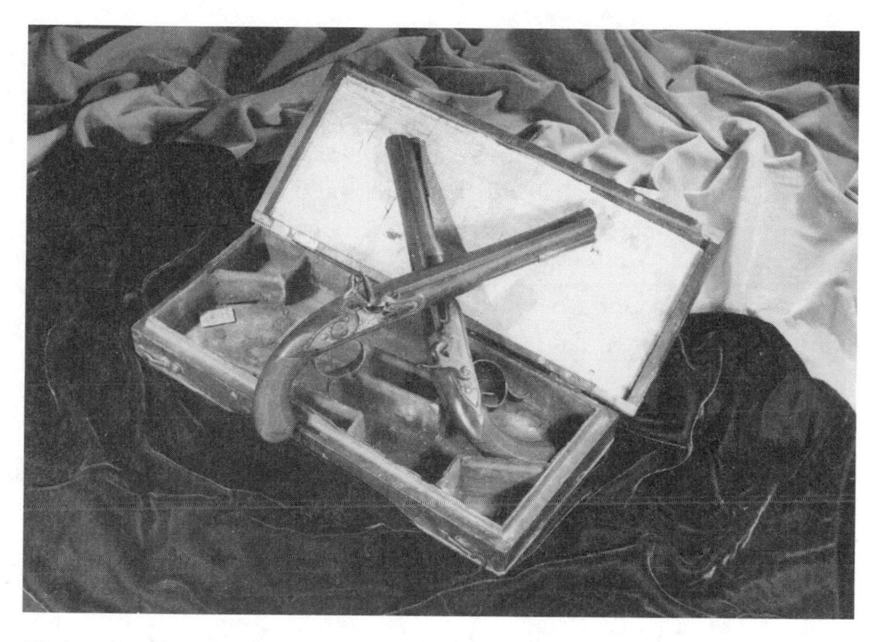

Fig. 27. Dueling pistols used in the Burr-Hamilton duel. Hamilton's brother-in-law John Barker Church lent this fine brace of pistols to Hamilton for his duel with Burr. During his own 1799 duel with Burr, Church shot a button off Burr's coat with these same pistols; they may also have been used by Hamilton's son Philip in his fatal 1801 duel. (Courtesy Chase Manhattan Bank Archives)

Morris gave Hamilton's eulogy, on July 14, the city was in a "frenzy." Hoping to discourage the public from committing some "outrage" against Burr, Morris avoided any mention of the cause of death. Later that day, he marveled, "How easy would it have been to make them, for a moment, absolutely mad!"[64]

Aware of public interest and anxious to protect their principals' reputations, Hamilton's and Burr's seconds began to draft an account of the duel almost immediately after Hamilton's death. By July 16, they had sketched out a statement of events on the dueling ground, though they did not "precisely agree" on which evidence to present or on the vital question of who fired first: Hamilton's second Pendleton claimed that his principal had involuntarily discharged his pistol in the air upon being shot, whereas Burr's second Van Ness asserted that Hamilton had taken aim and fired first.[65] Eager to exploit the public uproar to exalt Hamilton at Burr's expense, Pendleton pressed for immediate publication, but Van Ness demurred; with the coroner's inquest yet undecided and outrage at Burr unabated, he well recognized the advantage of delay. Though Pendleton attempted to address Van Ness's concerns, he ultimately published his statement without Van Ness's final approval; it appeared in the *Evening Post* on July 16. Van Ness countered with an account more favorable to Burr, published in the *Morning Chronicle* the next day.

Taking advantage of the controversy, Clintonians and Hamiltonians capitalized on public interest to achieve a political victory over Burr, their common foe. The *American Citizen* and the *Evening Post* joined in high praise of Hamilton and condemnation of Burr as a murderer. Contentious Clintonian editor James Cheetham charged Burr with violating the code of honor: he had practiced with a target beforehand; he had worn a coat made of silk—a material that was "impenetrable to a ball"; he had killed Hamilton in cold blood, knowing that Hamilton would not shoot; he had laughed as he left the dueling ground; he had thrown a party upon his return to New York;[66] he was, in fine, a dishonorable man. Burr was outraged that "thousands of absurd falsehoods are circulated with industry." But he understood why: "All our intemperate and unprincipled Jacobins who have been for Years reviling H. as a disgrace to the Country and a pest to Society are now the most Vehement in his praise, and you will readily perceive that their Motive is, not respect to him but, Malice to me."[67]

Although public outrage forced Burr to flee the state, his supporters continued to defend his reputation. Rather than justifying Burr's actions, they attacked Clintonians and Hamiltonians for their hypocritical and self-interested newspaper campaign against Burr. Writing as "Vindix," Van Ness lashed out at "officious intermedlers, who have neither the feelings of gentlemen nor the hearts of men." He was outraged at the "mountain of the most detestable fals[e]hood" propagated by writers for the "scurrilous columns of the Evening Post" and the "disgusting pages of the American Citizen." Asserting that silence would prove Burr's friends "worthy of this monstrous and merciless persecution," he pleaded with the public to hear his defense: "I demand it from their justice," he declared.[68]

After a month of controversy, rumors proved too powerful for a newspaper defense; the two seconds could not keep up with the constantly shifting stream of charges and countercharges, and the unfolding argument seemed to require a different forum, so the debate moved into warring defense pamphlets. On August 11, the *Morning Chronicle* noted that a pamphlet was "promised in further persecution of Mr. Burr and his friends, of which hint, I am disposed to avail myself. If therefore this task [defending Burr] is not undertaken by some gentleman of more leisure and superior talents, I will resume this subject in a pamphlet." Shortly thereafter, Van Ness anonymously published *A Correct Statement of the Late Melancholy Affair of Honor, Between General Hamilton and Col. Burr,* a pro-dueling defense of Burr's actions that scholars have entirely overlooked. *Evening Post* editor Coleman defended Hamilton in *A Collection of the Facts and Documents, relative to the Death of Major-General Alexander Hamilton;* unaware of Van Ness's publication, scholars have missed the political motives behind this compendium of documents as well.[69]

Because the two seconds had agreed publicly upon most of the duel's details, differences between the two defenses were subtle—implied by tone, word emphasis, or choice of evidence. For example, Van Ness and Pendleton had mismanaged the official delivery of Burr's challenge, leaving Hamilton unsure whether he had accepted it; Hamilton had attempted to offer Burr a final note of explanation, "if the state of the affair rendered it proper." Hamilton's defender Coleman stated that Van Ness had refused to receive the explanation because he considered Burr's challenge accepted, thereby blaming the duel on Van Ness for spurning an apology. In his defense of Burr, Van Ness claimed that he *had* offered to accept the note, but only if it contained "a specific proposition for an accommodation," thereby attributing blame to Hamilton for not offering an explicit apology.[70] As in other controversial duels, supporters manipulated the truth in the name of honor and reputation.

Hamiltonians had an easy task defending their chief. Presenting

Fig. 28. Alexander Hamilton memorial handkerchief, linen, 1804. This mourning handkerchief shows what Burr was up against after his duel with Hamilton. Washington's tomb stands in the background, suggesting that Hamilton is the second great leader to fall—and perhaps suggesting that he is second only to Washington. (Courtesy of the Museum of the City of New York, Gift of Mrs. Frederick S. Fish, 33.318)

their leader as a martyred hero, they augmented their account of the duel with laudatory eulogies and sermons from around the nation (fig. 28). Burrites had a harder task; they had to justify Burr's actions and exonerate his motives for dueling. To accomplish this, Van Ness supplemented his description of the duel with a lengthy essay entitled "A Candid Examination of the Whole Affair in a Letter to a Friend." Contradictory and defensive, this rare written justification of dueling reveals the duelist's point of view in a period of great ambivalence toward the practice.

Van Ness attempted to grapple with the essay's fundamental contradiction in his first few paragraphs. Proclaiming his opposition to the "evil" of dueling, he stated that the practice had unfortunately received "the sanction of the world," particularly of "the higher class of society." Because Burr was conforming to public opinion, he should not be blamed. Van Ness next signaled the limits of his investigation. He would answer only four questions: Did Burr have a right to question Hamilton about his comments, and did he do so correctly? Was Hamilton obliged to avow or disavow Burr's charge? Was Burr justified in bringing the dispute to the field of honor? By restricting himself to these four questions about the formalities of the code of honor, Van Ness clearly hoped to separate the duel from the duelist.[71]

Although Van Ness claimed that his essay would not defend the practice, he could hardly avoid doing so. In presenting Burr as an honorable man with a right to protect his reputation, Van Ness was validating the affair of honor. His essay contains many of the conventional arguments used to justify dueling. He claimed that the affair of honor prevented slander, malice, and vice from running rampant. He reminded readers that a man's reputation was his most valued possession and that political opposition never warranted an attack on another man's character. He maintained that any man who felt dishonored had "an unalienable right" to demand an explanation; the right to uphold one's honor was "a law of nature."[72] In the midst of fierce political strife, forced to justify the killing of a political rival, Van Ness could still argue that the code of honor ensured an honorable political world.

In spite of his supporters' efforts, Burr lost his battle for public approval. A duelist who killed his opponent could erase his crime only by proving himself a man of honor who had conformed with the rituals of the *code duello*. But in seizing on a vague offense and exhibiting uncompromising hostility in his correspondence, Burr left himself open to charges of dishonorable conduct. When Federalists and Clintonian Republicans branded him a murderer, he was left without effective defense.

Although he defeated his opponent on the field of honor, Burr thus became a failed duelist, for he was unable to sway public opinion in his favor. His fate demonstrates the power of public opinion. In challenging Hamilton, he had acknowledged his vulnerability to popular sentiment. In accepting his challenge, Hamilton had made the same admission. Hamilton fought, his second explained after the duel, because "his Sensibility to public opinion was extremely strong, especially in what related to his conduct in Public Office." As Hamilton himself said, *not* to defend one's honor was to "commit an act of political suicide."[73] Compelled by the mandates of politics and honor, dependent on an ill-defined public for political career and private sense of self, Burr and Hamilton dueled because they were afraid not to.

"I Hope the Grounds of His Proceeding Have Been Such as Ought to Satisfy His Own Conscience"

Gouverneur Morris and Matthew Clarkson understood why Hamilton had dueled with Burr. Several days after Hamilton died, Morris recorded Clarkson's explanation in his diary: "Clarkson . . . is extremely wounded. He said to me . . . just after our friend had expired: 'If we were truly brave we should not accept a challenge; but we are all cowards.' The tears rolling down his face gave strong effect to the voice and manner with which he pronounced this sentence. There is no braver man living, and yet I doubt whether he would so far brave the public opinion as to refuse a challenge."[74] Fear, not courage, had goaded Hamilton to duel. Morris assumed that Clarkson would have done the same thing for the same reason. Dueling was cowardly; Hamilton's honorable sacrifice to the public good was also a surrender to the power of public opinion. The shock of this realization brought tears to Clarkson's eyes. He had pierced the illusion of the duel.

An ambiguous blend of the selfless, the self-interested, the political, and the personal, the affair of honor was a peculiarly powerful yet elusive political tool. Its ambiguities often left politicians conflicted and guilt-ridden, unable to reconcile the competing demands of honor, politics, and morality. Hamilton was a virtual embodiment of this conflict. Recounting the confrontation of the duel, Burr later noted that Hamilton had "looked as if oppressed with the horrors of Conscious Guilt," assuming that Hamilton was ashamed of his political improprieties. But Hamilton's facial expression was his final testimony to the complexities of the affair of honor. Thinking of his status and reputation—anxious to restrain a political rival—convinced that he was acting in the public good—feeling the twinges of religious faith, personal morality, and familial responsibility, Hamilton was a duelist who refused to fire.[75]

For Hamilton, as for others, the affair of honor was a public servant's ultimate self-sacrifice. Even on his deathbed, he attributed his duel with Burr to public-minded motives. Yet Burr insisted that Hamilton was the miscreant, an ambitious politician who had violated the laws of honor.[76] Like other duelists, he saw his behavior as obligatory and community-minded. The charges and countercharges of unworthy motives were not unusual, but the duel's ultimate outcome was. By themselves, the combined efforts of Clintonians, Hamiltonians, and otherwise hostile Federalists and Republicans might have proven strong enough to effect Burr's political demise. But ultimately, it was Hamilton's apologia that ensured Burr's downfall. Hamilton closed his life with an intimate, heartfelt statement that professed his willingness to die for the public good; he depicted himself as an exemplary man of honor, compelled to fight, unwilling to kill, gaining nothing, sacrificing all. There was no more effective way to prove oneself a martyr and one's foe, by necessity, a fiend.

Burr perceived the ugly political reality underlying Hamilton's statement. He assumed that Hamilton's attempt to portray himself as a selfless public servant was politically driven—a final, brazen attempt to quash a longstanding rival. To his friend Charles Biddle, Burr fumed, "The last hours of Genl. H. (I might include the day pre[ceding] the interview) appear to have been devoted to Malevolence and hypocricy. . . . The friends of Genl. H. and even his enemies who are still more my enemies, are but too faithful executors of his Malice." Burr relied on "all Men of honor" to recognize the truth, to "see with disgust the persecutions which are practised against me."[77]

Killing Hamilton drove Burr into physical exile, but condemning him thrust Burr into intellectual oblivion, for few men shared his opinion, or at least said so in public. In the end Burr's fate forced him to perceive the truth—to discern the self-interest and political pragmatism underlying the laws of honor. Assuming an attitude of "defiant affectation," he taunted public men by pricking at their convictions about political honor. With "amazing nonchalance," his first biographer reported, Burr sometimes spoke of "my friend Hamilton — whom I shot," a blunt reminder of the duel's viciousness and the violent nature of American politics.[78]

In the long term, Hamilton's statement failed to accomplish what he intended. It did not prove his public-minded motives to posterity. It did not gain him eternal forgiveness for engaging in what he himself deemed an indefensible practice. Yet ultimately, his apologia succeeded in ways that he could not have foreseen. Superficially, it left to later generations the image of Burr the unprincipled politician, an image that retains its potency even today. On a deeper, less conscious level, it reveals much more, offering firsthand testimony to the significance of dueling among early national politicians. Convinced that Burr was a threat to the republic, personally invested in his public role to an extraordinary degree, Hamilton perceived the duel as both a public service and a personal sacrifice. It was also a self-serving attempt to preserve his political career and his private sense of self; ambitious, competitive, and suffering from the endemic insecurity of the self-made man, Hamilton could not risk dishonor. Yet in proving himself a man of honor, he violated his moral principles and afflicted his family, two things close to his heart. By not resolving these contradictions, by committing to paper a tangled mix of hopes and fears, Hamilton gave voice to the complexities of political leadership among men of honor. His apologia offers an insider's view of a ritualized, honor-bound, personal level of political interaction that persisted until the anonymity of formal national political parties altered the tone of politics forever.

5

An Honor Dispute of Grand Proportions

THE PRESIDENTIAL ELECTION OF 1800

Matthew Davis read Aaron Burr's letter of March 15, 1830, with a sense of foreboding. Here, again, was the cursed presidential election of 1800, a hotly contested campaign that had resulted in a tie between Republicans Burr and Thomas Jefferson, a deadlock in the House where the tie had to be broken, an outburst of intrigue and suspicion, Jefferson's election, and Burr's eventual downfall. The crisis had been sparked by the constitutional voting process, which did not differentiate between presidential and vice presidential candidates. Each elector cast two votes, and the man who received the most votes became president, the runner up vice president, regardless of their political affiliations; any candidate could win either office. This constitutional issue—later resolved by the Twelfth Amendment (1804)—joined with the period's distinctively personal politics of reputation to produce a controversy that would haunt participants for decades thereafter.

Burr's letter reported that a stranger named Richard Bayard was seeking his assistance in clearing the name of his father, James Bayard, one of the election's more controversial figures. For six days of excruciating indecision in February 1801, the House had voted again and again, unable to break the tie after thirty-five ballots, Federalists leaning toward Burr, Republicans standing behind Jefferson. In the final moment of crisis, Bayard was the Federalist who decided the election by negotiating a deal with Jefferson—or so Bayard believed. Not surprisingly, Jefferson vehemently denied this, venting some of his spleen in a memorandum later included in the "Anas." It was this memorandum, published the year before in the first edition of Jefferson's works, that Richard Bayard sought to refute. Unable to answer Bayard's queries, Burr asked Davis—his former political lieutenant—to handle the matter.

Davis complied, but reluctantly. The history of the election was "enveloped in thick darkness," he cautioned Burr. "Whether the period has yet arrived when an effort should be made to dispel that darkness is problematical." It was not that he lacked the evidence to refute all lingering suspicions; on the contrary, Davis assured his friend, "the means . . . exist of proving to the satisfaction of the most skeptical, what are the facts in the case." Rather, it was the impact of such a statement that concerned him. Even at a distance of thirty years, Davis felt compelled to wait for "a proper crisis" to undertake such an "unpleasant . . . duty," at which time, he vowed, he would recount the truth "fairly, impartially, and fearlessly."[1]

Thirty years after the fact, Davis, Burr, and Bayard were still emotionally tangled in the events of 1800, Davis afraid even to broach the topic, Burr eager to settle it, and Bayard unable to let it rest. A decade after the contest, John Adams had likewise fought the battles of 1800 with his *Boston Patriot* essays. Indeed, in the years following that fateful election, no fewer than ten people felt compelled to defend their actions publicly. Even as late as 1907, Bayard's descendants were still pressing the issue.[2] Though it is tempting to blame such peevishness on the disappointment of a lost election, at least one complainant, Maryland Republican Samuel Smith, had been on the winning side of the contest and had been offered the position of secretary of the navy upon Jefferson's election. Even Jefferson himself was still agitated about the election years later.[3]

Modern studies of this pivotal contest offer little insight into such long-lived anxieties, generally viewing the election as a signpost of political development. Pointing to the Federalist and Republican caucuses to name candidates, the organization required to manage massive national publicity campaigns, the party discipline that led to the tie between Jefferson and Burr (every Republican elector voted for both men), the first transfer of power from one party to the other, and the downfall of Federalism and its aristocratic, Old World order, most scholars depict the election of 1800 as the first "modern" presidential election featuring distinct national political parties. And there is no denying that this presidential election differed from the three that came before, particularly on a local level, where partisan mobilization and popular politicking had reached new heights. Even participants recognized the contest's significance, dubbing it the "revolution of 1800," in their minds an uprising as monumental in its consequences as the first.[4]

Clearly, however, there was an additional personal dimension to this election that resonated for decades thereafter, an ambiguity or complication that raised questions serious enough to demand a public refutation as much as a hundred years later. Wrapped up with questions of honor and reputation, the election of 1800 is a perfect case study of the period's distinctive political dynamic. It reveals the grammar of political combat in action.

The participants themselves never agreed on the precise events of 1800; indeed, it was their continuing attempts to understand them that transferred blame from one man to another for decades thereafter. But there was one underlying assumption that few contested: the corruption of Aaron Burr. Most assumed that Burr had schemed to win the presidency over Jefferson, his running mate; it was identifying his agents of influence that provoked continued controversy. Neither Burr nor his political intimates ever successfully dispelled the charge, ceasing their efforts only after he had departed on his self-imposed European exile in 1808; even Burr's duel with Hamilton was partly fueled by the shadow of the 1800 election. Nor had the accusation vanished when he returned in 1812. By that time, however, the fifty-six-year-old had accepted his role as the enfant terrible of American politics, skillfully shielding himself from the embarrassment of a personal snub by habit-

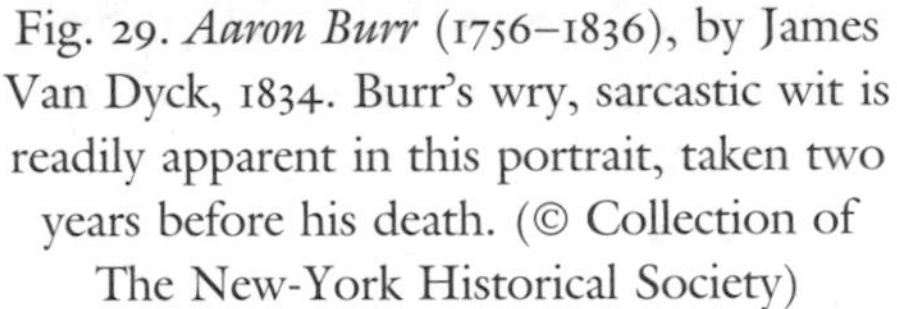

Fig. 29. *Aaron Burr* (1756–1836), by James Van Dyck, 1834. Burr's wry, sarcastic wit is readily apparent in this portrait, taken two years before his death. (© Collection of The New-York Historical Society)

ually averting his eyes when out in the street, responding to direct insults with a display of whimsical disregard that itself attracted comment (fig. 29).

Yet for Burr, as for many others, the election of 1800 remained an open wound—in his mind, the cause of his precipitous fall from power. Thus, upon learning of the "Anas" from Bayard, he obtained a copy for himself, eager to see what Jefferson had to say about this pivotal contest. What he found was profoundly upsetting. Even as late as 1806, Jefferson was denying his own guilt in the affair, raging against Burr's low tactics. Burr was "disgusted" that Jefferson had recorded their private conversations and repeated mere scandal as the truth; coming from Jefferson, such hearsay would be believed—this he knew. Even more infuriating, however, was that Jefferson was berating Burr for the very sins he himself had committed; in Burr's eyes, it was Jefferson who had bargained his way to victory.

To exonerate Burr one would have to incriminate Jefferson. It was the implications of such a charge that led Davis to beg Burr for continued silence. To question the terms of Jefferson's victory in 1801 was to invite the wrath of his many admirers; the former president's death four years earlier had only heightened concerns for his honor and reputation. There were wider repercussions as well. The animosities unleashed by the election had festered over time, becoming intertwined with the political folklore of the nation's founding. By 1830, the idea that democracy had triumphed with Jefferson's victory was central to America's self-perception as a New World haven for equality, justice, and the rights of the common man.[5] To modify the conventional narrative of the 1800 election was to tamper with national mythology. It was this historical investment that gave Davis pause.

Of course, it was this same historical investment that compelled Burr to respond to Jefferson's accusations, for Burr's reputation in the eyes of posterity was at stake. Thus, rather than greeting this attack with his customary composure, Burr became "much excited" by what he read in the "Anas" and shortly thereafter decided upon a counterattack: he would write his own history. Given the sad state of his reputation, he could not undertake such a task himself; the very charges that he was refuting would discredit anything issuing from his pen, no matter how persuasive his evidence. He thus approached Davis (fig. 30). Reading the "Anas" carefully, he marked the most offensive passages and gave the volume to Davis "with a request that I would peruse the parts designated by him," Davis later explained. "From this time forward," he continued, Burr "evinced an anxiety that I would prepare his Memoirs, offering me the use of all his private papers, and expressing a willingness to explain any doubtful points, and to dictate such parts of his early history as I might require."[6]

Preparation of Burr's memoirs began in 1830, one of many responses to Jefferson's "Anas."[7] The work did not proceed without a hitch; at least once over the course of the next six years, Davis pulled out of the project, unwilling to undertake the attack on George Washington's "military movements" that Burr desired. Work recommenced

Fig. 30. *Matthew Livingston Davis* (1773–1850), unidentified artist, ca. 1840. Burr's political lieutenant and the author of his memoirs, Davis was sixty-seven when this portrait was painted, four years after Burr's death. (© Collection of The New-York Historical Society)

only when Burr promised to take full responsibility for the narrative text of his memoirs. "With this understanding," Davis later explained, "I frequently visited him, and made notes under his dictation." During the summer of 1835, Davis also examined Burr's correspondence and public papers, with Burr's authorization to "take from among them whatever I supposed would aid me in preparing the contemplated book." The resulting two volumes, published in 1836–37, represent Burr's account of the events of his life, as edited and adapted by his friend Davis. They constitute the only attempt by one of the period's most cryptic political actors to explain the unfolding of his life and his reading of the events and personalities of the founding period.[8]

This alone would make Burr's *Memoirs* significant, for he was notoriously tight-lipped about his motives and intentions, even among his most intimate friends. He kept his correspondence concise and to the point, devoid of any direct references to political actors or events, and habitually wrote in cipher, a practice that dated back to his youth. As Davis put it, Burr was "desirous at all times of casting . . . a veil of mystery" over his correspondence, social life, and political movements.[9] But a close reading of the *Memoirs* offers more than biographical insight. Because the text is as polemical as it is personal, it reveals much about Burr's sense of himself as a public man—his entitlement to leadership, his priorities and principles (or lack thereof), and the key to his political victories. By defending himself against the many accusations that grew from his public career, he likewise provides invaluable information about the bounds of political propriety among early national politicians. Burr represented an extreme, and his contemporaries perceived him as such. Noting when he crossed a line exposes the rules and restraints of political interaction.

Valued and exploited for his political innovations and intrigues, Burr was distrusted and ultimately discarded because of these same talents and abilities. Ambitious self-promotion, intrigue, and secrecy seemed directly opposed to the public-mindedness and accountability at the heart of republican governance, yet they won political battles. This fundamental conflict between personal imperatives ("shoulds" and "should-nots") and political realities ("musts") was wrapped up in the figure of Aaron Burr. Condemning Burr's methods even as they yoked them to their cause, politicians fueled the process of political change. The clashing worldviews that led to these compromises created an atmosphere of hostility and mutual distrust, spawned misunderstandings and accusations, and ultimately led to Burr's destruction.

The Enigma of Aaron Burr

Aaron Burr was one of the most controversial men of his time, as renowned for wickedness in his later years as Washington was for probity or Jefferson for patriotic fervor. As Davis well recognized, defending the reputation of such a man would require more than mere disclaimers and denials. To convince readers that Burr was not the immoral fiend of legend, Davis would have to reveal the self-interested malice of Burr's foes. Only by incriminating these false friends—the Jeffersonians—could he dismiss their charges as malignant lies. In essence, Burr's *Memoirs* defends Burr's reputation by transferring blame, tracing his rise and fall at the hands of Jefferson and his spiteful, dissembling "Virginia junto."[10]

This strategy for political self-defense was not uncommon in the early republic. Rather than simply disproving incriminating charges, politicians often went a step further, reproaching their assailants for the baseness of their political methods. Such recriminations made sense, given the prevailing anxieties about the workings of national politics. Something seemed to be awry in the American political system, and someone had to shoulder the blame. Partisan conflict on a local level was disturbing, but translated onto a national scale and inflicted on a fragile and untested union, it became something more: it seemed to be rending the nation along partisan lines, threatening disunion and civil war.

Convinced of their own good intentions, national politicians explained this political crisis in two ways: either their opponents were not playing by the rules or the system itself was fatally flawed—or both. Burr's memoirs reveal a basic underlying assumption about his political world that he shared with his peers: his trials and tribulations were not simply the inevitable price of political competition but rather proof that something had gone fundamentally wrong.

Even the seemingly immoral Burr perceived a morality of politics. In his eyes, Jefferson and his Virginia friends were corrupt, self-interested, and hypocritically virtuous in their politicking; they were men without honor who lied and deceived. Burr's *Memoirs* contains numerous examples of what Davis termed "Mr. Jefferson's idea of *honour* and *morality,* as practiced by him and by his order." Burr himself, on the other hand, considered his own honor unsullied, for his politics were precisely what they seemed. Never malicious in the manner of the "junto," he was an ambitious and clever politician who always behaved like a gentleman. It was Hamilton's violation of such gentlemanly standards that prompted Burr's challenge in 1804; as Burr wrote to Hamilton during their duel proceedings, "Political opposition can never absolve Gentlemen from the necessity of a rigid adherence to the laws of honor and the rules of decorum."[11] Of course, Jefferson and his allies saw something quite different. They considered themselves men of honor who were dedicated to the public good. Burr was the immoral one, his self-interest so all-consuming that he did not even deign to couch his political sins in the guise of public service. Sacrificing all to his personal ambitions, he was disloyal, dishonest, and dishonorable—the very sins that Burr attributed to Jefferson.

Posterity has sided with Jefferson, depicting him as a disinterested servant of the people surrounded by villains like Hamilton and Burr (fig. 31). Yet there was some truth to Burr's perspective. Jefferson was indeed willing to compromise his personal integrity (or that of his friends) in the service of what he considered public-minded goals. He disclosed such impulses in 1799, in response to Federalist attempts to build up the nation's armed forces in preparation for war with France; this was the same controversy that had cost Adams his Federalist following and the presidency. To Jefferson, war with France (and a possible alliance with England) was bad enough, but a standing army was an even greater threat. Standing armies were tools of monarchy, funded by high taxes and justified only by constant and unnecessary warfare. Desperate to reveal the Federalists as the monarchists he thought they were, Jefferson urged James Madison to publish his notes from the Federal Convention, despite Madison's promise, as a member, to keep them private—a promise sworn for just this reason, to prevent the conversion of a controversial debate into political fodder. Publishing them would implicate Madison's character, Jefferson acknowledged, but because it was done in the service of the public (i.e., the Republicans), he considered it the "moral" choice. "The arguments against it will be personal; those in favor of it moral," he explained, taking a final swipe at Madison's conscience by noting that "something is required from you as a set-off for the sin of your retirement."[12] Clearly, like most of his peers, Jefferson had his own sense of political proprieties. An understanding of such personal standards helps explain the enigma of Aaron Burr.

There were any number of factors that shaped a man's personal

Fig. 31. *Thomas Jefferson* (1743–1826), by Gilbert Stuart, 1805. Toward the end of Jefferson's second term and continuing after his death, prints of this likeness enjoyed great popularity; in the public mind in an age before photography, this *was* Jefferson. (Courtesy of the National Portrait Gallery, Smithsonian Institution, and Monticello, Thomas Jefferson Memorial Foundation; Gift of the Regents of the Smithsonian Institution, the Thomas Jefferson Memorial Foundation, and the Enid and Crosby Kemper Foundation)

brand of politics: his rank, reputation, regional loyalties, principles, aspirations, and temperament, his friendships and enmities, his sense of public opinion, and the political demands of the moment. As demonstrated by the chorus of anxiety in correspondence, political decisions were shaped by an ever shifting array of influences, and politicians did not make such choices in partisan lockstep. Predictable as their decisions might appear to us today, they were products of the moment, entirely unpredictable in their outcome and implications. And what seemed virtuously public-minded and essential to one man could seem entirely corrupt to the next. This lack of well-defined standards in an unstable political environment convinced many politicians that the nation was in the throes of a moral crisis. The nature of their compromises—the underlying logic behind each politician's decisions and actions—explains how members of an aristocratic ruling elite gradually moved toward party politicking.

Studies of the period often reduce this ambiguous process of political self-definition to a conflict between two sets of rules and standards. On a cultural level, historians see a clash between deference and democracy; on a political level, they translate this cultural battle into a struggle between backward-looking, aristocratic Federalists and forward-looking, democratic Republicans. Within this larger narrative, the election of 1800 figures as a final victory for democracy when the leveling spirit of the Republican party gave birth to a new style of politics.

But this is a Whiggish historical narrative that obscures the process of change and distorts our understanding of the dynamics of early national politics. Politicians did not cling blindly to the past in the face of a tide of political change, nor did they simply abandon their long-held standards to grasp at political gain.[13] Rather, they were engaged in a subtle, multifaceted tug of war between ideals and realities, past and present, deference and democracy, Old World and New that must be understood before we can begin to grasp the pace and pattern of political change.

No politician reveals this more strikingly than Aaron Burr, an elite politician who dirtied his hands in the routine business of politics to an extraordinary degree. Unlike most others of his social standing, he was a campaign manager with an eye for detail and an exuberant love of the political game. Few of his colleagues would have converted their homes into a campaign headquarters, as he did in 1800, complete with round-the-clock coffee and mattresses on the floor for catnaps, nor would many acknowledge that campaigning afforded them "a great deal of fun and honor & profit."[14] How, then, was he accepted as a member of the political elite? And where was the inspiration for his unusual brand of politics? It certainly was not born of democratic fervor. His *Memoirs* reveals little interest in political principles; unlike the autobiographies and histories of virtually all his peers, it propounds no political philosophy and contains only vague references to his political leanings.

Indeed, Burr seems to have had little interest in the republican dimension of the American experiment in government. This is not to say that he shirked his duties while in public office; on the contrary, many consider his years presiding over the Senate as vice president his finest hours; his farewell speech was such an eloquent expression of his good wishes for the republic that it reduced his audience to tears. As a political combatant, however, he had little interest in the principles of republicanism that so restrained Maclay, making an occasional bow in their direction more as a gesture of politeness than a statement of principle. When contemporaries observed that he "had no theory," they meant that he had no commitment to republicanism, no intellectual line in the sand to restrain him from politicking according to Old World standards of corruption, ambition, and personal gain.[15] Their distrust in his character and discomfort with his politicking reveals the relative importance of such restraints of principle. Without them, a man was free to respond to the political demands of the moment unhampered by political proprieties; he could commit political sins with little compunction, provided they were not blatantly apparent to his more scrupulous peers. In comparison with such men, Burr seemed ambitious, self-interested, deceitful, and dishonest. Hence his reputation in the eyes of his peers.

Yet Burr was not devoid of principles, and it is here that modern assumptions about politics have preserved his enigma to the present day. For Burr governed his actions according to the mandates of honor, and this is why he was accepted by men who distrusted his high ambitions and questionable political methods. In his manner, attitude, upbringing, and way of life, Burr was one of them. He was indisputably a gentleman, questionable as his habits might be.

Of course, Burr himself never doubted that he was a man of honor and reputation, and he assumed that others would respect him for his strict adherence to the code of honor. As he noted to Hamilton during their duel proceedings, regardless of his many personal and political sins, he had never slandered an opponent's name, and indeed, one searches his correspondence in vain for the habitual mud-slinging and character assassination that peppers the letters of his peers. As a man of honor, he also assumed that his word was his pledge. It was a slap at this fundamental aspect of his sense of self that led Burr down the path of ruin in the election of 1800. Without an understanding of the culture of honor and its political impact, his actions remain illogical (or puzzling at best), preventing a full understanding of the contest that he considered the most crucial in his political career.

It is Burr's sense of himself as a man of honor that holds the key to his politics, for his democratic opportunism was born of his aristocratic pretensions. As he suggested to Hamilton on one occasion, he considered himself superior to the petty rules governing lesser men.[16] The grandson of Jonathan Edwards, the son and namesake of the president of the College of New Jersey (now Princeton), he was a scion of New England gentility and perceived himself as such; indeed, Burr's seeming claim to leadership, the product of his heritage, made his ambitions all the more threatening.[17] With Lord Chesterfield as his guide, he perfected the pose of the courtier: he was "fascinating" in manner, graceful in person, affable in conversation, gallant among women, and intent on winning honors and reputation, with the entitled air of one to the manor born. Friends and enemies alike considered him one of the most courtly public men of his generation. Following Chesterfield's cue, Burr also assumed the license of an aristocrat, presuming the world indulgent toward men of high station and trusting that knowledge of his character and background would refute attempted slanders.[18] Secure in his rank and eager for his just due, he felt free to adapt to the political demands of the moment, heeding the democratic pull of the public. Ironically, it was aristocratic tradition that fueled Burr's democratic politics—a seeming paradox that offers insight into the politics of many of his contemporaries.

Free to adapt to the demands of the moment, Burr practiced a seemingly modern politics of campaign management, aggressive self-promotion, and democratic appeals. His corps of devoted followers also seems modern in character. Joined to Burr by his personal magnetism and their ambitions for public office, devoid of any unifying principle other than self-advancement, they were a faction in the truest sense of the word: a personal following without any commitment to a higher cause. Young men ("mere boys," charged his opponents) impressed with Burr's worldliness and heroic war record, Burr's "loyal band" took risks that could be explained away by the excesses of youth. Free from the restraints of republicanism, their efforts seem like the victory-minded electioneering of the present day.

Yet at its core, Burr's politicking was as traditional as it was modern, for notwithstanding his democratic methods, he maintained an aristocratic detachment from the masses. It was his supporters, not he himself, who politicked among the multitude; when he made an exception to this rule in 1800, it was seen as evidence of his willingness to take extreme measures. Though his politicking was far more aggressive and self-promoting than a republican might allow, he electioneered like a gentleman, mingling among a limited circle of social equals who were charmed into supporting him. In a politics of friendship, this personal brand of politicking was extremely effective.

His followers also admired Burr for his aristocratic virtues rather than his democratic skills. As Davis explains, Burr's influence was largely a product of his image. The "generally young men" who congregated around him were inspired by his reputation as "a patriot hero of the revolution." It was among these "gallant" young men that Burr was "all-powerful," Davis continues, "for he possessed, in a preeminent degree, the art of fascinating the youthful."[19] It was his self-perceived identity as a valorous man of honor that earned him support, not his campaigning methods.

This understanding of Burr's politics reminds us of the difficulties of making sweeping generalizations about political practices in a society governed by fine distinctions of rank and reputation. A man's status depended on a number of factors: his heritage, his property, his record of public service, his profession, his friends and kin, his education, his manner of living, his talents, his temperament and manners, his appearance, his importance to a community, and the cultural assumptions that were distinctive to his region. Standards of political behavior were attuned with these subtleties of rank, restraining the elite from politicking in the same manner as those on the other end of the social spectrum. Between these two extremes, however, was a vast gray area of ambiguous and contested standards. Burr's particular talent was to position himself smack in the center of this nebulous code of political propriety, balancing precisely his rank and his politicking—at least for a time.

Ironically, given his historical reputation, to understand Burr one must understand the subtleties of honor; only then does he become more than a villainous archetype. More than anything else, this was the motive behind his *Memoirs:* to prove himself a man of honorable intentions who was often unwise but never corrupt. It was a message that Burr's opponents could never accept, for their political careers and reputations rested in part on their opposition to him. In the battle of reputations at the heart of the period's many histories, defenses, and memoirs, Burr carried a serious handicap. Murderer of Alexander Hamilton, corrupt deal-maker in the election of 1800, and would-be emperor of the American West in the eyes of his peers, Burr had earned a reputation that even the most authentic evidence could not overcome.

The Lessons of 1796

Although Burr's *Memoirs* purport to explain his public life, by our standards they contain surprisingly little politics. Progressing through what Burr considered the four major controversies of his life—his relationship with George Washington, the election of 1800, his duel with Hamilton, and his 1807 treason trial—the work details Burr's relationships with Washington, Jefferson, and Hamilton, the three men who had the greatest impact on his life. Looking back on his political career at the ripe old age of seventy-four, Burr saw a series of personal relationships rather than political acts. In this way, his *Memoirs* shares much with other personal histories of the founding generation. Biographical accounts that focus on friendships and enmities, loyalty and treachery, they reveal the personal nature of the early national political world.

A politics of friendships and enmities was fluid, unpredictable, and difficult to manage. Under the two umbrellas of principle known as Federalism and Republicanism lay a mass of shifting loyalties, no one figure ever entirely predictable in his actions or allegiances. At various points in their political careers, even men of seemingly ironclad principles like Jefferson and Hamilton were rumored to have abandoned their supporters to join with former foes.

For participants in the election of 1800, such fears defined the contest. Adams was worried about the loyalty of former Federalists in the wake of his negotiations with France and Hamilton's opposition; there was no telling how Federalists might vote. Burr was wary of the Virginia "friends" who were supposedly supporting him for vice president, deeming them "not to be trusted." (Years later, advising Andrew Jackson about running for president, he cautioned the general to beware the "insidious promises of boons & favors" offered by "the Virga. Junto.")[20] The powerful Republican George Clinton of New York was on the verge of betraying Jefferson by withholding his support because he believed that Jefferson had abandoned him four years earlier by declaring friendship for Federalist John Adams. And northerners and southerners entirely distrusted one another, fearful that allies from the opposite region would support regional favorites rather than partisan allies. Would northern Republicans vote for Republicans Jefferson and Burr or for northerners Burr and Adams—a Federalist? Would southern Republicans support southerners Charles Cotesworth Pinckney—a Federalist—and Jefferson?

To understand this political mindset, we must first come to terms with lessons learned four years earlier. For as they approached the 1800 campaign, politicians had behind them only one other contested presidential election, the competition between Adams and Jefferson in 1796. As the first presidential election after George Washington's retirement—the nation's "first competition," as one politician phrased it—the election of 1796 had raised a host of fears about the workings of national politics and the consequences of a political battle fought on so national a scale.[21]

More than anything else, however, that election had taught politicians about the frailty of national partisan bonds in the face of conflicting loyalties. Public men had selected a presidential candidate and campaigned for him nationally for the first time; as individuals, they had had to sift through a range of options and influences to assign their political loyalties. Ambivalent about party combat and unfamiliar with the personal implications and practical logistics of national politics, they had not necessarily placed partisan demands above all else: regional loyalties, local politics, career aspirations, friendships and enmities, personal honor, even apathy all held sway. Across the country, friends had betrayed friends and politicians had abandoned their political allies. Southerners and northerners had turned their backs on one another, while the politically timid had struggled to conform with the majority.[22]

Such decisions were by no means predictable. A public man might be trustworthy on most occasions, only to leap to the opposition when a conflicting loyalty took precedence. The Electoral College only magnified this unpredictability. Devised as a means of regulating and guiding an unwieldy national process, the institution, by its terms, discouraged national political organization. In the name of federalism and state autonomy, states could appoint electors in any way they chose, and electors were free to vote as they wished, regardless of the will of the people, a virtual guarantee of an ever-shifting, localized, and profoundly personal presidential contest.[23] As Connecticut Federalist Chauncey Goodrich wrote, only "a good Providence" would produce a single leader from among the nation's "numerous & unconnected assemblies."[24]

This is not to say that national partisan loyalties played no role in the 1796 election; indeed, participants were alarmed by their increased importance. As Maryland Federalist William Vans Murray observed, "In this county, I think I never knew an election so much of *principles*." Politicians habitually described the political landscape in black-and-white terms—a contest between "us" and "them"—though the labels they chose for the contending teams varied greatly. Republicans railed against monarchists, aristocrats, the "Eastern men," the "British party," and "Hamilton *& his party*." Federalists, in turn, battled anarchists, "disorganizers," Jacobins, the "Virginian party," the "French party," and "Jefferson's party."[25] But such epithets should not be taken to mean that political battles consisted of predictable teams fighting under banners of pure principle. Rather, they reveal the many loyalties that divided man from man—bonds of regionalism, friendship, and principle that did not necessarily coincide. The increased importance of partisan loyalties was simply one factor among many that guided political choices. Whether they were selecting candidates, electioneering, or voting in the Electoral College, politicians were sifting through a spectrum of options and loyalties, balancing them according to the individual logic of their lives.

The election's first major decision—the selection of candidates—involved a difficult and prolonged process. For one thing, there were basic questions about the nature of the presidency that had never before been considered because of the power of George Washington's symbolic presence (fig. 32). What sort of man ought to fill the executive office, and how was he to be selected? What were the mechanics of such a national contest? Should national politicians designate presidential candidates at closed-door meetings in the capital, or should each state be free to select its own? Vital as such questions might be, discussion was kept to a minimum until a mere two months before the election, when Washington formally announced his retirement. Poor channels of communication and ambivalence about party politicking and private meetings only increased the difficulty of reaching joint decisions and made it almost impossible to enforce them. Add the many local, regional, and personal factors that influenced political decisions, and the difficulties of selecting partisan candidates become clear.

The Federalists never reached more than a nebulous decision; by June "it seemed understood" that John Adams and Thomas Pinckney of South Carolina were the candidates of choice. Pinckney's relative obscurity, supposedly one of his strengths as a candidate, was likewise his greatest weakness. Although his reputation had been relatively untouched by recent political wrangling, as a result, few knew who he was. As late as November 2—even as electors were being chosen in his home state of Maryland—Federalist William Vans Murray did not know "who is thought of for a Vice President." When informed that Pinckney was the man, Vans Murray enthusiastically endorsed a national letter-writing campaign in his support. There was only one

Fig. 32. *"Look on This Picture, and on This,"* broadside, 1807. Washington's presence loomed over the presidency long after he retired. This Federalist broadside compares Washington and Jefferson, and finds Jefferson wanting. (© Collection of The New-York Historical Society)

problem: he did not know Pinckney's first name. Before any letters could be written, Pinckney's "*christian* name . . . would be *necessary*—though I could *find* it, yet I forget it." As late as September, some Federalists believed that John Jay or Patrick Henry were potential presidential candidates.[26]

Republicans had similar problems, never conclusively determining a vice presidential candidate. Contenders included New Yorkers Robert R. Livingston and Aaron Burr, John Langdon of New Hampshire, and South Carolinian Pierce Butler. To Federalist observer William Loughton Smith, Livingston appeared to "stand highest." Langdon lacked influence. Butler was a strong contender, but he was a "Southern man and as Jefferson is to be President, it won't do." Offended at his rejection, Butler departed the meeting in a huff. This left Livingston and Burr, a man whom many considered "unsettled in his politics" and therefore likely to "go over to the other side." Though ultimately the favored candidate, Burr never received solid support from the Republicans, whose ambivalence cooled to wary distrust during the course of the election. By November, Smith could report only that the Republican candidate for the vice presidency was "any other man, except Adams and Pinckney."[27]

Though ostensibly running for vice president, Burr and Pinckney were presidential candidates as well, at least in the eyes of a select few. Pinckney was supported by a mix of personal friends, fellow southerners (both Federalist and Republican), and northern Federalists who distrusted or disliked Adams. Burr's support base was even more varied. Committed to neither Federalists nor Republicans, he sought office at any cost and was happy to accommodate anyone willing to support him. Through a combination of personal charm and persuasion, he forged personal bonds with men of all political stripes, ultimately receiving support for both the presidency and the vice presidency from both Federalists and Republicans. A handful of New Yorkers even considered an Adams-Burr ticket. Such strange conglomerations of northerners, southerners, Federalists, and Republicans reveal the very personal nature of political decisions and the consequent difficulties in achieving partisan unity. No combination of candidates would have produced a straight Federalist or Republican ticket; any two would have linked together Federalist and Republican support.

The small degree of unity produced by informal caucuses quickly broke down in the face of private ambitions, personal friendships, and political realities on a local level—a seemingly insurmountable obstacle to electioneering, the second phase of the campaign. A group decision by congressmen at the nation's capital had little significance unless it could be communicated to supporters around the nation. Yet such coordination was almost impossible for a number of reasons. Poor roads, unreliable mail delivery, and limited channels of communication made it difficult to learn about political proceedings outside of one's own state reliably and regularly. When Congress was in session, local politicians kept themselves informed by corresponding with congressmen. Philadelphia was a national clearinghouse of political information where people from around the country met and exchanged local news gleaned from personal letters. When Congress was out of session, however, it was difficult even for political insiders to get a national perspective.[28] In 1796, Congress did not meet between June 1 and December 5, a six-month gap that left many scrambling for information.

Conducted largely through letter campaigns (even newspapers relied on personal letters for credible evidence), national electioneering depended on bonds of friendship, fragile networks that were vulnerable to apathy, misunderstandings, and the complicated logistics of long-distance communication. Thus, the greater the distance from the nation's capital, the less accessible was national political information. As Fisher Ames explained, "The government alone possesses information, and . . . the stage-horses alone are the pipes for its transmission to the printers, who are the issuing commissaries to the people." Without "the light of the newspapers, . . . we sit in darkness." William Vans Murray of Maryland was likewise uninformed about politics "East-[war]d or Southw[ar]d" because "no one hears of such things except at Philad. &, as I have no correspondent there who ought to trust to a letter by post, I am in the dark."[29]

For "country people" far removed from an urban center, the presidential election itself was easily forgotten. In Pennsylvania more people voted for governor than for president in 1796. In the few states that chose electors by popular vote, it was difficult simply to rouse rural farmers to vote, for they faced a long, often arduous trip to the nearest polling place. The little news that managed to reach the countryside was often mere rumor, distorted by the chain of conversations at the heart of political gossip. For example, a "Country man" visiting Boston expressed regret that John Adams could not be president. "They tell me that Mr Adams tho a Clever man will not do for president," he told a shopkeeper. Adams was qualified, the man admitted, but he was mute, and a president probably needed the power of speech.[30]

Logistical problems were complicated by personal, partisan, and regional considerations. This clash of loyalties is most apparent in attempts by national politicians to influence presidential electors. The real battle for the presidency was fought not in the nation's capital but in the states. Despite the best efforts of politicians to influence and coordinate electoral votes on a national level, it was local men fighting local battles—coached and prodded by their state's national representatives—who determined the election.

National politicians knew that victory depended on their influence over these 136 presidential electors, though states that chose electors by popular vote required added efforts and strategic creativity. In Pennsylvania, for example, John Beckley organized the election's most ambitious campaign, distributing handbills and ballots with the names of the Republican electors already written in; he ultimately distributed 30,000 ballots handwritten by family members of Republican politicians in a state where only 24,420 people voted.[31] However, Pennsylvania was hardly the norm. In most states, the choice of electors could be decided by a few influential men. Indeed, New Jersey Federalist Jonathan Dayton believed that the entire election could be decided by a handful of national politicians. Eager to promote Burr for president, Dayton sent a message to Massachusetts Federalist Theodore Sedgwick asking for his cooperation in swaying electors; in an attempt to pressure Sedgwick into compliance, he instructed the messenger to wait for a response. "I assure you," he wrote to Sedgwick, "that I think it possible for you & me with a little aid from a few others to effect this." Sedgwick refused, gently reprimanding Dayton for promoting Burr's election through "misrepresentation" and reminding him that Burr was unlikely to receive Republican support in either the North or South. "The party with which he has generally acted, although they covet the aid of his character & talents, have not the smallest confidence in his hearty union to their cause," Sedgwick explained. Indeed, Sedgwick was sure that Burr's political views were not only "distinct but opposite" to Republican principles; "They know, in short, he is not one of them."[32]

Dayton's efforts proved useless, as did those of many politicians who tried to organize a national campaign, even with the limited pool of electors. Personal influence could not always triumph over local loyalties. In the end, political organization relied on each politician's sense of personal and regional honor at least as much as on his commitment to a cause or candidate. Sedgwick disapproved of Dayton's election trickery in part because promoting Burr above Adams would dishonor New England and shatter the fragile trust joining North and South.

Honor likewise compelled South Carolina's Federalist electors to stick by Adams. They had promised him their support and thus to vote otherwise would be dishonorable—"and if no confidence can be placed in their honor, it is impossible even to act extensively, in concert."[33] If one could not trust the word of these electors now, how could one trust them in future? Destroy the bonds of honor between men, and you destroyed the Federalist party as a whole.

In the case of South Carolina, regional loyalty ultimately prevailed over partisan discipline, for all its electors voted for Jefferson and Pinckney. Such unpredictability characterized the entire presidential campaign. No alliance was too firm to be broken. Even electors of known political inclinations were targeted for conversion; like candidates for executive office, electors won their position more on the basis of character and political inclinations than partisan commitment. Although some potential electors publicly declared their choice of candidate, others did not, leaving them open to last-minute attempts at persuasion. Many were men of local prominence whose membership in the Electoral College marked a first step toward a national career.[34] For men with such ambitions, the attentions of a national politician and his allies could be seductive. With influential men clamoring for their vote, local constituencies voicing preferences, bonds of friendship tugging at their loyalties, and national prominence just beyond their reach, electors had to weigh carefully the consequences of their votes.

Throughout the autumn of 1796, national politicians attempted to secure electoral votes through a combination of promises, threats, and appeals to principle. Weapons of combat included social calls as well as pamphlets, newspaper essays, and personal letters, often hand delivered by local politicians with national connections; each represented a national-local link. Republican Tench Coxe was particularly methodical in his campaign to sway electors. Designating correspondents in New Hampshire, Connecticut, New York, New Jersey, Delaware, Virginia, and Maryland, he channeled electioneering pamphlets and letters to electors, his political agents often personally delivering them to their front doors—though not always on time. Frustrated at receiving Coxe's pamphlets three days after his state's electors had been chosen, Connecticut Republican Samuel Andrew Law swore to Coxe that had they arrived earlier, he "would have distributed the copies, even if I had rode from this place to Hartford," where the electors were due to meet. Moore Furman of New Jersey assured Coxe that his pamphlets were "in the hands of every one . . . except the Bergen [County] elector[,] who is in such an out of the way corner that I have yet had no opporty to [visit] him."[35]

More than any other candidate, Burr waged political warfare using personal interviews. The exception to almost every rule, he campaigned in New England—ostensibly for Jefferson—for several weeks, meeting with powerful state politicians who might influence the selection of electors. In Boston, Abigail Adams observed that Burr had been "constantly closeted" with Republicans Charles Jarvis, Benjamin Austin, and William Eustis. In Ulster County, New York, he met with powerful Federalist Ebenezer Foote, who later described Burr as "a mighty winning fellow." On occasion, Burr electioneered through agents, as when his friend Peter Van Gaasbeek spent "the greatest part of [the] Night" in an "interview" with New York elector Johannes Miller. Burr likewise urged his friend Eustis to talk with Massachusetts elector Elbridge Gerry.[36]

Direct manipulation of electors was tricky, for too overt an attempt to affect their votes would appear to be thwarting the popular will, a charge that could destroy a candidate's reputation. Even Burr, typically unconcerned with appearances, felt compelled to watch his words in a letter to Gerry, offering him advice "if not deemed improper." News of such letters spread quickly. Thus, Adams learned of Hamilton's electioneering letter to Massachusetts Federalist Stephen Higginson within two weeks of its initial posting. Higginson, in turn, knew that New York Republican Melancton Smith had written letters to electors in both Massachusetts and New Hampshire.[37]

This tension between personal and political loyalties pervaded every electoral contest. In New York, George Clinton hoped that "the Influence of personal Attachment" would induce a few Federalist electors to vote Republican. In South Carolina, William Loughton Smith noted that Republican Edward Rutledge was "tampering" with his cousin Benjamin Smith, though he had hopes that Rutledge would fail. In New Jersey, Moore Furman noted that one elector "might be detached" from his Federalist friends but would probably vote with them because "he must go with the multitude." William Vans Murray thought that Maryland's one stray vote for Jefferson resulted from the elector's unpaid debts to British merchants. Stephen Higginson, Hamilton's main source of influence in Massachusetts, noted that three electors each refused to give one of his votes to Pinckney because of "interested & personal motives" and the influence of "Adams's particular friends."[38]

A brief glance at the votes of the Electoral College reveals the effects of these shifting loyalties. In the final tally, only 8 out of 16 states voted a straight Adams-Pinckney or Jefferson-Burr ticket; 52 out of a total of 136 electors did not abide by the national caucus decision.[39] The distribution of votes likewise reveals the unstructured nature of the 1796 election. A total of 13 candidates received electoral votes, some of them regional favorites, others of national repute. Many of these late additions received votes as a form of protest against another candidate. For example, Virginia electors who distrusted Burr voted against him by casting one of their votes for Jefferson and the other for Sam Adams. Republican John Beckley tried to unite southern Republicans against Burr—pitting regional ties against partisan loyalties—and achieved some degree of success, but, notably, those who voted against Burr did not even attempt to agree on an alternative. Southern opposition to Burr was one thing, uniting behind a single candidate was another. Such regional differences would play a pivotal role in the election of 1800.

Both the campaign and the results in the Electoral College show that a politics without sharply defined permanent parties was indeed like a war without uniforms; it was difficult to distinguish friends from foes and often impossible to predict the strange combinations of circumstances that could alter a man's political loyalties or lead to an alliance between former enemies. Desperate to differentiate true Republicans from Federalists in disguise, Tench Coxe pleaded with printer Philip Freneau for a list of Federalists who had written deceiving articles in the *National Gazette*. Aware that such a disclosure would discourage contributors from trusting him in future, Freneau refused. So uncertain were Patrick Henry's political inclinations that he was simultaneously supported by Federalists as a potential presidential candidate and by Republicans as a potential elector.[40] And perhaps most astonishing of all, for a brief period in the campaign, some Republicans believed that Hamilton was advancing Jefferson for president. As John Browne Cutting told Massachusetts Federalist George Cabot, Hamilton had told him that "Mr. Jefferson must be supported, as the only way of appeasing France" and saving the Union. John Beckley thought that such news deserved publication in Pennsylvania newspapers.[41]

In such an unstable political world, it is no wonder that Burr's lack of political commitments hurt his electioneering efforts as much as it helped them. Though skilled at garnering votes and victories, Burr was ultimately untrustworthy, a friend to everyone and thus a friend to no one. Where political bonds were premised on the mutual confidence of friendship, and the conduct of one friend could influence the reputations of all, few politicians would willingly risk an explicit political alliance with Aaron Burr. Even when Virginia Republicans offered him support in 1800, they remained detached enough to throw him over when he became a political liability. This was how Burr perceived the Virginians' behavior during both contests: as a betrayal of friendship.

It was the possibility for dramatic political conversions—the result of the politics of the moment—that accounts for the extreme anxiety produced by newly elected Vice President Jefferson's seemingly simple offer of friendship to President-elect Adams. Republicans and Federalists alike took alarm at the possibility, for there was no telling how such an alliance might change the political landscape. To some Republicans Jefferson's gesture seemed a betrayal of the worst sort. After months of active campaigning against Adams, they could hardly expect to be in his favor during his presidency; by extending a hand of friendship to Adams, Jefferson appeared to be abandoning his Republican friends.[42]

Many Federalists were equally unhappy with Jefferson's gesture of friendship, and most came to the same conclusion: the vice president was taking advantage of Adams's antipathy toward Hamilton to sway Adams to the Republican cause. As Theodore Sedgwick explained, "A new scene of intrigue is exhibiting on the political theatre—the attempt is to gain the new President by flattery. . . . Hence the indust[r]ious attempts to induce him to believe that Hamilton & his party, as they express themselves, did not wish but insidiously opposed his election."[43] Jefferson's comments suggest that the Federalists were right. "There is reason to believe that he [Adams] is detached from Hamilton and there is a possibility he may swerve from his politics," Jefferson wrote in January 1797. "If so, we must counteract with defensive addresses." Virginia Republican Joseph Jones, friendly with both Madison and Jefferson, likewise hoped that Adams "may be induced" to throw off his monarchical prejudices."[44]

The remarkable fluidity of partisan alliances helps explain these puzzling hints of collaboration between Adams and Jefferson after the election. Historians usually dismiss the possibility of an alliance between the two men, conceding, perhaps, that personal friendship took precedence over political differences for the briefest of moments. Jefferson's December 1796 letter of friendship to Adams, withheld at Madison's suggestion, is seen as a glimmer of emotional sincerity that was quickly stamped out by political practicalities, a remembrance of the admiration and respect Jefferson had felt for Adams when the two men had struggled for independence twenty years past. And if we presume the inevitability of political parties and locate their origin in the 1796 election, such a union does, indeed, seem implausible. But if we examine it in the context of the period's ever-shifting political alliances, understanding it as an attempt at cooperation rather than partnership, the alliance is not beyond belief. Indeed, Adams's political loyalties were unpredictable enough to encourage both the French and British ministers to consider his election good news.[45]

Nor was Jefferson's overture of friendship abandoned with the withdrawal of his letter. Madison wanted to moderate the tone and implications of Jefferson's statement, not cancel it altogether. Most of all, he wanted to avoid giving Adams "written possession" of Jefferson's feelings in a signed personal letter that could demonstrate the vice president's lack of integrity in future. So the two men leaked Jefferson's sentiments to Adams through known channels of political gossip. In addition, Jefferson wrote a suggestive letter to New Hampshire Republican John Langdon, counting on the fact that Langdon would show it to Adams. The letter contained "exactly the things which will be grateful to Mr. A. & no more," Jefferson swore to Madison. Adams replied in kind, expressing his friendship through mutual friends.[46] The elaborate planning necessary for this seemingly simple declaration of friendship reveals the political significance of such bonds, as well as the importance of deploying the appropriate weapon.

Adams and Jefferson believed of each other what many politicians believed about many political chiefs: the most honest republican could become a rabid partisan under the influence of his friends. As Maryland Federalist Charles Carroll said of Jefferson, "If left to himself he may act wisely: but, as he will be elected by a faction, it is apprehended he will consider himself rather as the head of that faction, than the first magistrate of the American People." Indebted to his friends for his office, Jefferson would give their demands precedence over the public good. Joseph Jones said the same thing about Pinckney: he hoped that Pinckney would "stamp his administration with the Character of Republican," but feared that "this Gent. will be disposed to take council from those men who have had too much influence hitherto in our councils and will practice every art and stratagem to continue it." Jefferson used the same logic in his strategy toward Adams, hopeful that "detached from Hamilton . . . he may swerve from his politics"; when his efforts at cooperation failed, Jefferson blamed it on the corrupting influence of Adams's cabinet members.[47] For all these men, it was the corruption of faction, the intrigue and persuasion of power-hungry friends, that led politicians astray.

Rather than moments of extreme party discipline—the building blocks of a party system—presidential elections thus were unsettling periods of political conversion that tested loyalties, forged new alliances, and destroyed old ones. Each election reshaped the political landscape, revealing a new cast of characters fighting under each banner. The brief hiatus of partisan strife during the first few months after Adams's election was the product of just such a political reshuffling. Uncertain of new political alliances and enmities, curious to see how

Jefferson, Adams, and their political friends would align themselves, the political community waited and watched; even radical Republican newspaper editor Benjamin Franklin Bache declared an official cease-fire in his Philadelphia *Aurora*.[48]

As bodies of principles, Republicanism and Federalism held reasonably constant, but individual commitments remained unreliable and unpredictable. Elections forced politicians to declare their loyalties; in a murky world of shifting alliances and undeclared intentions, they were bursts of light that revealed in a flash the lay of the political landscape.[49] In 1800, national politicians revisited this disturbingly unpredictable landscape, determined to prevent a recurrence of the problems of four years past. Looking back at the election of 1800 in his later years, Burr would regret that he had not heeded more closely the lessons of 1796.

The Election of 1800

For Burr the election of 1796 had been a painful experience—so humiliating, in fact, that he excluded it from his memoirs. Encouraged by his Virginia friends only to be betrayed at the height of the contest, Burr remembered this emotional lesson when Republicans invited him to run for vice president again in 1800. When John Nicholson asked him whether he cared to run, the normally self-possessed Burr "appeared agitated[,] declared he would have nothing to do with the business[,] that the Southern States had not treated him well on a similar occasion before, that he thought their promise could not be relied on." He repeated his sentiments to John Taylor of Caroline in a more characteristically sardonic strain. "After what happened at the last election (et tu Brute!) I was really averse to have my Name in question," he explained. But he had finally agreed, though he warned Taylor that he "should not choose to be trifled with."[50] Written to a Virginian who was intimate with Jefferson, this caution was almost certainly intended for eyes beyond Taylor's.

Burr and his peers emerged from the 1796 election predisposed to distrust political friends, for above all else the contest had revealed the tenuousness of national partisan ties. Taken beyond the capital and extended across state lines, political loyalties were weaker than expected and regional biases stronger, breeding an atmosphere of distrust between North and South that worsened over the next four years. The sectional nature of national alliances cloaked this regional distrust in the guise of partisanship but did not erase it. There were complications of federalism as well. The often lackluster response of local politicians to the urgings of national leaders revealed an alarming gap between the two levels of politics. By definition, national politicians had a broader political perspective than their friends at home. Clustered together in the nation's capital and forced to develop working relationships with men from other regions, they likewise could better envision national cooperative efforts. But communicating this outlook to their colleagues back home proved harder than expected. By demanding partisan loyalty on a national scale, the election of 1796 thus exposed the many rifts and disjunctures that divided the nation.[51]

The contest also revealed the inadequacies of many political methods and strategies. The adjournment of Congress virtually dissolved the national base of the Federalist and Republican persuasions; without an informational clearinghouse at the capital, it was difficult to gain a national perspective and almost impossible to adapt to the shifting conditions of a national campaign. Those few politicians whose long-distance correspondence sustained lifelines of nationalism were stymied by the uncertainty and slowness of the mails. Newspapers formed a partial bridge, but they were increasingly beyond the control of the ruling elite. Ultimately, this first presidential contest was fought in a series of regional battles between locally defined Federalists and Republicans, with little effective guidance from national politicians, who had not yet determined how to exert their influence.

In a sense the election of 1796 had followed a republican script: the various state contests had selected the "best" men for office—Federalist John Adams as president and Republican Thomas Jefferson as vice president—who happened to have opposing politics, thereby discouraging partisan rule. Was this not the embodiment of James Madison's "extended republic" as delineated in *The Federalist* No. 10, in which local party battles worked against the formation of national parties? The problem with this scenario was the equivocal status and role of national politicians. In attempting to coordinate local politicking on a national scale—however public-minded their efforts might be—they were promoting what they most feared: national political parties. This fundamental conflict between the demands and proprieties of national politics fostered the crisis mentality that so characterized the period's politics.

National politicians were caught in a vicious circle. Driven by fears of civil war, disunion, and the collapse of their cause and careers, they felt compelled to risk all in the name of the public good, leading them to violate many of their most deeply held ideals and standards. The cause of liberty certainly had justified extreme measures before; with both sides convinced that they were defending the promise of the Revolution, it was no great leap to conclude that their present combat demanded more of the same. As Hamilton wrote during the 1800 election, "In times like these in which we live, it will not do to be overscrupulous. It is easy to sacrifice the substantial interests of society by a strict adherence to ordinary rules." Connecticut Republican Gideon Granger felt the personal impact of this mentality during a congressional debate in 1800. As he explained to Jefferson, a Federalist representative had been "insolent enough to dictate to me that tho' he esteemed me as a Man, yet we must all be crushed and that my life was of little Importance when compared to the peace of the State."[52]

Extraordinary times demanded extraordinary actions. Such supposed moral lapses, in turn, fostered anxiety about the fate of the republic. Because their actions were so extreme and seemingly improper, politicians spent an inordinate amount of time analyzing and rationalizing them, thereby documenting the process of political change. A crisis mentality greased the wheels of political innovation, premised on each man's assumption that his was the righteous cause. If the Union fell, it would be the fault of his foes, desperate men who had forsaken the public good to win power, fortune, and influence.

The election of 1800 certainly qualified as a crisis. As Matthew Davis wrote to Albert Gallatin in the spring of 1800, this election would "clearly evince, whether a Republican form of Government is worth contending for" and decide "in some measure, our future destiny." Many Federalists were likewise uneasy as the contest approached, convinced that this would be the last election. Even President Adams assumed that some of his colleagues sought the destruction of the republic and a new constitution. As early as May, months before a vote was cast, there had been anxious talk of civil war.[53] The fuel for these fears was the seemingly implacable opposition of Federalists and Republicans, largely a battle between northerners and southerners. With partisan animosity soaring and no end in sight, many assumed that they were engaged in a fight to the death that would destroy the Union.

Motivated by the impending crisis and guided by the lessons of 1796, politicians prepared for this pivotal contest early and energetically.[54] Jefferson took a far more active role in this campaign, protecting his reputation all the while. His most vigorous campaigning was in the capital, where it could be inconspicuously incorporated into his daily routine. There, the blurred bounds between socializing and politicking helped obscure his efforts. At his mountaintop home in Virginia, however, where his movements were far more conspicuous, this same ambiguity gave his every word and action political significance, as it had in 1796, when a visit from Burr drew charges of intrigue for months thereafter. So in 1800, Jefferson's most vigorous efforts abruptly ceased when he left Philadelphia. Although he was eager to establish a national Republican newspaper in the capital, for example—canvassing the idea among friends and supporters until the day of his departure—he refused to involve himself in such efforts at Monticello, even when he was asked. As he explained to Tench Coxe, "My situation exposes me to so much calumny that I am obliged to be cautious of appearing in any matter however justifiable . . . if it be of a nature to admit readily of miscon[duct]." Even a visit to Madison at Montpelier became impossible once Jefferson was ensconced at Monticello, for it too was apt to invite charges of conspiracy and self-interest. Such a visit "wod. certainly compromit you both," agreed James Monroe, "as it wod. immediately appear throughout the continent."[55] To protect his reputation—and of course, his cause—Jefferson had to appear passive.

Appearances mattered more than actions, for in Jefferson's mind, his politicking was not only acceptable but essential: Republican failure would mean the end of republican governance. Thus, on the occasions when his actions were less visible and thus less likely to invite attack, he became more willing to take risks and bend rules. For example, in the spring of 1800 he considered arranging a "spontaneous" demonstration of support for himself on his way home from the national capital. As he explained to Monroe, he hated ceremony and preferred to avoid occasions "which might drag me into the newspapers," yet Federalists "had made [powerful?] use" of such demonstrations, and there was "a great deal of federalism and Marshalism" in Richmond. Was a reliance on "the slow but sure progress of good sense & attachment to republicanism . . . best for the public as well as [myself]?" Torn between political proprieties and the demands of the moment, Jefferson opted for the latter. Monroe's response must have brought a twinge of pain. After inquiring "in a way wh[ich] compromitted no one"—collecting public opinion on the subject—Monroe discouraged a public demonstration, for "it was feared . . . that the zeal of some of our friends . . . had abated by yr. absence"—an interesting comment on the supposed wave of sentiment that swept Jefferson into office.[56]

This same compromise between political proprieties and the demands of the moment influenced Burr's extraordinary electioneering efforts in 1800. Given Burr's perverse pleasure in violating prevailing standards and norms, it is difficult to ascribe his actions to a process of tortured compromise, but he did dirty his hands in street campaigning to a remarkable degree. As Davis explains, because "it was universally conceded" that New York would decide the election, and that New York City would guide the rest of the state, Burr decided to "address the people" in person, an unprecedented act that both shocked and impressed Davis.[57] Significantly, Burr was responding to a similar decision by Hamilton, who had previously announced his intentions to campaign in the same manner.

During the three-day voting period, the two men argued "the debatable questions" before large assemblages at polling places, each man politely stepping aside when it was the other's turn to speak. Between their debates, they rushed from ward to ward, encouraging voters for twelve to fifteen hours at a stretch, their friends hard put to keep up with them. These bold democratic gestures are unremarkable by modern standards, but the partisan press recognized their novelty. How could a "would be Vice President . . . stoop so low as to visit every corner in search of voters?" asked the Federalist *Daily Advertiser*. The Republican *Commercial Advertiser* likewise commented on the "astonished" electorate that greeted Hamilton's efforts: "Every day he is seen in the street hurrying this way, and darting that; here he buttons a heavy hearted fed, and preaches up courage, there he meets a group, and he simpers in unanimity, again to the heavy headed and hearted, he talks of perseverance, and (God bless the mark) of virtue!" Though as energetic as Burr, Hamilton electioneered with a decidedly Federalist flair. On at least one occasion, he supposedly offended the crowd at a polling place by appearing on horseback, prompting one disgruntled observer to literally force Hamilton off his high horse; at other polling places, he was supposedly greeted by cries of "scoundrel" and "villain."[58]

Hamilton's polling-place debacles are reminders of the discomforts of democratic politicking among the political elite. It was one thing to preach the political gospel to a crowd, as Hamilton tried to do during the 1795 Jay Treaty rally; it was quite another to mingle with the multitude. Increasingly during the 1790s, men accustomed to leadership had to reevaluate and revise their political methods, and some managed it better than others. This was Burr's genius—the accomplishment that won him the vice presidency. Through his corps of mobilized young lieutenants, Burr directed a popular political campaign from on high, and the result was a stunning Republican victory in one of the election's most crucial contests. He purportedly compiled a roster with the name of every New York City voter and portioned it out to his young followers, who literally electioneered door-to-door. He dispatched German-speaking Republicans to the predominantly German seventh ward to "explain" the election in the voters' native tongue. This electoral magic made Burr an invaluable ally in a political war. Few of his station could or would do the same—and for that same reason, Burr was distrusted. Ambivalence about Burr was ambivalence about the changing nature of politics.

This struggle between political proprieties and the demands of the moment is particularly apparent in the many attempts to tamper with the Electoral College. Electors in 1796 had been unpredictable, frustrating attempts at national coordination. So in 1800, rather than wooing electors, national politicians focused their efforts on the selection process, hoping to install properly loyal men. Given the sense of crisis, such measures seemed imperative, yet they were blatant violations of the republican morality of free elections, producing an outpouring of anxious self-justification. Pleading for immediate electoral reform in Virginia, North Carolina, Kentucky, and Tennessee, South Carolina Republican Charles Pinckney insisted, "I tell you I know nothing else will do and this is no time for qualms." Maryland Federalist Charles Carroll likewise encouraged such reform, though he disapproved of "laws & changes of a moment." The entire Massachusetts congressional delegation urged similar reform for their state. Assuming that their home audience had no national perspective on the contest, the delegates explained the urgency of their request in a circular letter, including an apology for their actions: "Excuse us for suggesting these ideas; our anxiety for the event of the election must be our apology."[59]

Other politicians waited until their states had elected new legislatures; if their party had a clear majority, they lobbied to convene it immediately for the selection of electors, before their opponents could organize resistance. Hamilton urged the reverse. Alarmed that the incoming New York legislature was largely Republican and would select Republican electors, he wrote to Governor John Jay pleading for drastic measures: the old legislature needed to be called immediately and the mode of choosing electors changed to popular voting by district. Hamilton was "aware that there are weighty objections to the measure," but the "scruples of delicacy and propriety . . . ought to yield to the extraordinary nature of the crisis. They ought not to hinder the taking of a *legal* and *constitutional* step, to prevent an *Atheist* in Religion and a *Fanatic* in politics from getting possession of the helm of the State." Jay did not know the Republicans, Hamilton insisted: they were intent on either overthrowing the government "by stripping it of its due energies" or effecting a revolution. Given the threat to the republic, the "*public safety,*" and the "great cause of social order," it was their "solemn obligation to employ" any means in their power to defeat these wrongdoers. There could be no hope for a popular government "if one party will call to its aid all the resources which *Vice* can give and if the other, however pressing the emergency, confines itself within all the ordinary forms of delicacy and decorum." His closing—"Respectfully & Affec[tionatel]y"—reveals him appealing to Jay as both governor and friend. Jay was not persuaded, writing on the bottom of the letter, "Proposing a measure for party purposes wh[ich] I think it wd. not become me to adopt."[60]

Although historians often lambaste Hamilton for this suggestion, he was only one among many willing to compromise their principles. The difference in Hamilton's case was that he urged his reform after the Republicans had won a majority in the state legislature—the very maneuver that politicians in other states were resisting when they lobbied for the legislature to meet immediately and select electors. Like Jefferson, these politicians justified their actions by declaring them high-minded during a time of crisis; rather than abandoning their republican morals, they were clinging to them as justification for their political sins.

Other innovations were less blatantly improper. For example, remembering the fragmented campaigning of 1796, politicians tried to forge reliable national networks of communication. Federalists focused their efforts on establishing a regular correspondence among the nation's leading men. As Hamilton explained in a letter to Carroll, the "true & independent friends of government must understand each other." South Carolina's Robert Goodloe Harper, far removed from the stronghold of Federalism, also recognized the need for "certain & regular information from our friends every where." Jefferson likewise attempted to cultivate a correspondence with men around the nation.[61] As suggested by their choice of words, these politicians envisioned themselves as uniting a group of "friends," not organizing a national party.

Republicans went a step further through their use of newspapers. As Jefferson put it, in their electioneering efforts, "the engine is the press." Tools of mobilization as well as communication, newspapers were an invaluable means of nationalization. Reading the same news, joined by their shared "membership" as subscribers, Republicans forged links across the nation. Indeed, in the absence of an effective national political organization, newspapers were one of the few acceptable means of promoting national unity. Although the national elite were not in control of this powerful engine, they made use of it. Thus Jefferson's efforts on behalf of the Washington *National Intelligencer* and the *Universal Gazette,* both intended to be national newspapers. The nationalizing influence of newspapers would be one of the most fundamental lessons that the Federalists took away from their defeat in 1800. As Fisher Ames wrote, "The Jacobins owe their triumph to the unceasing use of this engine. . . . We must use, but honestly, and without lying, an engine that wit and good sense would make powerful and safe." He hoped that the *New England Palladium* would serve this purpose.[62]

Honor: The Bond of Party

Correspondence and newspapers solved some of the problems, but they could not address a fundamental challenge: how to deal with the unstable loyalties of the national political elite. In fact, among the national elite, mutual distrust was perhaps the most significant legacy of the 1796 election. Even the candidates were not exempt. Given his suspect loyalties, Burr was naturally eyed with care in 1800. But after the scare of Jefferson's overtures to Adams, many of their "particular friends" were also loath to trust these two men a second time. Asked to support Jefferson in 1800, for example, New York Republican George Clinton declared him an untrustworthy man who had used his friends to gain office and then abandoned them by declaring friendship to Adams. In Burr's memoirs, Matthew Davis—present during attempts to sway Clinton—offers a substantially cleaned-up version of what Clinton *really* said, which Davis recorded in a memorandum. "At the last interview, after we had urged him very hard, he became violently Enraged," Davis recorded in his notes. Turning to Burr, Clinton "exclaimed, in most infuriated tones, 'If you, Sir, was the Candidate for President, I would serve with pleasure; but to promote the election of Mr. Jefferson, I will not. . . . Sir, at the last contest we supported him, in opposition to Mr. Adams. We were unsuccessful, but he was elected Vice President. What did he do? His first act in the Senate was, to make a *damned time serving trimming speech,* in which he declared, that it was a great pleasure to him, to have an opportunity of serving his Country under such a tried patriot as *John Adams,* which was saying to his friends—I am in; Kiss my --- — and go to H-ll.'"[63] Here was the emotional impact of political betrayal.

Clearly, Jefferson's praise of Adams had a lingering impact. Madison had been right to discourage Jefferson from putting his feelings in writing; even in spoken form, they were problematic. As Maryland Republican Gabriel Duvall explained to Madison, after asserting for months that Adams was a monarchist, he and his friends were "now placed in an awkward situation by the opinion of Mr. Jefferson himself," whose friendliness with Adams suggested his full confidence in Adams's republicanism. Where political alliances were envisioned as friendships, a friendly gesture could signal a political alliance. Under such circumstances, even Jefferson's inaugural declaration that "We are all federalists, we are all republicans" had troublesome implications. Jefferson's conciliatory attitude toward the Federalists had "disgusted, beyond expression, the leaders of his own party; because it gave the lie to all those slanderous misrepresentations by which his elevation had been secured," claimed Federalist Theodore Sedgwick. To Sedgwick, Jefferson's "violent removals" of Federalists from lucrative offices were attempts to repair the damage. "The wit of man could probably devise no measure more fitted to render party animosities incurable," he declared. "This is 'healing the wounds of party divisions' with a witness."[64]

Distrust of John Adams, intensified by his French peace mission toward the end of his presidency, was even more marked. A surprisingly large number of Federalists and Republicans believed that Adams was forging "a coalition" with "Mr. Jefferson's friends," or worse, attempting to form his own faction. "We are betrayed if there is any understanding" between Adams and Jefferson, fretted Delaware's James Bayard, "and to believe that, is to credit but a small portion of what is said." Could Adams's French peace mission and the firing of his cabinet be deliberate bids for Republican support? And why were Republicans in the capital so eager to talk with Adams? Why had Jefferson remained in Philadelphia longer than usual? How did Republican newspapers obtain advance notice of Adams's actions? To Federalists the answer seemed obvious. Even some Republicans harbored such suspicions, Burr reporting as late as September 1800 that Adams would serve as Jefferson's vice president if elected. Charging that Adams had proven himself "unworthy of trust," many Federalists were prepared to abandon him in 1800.[65]

With personal and regional distrust endemic, it is no wonder that one onlooker believed that "the party spirit amongst us is geographical & personal."[66] Clearly, to ensure an electoral victory in 1800, national party bonds would have to be strengthened. Politicians responded to this dilemma by holding national caucuses in May, just before the adjournment of Congress. Most accounts of the election cite these gatherings as proof of increased partisan fervor, yet the truth is just the opposite: the caucuses of 1800 were attempts to bolster national alliances that were dangerously divided along regional lines.

The first hint at the purpose of these meetings can be found in the words that politicians used to describe them. Though they sometimes referred to them as caucuses, they also used such terms as "the agreement," "the promise," "the compromise," and "the pledge," to which they would be "faithful" and "true."[67] Obviously, these caucuses involved negotiation and compromise between men of differing views, rather than the simple confirmation of a presidential ticket. The result of the compromises—electoral tickets featuring a northerner and a southerner—were not foregone conclusions, regardless of how obvious this strategy might appear. A cross-regional ticket was risky, for it required a high degree of national party loyalty and mutual trust between North and South. Many politicians later regretted their faith in such a scheme. John Adams's son Thomas attributed his father's loss to the treachery of southern supporters of Charles Cotesworth Pinckney. "It ought never to have been the plan of the federal party to support a Gentleman from the South, merely for the sake of securing the interest of [any] Southern State in favor of the federal ticket. There was evidence enough on the former trial, what result might be calculated upon in making another." Adams now had no "confidence in the Southern people." Although southern Republicans remained true to their promise, supporting both candidates equally, they regretted their actions once the tie between Jefferson and Burr was announced. To Maryland Republican John Francis Mercer, the lesson was obvious. As he wrote to Madison, "It all amounts to this, that we are *too honest*."[68] They should have thought first of themselves.

The national caucuses of May 1800 were attempts to create national party unity, not expressions of it. Indeed, as suggested by such words as *pledge* and *promise,* national party loyalty was so weak that it had to be supplemented by personal vows. To attain partisan unity, politicians had to commit themselves personally, pledging their word of honor and their reputations; the only way to unite North and South was to appeal to politicians as gentlemen rather than as partisan allies. Honor was the ultimate bond of party when all else failed, the only way to supersede the many conflicting regional and personal claims that tore at a man's commitments of principle. Unfortunately, as the unfolding of the electoral tie would reveal, personal honor proved to be an ambiguous, subjective thing that could compel like-minded men to take very different courses of action.

Throughout the campaign, politicians clung to their bonds of honor as the only hope for national partisan unity. When Hamilton began to urge Federalists to abandon Adams in favor of Pinckney, he was reminded repeatedly that they could not do so without going back on their word. *"We are pledged"* to give Adams *"the full chance of the united vote concerted at Philadelphia,"* urged George Cabot. Cabot again reminded Hamilton of their vow when the latter was contemplating his pamphlet attack on Adams. "Good faith wou'd & ought to be observed as the only means of success," he insisted, for if Adams was dropped, his friends would drop Pinckney in return.[69]

All over the nation, Federalists knew that if they reneged on their half of the agreement—if they dropped the candidate from outside their region—that man's supporters would do the same in return, and the Federalist cause would collapse. Everything depended on the personal honor of individual politicians. Thus, throughout the election, they pledged their faith to men from other regions, hoping for similar reassurance in return. South Carolina's John Rutledge, Jr., described one such exchange to Hamilton. Shortly after arriving in Rhode Island, he received a "pressing invitation" for an "immediate" discussion of the election. When he explained that he could not journey into town, "the old Gentleman" who had requested the meeting traveled out to Rutledge for "an hours conversation." The man asked Rutledge "to declare [for] the information of his friends . . . whether I really thought Mr A[dams] would have the votes of So Carolina. I told him I had on my return there fulfilled the promise I made at the Caucus held at Philada., & used every exertion within my power to induce the federalists to suport Mr A equally with Genl P. . . . He seemed pleased with this information—said we might rely upon P's getting all the votes in this State."[70] This "old Gentleman" was desperate for personal reassurance of South Carolina's fidelity. Only then could he claim confidence in the national cause. Such personal pledges of honor were virtually the only thing binding North and South.

Northern and southern Federalists exchanged vows of loyalty in their correspondence as well, nervously reminding one another of their sworn duty to abide by the Philadelphia agreement. Their worries centered around Massachusetts and South Carolina, the home states of the two candidates, for it was these states that were likely to succumb to regional prejudice and abandon one candidate in favor of the native son. "I fear you and your friends in Boston are ruining every thing," wrote South Carolinian Robert Goodloe Harper to Harrison Gray Otis of Massachusetts. "The federalists . . . in South Carolina, are making the fairest & the most zealous exertions in favour of Mr. Adams. . . . But can it be expected that they will continue the same efforts" if they know that Massachusetts has abandoned Pinckney? Virginian Bushrod Washington—George Washington's nephew—likewise wrote a frantic letter to Oliver Wolcott in Connecticut, assuring him that South Carolina would support both Adams and Pinckney, for "they consider themselves imperiously urged to pursue this conduct by the soundest principles of good faith & of good policy." Even Pinckney was behaving "like a man of honor" by supporting Adams, Washington insisted. Should "distrust take place between the friends of the two federal candidates," he warned, "all must end in the election of Mr. J[efferson]—which God forbid."[71]

So important were such personal reassurances that Wolcott began a letter campaign, quoting Washington's letter to friends throughout the North. Pinckney himself wrote a similar letter to James McHenry in Maryland, assuring him that South Carolina would abandon Adams only if New England did so first—an interesting insight into Pinckney's ambitions. All these men recognized what James Bayard put into words: the Federalist party's "efforts can not be united, but thro' mutual confidence," and the best way to ensure such regional trust was through pledges of personal honor.[72]

Republicans, too, clung to their caucus pledge as their only hope of surmounting regional differences. Like the Federalists, their concerns focused on the home states of the candidates, New York and Virginia, where regional biases would be strongest. Thus, throughout the election, a slew of anxious correspondence passed between New Yorkers and Virginians, each seeking reassurance that the other's honor was pledged. Burr's friend David Gelston—well aware of Virginia's disloyalty four years earlier—was particularly nervous about that state's intentions, writing several anxious letters to Madison during the course of the election. "*Can we, may we* rely on the integrity of the southern States?" he wrote in October. "We depend on the integrity of Virginia & the southern States as we shall be faithfull & honest in New York." Six weeks later, agitated by reports that Virginia was going to drop a few votes for Burr to ensure Jefferson's victory, he wrote again, reminding Madison that honor was at stake. "I am not willing to believe it possible that such measures can be contemplated," he wrote, suggesting just the opposite. "We know that the honour of the Gentlemen of Virgina. and N. Y. was pledged at the adjournment of Congress," and to violate such an agreement would be "a sacrilege." A letter from Madison to Jefferson reveals that Gelston's fears were well founded. Gelston "expresses much anxiety & betrays some jealousy with respect to the *integrity* of the Southern States," Madison wrote. "I hope the event will skreen all the parties, particularly Virginia[,] from any imputation on this subject; tho' I am not without fears, that the requisite concert may not sufficiently pervade the several States." Such fears eventually compelled Jefferson himself, as he later explained, to take "some measures" to ensure Burr Virginia's unanimous vote.[73]

This mistrust between North and South tainted the reputation of Massachusetts Republican Timothy Green, one of the election's many victims. A friend of Burr's who traveled to South Carolina in the middle of the campaign, he was accused of attempting to secure that state for Burr. According to Clintonian newspaper editor James Cheetham, Burr had sent Green to South Carolina on his behalf because he himself was "scarcely known in that state." Serving as Burr's "eulogist" and "intercessor," Green supposedly reported to Burr through letters to their mutual friend John Swartwout. Green insisted that his trip had been personal in nature, his letters mere reassurance for political friends, and his political activities limited to pleas for "union and good faith" among South Carolina Republicans. But given the prevailing distrust between North and South, a northern Republican urging "good faith" to South Carolinians would seem to have one purpose in mind—the support of Aaron Burr.[74] Likewise, even if they were not explicitly political in purpose, letters of reassurance about South Carolina could not help but have a political impact among distrustful northerners; as Burr himself wrote, Green's letters were "much relied on" in New York. The personal nature of political bonds made it virtually impossible to differentiate socializing from politicking.

In 1800 honor united national politicians more than partisan loyalty. Politicians could agree upon political priorities and principles locally far more readily than they could across regions. And indeed, local political parties were more organized in 1800 than they had ever been before, creating statewide committees of correspondence and networks of influence. On a national level, such organization proved more problematic, for it seemed to threaten the very Union itself. In the face of such conflicts, national politicians turned to what they knew best, guiding their actions according to the mandates of honor. It was their reliance on aristocratic customs of the past that enabled politicians to adapt to the demands of a democratic politics. In Burr's case, the importance of honor would compel him to make the worst mistake of his political career.

The Complications of Honor: The Electoral Tie

The most controversial aspect of the election of 1800 was the tie in the Electoral College in February 1801. As devised in the Constitution, presidential elections were determined by a straight vote count. Each elector cast two votes, and the candidate with the most votes became president; the runner up became vice president. When two candidates were tied, the election was thrown into the House, where each state had one vote, to be decided by a majority of the delegation.

In 1800, even this backup procedure proved problematic. Republican congressmen stood steadfast behind Jefferson—the man they had intended to elect president—while Federalists supported Burr as a viable alternative to a man they detested. The result was a six-day, thirty-six-ballot deadlock. It was the onus of Burr's actions during that time that plagued him to the end of his days and inspired him to compile his memoirs to argue his case thereafter. To Davis the events of 1801 "fixed the destiny of Colonel Burr. . . . Subsequent events were only consequences resulting from antecedent acts."[75] For Burr, as for many others, this three-week period would constitute the defining moment of his political career.

Among politicians bound to one another through friendship and honor, the tie was destined to be a crisis, for it forced them to declare their loyalties in a definitive way. In a sense, the tie was a stress test of loyalties, priorities, principles, and ambitions; as in the election itself, a demand for partisan unity revealed the precise opposite. The result was a complex and tortuous process that resulted in mutual recriminations for decades thereafter.

The tie between Jefferson and Burr has long been attributed to intense party discipline: so loyal were Republican electors to their party ticket that they unexpectedly caused a tie by all voting for their two candidates. Yet there is another way of interpreting such unanimous support, as suggested by Connecticut Federalist Uriah Tracy. Writing from the capital, Tracy reported that Republicans were in a rage "for having acted with good faith . . . each declaring, if they had not had full confidence in the treachery of the others, they would have been treacherous themselves; and not acted . . . as they promised . . . to act—at Philada. last winter."[76] In other words, no Republican had dared drop a vote because each assumed that others would prove disloyal. To drop a vote would be to invite retributive vote-dropping elsewhere, thereby destroying whatever national party unity existed and probably throwing the election to the Federalists. This was hardly a great stride in national party commitment. Indeed, regional distrust and personal differences only increased during the course of the election, as did partisan enmity, eventually flaring into anxious talk of civil war.

Concern about disunion and armed conflict had in fact emerged as early as May, but it was not until the electoral tie that politicians began to seriously contemplate such threats. Pennsylvania Republican Hugh Henry Brackenridge envisioned an army led by Hamilton seizing control of the government.[77] Federalists were equally nervous. The Republicans would destroy the government rather than surrender Jefferson's victory, charged Senator James Gunn of Georgia.[78] Of course, the Republicans gave Federalists good reason for such concern. According to New York Republican Edward Livingston, the Virginia legislature had "pledged themselves to resist the authority" of any attempt to usurp the government, "decisively and effectively." As Jefferson later explained, this "decisive" action was a call to arms. Though it is difficult for us to take such a threat seriously, Jefferson considered it convincing enough to win him the election. "The certainty that a legislative usurpation would be resisted by arms" convinced the Federalists to surrender, he explained to Madison and Monroe.[79]

The inspiration for such desperate action was the prevailing fear that the Federalists would usurp the government, appointing a president pro tem until they devised another plan; Federalist correspondence shows that this option received serious consideration for quite some time.[80] Yet Republicans held on to the slim hope that the Federalists would ultimately follow the public will and elect Jefferson. James Monroe felt sure that after an initial outburst of spleen, Federalists would assume "more correct views" and install Jefferson as president. The alternative was unthinkable: surely they would not usurp the election, for such a move "wod. require a degree of . . . wickedness in that party wh. I do not think it possessed of." Madison agreed: "Certainly" the Federalists would put things right.[81]

Many Federalists used this same logic when contemplating the possibility of having Jefferson or Burr as president: surely these men were not as bad as Federalists had been led to believe. Faced with a national emergency, politicians revealed that beneath all their partisan name-calling and threats, they thought that their opponents would act for the public good; by threatening the Union, the crisis of 1801 forced both sides to acknowledge their mutual commitment to it. In the same way that calls for national unity revealed dangerous divisions, the threat of disunion revealed bonds of nationalism, tenuous as they might be.[82]

This jumble of suspicions and expectations—partisan, regional, personal, ideological—was at the heart of the subsequent controversy over the tie between Jefferson and Burr. Forced to take a stand with their votes, congressmen found themselves torn between conflicting aspects of their public identity. Voting along partisan lines might do a disservice to one's region; voting along regional lines could endanger the Union; and either of these paths could damage one's public career. There was no single correct course of action, but a poor choice could bring dishonor, defeat, and disunion. In the end, most men remained true to partisan demands. Republicans voted for Jefferson, and Federalists withheld enough votes to allow him to win. But resolution came only after six days of conflict, questions, persuasion, and suspicion.

Considering the distrust between northern and southern Republicans, it should be no surprise that during the balloting, at least one New Yorker tried to entice New York and New Jersey Republicans to abandon Jefferson in favor of Burr. As Maryland Republican Samuel Smith told Burr, "a Mr. Ogden" had recently "Addressed the York Members on your Acct. directly & boldly," suggesting "how much New York would be benefited by having you for the President," and made similar suggestions to a New Jersey representative. Already predisposed to distrust New Yorkers, many southern Republicans assumed that David Ogden had been sent by Burr to sway the election in his favor. The same was suggested of northern Republicans Edward Livingston and Abraham Bishop. A New Yorker who was friendly with Burr, Livingston was assumed to be assisting Ogden as Burr's "confidential agent" in wooing Vermont and Tennessee delegates; Bishop was accused of traveling to Pennsylvania with similar intentions.[83]

Regardless of the truth of such claims, New York and New Jersey Republicans clearly feared the lure of a regional victory, for shortly after Ogden's departure, they called a caucus "to pledge themselves to each other." In the face of such temptation, their loyalty to the national cause required the reinforcement of a personal pledge of honor. Once again, honor was the ultimate bond of party. This type of ceremonial vow, entirely overlooked by modern accounts, meant enough to inspire at least one Virginia representative with hope.[84]

A group of Federalists made a similar pledge but for very different reasons. As Representative George Baer explained, six men held the election in their hands: Baer himself, William Craik, John Chew Thomas, and John Dennis of Maryland; James Bayard of Delaware; and Lewis Richard Morris of Vermont. Representatives of small states with small delegations, they could conceivably carry their own state and decide the election. Aware that they would be held responsible for the outcome of the contest, unsure about Burr's viability, their votes courted on all sides, they made "a solemn and mutual pledge" to act together; conscious that their seemingly disloyal actions could destroy their reputations and careers, they committed themselves to a difficult course of action. They would "defer to the opinions" of their "political friends" and support Burr as long as possible, but as soon as it was "fairly ascertained" that he could not be elected, they would allow Jefferson to win; far better to have an unfit president than to be personally responsible for disunion and civil war.[85]

Bayard had an additional reason for such a strategy: the best interests of his home state relied on the continuing existence of the Union. As he explained to John Adams after the election, "Representing the smallest State in the Union, without resources which could furnish the means of self protection, I was compelled by the obligation of a sacred duty so to act as not to hazard the constitution upon which the political existence of the State depends."[86] Compelled to decide between loyalty to Federalism and to his home state, Bayard abandoned Federalism.

The lone representative from Delaware, Bayard felt particularly responsible for the election's outcome, for he had an entire state's vote in his power. The difficulty of his decision, joined with the controversy that surrounded it in later years, led him to document his reasoning in great detail, offering invaluable insight into the internal logic of one of the period's many personal compromises. A letter to Hamilton written shortly after the tie was announced suggests that Bayard viewed national politics through two lenses. First and foremost, he considered himself a Federalist who would require "the most undoubting conviction" before he separated himself from his friends. He also thought of himself as a northerner whose intense dislike of Virginia seemed to make Burr the preferable choice.[87] Under normal circumstances, these two perspectives were in accord, for the Federalists were largely a northern party with a particular hatred of Virginia, the heart of their Republican opposition.

Bayard's problems arose when he perceived a conflict between national partisan considerations and concern for the welfare of his state. New England Federalists seemed willing to sacrifice the Union rather than install Jefferson as president, a desperate act born of regional hatred that compelled Bayard to redefine his priorities. Confronted with a regional faction that threatened the interests of his state, he first joined with Federalists from the middle states to protest these desperate measures. When the interests of Delaware seemed to stand alone, Bayard went one step further. As he explained when describing the violent Federalist reaction to his decision to support Jefferson, "I told them that if necessary I had determined to become the victim of the measure. They might attempt to direct the vengeance of the Party against me but the danger of being a sacrifice could not shake my resolution."[88] In the final moment of crisis, Bayard abandoned national Federalism.

Bayard was experiencing firsthand the complications of federal governance. For Bayard, as for most others, the choice was obvious though difficult: if national policy endangered one's home state or region, local considerations must prevail. New England Federalists used the same logic when they debated abandoning the Union rather than inflicting Jefferson on New England; so did Jefferson and his fellow Virginians when they vowed to take arms rather than deprive Virginia of the presidency. The bonds that formed national political parties were untested, unstable, undefined, and largely personal. In the pressure-cooker atmosphere of the capital in February 1801, they readily gave way to local and personal concerns.

A crisis justified desperate measures, freeing politicians to act as they saw fit; significantly, given the choice, most of them were willing to abandon national allies. Bayard and his five colleagues vowed to split with the Federalists at the final crisis. According to Bayard, representatives from New York, New Jersey, Vermont, and Tennessee made the same promise: they would "vote a decent length of time for Mr. Jefferson, and as soon as they could excuse themselves by the imperious situation of affairs, would give their votes for Mr. Burr, the man they really preferred."[89] As we shall see, at the height of the crisis, even Jefferson made a compromise. National bonds were dissolving into geographical and personal alliances.

In the midst of this partisan shuffling and reshuffling, what of the seemingly bipartisan Burr? From a modern perspective, his actions seem inconsistent, irrational, or frustratingly enigmatic. Yet understood in the context of personal honor, they are not only understandable but logical. Like other national politicians of the period, Burr governed his public life according to certain fundamental assumptions about his character and reputation. He considered himself a gentleman, a man of honor, and a deserving member of the ruling elite; he likewise assumed that others recognized him as such. As a gentleman, there were any number of sins that Burr could commit without destroying his reputation, and over the course of his life he committed many of them: extravagance, licentiousness, debauchery, womanizing. As Davis noted in Burr's *Memoirs,* Burr was "regardless of the consequences in the gratification of his desires."[90]

There was one sin, however, that even Burr felt compelled to avoid. He did not break his word—the core of his gentlemanly status. A gentleman was a man whose strength of character ensured that his word was his pledge; it was not the civil law, but the higher, self-imposed law of honor that governed his actions and made him a trustworthy and reliable man among equals.[91] As stated in the code duello, the worst insult for a man of honor was to be charged with lying or breaking one's word; "the lie direct" justified an immediate challenge.

It was this assumption, among others, that guided Burr's actions during the electoral tie. When he had accepted his candidacy for the vice presidency, Burr had agreed to join Jefferson and his friends in a joint campaign, each man trusting the other to defend their shared cause. In essence, Burr gave his word that he would support Jefferson for president. He repeated this promise when the possibility of a tie made southern Republicans uneasy about Burr's intentions, issuing a pledge that he would "utterly disclaim all competition" with Jefferson—yet another use of personal honor as a political bond. To this reassuring pledge, however, he added a warning: any "friends" who suspected that he might "submit to be instrumental in Counteracting the Wishes & expectations of the U.S. . . . would dishonor my Views and insult my feelings."[92]

As a man of honor, Burr expected his word to be trusted. Throughout the campaign's many twists and turns, he never went back on this promise, doing nothing to *actively* draw the presidency away from Jefferson. On a more passive level, however, his actions were more questionable; he never promised to decline the office if it were offered. Indeed, considering his assumptions about his merit and talents, he thought it ridiculous to assume that he would. As he explained to his friend William Eustis, his public denial of "competition" with Jefferson was "a pledge of good faith only"—it was "absurd & unpardonable" for anyone to assume that he would resign if chosen in Jefferson's place, and most Republicans would agree. Thus, although he did not campaign against Jefferson, he did not hide his willingness to replace him. In his mind, the contest was entirely in the hands of the Federalists; he could do nothing, but they could "make their election and . . . coerce" the Republicans to "abandon J[efferson]" if they so chose.[93]

Regional distrust quickly complicated this standoff. Southern Republicans, already leery of Burr, worried about the loopholes in his pledge, aware that he had not forsworn all interest in the presidency. Fearful that he might come to an understanding with the Federalists, they began to murmur about his intentions. When Samuel Smith asked for confirmation of his loyalty, Burr's protestations about his honor rose to a still higher pitch. "I think I could hardly forgive any democrat who could for a Moment doubt about the line of Conduct I shall pursue." Five days later, after receiving more pressing demands for reassurance, Burr exploded. He had received "a great Number of letters on the subject of the election," he complained, and perceived "a degree of Jealousy and distrust and irritation by no Means pleasing or flattering." Most of the questions in these letters had been answered in previous letters to Smith, but "one Gentleman (of our friends) has asked me whether if I were chosen president, I would engage to resign." To Burr, this was too much; to the injury of questioning his word, Republicans added the insult of suggesting that he did not merit the presidency. If the House determined to offer him the job, why should he refuse it? He was certainly as capable as anyone else to fill the position. Such a question "was unnecessary, unreasonable and impertinent," Burr fumed, "and I have therefore made no reply"—though the answer, he informed Smith, was that he would not resign.[94]

Matters were not helped when Virginian pride rose to the surface. As the Federalists were delighted to report, they had heard of a letter from Madison which spoke of "America being degraded by the *attempt* to Elect Burr President." Thus, when Burr and Smith met in Philadelphia five days later by prearrangement, the offended Burr insisted even more firmly that he would accept the presidency if it were offered. As Smith later recalled, Burr said "that at all events the House could and ought to make a choice, meaning if they could not get Mr Jefferson they could take" Burr.[95] Ironically, it was the mandates of honor that led Burr to destroy his reputation.

This account of Burr's actions reveals that his self-defense in his *Memoirs* is essentially correct. Contrary to the expectations of friends and foes, he did not explicitly scheme to usurp the presidency. He did, however, make one fundamental mistake: he did nothing to hide his interest in the office. The proper stance for a candidate for high office—particularly the presidency—was complete and utter silence, the sort of republican display of obeisance to the public will that came so naturally to Jefferson. Fifteen years after the election, Burr passed this lesson on to another potential presidential candidate. Hopeful that Andrew Jackson would run for president and displace the "Virginia junto," he had one key piece of advice: Jackson "ought first to be admonished to be passive."[96] As Burr learned too late, a single such mistake could mean eternal damnation as an ambitious, self-interested man.

Eager for the presidency but unable to break his word by negotiating for it, Burr was in an impossible situation. Federalists who knew his character and ambitions were baffled; in their minds, there was nothing to hold him back—surely he could feel no commitment to Virginians, who had never shown any commitment to him. A sudden case of conscience seemed equally unlikely, for Burr was a man who habitually violated political conventions. So unimaginable was Burr's lack of interest that Federalists simply dismissed his pledge as "a cover to blind his own Party." In their minds, the main problem was one of logistics: How could they negotiate with Burr when such an act would condemn both Burr and the Federalists as self-interested and oblivious to the public will? When Federalists later attempted to negotiate with Jefferson, they faced the same problem. The prevailing distrust of such private bargaining was an immense obstacle complicating all efforts to resolve the tie.

The crucial moment of decision came after the Federalists had relinquished their hopes for Burr, finally taking his silence as lack of interest. Rather than simply surrender the battle, however, some Federalists—most notably, James Bayard—tried to strike a deal with Jefferson, to get his assurance concerning a few basic Federalist demands. Specifically, they wanted to be sure that he would support the navy, maintain public credit, and retain some Federalists in public office. Most accounts of this key moment in the election crisis give short shrift to this negotiation. Historians recognize that Bayard decided the election but are unclear about the precise chain of events that led to his decision, some suggesting that he misunderstood Jefferson's response and threw the election under the false assumption that they had come to an agreement.[97] The truth, however, is far more complex—and it is Jefferson, not Bayard, who took the most decisive course of action.

As Bayard himself later explained it, after weeks of balloting, he made a last attempt to "obtain terms of capitulation" from one of the candidates. Unable to speak directly with them without appearing to scheme, he intimated his intentions to Edward Livingston, Burr's friend and supposed agent, and John Nicholas, Jefferson's "particular friend." Livingston denied having any influence with Burr, leading Bayard to give up on the New Yorker. Nicholas, however, was willing to discuss Federalist terms and, having heard them, declared them rea-

Fig. 33. *James Bayard* (1767–1815), by Charles Balthazar Julian Fevret de Saint-Memin, 1801. This portrait was painted the same year that Bayard played a key role in settling the electoral tie between Jefferson and Burr. His children, grandchildren, and great-grandchildren were defending his name from the taint of this election as late as 1907. (Courtesy of The Baltimore Museum of Art, Bequest of Helen Bayard)

sonable. Assuring Bayard that he was friendly with Jefferson and the men who would be "about him" as president, Nicholas stated that he could "solemnly declare it as his opinion" that Jefferson would abide by Bayard's demands. Bayard, however, refused to change his vote without Jefferson's direct confirmation, which Nicholas refused to seek.[98] Before he conceded the election, Bayard wanted Jefferson's personal pledge; once again, honor was the ultimate bond of political trust (fig. 33).

Unable to coax more out of Nicholas, Bayard repeated his terms to Samuel Smith, who was likewise intimate with Jefferson. At the instigation of two other Federalists, Smith had already spoken to Jefferson twice about these same terms, and he repeated Jefferson's comments to Bayard. Though this conversation has been left out of virtually all modern analyses of the 1800 contest, the manner in which Jefferson communicated his thoughts to Smith was what ultimately determined the election. As Smith later recounted it, when he approached Jefferson with the Federalist terms, the Virginian first declared that "any opinion that he should give at this time might be attributed to improper motives"—in other words, he did not want to seem guilty of negotiating his way into the presidency. Then, with a crucial twist of logic, he added that "he had no hesitation" in discussing his sentiments privately with Smith. Engaged in mere conversation, Jefferson then responded to each Federalist proposition in turn, backing up his statements with references to his writings and political career.[99] In essence, Jefferson took advantage of the blurred bounds between politicking and socializing to make an official statement by unofficial means.

The ambiguity that enabled Jefferson to negotiate in this manner spawned controversy when Bayard and Smith interpreted Jefferson's words in different ways. Bayard heard an official commitment to an agreement and therefore convinced his Federalist small-state pledgemates to withhold their votes and allow Jefferson to win (fig. 34). Smith insisted that he had simply relayed Jefferson's informal thoughts without any intention of making a deal. Of course, both men were right, as was Jefferson—in a formal sense—when he angrily declared that he had not bargained with Bayard (though he went too far when he asserted that the Federalist had invented the charge without "any other object than to calumniate me").[100] At fault were the ambiguities of a politics of friendship that blurred the public, the private, the political, and the personal. Depending on one's worldview, Jefferson's comments could be interpreted as anything one wanted them to be.

Thus, Burr's *Memoirs* is essentially correct. From Burr's point of view, Jefferson *did* intrigue for the presidency, and Davis cited direct

Fig. 34. Election banner, 1801. This rare piece of political paraphernalia from the presidential election of 1800 celebrates Jefferson's victory. Surrounding Jefferson are the words "T. JEFFERSON President of the United States of AMERICA******JOHN ADAMS is no MORE." (Courtesy of the Museum of American History, Smithsonian Institution)

testimony from Bayard and Smith to prove it. Indeed, angered by reading Jefferson's protestations in the "Anas," John Quincy Adams said that he had heard this same testimony from Bayard himself.[101] Yet Jefferson likewise could truthfully deny such a claim, asserting that he had done nothing more than talk informally with a friend. The reverse was true as well. Jefferson could correctly accuse Burr of attempting to win the presidency—and Burr could just as truthfully deny that he had any such intentions. A politics of friendship was a politics of deniability. Where the most political actions seemed personal in nature, it was easy to deny political ambitions, even to oneself.

The Legacy of 1801

The taint of the electoral tie remained with Burr to the end of his days. Even when he revealed the "truth" in his memoirs, his peers and posterity remained unconvinced. In part, this stemmed from Burr's unfortunate failings of character. Heedlessly ambitious and cheerfully sly, he made it virtually impossible to believe that he had not schemed for the presidency. His resultant dishonor affected the reputations of almost everyone he associated with during the course of the election. Smith, Ogden, Livingston, Green, Bishop, and Bayard all suffered guilt by association in later years, compelled to defend their names in newspapers and private letters; even Burr's family was contaminated by his dishonor, as demonstrated by a newspaper attack on Burr's uncle Pierpont Edwards. Indeed, because national politics was organized around networks of friends, the shadow of the controversy reached beyond the small circle of Burr intimates who were directly involved in the contest to cloud the reputations of many of their friends as well. To a lesser degree, the same held true of Jefferson; long after the election, some of his supporters were saddled with charges of intrigue and self-interest. The power of such a charge is apparent in the long-lived impact of the controversy. Indeed, it is remarkable how often those involved were raked over the coals for actions long past—and because of the network of friendships that defined this political event, an attack against one man was an attack against all.

Of course, Burr was always at the center of the controversy. After circulating for months as a whisper campaign, rumors about his supposed intrigue for the presidency were committed to print in early 1802, at the outset of a two-year pamphlet war between Clintonians and Burrites in New York City. Confronted with concrete evidence of the tattered state of his reputation, Burr tried to repair the damage in every way possible. He made a public statement about the circulating "charges and insinuations" in a letter to New Jersey governor Joseph Bloomfield that was published in newspapers around the nation. He solicited a written denial of any wrongdoing from Edward Livingston, and convinced Hamilton to take back some of his accusations in a brief statement in the *Evening Post*.[102] To bolster his reputation by association, he joined the Society of the Cincinnati, an organization of Revolutionary War officers, asserting his membership among the political elite.

In addition to Burr's personal campaign, his friends defended his name in pamphlets and newspapers, attempting to discredit circulating rumors by attacking Burr's attackers. As could be expected, such charges and countercharges of honor and dishonor produced a rash of honor disputes—including a near encounter between Hamilton and Burr. (Recall that during his 1804 duel negotiations with Hamilton, Burr claimed that he had almost challenged Hamilton twice before but that Hamilton had "anticipated me by coming forward Voluntarily and making apologies and concessions.") Hamilton's vaguely worded *Evening Post* denial, stating that "he had no *personal knowledge* of any negotiation between Colonel Burr and any person whatever" respecting the presidency, was probably Hamilton's concession to avoid armed conflict.[103]

Burr took his boldest action in February 1802, by chance on the one-year anniversary of his loss to Jefferson. Invited by Bayard to attend a Federalist celebration of George Washington's birthday, he seized the opportunity to throw the gauntlet before the Virginians who had betrayed him; as with many such social events, the 1802 fete was unquestionably political as well. Taking advantage of the stunned silence that greeted his arrival, he offered a toast—"An *union* of all *honest* men"—a somewhat cryptic statement that becomes clear in light of the 1801 controversy. His comment was a deliberate slap at Jefferson and his friends, who, by Burr's account, had raised themselves to power through dishonest means, as well as a welcome call to others who shared his distrust of the Virginians. Burr was taking advantage of the North-South divide in national politics to position himself as the potential leader of a northern party.

The reverberations of Burr's 1802 defense campaign were unavoidably far-reaching. He himself involved Livingston, Hamilton, Jefferson and his friends, and several of his own intimate friends, who in turn pulled others into the controversy. Timothy Green, Abraham Bishop, and John Swartwout all felt compelled to defend themselves in the newspapers, as did Samuel Smith, who eventually filed a libel suit against an attacker. Bayard likewise revisited the events of 1801 in 1802, attacking Jefferson on the floor of the Senate for intriguing his way into office; indeed, Bayard invited Burr to the Federalist celebration of Washington's birthday as a deliberate attack against Jefferson and "the proud and aspiring Lords of the Ancient Dominion." A few weeks later, an anonymous writer defended Jefferson by attacking Bayard's speech in a pamphlet.[104]

Such charges and countercharges did not stop here. Rather, they ebbed and flowed with the current of political events, reemerging when sectional divisions arose or when one of the participants was under attack. For the ever ambitious and competitive Burr, they were never entirely out of view. His efforts to clear his name took on a new urgency in January 1804, as he looked toward New York's gubernatorial campaign—his last stab at public office. So desperate was he to remove the stain of 1801 that he actually turned to Jefferson. Burr's enemies were using Jefferson's name "to destroy him," Burr explained in a personal meeting (carefully documented in one of Jefferson's memoranda). "Something was necessary" from Jefferson "to prevent and deprive them of that weapon, some mark of favor . . . which would declare to the world that he retired" with the president's confidence. Not surprisingly, Jefferson refused.[105]

Two weeks later, Burr tried a different approach, filing a libel suit against James Cheetham, the man who had first published the rumors about his intrigue. His efforts spawned yet another burst of controversy, for in the course of preparing for trial, Cheetham's counsel obtained depositions from several key players in the 1801 controversy, including James Bayard and Samuel Smith. Burr even committed a crime in the service of his reputation, attempting to doctor Smith's written testimony; as with any matter of honor, what mattered to Burr was his reputation in the eyes of others, not the means by which he defended it. Outraged by Burr's libel suit, Jefferson vented his spleen in a memorandum that ultimately attracted the attention of Bayard's son, whose counterattack, in turn, led Burr to compile his *Memoirs*.[106]

Despite Burr's efforts, the stain on his reputation proved indelible. His most extreme attempt to clear his name took place on July 11, 1804, when he met Hamilton on the field of honor, spurred by his desire to refute the claim that he was capable of "despicable" actions; indeed, an awareness of Burr's ongoing struggle to redeem his reputation explains the anger and desperation that led him to issue that fateful challenge. Over the course of the next two decades, other participants in the 1800 contest suffered a similar fate, defending themselves repeatedly against charges of disloyalty, dishonesty, and self-interest. But it was not until 1830 that the controversy of 1801 received a serious public airing, the stakes suddenly raised by the publication of Jefferson's history, which seemed to declare as fact what many regarded as the warped personal vision of Thomas Jefferson.

The impetus for this hearing was a sectional dispute in the Senate over the development of public lands. In the course of defending the South, South Carolinian Robert Hayne cited Jefferson's "Anas" as historical evidence. Two days later, sparked by Hayne's claim that the "Anas" was a record of fact, John Clayton of Delaware stated that he wanted to disprove a charge in that same volume that dishonored the memory of James Bayard, an "illustrious statesman" from his home state whose dishonor tainted Delaware as well. He then read aloud Jefferson's memorandum of February 12, 1801, in which Edward Livingston told Jefferson that Bayard had tried to bribe Samuel Smith to vote for Burr. Dramatically turning to the aged Livingston and Smith—both senators—Clayton demanded that they disprove the accusation. Smith replied that Bayard had been too honorable to make such a proposition, Livingston claimed to have no memory of the transaction, and Clayton declared his purpose served. But the attack on Jefferson's veracity was too much for Thomas Hart Benton of Missouri, who jumped to his feet to defend the Virginian's name, as did Hayne at the Senate's next meeting. Clayton concluded the matter by explaining that he meant no disrespect to Jefferson but that "at every hazard—let the consequences fall where they may," he would "repel every imputation, like that contained in the memoir, upon the memory of Mr. Bayard . . . whose honor in that transaction cannot be touched without a reflection on the State herself."[107] Richard Bayard and his brother James later continued this argument in a defense pamphlet entitled "Documents Relating to the Presidential Election of the Year 1801," which John Quincy Adams encouraged editor Hezekiah Niles to publish. And as in days gone by, the aged James Madison came to Jefferson's rescue in the *National Gazette,* loyally defending Jefferson's reputation.[108]

Benton's response to Clayton's defense shows that one man's reputation could not be defended without affecting another's. By asserting Bayard's innocence, Clayton had suggested that Jefferson was a liar. In life, Bayard and Jefferson had been bitter opponents; now, in death, their reputations were perpetually linked, their two worldviews diametrically opposed. The same held true of other political opponents, such as Hamilton and Jefferson. So intertwined were their reputations by 1830 that one Hamilton sympathizer invited Hamilton's son James to witness the senatorial attack on the "Anas" as a vindication of his father's name; James Hamilton was seated in the gallery on that day and later recounted the event in his own memoirs for precisely this purpose.[109]

For these men, as for others, there was little room for compromise in their political viewpoints; indeed, national political combat was premised on such intolerance. Republican political fervor was justified by the threat of Federalism, and vice versa. Among men who distrusted and disapproved of national party combat, only dire threats to the republic could justify their own partisan politicking. It was their absolute conviction in the righteousness of their cause—a cause premised on the corruption of their foes—that enabled national politicians to justify their partisan activities to themselves and, ultimately, to posterity. Such logic enabled Jefferson to explain away his most questionable political maneuvers, even to himself. Hamilton, too, justified his most questionable political acts as public-minded attempts to stem a national crisis; after the Federalist defeat in 1801, he became particularly strident in his attempts to convince Federalists to temporarily violate political proprieties for the public good. Indeed, many national politicians saw their most reprehensible politicking as extreme measures aimed at serving the public in a time of crisis. A crisis mentality fueled the process of political change; ironically, republican adherence to the general good contributed to the development of democratic partisan politicking.

A man's public-minded political sins were justified by the crimes of his opponent. It is these bonds of reputation between enemies as well as friends that explain Burr's treatment at the hands of his peers. For Jefferson, Hamilton, and their supporters, Burr's every political victory was a slap at their worldview—a suggestion that their political sins were unwarranted. This was the driving force behind Jefferson's seemingly pathological hatred of Burr. After the 1800 election, Burr's very existence attested to Jefferson's worst political behavior—his faithlessness, his self-interest, his regional bias. In a sense, Jefferson was haunted by his own reflection as cast back at him through the distorted looking glass of Burr. Thus the intensity of Jefferson's desire to crush Burr at his 1807 treason trial: to destroy Burr would be a personal act of self-defense. Jefferson's rancorous hatred of Burr was, at heart, inspired by his intense concern for his honor and reputation in the eyes of his peers and, even more pressingly, in the eyes of history. The same holds true for Hamilton's hatred of Burr and, indeed, for many other seemingly pathological political rivalries of the period.

The difference, with Burr, was his lack of public-minded motives, for without any personal "theory" of republicanism, his actions could be attributed to nothing other than self-interest. In the conclusion of his account of the 1800 election, Davis claims that Burr's greatest mistake was in "permitting his reputation to be assailed, without contradiction, in cases where it was perfectly defensible"—a claim that is only half true. Burr should have attended more to his *political* reputation in the eyes of his peers, professing (if not feeling) an interest in the public good, rather than relying on his status to excuse his politics. In neglecting to do so, he destroyed his personal reputation as well as his public career. His precipitous fall from power reveals the continued importance of republican principle and personal honor in early national politics.

The long-lived nature of the 1801 controversy suggests the fundamental ways we have misunderstood early national politics, including one of its most defining features: the intensely personal nature of political combat. Party bonds were personal above all else; they were voluntary ties of trust and commitment—friendships, by every sense of the word. Political combat forged, tested, and destroyed these bonds of friendship, eliciting a level of fear, suspicion, and rancor that often seems exaggerated or delusionally "paranoid." Yet to men who were personally involved in a high-level political experiment of their own making, with public careers, private lives, and personal reputations all at the mercy of the tides of politics and the opinions of the masses, it would have been irrational *not* to display such feelings.

In 1800, growing awareness of the fragility of national partisan bonds drove politicians to cling to these loyalties all the more tightly. When political friendships proved too weak to sustain a national party, politicians reduced partisan ties to their bare minimum, defining them as commitments of personal honor, if nothing else; in the face of flagging partisan loyalty, at least they could rely on the instinct for self-preservation that would compel any man of honor to remain true to his word. It was this instinct to protect one's reputation that *The Federalist* cited as the ultimate assurance that high officeholders would behave. To a certain extent, the assumption proved valid. The mandates of personal honor determined Burr's equivocal middle course, restrained Jefferson from openly negotiating with the Federalists, compelled Bayard to fulfill his "sacred duty" to the state of Delaware, and cemented the many caucuses that emerged during the election. Unfortunately, as national politicians discovered amid the tensions of the election, the path of honor was exceedingly subjective; what was honorable to one man was opportunism or personal betrayal to another. The result was a maelstrom of conflicting accusations, none of them patently true or false.

At the heart of this whirlpool of dissension was the charge of disloyalty. In a political world structured by personal friendships, disloyalty to one's party was a betrayal of one's friends that proved a man faithless, self-interested, and dishonorable. Every pledge of honor sworn during the election testifies to this link between personal honor and political loyalty. It is this interconnectedness that is most foreign to modern sensibilities. To national politicians, politics was about friendship, not party; it involved honor as much as ideology; it relied on bonds of personal loyalty, not partisanship; and it was fueled by a concern for the public good, not by party spirit. In looking for the onset of the competitive self-interest or "liberalism" of the modern world, we have obscured the process of political change.

This realization reveals the ground-level reality of the period's cultural shift from deference to democracy. Politicians did not abandon their aristocratic pretensions and republican ideals on their way to a more glorious democratic future; they did not stifle their sense of political morality in the face of electoral realities. Rather, they adapted their assumptions and expectations to the situation at hand, struggling to accommodate their ideals and their actions. This link between honor and politics, the personal and the political, gave early national political combat its passion and its sting, for it bound together a politician's personal character with his political principles and actions; in essence, it instilled into politics a moral and personal dimension that is often overlooked. This personal process of accommodation among a variety of populations constitutes the reality of political change.

It also reveals the link between early national politics and the "party systems" of later years. When alliances of friends had become established enough to be almost institutional—when men could rally under the banner of a party name rather than the reputation of a political chief—politics became a war between opposing armies rather than a personal contest of reputations. For the very reasons that *The Federalist* No. 70 suggested that group politicking was dangerous—it hid each man's personal failings behind a blur of joined reputations—it was also eminently useful. In essence, there was only one way out of this endless battle of reputations: the anonymity of party warfare. The shift toward a national politics of party was a gradual process that took place one decision at a time, making it virtually impossible to declare a single defining moment of birth. Reconstructing the logic of these decisions reveals the evolution of American politics.

Epilogue
Constructing American History

To self-conscious, reputation-minded national politicians, only one thing could be more volatile than the partisan battles of the 1790s: documenting them in the historical record. By declaring winners and losers, heroes and villains, a history of the founding could shape national character to an extraordinary degree. Equally alarming, it could destroy reputations with the stroke of a pen. Yet the founding era was slipping from view. Washington's death in 1799 and Jefferson's "revolution" of 1800 were unquestionable heralds of historical change, particularly to those who had been overthrown.

William Plumer of New Hampshire was one such Federalist. Tall, spare, simple in dress and manner, and largely self-educated, he was a lawyer with extensive experience in local politics—much like William Maclay—who had never been farther from home than Boston (fig. 35).[1] Elected to the Senate in 1802, he arrived in Washington impressed—and depressed—by the spirit of change. A powerless victim of a political revolution, Plumer knew that he was witnessing a far-reaching transition. Sensing that the ground was shifting beneath his feet, his thoughts turned to the historical record. As he explained it, "With the changes & revolution of time & of parties," invaluable "facts & opinions . . . are rapidly hasting to oblivion."[2] The Federalist worldview was dying, perhaps never to rise again.

This gloomy prognosis struck him with unexpected force shortly after his arrival in the capital, the result of a chance encounter. Glancing into the congressional lumber room, Plumer saw a horrific sight: an enormous cache of discarded congressional documents, tossed about in stunning disarray. Consisting largely of spare copies of reports and

Fig. 35. *William Plumer* (1759–1850), by Charles Balthazar Julian Fevret de Saint-Memin, 1804. Painted roughly two months after Plumer arrived in Washington, D.C., this drawing shows something of his moderation, congeniality, and good temper. He considered it "a correct likeness." (Courtesy of the New Hampshire Historical Society)

papers left in desks by departing congressmen, the pages "lay on the floor without any order—covered & mixed with dirt, plaster, and rubbish." Water leaked onto them during rainstorms; workmen trod them underfoot.[3] Upon examination Plumer discovered that some of them dated as far back as the First Continental Congress. The Federalist era was disintegrating before his eyes.

Distressed that something "so valuable, should be suffered thus wantonly to be destroyed," Plumer determined to collect "a compleat sett" for himself. Over the course of the next four years, he spent hours at a time sifting through documents, eventually filling several trunks.

He also solicited correspondence from colleagues and copied notes from the Senate's Executive Journal; when Senate secretary Otis—the same Otis who had bedeviled Maclay—became nervous about Plumer's note taking, the determined senator memorized excerpts instead, transcribing what he remembered at night. By the end of his term of office, he had accumulated the journals of every Congress from 1774 to his own, as well as enough documents to fill between four and five hundred bound volumes—one of the largest collections of government papers held by a private citizen, even after he donated a large box to the Massachusetts Historical Society, and a trunkful to a friend. "I greatly rejoice that I have fulfilled the task I imposed upon myself—& that I have rescued so many useful papers from inevitable ruin," he wrote at the close of his efforts.[4] In his mind, he had salvaged the nation's history from an ignominious death in the cold, damp depths of a storeroom.

In one form or another, Plumer would continue his historical quest for five decades. It gave meaning to his useless national tenure, carried him through later controversies, and structured his retirement and old age. The conviction that he was assisting in the construction of American history gave his life purpose; his historical writings would be his contribution to the world. Over the course of fifty years, Plumer's personal investment in American history never faltered, though his methods changed. First an archivist, then a diarist, a historian, a biographer, and an autobiographer, he reached for historical truth in a variety of media, eventually discovering it in his own life and career. To Plumer, in the end, reputation and character mattered above all else.

Attempting to capture the essence of America's difficult founding, Plumer revealed far more than he intended. His efforts document the onset of a period of intense historical consciousness, as the aging founding generation wrestled with their accomplishments and legacy. Plumer was keenly aware of the significance of this moment, investing inordinate amounts of time and energy into his own historical endeavors and responding to those of his contemporaries as they were published, one by one. In essence, he documented a historical debate as the period's most renowned politicians and their progeny grappled with the meaning of their life's work. No two of these histories exactly agree. Yet they contain an emotional truth that would be impossible for later generations to recapture. Partisan, personal, and aggressively self-promoting, they are the 1790s writ large, as politicians and their descendants overstated their cases in a desperate attempt to shape the historical record—and their own reputations—one last time.[5]

Politics as History

Plumer did not begin his historical enterprise to bolster his reputation. In fact, fueled by a preservationist concern for documentary evidence, he was all but invisible in his earliest efforts. But the varied outrages of Jefferson's administration soon spurred him to invest more of himself in his work. In fact, it was the 1803 Louisiana Purchase that set Plumer's pen in motion. Although Congress was not due to meet until November, Jefferson had convened it early to discuss the treaty that would cede the territory, hoping for quick Senate approval. It was Jefferson's apparent haste that alarmed Plumer; the president seemed determined to railroad the treaty through the Senate with barely a pause for consideration, despite the many loopholes, ambiguities, and dangerous precedents that Plumer saw throughout. Unable to stop the Republican tide and enraged by Jefferson's dictatorial attitude, Plumer watched in horror as the Senate advised ratification within three days of receiving the treaty—he and the five other New England Federalists casting the only negative votes. It was Plumer's helpless displeasure in the face of this outrage that compelled him to start keeping records.

There were any number of reasons for such efforts. In part, Plumer was documenting legislative mistakes that were bound to have serious repercussions. When disaster struck, the Republicans would be only too eager to transfer blame, but Plumer's notes would preserve their words and actions for the record. He paid equal mind to presidential messages and addresses, for there was no telling how Jefferson might twist their ambiguities into whatever would "best suit his crooked policy." Plumer's notes were also an outlet for ideas and emotions that he could not voice on the Senate floor, for reasons both practical and personal. A minority member with little hope of success, he found it difficult and often unwise to air his unpopular views. Equally problematic, he was too intimidated to speak on the national stage, a failing that "surprized & mortified" this veteran of New Hampshire politics, who had "long been in the habit of speaking freely in public."[6]

Thus from October 17, 1803, through the end of his six-year term, Plumer diligently documented congressional proceedings, taking cursory notes during the day and fleshing them out in a journal at night. The resulting three volumes fill 643 pages in published form.[7] An eyewitness account of a New England Federalist's experiences during Jefferson's administration, Plumer's notes offer invaluable insight into a range of subjects. As a historical record, they contain a detailed account of Senate proceedings in the Seventh through Ninth Congresses, a valuable addition to the two other congressional chronicles of this period, the *Annals of Congress* and the diary of John Quincy Adams. They also suggest the flavor of political life in early Washington — the barely suppressed chaos of congressional debate and the choreographed charm of Jefferson's dinner parties, the crowded boardinghouses and the mania for horse races (the Senate clock was set thirty minutes ahead to give senators time to get to the racetrack after adjournment). Considering the wealth of information within their pages, they have received remarkably little scholarly attention.[8]

A somewhat obscure local politician — now senator — whose insecurities and fears inspired him to keep a journal, Plumer bears a striking resemblance to another dismayed senator of fourteen years past: William Maclay. The two men adopted the same method, filling several volumes with observations extracted from cursory notes. Both documented the tone and content of congressional debate and the details of everyday life. Members of a beleagured minority, both felt dwarfed on the national stage, powerless to stem what they perceived as a tide of destruction. Maclay saw monarchists constructing walls and Plumer saw democrats tearing them down, but both men poured their concerns onto paper each night.

Yet there is one fundamental difference between the two journals. Maclay wrote for an audience of state legislators. His purposes were immediate: by revealing the truth of his term of office, he would thus demonstrate his public-mindedness, expose his aristocratic foes, redeem his reputation, and win reelection. Plumer did the precise opposite. His notes were private, at least for the present. He was looking to the future; as he suggested on the title page of his first volume, he was recording "memoranda"—records intended for later use. In essence, Plumer's intentions reflect the impact of a decade of national governance. Caught up in the founding moment, Maclay wrote for the present; watching that moment slip from view, Plumer wrote for the ages. His memoranda thus lack the emotional rawness of Maclay's diary, for Plumer was building a historical archive of events and personalities, not chronicling his efforts in the hope of reelection. An 1804 entry reveals the direction of Plumer's thoughts: it is misdated Wednesday, November 28, 1784.[9]

Plumer's obsession with history represents an enormous mental shift. In his mind, something momentous had already been accomplished; to Maclay, everything had yet to be done. President Jefferson's political delusions might destroy their experiment in government, but regardless of its fate a generation of men had made a breathtaking leap of logic, staking their lives, fortunes, and sacred honor on a new and unproven mode of governance that had endured a decade of crises. Proud of their achievements and eager to preserve them for posterity, they were exceedingly paper-minded: notes must be taken, documents preserved, correspondence collected and organized. This impulse to inform and educate posterity made the founding generation instinctive archivists; it fueled Madison's detailed notes of the Federal Convention, drove Jefferson to tinker with his correspondence until his dying days, and compelled Hamilton, Burr, Adams, and countless others to put pen to paper to set the record straight. Their historical significance was never far from their minds, a current of anxiety that invested politics-as-usual with the weight of history. Plumer's archival efforts thus were not unusual, though he undertook them with a rare energy and focus.

Initially restricting his notes to interesting or significant debates, Plumer changed his strategy toward the start of his second session as part of an overall shift in his political method. Aware that he had no "rational prospect of doing good" and unwilling to humiliate himself

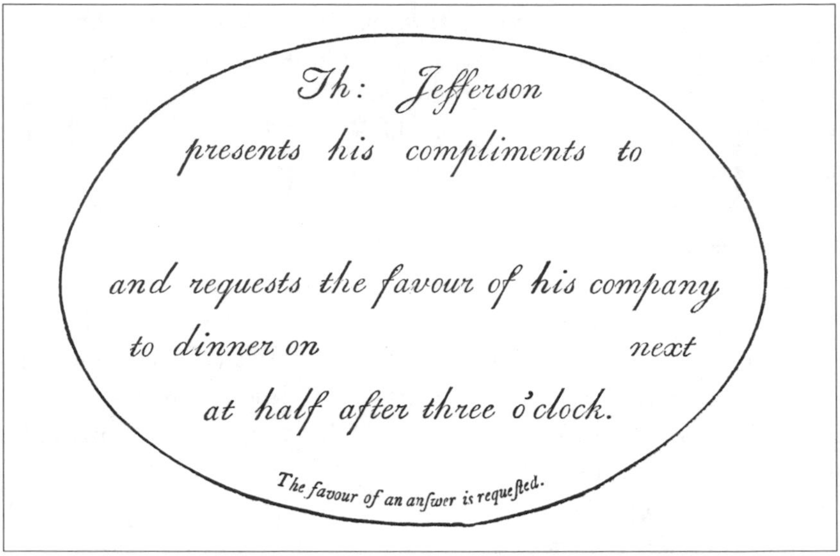

Th: Jefferson
presents his compliments to

and requests the favour of his company
to dinner on next
at half after three o'clock.

The favour of an answer is requested.

Fig. 36. Thomas Jefferson's invitation to dinner, undated. (Sol Feinstone Collection, David Library of the American Revolution, on deposit at the American Philosophical Society)

on the national stage, he decided that it was "imprudent" to enter into debates. Better to become an expert listener. His decision increased the length, intimacy, and subject matter of his memoranda; as the only record of his conversational gleanings, they became more anecdotal. Now he described the exotic costumes of foreign ministers and Indian chiefs, critiqued his colleagues' oratory, mused about their motives, and commented on affairs of honor and Jefferson's pretentiously modest presidential etiquette. He found the wording of Jefferson's dinner invitations particularly grating: "It is *Th:Jefferson* not the *President* that invites—& yet were he not the President I presume I should not be invited" (fig. 36). In his third and final session, such entries multiplied, including more transcribed conversations and political gossip, the product of his fully refined political style. As he explained it, "I speak none . . . & yet my influence on many subjects is not confined to my own vote. I am industrious in all private circles."[10] Proficient at politicking in one-to-one conversations, Plumer filled his notes with his conversational spoils.

Although historians have identified only three volumes of these memoranda, there is in fact a fourth that has been overlooked. Titled "Repository," it is a collection of observations about the personal character of Plumer's peers—*character* meaning both their reputations and their true nature. As Plumer explained it, "*My design* in writing these sheets is meerly to put down some facts—& give some outlines of the character of some of the Rulers of the day." Composed of anecdotes gleaned from private conversations (largely with beleaguered Federalists), it is a catalogue of political gossip—a Federalist version of Jefferson's "Anas."[11] Like Jefferson, Plumer collected anecdotes as insights into character, meticulously documenting their sources. Unlike Jefferson, he was more interested in revealing personal qualities than in exposing political sins, another product of his historian's sensibility.

Each anecdote in the "Repository" offers a flash of insight about a politician's innermost character; although Plumer recorded most of them without interpretation, their implications would be apparent to anyone attuned to the Federalist point of view. Connecticut Senator James Hillhouse told Plumer that at a presidential dinner he heard Jefferson confess that in his youth, news of an Indian war had sent him scurrying "into the woods," where he "dug a hole to hide myself"—evidence of Jefferson's cowardice (fig. 37). Observing Burr's virtual isolation from Jefferson and his cronies, Plumer asked Burr "how he left his friends" and Burr replied, "*They have left me*"—an indictment of the Republicans as false friends. Jefferson's affair of honor with John Walker received lengthy commentary, as did other honor disputes that revealed Republicans behaving badly, suggesting that Jefferson and his friends were not men of honor. Spanning the year covered in Plumer's first and least anecdotal memorandum book, the "Repository" is a companion volume, focusing on character rather than events for the same archival purpose: "to preserve facts that are fast fleeting down the current of time to oblivion to which we are bound."[12] To Plumer the character of the nation's founders was a crucial part of the historical record, an assumption that would have its full impact in years to come.

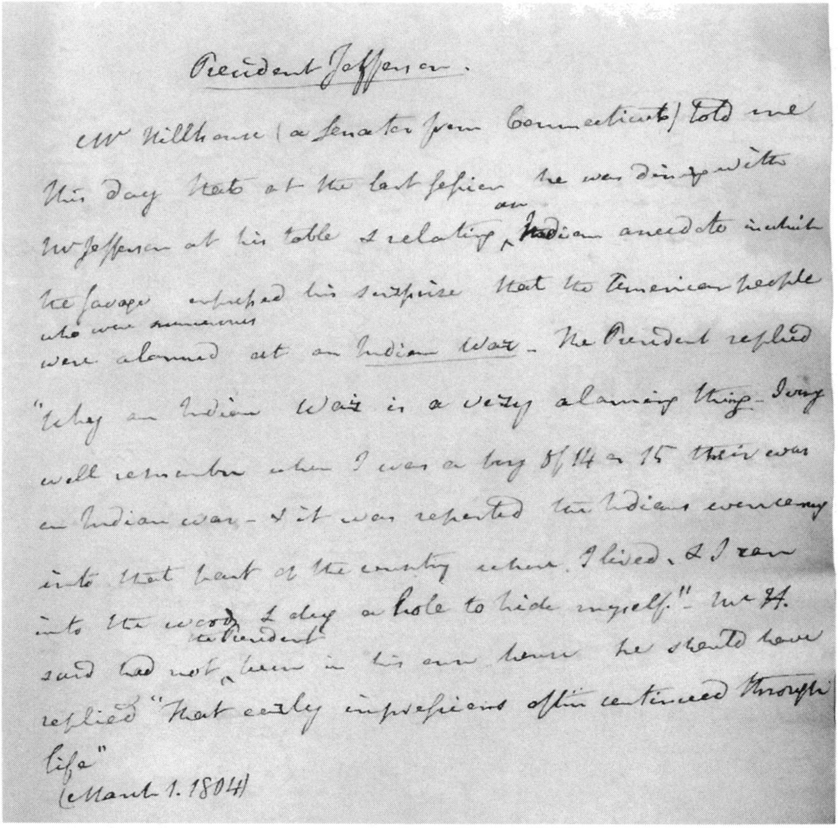

President Jefferson.

Mr Hillhouse (a Senator from Connecticut) told me this day that at the last session he was dining with Mr Jefferson at his table & relating an Indian anecdote in which the savage expressed his surprise that the American people who were numerous were alarmed at an Indian War — The President replied "Why an Indian War is a very alarming thing — I very well remember when I was a boy of 14 or 15 there was an Indian war — & it was reported the Indians were coming into that part of the country where I lived, & I ran into the woods & dug a hole to hide myself." Mr H. said had not the President been in his own house he should have replied "that early impressions often continued through life"
(March 1. 1804)

Fig. 37. Page from Plumer's "Repository," March 1, 1804. In this Federalist version of Jefferson's "Anas," Plumer recorded gossip and observations about his foes. Here, Connecticut Senator James Hillhouse relates a dinner conversation with Jefferson, who recalled that as a boy he had once fled into the woods in fear of Indians "& dug a hole to hide myself." Hillhouse wished that he had replied "that early impressions often continued through life"—or in other words, once a coward, always a coward. (Courtesy of the New Hampshire Historical Society)

Modern chroniclers assume that Plumer's significance ends with his note taking, but in fact, his historical mission extended much further. Throughout most of his Senate tenure, he had been amassing the pieces of a puzzle to be sorted by a future historian. His intentions are apparent in the words that he used to describe his writings; *memo-*

randum, register, and *repository* all refer to a rough record of observations intended for future use.[13] His thoughts changed, however, with the approach of his final term of office. Considering his prospects as he traveled home at the break before his last session, Plumer realized that he himself might be that future historian. Over the course of the next few weeks, he gave the idea serious consideration, characteristically recording his thoughts in a lengthy memorandum.

His ambition was to attempt something new and necessary: a history of the government of the United States. Although there were histories of the Revolution and of individual states, there was no study of national governance, its structure, dynamic, evolution, and leaders. Such a work would doubtless guide future statesmen. If it were well written, it might also improve the poor reputation of American literature on the world stage. Not to mention the personal gains that would accompany such an effort. "If well executed it would be an imperishable monument that would perpetuate my name more effectually than anything I could do," Plumer reasoned. "It would exist when columns of marble are dissolved & crumbled to dust."[14]

Plumer could earn lasting fame. But he might also "tarnish & destroy much of the little fame" he had earned—one of many arguments against the project. He was too old and weak to undertake such an enormous task; he did not have enough documentary evidence (even with his unparalleled archive); he would need "indefatigable industry" and patience; he would have to read and evaluate a library of books; his wife was ill; his children required his attention; the book's sales would never recuperate the project's great expense; he was no scholar, read no second language, knew little about geography and science, and wrote slowly. Despite all these considerations, however, the prospect of being "useful to others and honorable to myself" won out. By the end of his lengthy memorandum, he was wondering whether to divide the book into chapters or letters, and his project had expanded to encompass "a general history of the United States, to commence from the first discovery of America by the Europeans," including the "biography of eminent Americans."[15]

In many ways, Plumer was ideally qualified for the task. Although he arrived in Washington an embittered, true-blue Federalist, he had become more moderate by the end of his term. As he reflected upon learning of his failed reelection, "I am too much of a federalist to have republican votes, & too much of a Republican deeply to interest federalists in my favor." Temperate in his politics and friendly with congressmen of all stripes, he intended to be an impartial historian, favoring neither Republicans nor Federalists. He sought truth; the word rings like a watchword throughout his writings. "An historian, like a witness, is bound to relate the truth, the whole truth, & nothing but the truth," was the epigraph on the first page of notes for his history.[16] This was to be no partisan diatribe. Plumer assured others of as much when he solicited their assistance. He was not going to attack or defend but rather reveal and explain.

To veterans of the contentious, strife-ridden 1790s, however, historical truth could be problematic. The national government's first decade had been a period of extremes, in emotion, actions, and accusations. Although public figures had often acted as they saw best for the public good, their behavior could seem less admirable in hindsight, examined in the cool light of day. Exposed by an unfriendly observer out of context, the sins of the 1790s could cut a reputation to ribbons. For America's self-declared Founders, political history was thus intensely, dangerously personal. Not only would it shape national character and governance, but it would determine their status as Founding Fathers.

The construction of a national history was crucial to their lives and legacies, an obsession of their old age. There were unpleasant truths to reveal and records to set straight, accomplishments to document and credit to claim. By transcribing their achievements for future generations, politicians were demanding their place in the annals of history, proving themselves Founders, like Plutarch's heroes of old. The personal stakes were high, worthy of intense efforts and energies, and a conflicting account demanded passionate resistance. The result was an ongoing biographical feud of clashing reputations and conflicting points of view. The person who took a stand in this war was playing with fire.

Plumer learned this for himself when he confronted President Jefferson with his own writing plans. Determined to take advantage of his last months in office, Plumer decided to discuss his history with the men who would people it, in the hope of getting access to their papers. Aiming high at the outset, he spoke with Jefferson first. To alleviate any fears of a Federalist bias, Plumer began by stating his goal of impartiality: it was his "intention to state facts & delineate characters fairly & impartialy" so that "the *reader* should not be able to ascertain, from the work, to what sect or party" he belonged. These comforting words produced a strange reaction. "I observed the countenance of the President repeatedly changed. At some moments there was the appearance of uneasiness and embarrassment—at others he seemed pleased—He alternately looked at me, & then fixed his eyes on the floor. I could perceive his mind was agitated with different emotions."[17] Attributing this odd display to displeasure (barely) repressed, Plumer departed, hungry for an explanation.

He received one a few days later from John Quincy Adams. Plumer had great admiration for Adams, who shared his aversion to "rigid" partisans of any persuasion. So after requesting (and receiving) access to Adams's papers, Plumer questioned him about Jefferson's puzzling display. "The President cannot be a lover of history," Adams responded. "There are prominent traits in his character, & important actions in his life, that he would not wish should be delineated, & transmitted to posterity." Madison would be equally displeased, Adams predicted. "He will suffer in history."[18] Plumer had observed Jefferson's visceral reaction to his political past, Adams suggested; the thought of his reputation suffering before the eyes of posterity had produced a visible shudder.

Jefferson was not alone in his feelings. To America's self-conscious founders, historical dishonor was the ultimate threat, condemning its victims to an eternity of abuse. A lifetime of work, sacrifice, and vigilant protection of one's reputation could be undone with the stroke of a pen. Such a staggering blow could not help but invite retribution, making history writing a risky business. So *National Intelligencer* editor Samuel H. Smith cautioned Plumer upon learning of his plans. Smith advised against "publishing that part of it which is the most important, *our own times*." Better to "write it & leave directions to have it a posthumous work," for if Plumer published the book while living, he "must necessarily give mortal offense—& must retire from the world." Such a "cotemporary history could not be published with truth and safety," agreed John Quincy Adams, his use of the word *safety* hinting at the threat of gunplay. No matter how impartial Plumer intended his history to be, the only escape from the barbs of partisanship was the detachment of death, as Jefferson well knew when he planted his history among his papers to be discovered after his demise.[19]

If Plumer had written about his own times, he might have confronted such weighty decisions, but he never made it that far. Although he worked diligently for nine years, after 260 pages he had barely reached the seventeenth century. Given his ever-expanding literary ambitions (he ultimately began his history with the invention of hieroglyphics), he did not have sufficient materials or time to produce a work to his own satisfaction.[20] The more historical context he sought, the wider he felt compelled to cast his intellectual net, and the further his text drifted from its purpose. Historical truth seemed beyond his reach. Putting his project aside when he became governor of New Hampshire in 1816, he never resumed it. But his desire to leave his mark on the historical record had not abated.

History as Politics

Chronicling historical events had proven difficult, time-consuming, and ultimately unsatisfying. At the outset of Plumer's efforts, he had expressed interest in two things: the creation and evolution of the national government and the biographies of its first officeholders. Never extending beyond John Smith and the establishment of Virginia, Plumer's history included neither. So in the 1820s, Plumer changed strategies, transferring his energies to a second project that he had begun in 1808: a series of biographical portraits of every eminent American from the time of Columbus.[21] Forced by his unwieldy history to distill American history to its essence, Plumer focused on character above all else.

His first efforts in this vein had been inspired by the spate of George Washington biographies that appeared shortly after the first president's death; like Jefferson, Plumer considered Marshall's much-acclaimed *Life of Washington* particularly problematic. "There is in the whole of this ponderous work scarce an anecdote or observation that relates to the private life of Washington," Plumer complained after finishing it. The work resembled "more the reasoning used in treatises on particular subjects, than the plain, direct, dignified style of history, or the simple, familiar narrative of biography." To Plumer, Marshall's partisan objectives obscured the point of biographical writing: encapsulating a person's public and private character in order to inspire, memorialize, and instruct. "The sun is not less glorious for its spots," he declared; Washington's flaws were part of his character and deserved to be noted. Intent on portraying "the *whole truth*," Plumer undertook a "volume of portraits," with Washington as his first entry.[22] Dissatisfied, outraged, or encouraged at Marshall's Federalist bias, other would-be historians also took up their pens.

The founding generation was rushing headlong into a historical discussion; given the personal and violently partisan events it described, it rapidly became more of an argument than a conversation. There was no single narrative, no absolute truth. So Marshall could depict Republicans of the 1790s as small-minded provincials and Jefferson could insist that they were liberal defenders of the Revolutionary flame. Adams could present himself as an independent-minded hero, and Hamilton could declare Adams a loose cannon guided by his lust for high office. Burr could accuse Jefferson of scheming for the presidency and Jefferson could accuse Burr of the same sin. Self-consciously constructing an American history to shape future generations, public-minded national politicians could not help but present it from a personal point of view.

One man's history was another man's partisan diatribe, an accusation that reverberated throughout the first half of the nineteenth century, a period of prolific history writing. The founding generation was dying, taking invaluable and irreplaceable insights with them. Documentary evidence was being mislaid or destroyed. At the outset of the nineteenth century, the politically minded came to a common realization: a history of the nation's founding had yet to be written, and the clock was ticking. The repercussions of this conclusion were immediate and far-reaching. Historical societies were established; records were collected, catalogued, and deposited with them. Surviving participants, looking ahead to their imminent demise, began organizing their papers for publication after death. Jefferson was particularly diligent on this front, carefully structuring his reputation in the eyes of posterity; but he was not alone. Adams, Madison, and a host of others did the same. Burr and Hamilton were marked exceptions to this rule—Hamilton because of his sudden death and Burr because of a chronic distrust of things written. It is not surprising that the reputations of these two men have suffered accordingly, particularly that of Burr, the least paper-minded of his peers.

As suggested by Plumer's reading notes, Washington's death triggered the opening salvo in this historical onslaught: Marshall's *Life of Washington,* replete with documentary evidence culled from Washington's papers. To those who disagreed with Marshall's markedly Federalist perspective, the work posed a sizable threat, for how could one argue with personal letters written by the Father of His Country? Of course, letters could be doctored or quoted out of context; Jefferson accused Marshall of as much. Plumer charged Jefferson with the same crime when he read his *Memoirs* in 1830: "It is apparent [that Jefferson's] letters were prepared by himself for the press; & I have reason to beleive that some of these letters are different from what he wrote to his correspondents." Such trickery might "raise his character in the estimation of some who read them; but they have not that effect on me." Henry Lee, Jr., made the same accusation in a defense of his father entitled *Observations on the Writings of Thomas Jefferson*. Monticello was a "great mint of *press copies*" where letters could be "readily coined" for any purpose, Lee claimed.[23] As suggested by both Plumer and Lee, the only way to refute documentary evidence was by proving the writer—or his biographer—a liar.

The biographical war of the early nineteenth century was thus inescapably bound up with issues of honor. Not only would the losers be banished from the pages of history, but they would be proven dishonorable in the process. Intertwined with the reputations of their subjects and writers, these histories pitted personal characters against one another in a contest for credibility before the public eye. As Timothy Pickering put it, the value of his historical testimony would "depend on the estimate formed of my character by my contemporaries." James Madison's face revealed the pain of such invalidation when he heard of an upcoming biography of Alexander Hamilton. Informed that the work would deny "the authenticity of his (Mr. M's) report of Colo. H's speech in the Federal Convention" and assert that Madison had "abandoned" Hamilton in the 1790s, Madison flashed a look of "painful surprise" followed by a long silence. It speaks well of Madison's character that he refused to consider these charges anything other than honest mistakes.[24]

As both Republicans and Federalists realized, the party that won this literary debate would claim the soul of the republic; by shaping popular conceptions of the nation's founding, they would have a long-reaching influence on later events. History was personal, immediate, and politically significant; in fact, history *was* politics. Thus the impassioned and volatile biographical feud that continued for decades. The argument's thread is intricate and difficult to follow, but its outlines are revealing. Marshall's "five-volumed libel" prompted Jefferson's strategically arranged history; Thomas Jefferson Randolph, the editor of Jefferson's *Memoir,* dismantled this history and concentrated its most scandalous contents—Jefferson's gossip-filled memoranda—into one volume, a historical bombshell even more thunderous than Marshall's. "The fourth volume of Jefferson's *Memoirs,* lately published, has produced considerable excitement here," New Hampshire Representative Samuel Bell wrote to Plumer on January 30, 1830. "It contains a great deal of *little tattle,* and some slanders against the public men of that day, still upon the stage."[25] Only two days earlier, Bell had been privy to a real-life demonstration of the power of Jefferson's "tattle," when Delaware Senator John Clayton had brought Edward Livingston and Samuel Smith to their feet to avow or deny Jefferson's charges about the 1800 election.

Attacking the private characters of many of his contemporaries, Jefferson's *Memoir* inspired a slew of responses, prominent among them Burr's *Memoirs;* indeed, Burr set his memoirs in motion by marking the offensive passages in Jefferson's "Anas." Both Henry Lee's defense of his father and Theodore Dwight's *The Character of Thomas Jefferson as Exhibited in His Own Writings* (1839) adopted a similar strategy, as suggested by their titles. Other writers (largely New Englanders) countered Jefferson's memoirs with conflicting memoirs of their own, such as George Gibbs's *Memoirs of the Administrations of Washington and John Adams Edited From the Papers of Oliver Wolcott, Secretary of the Treasury* (1846); John T. S. Sullivan's *The Public Men of the Revolution . . . in a Series of Letters by the Late Hon. Wm. Sullivan* (1847); and Samuel Goodrich's *Recollections of a Lifetime* (1856). Quotations from Jefferson's papers run throughout these works in an attempt to turn his words on himself. Sullivan's *Public Men of the Revolution,* written in 1834 shortly after the publication of Jefferson's *Memoirs* but not published until 1847 by his son, sets forth the logic behind this strategy: "*Familiar letters*" allowed the sort of "personal descriptions and particular illustrations, which the 'Memoirs and Writings of Thomas Jefferson' make indispensable."[26] Personal musings enabled these writers to counter Jefferson's character attacks with character attacks of their own.

Some "Anas" attackers adopted a different strategy, masking their personal diatribes as objective history. Alden Bradford's *History of the Federal Government* (1840) is one such example, though none surpasses John Church Hamilton's massive seven-volume *History of the Republic of the United States* (1857–64), an attempt to trace "the origin and early policy of this GREAT REPUBLIC" in the life and writings of John Church's father, Alexander Hamilton. Vindicating Hamilton in the text and refuting the "Anas" in the footnotes, the *History of the Republic* was, in truth, an aggressive, brash, no-holds-barred defense of the man who virtually embodied Federalism, an eerily accurate echo of the defensive arrogance of Alexander Hamilton himself. The work's concluding sentence reveals its real subject of study: "At two in the afternoon, my father died." Hamilton's older son James published his own memoirs for similar reasons, intending "to do justice to his Father against the aspersions of Mr. Jefferson, and more recently of Martin Van Buren, in his Inquiry into the origin of Political parties of the United States."[27]

The fist-clenched defensiveness of Hamilton's sons reveals the power of these dueling histories. Sons shared in the disgrace of their fathers; hence the many filiopietistic memoirs written by sons eager to protect their family honor. James and the younger Alexander Hamilton even competed with each other to defend their father's name.[28] Biased, personal, partisan, and focused on honor and reputation, these histories perpetuated the political feuds of decades past, embroiling the second generation in the process. Their father a virtual lightning rod for attacks on the defunct and seemingly corrupt Federalists—Federalist talk of secession in 1804 and 1814 tarring them as traitors as well—several second-generation Hamiltons almost fought duels in his defense. Hamilton's oldest son, Philip, had been mortally wounded in an 1801 duel provoked by an attack on his father. In 1809, James issued a challenge in defense of his father which was rejected, resulting "as was usual at that time, in his [attacker] being posted in the newspapers as a coward." Eager to prove his father's role in writing George Washington's farewell address, James's younger brother John Church almost provoked a duel with his father's dueling adviser of years past, Rufus King.[29] And one unknown joker tried to provoke James into a duel with Aaron Burr. According to Hamilton, his father's old friend Robert Troup appeared in his office and wordlessly handed over a note that read, "Aaron Burr—Sir: Please to meet me with the weapon you choose, on the 15th May, where you murdered my father, at 10 o'clock, with your second. James A. Hamilton." Excited and upset, Hamilton declared the note a forgery but added that if Burr had accepted the challenge, Hamilton would adopt it as his own. Troup insisted that he was not present as Burr's second but simply wanted to confirm that the note was forged, and the matter ended.[30] In attempting to redeem their father's reputation, Hamilton's sons were reliving his life.

Not all works centered around Hamilton and Jefferson, though most either praised or condemned the two as partisan stand-ins for Federalism or Republicanism. Not surprisingly, Burr's *Memoirs* were as controversial as his life, some reviewers complaining that editor Matthew Davis didn't censure him for his sins, others complaining that the work didn't reveal the inner Burr.[31] John Adams likewise attracted his share of controversy. The publication of E. M. Cunningham's "Correspondence Between the Hon. John Adams, Late President of the United States, and the Late Wm. Cunningham, Esq." (1823) enraged arch Federalist Timothy Pickering enough to write his lengthy vituperative response with the deceptively restrained title "Review of the Correspondence Between the Hon. John Adams . . . and the Late Wm. Cunningham, Esq." (1824).

Pickering considered his work both a historical memoir and a "formal vindication" of not only himself but also Hamilton. Adams was a liar, Pickering declared, though he avoided that charged word, accusing Adams of making "unfounded assertions" that one "might designate by a harsher term." For Pickering, it was his duty as a historian to reveal Adams's true nature to the world. "What is history?" he mused. "A mere detail of events may engage curiosity; but it is the characters of the actors which especially interest the reader; and the exhibition of their actions, whether these be good or bad, which furnishes useful lessons of instruction." History was a moral tale with heroes and villains. Protecting the truth was thus not only noble but necessary, for without such efforts, libelous immorality would prevail. The wrong men would be "blotted from history" or eternally tainted with corruption, their friends and families tarred by the same brush of dishonor.[32]

An active correspondence among survivors of the 1790s and their progeny accompanied this historical impulse, for sometimes only participants—or the familial guardians of their reputations—could be trusted as possessing the truth. At various points in his historical mission, Plumer sought testimony and evidence from James Bayard and John Quincy Adams, among others. William Maclay's nephew George Washington Harris likewise went straight to the source when contemplating the publication of his uncle's diary, corresponding with descendants of Tench Coxe and Alexander Hamilton, as well as with Joseph Gales, Jr., and William Seaton, the editors of the debates of the early federal congresses.[33] Hamilton's sons solicited biographical fodder from a wide range of sources; refuting charges against their father even as they sought assistance, they left a trail of offended correspondents in their wake.

Plumer was so insulted by one such "long abusive, & virulent" letter from Alexander Hamilton, Jr., that he almost ignored it, answering it only out of respect for the writer's father. Hamilton's letter related to information that Plumer had revealed in support of his friend John Quincy Adams. When Adams—defending himself against 1828 campaign charges—outraged New England Federalists by discussing their secessionism, Plumer jumped to his aid with evidence culled from his memory and memoranda. The first eyewitness testimony of the Federalists' 1804 flirtation with secession, Plumer's account drew an onslaught of abuse. He returned to his treason "like a dog to his vomit or the sow to her wallowing in the mire," charged the *New Hampshire Patriot*.[34] It was Plumer's claim that Alexander Hamilton was involved in this secessionist plot that invited his son's ire; by demanding "satisfaction," the young Hamilton made it clear that this was a matter of family honor.[35]

Ultimately, this clash of histories pulled the Federalist-Republican conflict of the 1790s and its personal implications well into the nineteenth century. As Oliver Wolcott's memoirist George Gibbs put it, "To the historian there is no statute of limitations against political crimes." In 1836, Burr was still fuming about his relationship with Washington sixty years earlier and refuting charges about the 1800 election. In 1809, John Adams still felt the sting of Hamilton's universally condemned 1800 "Letter"—and Hamilton's animosity had stemmed from Adams's behavior for years before that. The campaign to redeem James Bayard from the shadow of 1800 was particularly long-lived, still active as late as 1907. Timothy Pickering fretted about his place in the historical record even on his deathbed, gasping that he had hoped to live longer, for there were yet some "truths, important in an historical point of view," that should be known. Plumer also turned to history in his final moments, insisting that his writings were impartial "in every case."[36] Burr, too, grasped at the historical record in his dying hours, anxious that through his memoirs, "at last, his countrymen should know him as he was."[37]

Jefferson went to his grave struggling to cast his relationship with Hamilton in the right light, trying to depict himself as a liberal, right-minded leader rather than the petty and vindictive politician he often appeared to be. It was concern for his reputation that inspired him to put Hamilton's bust in the main entrance way to Monticello; there could be no nobler act than to acknowledge the greatness of one's enemies—and only the greatest of men could defeat such a foe. Positioned in Jefferson's American museum alongside Indian artifacts and moose antlers, Hamilton's bust is a political hunting trophy, evidence of the path not taken and the superiority of those who chose the right course.

These histories were personal, emotional, accusatory, defensive, partisan, and often petty. They make outrageous claims and deny demonstrable truths. They depict the 1790s as a Manichaean battle between right and wrong, true and false, us and them. Beneath their congratulatory self-promotion flows a vein of desperation, the fate of the republic and personal reputations at risk. In essence, these histories perpetuate the mood of the 1790s; in this sense, they are indeed the most accurate historical truth that can be found. They offer a blind, chaotic emotional truth in a manner that no objective history could match.

For a generation who conceived of themselves as "Founders," the history of the republic was a history of their reputations, a conclusion that Plumer reached with the ultimate product of his historical mission: his autobiography. More than four hundred handwritten pages long, it consists of his memoranda in narrative form, transcribed almost word for word, with the addition of some insights and stylistic revisions. When describing Jefferson's odd reaction to Plumer's intended history, for example, Plumer gave his literary persona some added insight. Jefferson "might have considered it a mere political project to aid the views of party," the autobiographical Plumer reasoned, "or he might feel an aversion to a full exposition of his own character & conduct."[38] At the time, Jefferson's actions had baffled Plumer, but with twenty years of hindsight, they became more understandable. Jefferson, like Plumer, was focused on the historical record. From his archival forays into the congressional lumber room to his memoranda, his aborted history, his biographical essays, and finally, his autobiography, Plumer had made his way toward a fundamental truth: the history of the founding was about personal reputations, including his own.

In the passage of two centuries, the winners and losers of this battle for fame have been ever changing, individual reputations rising and falling with the political tides of the times.[39] Different ages have turned to different Founders for historical ballast according to their values and needs. Those twin symbols of clashing ideologies Jefferson and Hamilton have gone in and out of favor repeatedly, one man rising in popularity as the other falls. In the 1830s, Jefferson was the darling of Jacksonian Democrats; during the Civil War, Hamilton the nationalist rose to the fore; he was also enormously popular during the business- and industry-oriented 1890s, a period which seemed to be the fulfillment of Hamilton's vision. America's growing imperialism at the turn of the twentieth century turned the spotlight back to Jefferson, overseer of the Louisiana Purchase; Jefferson the god of democracy reigned throughout the Cold War; but recently, caught up in heated questions of race because of his relationship with Sally Hemings, he has fallen enough to make room for Hamilton, whose star is now rising with a burst of new histories.[40]

Strangest of all is the current resurrection of Aaron Burr.[41] Praised by several writers for being clear-eyed and practical in an era of political posturing, Burr is perfectly suited to an age of jaded distrust in campaign promises and self-righteous principles. Long the enfant terrible of the founding period, Burr may finally be coming into his own.

Clearly, history is in the business of making or breaking reputations, and few fall so low that they cannot rise again. In this America's Founders share much with politicians and personalities up to the present day. The difference, for the founding generation, was their understanding of their audience and the significance of their performance. Like any gentlemen of the period, early national politicians lived for their reputations; their sense of self, their sense of accomplishment, the essence of their manhood depended on it. For these men to play the high-risk game of politics before a national audience was a high risk indeed. For men of honor, political losses or public humiliations were no temporary setbacks; they struck at a man's core and threatened to rob him of his self-respect as a man and his identity as a leader, a threat profound enough to drive him to the field of honor.

The resulting style of politics—self-conscious, anxious, and intertwined with the rites and rituals of the honor code—fell to the wayside with the acceptance of political parties. Not that political gossip and the power of public opinion were excised from political combat. As any political pundit can attest, mudslinging and publicity campaigns are still the stuff of politics, our ever-expanding media network only broadening their audience and impact.[42] It is not the essence of politics that changed but rather the experience of being a politician. The political elite in the early republic wielded their reputations as their most formidable weapons; they were individual men of honor, in league with like-minded men, perhaps, but individually responsible for their words and actions, nonetheless.

Institutionalized parties forever altered this political dynamic, creating groups of loyal combatants whose organization and number were more important than the identity of any one man. A politician could fight anonymously under a party banner, freed from personal responsibility for party directives. There was safety in numbers—a primary argument against a joint national executive. As Hamilton argued in *The Federalist* No. 70, with more than one man as the national executive, blame for "pernicious measures" could be "shifted from one to another with so much dexterity, and under such plausible appearances, that the public opinion is left in suspense about the real author." Uncomfortable with the implications of entrenched national parties, politicians of the 1790s and early nineteenth century enjoyed no such camouflage.

Public figures whose careers collapsed with the reputation of their political chief were among the first to perceive the security and anonymity of party membership. As Matthew Davis wrote to William P. Van Ness after their public careers had been sabotaged by Burr's downfall, "On the subject . . . of attachment to men, both of us, I think, have learned sufficient to know the folly of connecting our political destiny with that of any Individual; and more especially when the views and conduct of that Individual is not in unison with the wishes and expectations of the party."[43] For Davis, as for other national politicians, party politics made sense. Only by understanding the honor-bound combat of the 1790s can we fully understand the appeal of party politicking in the nineteenth century.

But national politicians did not march into party formation with their eyes open. As the election of 1800 reveals, they backed their way into it one decision at a time, making exception after exception to political proprieties amid a continuing series of crises. To save the republic, they were willing to stretch the rules to the breaking point, but they did not abandon them entirely. Rather than discarding past habits, ideals, and assumptions on their way to a glorious democratic future, the political elite made a series of personal compromises, adapting their politics to the crises at hand, struggling to adapt to the evolving demands of an increasingly powerful populace. This crisis mentality is a vital component of the process of political change. There were no assurances, no guarantees of success, and a constant fear that the entire structure would come crashing to ruin. Imposing patterns on the period in hindsight, we often forget that this was a world of chance and circumstance, where voting patterns and probabilities that seem obvious to us were obscured in a cloud of uncertainties and fears.

Viewed in their proper context, these crisis-bound decisions of the moment do not reflect a sudden embrace of a "modern" party politics. Rather, they reveal a leadership learning how to practice a national politics. When the changing political landscape seemed to demand more organization, politicians formed personal alliances—sometimes called parties—on the assumption that they did so voluntarily, in mutual trust and friendship, and driven by concern for the public good. Contrary to our expectations about American politics, faith in the culture of honor and the mandates of republicanism helped elite politicians adapt to democratic politicking without violating their sense of political propriety. In their minds, there was a vast difference between a "party" of right-minded friends striving for the general good and a structured and institutionalized partisan "squadron" devoted to selfish interests. Indeed, it was the difference between these two conceptions of party—the ambiguously personal nature of the former versus the regulated impersonality of the latter—that defined and structured their political world.

Honor is at the core of this process of political transition. The language of honor set the terms of debate; the rituals of honor channeled dangerous passions; the logic of honor shaped political strategy;

and the significance of honor gave weapons their power and sting. The full story of early national politics cannot be told without the culture of honor, a shared body of assumptions and rituals that framed the bustle and confusion of the national political world. It is a key that unlocks countless mysteries of the period, rationalizing the seemingly irrational, justifying the seemingly petty and perverse, and recasting our understanding of America's founding.

The political significance of honor also alters some basic definitions at the heart of the historian's craft, redefining such concepts as "politics" and political evidence, which encompass far more than elections, legislation, debate, and compromise. Politics was personal; politics was everywhere, shifting among different populations, different cultures, different places, and different times. It is an idea with implications that historians of different eras and populations are currently exploring—one that holds the potential to reveal similarities as well as differences between cultures.

A collection of beliefs and rituals with long-lived roots in civilizations past, the culture of honor also reminds us that the American republic did not spring to life from the brow of Washington, fully formed. There were cultural and political rites, traditions, and assumptions that Britain's North American colonists inherited and adapted on a distant stage. The tone of America's politics of reputation harkens back to Britain as well, which had a long and illustrious history of political bludgeoning through satire and character attack.[44]

Of course, there were American differences as well, and nowhere are these differences more obvious than in the publicity campaigns that followed political duels. National politicians were not grappling for prizes and privileges in a royal court. They were learning the art of popular politics, with mixed results. This shifting interaction between leader and citizen—the ways that different groups in this discussion received messages and voiced their own—reveals the ground-level reality of political change. Ironically, an understanding of an aristocratic culture of honor holds new insights into the evolution of our democratic two-party system.

Looking back on this process, the founding generation imposed a structure that exists only in hindsight. Theirs was an outlook born of reflection on past battles; from a distance of several decades what once seemed like a chaotic scramble for the soul of the republic came to feel like an organized war between two defined armies. Formerly unpredictable loyalties were now long known. Outcomes were clear. Enough time had passed for patterns to emerge. And the republic's continued survival suggested that perhaps team combat was not so destructive after all. As they waged historical warfare in their histories, biographies, and memoirs, the founding generation codified this mentality page by page; even as they defended their reputations, they were committing to paper their political learning process.

To understand the political importance of honor culture is thus to uncover the emotional reality of being a national politician during America's founding years. The knee-jerk sense of panic, the rampant suspicions, the high passions and shrill accusations were not irrational; they were a natural product of a politics of reputation that blended personal identity, public office, and political experimentation in a volatile mix. Neither were prevailing assumptions about the immorality of party politics naive; politicians were learning how to conduct national politics one decision at a time. There was an emotional logic to their actions and reactions that is apparent only in the context of their time.

Of course, logical decisions can be bad decisions, as the men who people these pages discovered. One can make rational choices for all the wrong reasons, or reason one's way into the wrong path. Honor-bound politicians were not always honorable—and this is precisely the point. Too often, the Founders are praised to the skies as saintly deities of governance or condemned as self-interested elitists who cared for money and power above all else. In reality, they were something of both. They sincerely strove to create a great nation grounded on popular will and the rights of man. They were also obsessively concerned with their interests, careers, reputations, and pocketbooks, practicing down-and-dirty politics in their efforts to get ahead. This is a distinction that makes a difference. If the founding generation were a band of angels, American politics has been in a state of free-fall ever since; if they were little more than greedy power-mongers, there is little hope that America can rise to much more. However, as real people who struggled with a difficult task, sometimes inspired to high purpose, other times feeding their meanest appetites, they extend to posterity the gift of hope. If these fallible, flawed people could accomplish great things, perhaps future generations can do so as well. It is the logic that inspired their greatest hopes for the future, the ultimate message they hoped to impart.

So, in ways that the founding generation realized all too well, history *does* matter. As suggested by the passion they devoted to their histories, memoirs, and biographies, the future is shaped by its understanding of the past. Though later generations have long overlooked or misunderstood these heartfelt final addresses to posterity, they were efforts well taken. For regardless of whether we praise or condemn their biased views of the past, they remind us that history—like politics—is subjective, contested, and fueled by personal agendas. They remind us that history is a story that we tell about ourselves.

A Note on Method

This book approaches politics in an unusual way. It does not examine political events or personalities in isolation or reduce them to the level of historical anecdote. Nor does it tackle so broad a theme as to lose sight of a participant's perspective. Aiming at a midpoint between broad cultural history and detailed analysis of the political narrative, it uses the vantage point of an ethno-historian, identifying and interpreting patterns of thought and behavior among a select group of elite public figures. In doing so, it reveals the overriding influence of honor on national politics, as well as the profound shaping influence of cultural imperatives on the political process. Every population shares a code of conduct, a mutual understanding of constraints, fears, expectations, and demands. It is impossible to fully understand political interaction without considering the impact of these cultural imperatives on decisions and actions, political and otherwise.

To detect and decode these shared understandings, this study uses seemingly unconventional forms of evidence. First and foremost, it relies on human emotion. Feelings represent individual attempts to grapple with the realities of a given moment. Regardless of whether these feelings are realistic or understandable to later onlookers, they represent an instinctive, human response to immediate demands and expectations. Sincere or feigned, they required shared standards and cultural assumptions to be understood. Close study of emotions is thus an invaluable pathway to core beliefs lurking beneath the surface of everyday event, beliefs so familiar and accepted that they were rarely committed to paper. Although historians typically dismiss such evidence as personal, idiosyncratic, and trivial—useful for little more than spicing up biographies and historical narratives—feelings are vital passageways to an intuitive level of thought.[1]

This is not to say that individual emotions studied in isolation are historically representative. It is emotional *patterns* that reveal larger cultural truths. If masses of people in a given place and time were amused, disgusted, or frightened in similar ways on similar occasions, this suggests larger, shared assumptions that require exploration. Outrage and shock are particularly useful indicators, revealing shared standards through their violation, but even subtle emotions offer vital insights.

The study of dueling is a perfect example of this theory in practice. Taken in isolation, individual duels seem to be little more than irrational outbursts fueled by psychotic rage or rampant insecurities; issuing or accepting an invitation to kill or be killed seems to defy all logic. Hence the tendency of many writers to attribute duels to mental illness or emotional instability. The Burr-Hamilton duel, in particular, invites such conclusions in abundance; how else can we explain such seemingly illogical behavior by two leading American statesmen? But thousands of Americans—and tens of thousands of people the world over—felt compelled to engage in this deadly ritual. Unless we are prepared to conclude that *all* these people were mentally unstable, we must concede that there was a larger logic underlying the duel, a belief so strong that it compelled men to hazard their lives. Acknowledging and synthesizing the feelings that drove men to issue and accept challenges exposes this internal logic, revealing the fears and desires that made this seemingly illogical practice seem logical to its practitioners.

Writers who impose modern feelings on historical characters trap themselves permanently in the present, grounding their conclusions on little more than subjective character judgments that ill apply to people of other places and times. Recognizing the emotional integrity of historical actors gets us beyond such ahistorical claims, explaining apparently erratic or incomprehensible acts, rather than condemning them as irrational, inappropriate, or primitive. When the scholarly consensus dismisses an event or action as inexplicable, crazy, or idiosyncratic, it is a red-flag indicator that there is a deeper logic waiting to be understood. Even decidedly stupid decisions were the product of a process of reasoning that deserves study.

The close analysis of emotional patterns is not the same thing as psychohistory. In fact, in many ways, psychohistory is the exact opposite of this historical method. Psychohistorical studies plumb the depths of a historical figure's soul in search of the personal hobgoblins that shaped his or her thoughts and actions. Placed within the proper historical context, such conclusions can offer valuable insight into both character and event. But too often, writers psychoanalyze their subjects in a historical vacuum, forgetting other behavior-shaping factors that are distinctive to a given place and time; without this vital contextual backdrop, practices or beliefs common to whole populations become symptomatic of a single flawed psyche. Only after ruling out the influence of shared assumptions and immediate demands can scholars use individual psychology as a motivating force with any accuracy.

Moments of choice are as evocative a form of historical evidence as personal emotions; indeed, the two are interlinked. When historical figures debated a course of action with any degree of seriousness, they were setting priorities, sifting through the demands and constraints of a particular situation, considering their options, and arriving at a decision they considered logical; when they sought the counsel of friends, they committed this process to paper. The "shoulds" and "should-nots" that governed these decisions are vital evidence in the quest to decode past behavior. They are written representations of a shared mentality as its practitioners understood it. Without at least a basic understanding of such distinctive behavioral bounds, it is impossible to fully understand individual action or agency. History represents a long series of choices by a wide range of individuals, bound in by constantly shifting cultural imperatives. Close study of these choices takes us beyond broad generalizations about a unified cultural consensus or defined "-ism," bringing us one step closer to the perspective of our historical subjects.

The ethno-historical study of patterns of thought and behavior requires a broad sampling of written and situational evidence. This study is grounded on thousands of letters, diaries, pamphlets, newspaper essays, and other assorted writings by roughly three hundred national political figures, their families, and friends—a wide sampling, given that Congress, the president, and his cabinet were roughly one to two hundred in number during any given point of the period. In examining these documents, I sought several types of evidence. Initially, I looked for judgmental statements about friends and enemies, hoping to find open declarations of shared attitudes, but a month of fruitless research led to a key realization: politicians knew better than to commit such judgments to paper. They were too dangerously personal, too likely to wind up as political fodder in enemy hands. For the accuser, it was better to hint at accusations and reserve the details for future conversations; for the victim, it was better to rage against them obliquely than to commit them to paper and widen their reach. Rather than outright judgments and declarations, I discovered what I came to call "the ouch factor": the wake of pain and outrage provoked by the passage of political gossip. Follow the path of outrage, and you reconstruct national networks of political friends and enemies. In essence, you expose the foundations of the national political process in the republic's early years.

Most useful of all were violations of this shared standard of caution, sporadic as they might be, for the resulting outrage often compelled onlookers to discuss rules and standards that normally went unmentioned. Jefferson's "Anas" is a prime example of this phenomenon. The shock that followed its publication offered the precise sort of judgmental declarations that I initially sought. Jefferson's "Anas" violated shared imperatives of political behavior that its victims were more than eager to discuss. Even Jefferson's friends were hard-put to defend his actions. Here was a violation that exposed a host of assumptions about political combat.

Beneath all these methodological suggestions is one underlying imperative. It is almost too simple to state, but so essential that it requires mention. To as great a degree as possible, *assume nothing* and willingly surrender even the most basic lingering assumptions at the demand of evidence. Searching for predetermined patterns of behavior obscures the seemingly impossible and the unknown, trapping the historian in the limited perspective of his or her own time. Searching for my definition of political gossip produced nothing; observing patterns of evidence revealed a world. Clinging to the touchstone of political parties would have been equally fatal, but when I abandoned my assumptions about the existence or absence of parties, I uncovered political logic and practices that were entirely unexpected. Even the types of evidence I used were affected by this mindset, for given the personal nature of political interaction in the early republic, seemingly personal confessions and private exchanges were often the most political of all.

This leads me to one final caution about historical evidence. Given the political nature of personal writings in the period under study in this book, documentary collections limited to "political correspondence and public papers" do readers a grave disservice, shearing off an entire body of crucial political evidence. Comprehensive documentary editions like the Franklin, Washington, Madison, Hamilton, and Jefferson Papers are thus essential entries into a full understanding of our nation's founding, offering readers a full immersion in the language and logic of another time.

Notes

When quotations are given, the first word of the quotation is silently capitalized or set in lowercase according to the syntax of the sentence. All other punctuation and spelling are as in the original unless bracketed. Angle brackets used in some documentary editions to supply omitted letters have been dropped.

Introduction

1. Unless otherwise noted, quotations are from *The Argus, or Greenleaf's New Daily Advertiser,* July 20, 1795. For excerpts of Hamilton's resolution, see John C. Miller, *Alexander Hamilton: Portrait in Paradox* (New York: Harper and Brothers, 1959), 424. The *Argus* does not mention the rock throwing incident, so it may be apocryphal; but see George Cabot to Rufus King, July 27, 1795, regarding an attempt to "knock out Hamilton's brains." Charles R. King, ed., *The Life and Correspondence of Rufus King,* 6 vols. (New York: Putnam's, 1895), 2:20. See also Harold C. Syrett, ed., *The Papers of Alexander Hamilton* [hereafter *Hamilton Papers*], 27 vols. (New York: Columbia University Press, 1961–87), 18:484, note 33; Broadus Mitchell, *Alexander Hamilton,* 2 vols. (New York: Macmillan, 1957–62), 2:683, note 42. Mitchell claimed that he had discovered no contemporary account of the rock-throwing incident, but he did not mention Cabot's comment to King.
2. For Hamilton's account of the Nicholson clash, see [Drafts of Apology Required from James Nicholson], [July 25–26, 1795], *Hamilton Papers,* 18:501–3. See also Edward Livingston to Margaret B. Livingston, July 20, 1795, Robert R. Livingston Papers, New-York Historical Society.
3. On "gentle identity," see Steven Shapin, *A Social History of Truth: Civility and Science in Seventeenth-Century England* (Chicago: University of Chicago Press, 1994), chaps. 1–3.
4. A handful of studies address the culture of honor outside of the South: Evarts B. Greene, "The Code of Honor in Colonial and Revolutionary Times, with Special Reference to New England," *Publications of the Colonial Society of Massachusetts* 26 (1927): 367–88; Bertram Wyatt-Brown, *Southern Honor: Ethics and Behavior in the Old South* (New York: Oxford University Press, 1982), xv–xvi, 19–20; Joanne B. Freeman, "Aristocratic Murder and Democratic Fury: Honor and Violence in Early National New England," paper delivered at the annual meeting of the American Historical Association, New York City, January 1997; and David Hackett Fischer, *Albion's Seed: British Folkways in America* (New York: Oxford University Press, 1989), 188, 582, 814. My next book will explore the national ramifications of honor culture.
5. Classic studies of the period's political violence include Marshall Smelser, "The Federalist Period as an Age of Passion," *American Quarterly* 10 (1958): 391–419; and John Howe, "Republican Thought and the Political Violence of the 1790s," *American Quarterly* 19 (1967): 147–65.
6. This is not to say that the Sedition Act had nothing to do with Federalist ideology or partisanship; rather, honor culture shaped the ways that Federalists (and Republicans) grappled with ideologies and politics. Leading studies of the Sedition Act include Leonard W. Levy, *Emergence of a Free Press* (New York: Oxford University Press, 1985); and James Morton Smith, *Freedom's Fetters: The Alien and Sedition Laws and American Civil Liberties* (Ithaca, N.Y.: Cor-

nell University Press, 1956). See also Norman L. Rosenberg, *Protecting the Best Men: An Interpretive History of the Law of Libel* (Chapel Hill: University of North Carolina Press, 1986), chaps. 4 and 5. See also Leonard W. Levy, *Jefferson and Civil Liberties: The Darker Side* (Chicago: Ivan R. Dee, 1989), chap. 2.

7. For a strikingly similar example of "a working solution in one area of the culture (gentlemanly society)" being "transported into another . . . to act as a local resolution of a pervasive problem," see the discussion of honor culture and eighteenth-century scientific debate in Shapin, *Social History of Truth,* quote at 42; also Jonathan Powis, *Aristocracy* (Oxford: Blackwell, 1984), 3. James Sterling Young sees no mechanism for resolving and limiting conflict on the national stage, but clearly, honor culture filled this gap. Young, *The Washington Community: 1800–1828* (New York: Harcourt, Brace, Jovanovich, 1966), 152.
8. Whether they embrace the idea of a party system or discuss the absence of such a system, most studies of early national politics center around the touchstone of party, acknowledging the unstable nature of political ties, but still dividing national politics into two cohered "proto-parties," to use James Roger Sharp's epithet. Sharp, *American Politics in the Early Republic: The New Nation in Crisis* (New Haven: Yale University Press, 1993); see also Stanley Elkins and Eric McKitrick, *The Age of Federalism* (New York: Oxford University Press, 1993); and Ronald P. Formisano, "Federalists and Republicans: Parties, Yes—System, No," in Paul Kleppner, et al., *The Evolution of American Electoral Systems* (Westport, Conn.: Greenwood Press, 1981). The foremost proponents of the first party system are William Nisbet Chambers, *Political Parties in a New Nation: The American Experience, 1776–1809* (New York: Oxford University Press, 1963); and Joseph Charles, *The Origins of the American Party System* (New York: Harper and Row, 1961).
9. On credit, see Jay M. Smith, "No More Language Games: Words, Beliefs, and the Political Culture of Early Modern France," *American Historical Review* (December 1997): 1413–40; on fame, see Douglass Adair's seminal article, "Fame and the Founding Fathers," in Trevor Colbourn, ed., *Fame and the Founding Fathers: Essays by Douglass Adair* (New York: Norton, 1974), 3–26. Also Peter McNamara, ed., *The Noblest Minds: Fame, Honor, and the American Founding* (Lanham, Md.: Rowman and Littlefield, 1999); Gerald Stourzh, *Alexander Hamilton and the Idea of Republican Government* (Stanford: Stanford University Press, 1970), 95–106; and Mark E. Kann, *A Republic of Men: The American Founders, Gendered Language, and Patriarchal Politics* (New York: New York University Press, 1998), 119–24. Major studies of honor include Frank Henderson Stewart, *Honor* (Chicago: University of Chicago Press, 1994), pt. 1; Julian Pitt-Rivers, "Honour and Social Status," in *Honour and Shame: The Values of Mediterranean Society,* ed. J. G. Peristiany (London: Nicholson, 1966); Wyatt-Brown, *Southern Honor;* Kenneth S. Greenberg, *Honor and Slavery* (Princeton: Princeton University Press, 1996); Pieter Spierenburg, ed., *Men and Violence: Gender, Honor, and Rituals in Modern Europe and America* (Columbus: Ohio State University Press, 1998), esp. the introduction; Steven M. Stowe, *Intimacy and Power in the Old South: Ritual in the Lives of the Planters* (Baltimore: Johns Hopkins University Press, 1987), chap. 1; and Shapin, *Social History of Truth,* chaps. 1–3.
10. Rufus King, undated essay, *Correspondence of Rufus King,* 5:96, note; Alexander Pope, *The Rape of the Lock* (1712), canto III, l. 16.
11. Examples include Sarah C. Chambers, *From Subjects to Citizens: Honor, Gender, and Politics in Arequipa, Peru, 1780–1854* (University Park: Pennsylvania State University Press, 1999); Nancy Shields Kollman, *By Honor Bound: State and Society in Early Modern Russia* (Ithaca, N.Y.: Cornell University Press, 1999); J. E. Lendon, *Empire of Honor: The Art of Government in the Roman World* (Oxford: Clarendon, 1997); Christopher J. Olsen, *Political Culture and Secession in Mississippi: Masculinity, Honor, and the Antiparty Tradition, 1830–1860* (New York:

Oxford University Press, 2000); and William M. Reddy, *The Invisible Code: Honor and Sentiment in Postrevolutionary France, 1814–1848* (Berkeley: University of California Press, 1997).

12. Hamilton, [Draft of Apology Required from James Nicholson], [July 25–26, 1795], *Hamilton Papers,* 18:501–3.
13. James Monroe to James Madison, June 8, 1798, *The Papers of James Madison* [hereafter *Madison Papers*], ed. Robert Rutland and J. C. A. Stagg, 17 vols. (Charlottesville: University Press of Virginia, 1962–), 17:145–47. See also Madison to Monroe, June 9, 1798, ibid., 17:148–50. In the end, Monroe took none of these options, although he considered running for Congress as a way of dealing with Adams.
14. For example, see Simon P. Newman, *Parades and the Politics of the Street: Festive Culture in the Early American Republic* (Philadelphia: University of Pennsylvania Press, 1997); Len Travers, *Celebrating the Fourth: Independence Day and the Rites of Nationalism in the Early Republic* (Amherst: University of Massachusetts Press, 1997); David Waldstreicher, *In the Midst of Perpetual Fetes: The Making of American Nationalism, 1776–1820* (Chapel Hill: University of North Carolina Press, 1997). This book focuses on elite national officeholders, but they were not the only performers on the national stage; see Jeffrey L. Pasley, *"The Tyranny of Printers": Newspaper Politics in the Early American Republic* (Charlottesville: University Press of Virginia, 2001).
15. Norbert Elias notes that the empowerment of a society's lower strata often spurs its elites to emphasize their differences and privileges. According to this logic, the rise in political honor disputes in the 1790s might represent the reaction of the nation's political elite to the growing empowerment of the body politic. Elias, *The Civilizing Process,* trans. Edmund Jephcott (Oxford: Blackwell, 1994), 507–8. Elias's ideas about the study of elite politics are worth repeating: scholarship often concerns itself "only with the constraint to which less powerful groups are exposed. But in this way we gain only a one-sided picture." Because every society has a kind of "circulation of constraints, exerted by groups on groups, individuals on individuals, the constraints to which lower strata are exposed cannot be understood without also investigating those affecting the upper strata." Elias, *Court Society,* 266 (see also 212, 271).
16. Seminal studies of the link between politics and culture include Elias, *Court Society;* Lynn Hunt, *Politics, Culture, and Class in the French Revolution* (Berkeley: University of California Press, 1984); Jean H. Baker, *Affairs of Party: The Political Culture of Northern Democrats in the Mid-Nineteenth Century* (Ithaca: Cornell University Press, 1983); Michael E. McGerr, *The Decline of Popular Politics: The American North, 1865–1928* (New York: Oxford University Press, 1986). Young moved in this direction in his study of the geography of power in early Washington, D.C. Young, *Washington Community.*

Prologue

1. Abraham Baldwin to Joel Barlow, March 1, 1789, Misc. Collections, Sterling Library, Yale University; Fisher Ames to George Richards Minot, May 27, 1789, in *Works of Fisher Ames, as Published by Seth Ames,* ed. W. B. Allen, 2 vols. (Indianapolis: Liberty Fund, 1983), 1:633. For typical reactions see August 29, 1789, *The Diary of William Maclay and Other Notes on Senate Debates,* ed. Kenneth R. Bowling and Helen E. Veit (Baltimore: Johns Hopkins University Press, 1988) [hereafter *Maclay's Diary*], 141; Pierce Butler to James Iredell, August 11, 1789, in Ulrich B. Phillips, "South Carolina Federalists, II," *American Historical Review* 4 (July 1909), 731; Fisher Ames to George Richards Minot, May 27, 1789, *Works of Fisher Ames,* 1: 633; Paine Wingate to Jeremy Belknap, May 12, 1789, Jeremy Belknap Papers, Massachusetts Historical Society.

2. For a beautifully rendered assemblage of their portraits, see the catalogue to the 1989 National Portrait Gallery exhibition: Margaret C. S. Christman, *The First Federal Congress, 1789–1791* (Washington, D.C.: Smithsonian Institution Press, 1989).
3. January 31, 1791, *Maclay's Diary,* 372; Ames to George Richards Minot, May 27, 1789, *Works of Fisher Ames,* 1:633. For similar thoughts in early Washington, D.C., see Young, *Washington Community,* esp. chaps. 2, 3, 5. By 1800 these feelings had evolved, though Young does not note this change, applying, for example, Maclay's 1789 commentary to 1800 Washington. See also the Epilogue, below.
4. Ames to George Richards Minot, March 25, 1789, *Works of Fisher Ames,* 1:560–61; Christman, *First Federal Congress,* 105. On the first federal elections, see R. B. Bernstein, "A New Matrix for National Politics: The First Federal Elections, 1788–1790," in *Inventing Congress: Origins and Establishment of the First Federal Congress,* ed. Kenneth R. Bowling, Donald R. Kennon (Athens: Ohio University Press, 1999): 109–37. On the "old Congress" generally and congressional malaise specifically, see Jack N. Rakove, *The Beginnings of National Politics: An Interpretive History of the Continental Congress* (New York: Knopf, 1979), esp. 198–200, 354–59. Also Edmund Cody Burnett, *The Continental Congress: A Definitive History of the Continental Congress from Its Inception in 1774 to March, 1789* (New York: Norton, 1964).
5. Ames to George Richards Minot, March 25, 1789, *Works of Fisher Ames,* 1:560–61; Washington to Henry Knox, April 10, 1789, in *The Papers of George Washington: Presidential Series* [hereafter *Washington Papers*], ed. Dorothy Twohig (Charlottesville: University Press of Virginia, 1987–), 2:46; August 29, 1789, *Maclay's Diary,* 141. See also Butler to Iredell, August 11, 1789, "South Carolina Federalists, II," 731.
6. The contrast of this ambitious hunger with the ambivalence of members of the Continental Congress is striking. See Rakove, *Beginnings of National Politics,* 216–39.
7. April 2, 1790, *Maclay's Diary,* 234.
8. Adams to Benjamin Rush, June 9, 1789, Adams Family Papers, Massachusetts Historical Society; Madison [Congressional debate of July 16, 1789], *Madison Papers,* 12:293. See also February 24, 1791, *Maclay's Diary,* 388–89; Hamilton to Edward Carrington, May 26, 1792, *Hamilton Papers,* 11:433; see also Oliver Wolcott, Jr., to Jeremiah Wadsworth, August 15, 1789, *Memoirs of the Administrations of Washington and John Adams,* ed. George Gibbs, 2 vols. (New York, 1846), 1:19.
9. Fredrika J. Teute and David S. Shields, "The Republican Court and the Historiography of a Woman's Domain in the Public Sphere," paper delivered at the Annual Meeting of the Society for Historians of the Early American Republic, July 16, 1994, Boston, Massachusetts; Rufus Wilmot Griswold, *The Republican Court, or American Society in the Days of Washington* (1867; New York: Haskell House, 1971).
10. Rush to Adams, July 2, 1788, *Letters of Benjamin Rush* [hereafter *Rush Papers*], ed. L. H. Butterfield, 2 vols. (Princeton: Princeton University Press, 1951), 1:468–70. Jay Fliegelman notes that "emulation permitted the expression of ambition in the context of a larger reverence for the models of the past." Fliegelman, *Declaring Independence: Jefferson, Natural Language, and the Culture of Performance* (Stanford: Stanford University Press, 1993), 180.
11. Fisher Ames to Theodore Sedgwick, October 6, 1789, Sedgwick Papers, Massachusetts Historical Society; Abigail Adams to Mary Cranch Smith, January 8, 1791, *Letters of Mrs. Adams,* ed. Charles Francis Adams (Boston: Little, Brown, 1840), 2:212; Henry Lee to James Madison, April 3, 1790. *Madison Papers,* 13:136–7; Clymer to Henry Hill, March 7, 1790, Signers' Collection, New-York Society Library. For a catalogue of regional diversity, see David Hackett Fischer, *Albion's Seed: Four British Folkways in America* (New York: Oxford University Press, 1989). See also Young, *Washington Community,* 91–92.
12. Rush to James Madison, July 17, 1790, *Madison Papers,* 13:279–80; Rush to John Adams, February 21 and June 4, 1789, *Rush Papers,* 1:501–3, 513–15; Rush to James Madison, September

15, 1789, *Madison Papers,* 12:403. See also Louis-Guillaume Otto to Armand Marc, comte de Montmorin Saint-Herem, July 12, 1790, in Margaret M. O'Dwyer, "A French Diplomat's View of Congress, 1790," *William and Mary Quarterly* (July 1964), 441. For a New Yorker's view of the contrast between New York and Philadelphia manners, see *New York Weekly Museum,* October 30, 1790.

13. Smith to Edward Rutledge, December 6, 1793, "The Letters of William Loughton Smith to Edward Rutledge, June 8, 1789–April 28, 1794," *South Carolina Historical Magazine* 70 (January 1969), 50.
14. January 7, 1790, *Maclay's Diary,* 179; Madison to Jefferson, June 30, 1789, *Madison Papers,* 12:268; Washington to Graham, January 9, 1790, *Washington Papers,* 4:551–54. See also Benjamin Rush to John Howard, October 14, 1789, *Rush Papers,* 527–28; Madison to James Madison, Sr., July 5, 1789, *Madison Papers,* 12:278.

1
The Theater of National Politics

1. Maclay's other public offices included a justiceship in Northumberland County (1772–86), deputy surveyor for Berks County (1764–90); and prothonotary, register, recorder, and clerk of the Northumberland County courts (1772–77). He also played a large role in the laying out of Northumberland County and the towns of Sunbury and Harrisburg. For an account of Maclay's life, see *Maclay's Diary*, 431–41; and Heber G. Gearhart, "The Life of William Maclay," *Proceedings of the Northumberland County Historical Society* 2 (May 1930): 46–73. For more obscure biographies, see *Maclay's Diary,* 432, note 1.
2. The quote is attributed to a "Mr. Harris of Harrisburg," probably a relation, since Maclay married into the family when he wed Mary Harris in 1769. Gearhart, "Life of William Maclay," 73. In addition to Maclay and fellow Pennsylvania senator Robert Morris, the Assembly considered Benjamin Franklin, William Irvine, John Armstrong, Jr., and George Clymer. For the maneuverings and counter-maneuverings that resulted in the choice of Maclay and Morris, see Harry Marlin Tinkcom, *The Republicans and Federalists in Pennsylvania, 1790–1801* (Harrisburg: Pennsylvania Historical and Museum Commission, 1950), 25.
3. April 29, 1789, and December 31, 1790, *Maclay's Diary,* 10, 351; May 17 and June 21, 1790, ibid., 270, 299. The weekly Pennsylvania dinners began in February 1790. See February 22, May 3, 17, and 24, June 7 and 21, 1790, ibid., 207, 259, 270, 274–75, 285, 299. On congressional "mess days," see Young, *Washington Community,* 98–102. Maclay's capitalization and punctuation are extremely erratic; with the exception of the first word in a quote where, as noted above, we have silently set a cap or lowercase to fit the sentence strucure, all Maclay's idiosyncrasies have been retained.
4. December 22, 1790, *Maclay's Diary,* 345; April 29, 1789, ibid., 10.
5. April 27 and 30, 1789, ibid., 7–8, 11–12; Maclay to Benjamin Rush, April 23, 1789, Rush Papers, Library of Congress.
6. May 8, 1789, and February 26, 1791, *Maclay's Diary,* 29, 395.
7. April 29 and June 4, 1789, ibid., 10, 66.
8. April 25, 1789, ibid., 5. For the drawing of Maclay's ballot, see May 15, 1789, ibid., 40. The measure was intended to prevent the entire Senate from departing at the same time; staggering the term lengths provided some continuity.
9. June 4, 1789, ibid., 66.
10. Maclay made no entries for June 7 and August 23, 1789, September 9–12, 1789 (when he was sick), December 11–12, 1790 (when the Senate was adjourned), and February 19–22, 1791 (when he was too busy—and unsure of the ultimate good of his diary).

11. Elkins and McKitrick, *Age of Federalism,* 46. See also Forrest McDonald, *The Presidency of George Washington* (Lawrence: University Press of Kansas, 1974), 29–31.
12. *Maclay's Diary,* xvi.
13. Abigail Adams in ibid., xiii.
14. John Adams, diary entry, in Andrew Trees, "'A Character to Establish': Personality and National Identity in the New American Nation" (Ph.D. diss., University of Virginia, 1999), 151. For the "first four decades of national government between one third and two thirds of the congressional community left every two years not to return." On average, 41.5 percent of the total membership left office every two years. Young, *Washington Community,* 89–90.
15. April 28, May 6, and June 11, 1789, January 20, 1791, April 3, 1790, *Maclay's Diary,* 9, 25, 74, 365, 235. On the link between nationalism and sectionalism, see Peter S. Onuf, "Federalism, Republicanism, and the Origins of American Sectionalism," in *All Over the Map: Rethinking American Regions* (Baltimore: Johns Hopkins University Press, 1996), 11–37; John Murrin, "A Roof Without Walls," in *Beyond Confederation: Dimensions of the Constitution and American National Identity,* ed. Richard R. Beeman, Stephen Botein, and Edward C. Carter II (Chapel Hill: University of North Carolina Press, 1987); and Young, *Washington Community,* 97–100.
16. April 26, 1789, *Maclay's Diary,* 6–7. See also April 4, 1790, ibid., 235–36. Fisher Ames also considered Fitzsimons "artful," describing him as "one of those people whose face, manner, and sentiments concur to produce caution, if not apprehension and disgust." Ames to George Richards Minot, May 18, 1789, *Works of Fisher Ames,* 2:627–28.
17. March 27, April 4, and May 9, 1790, *Maclay's Diary,* 229, 236, 263. For a similar comment regarding Clymer and Wynkoop, see also March 31, 1790, ibid., 232; September 28, 1789, ibid., 169; see also June 5, 1790, ibid., 284.
18. Gerry to unknown correspondent, March 22, 1789, Elbridge Gerry Papers, Library of Congress; Ames to George Richards Minot, May 29, 1789, *Works of Fisher Ames,* 1:638–39; Thomas Hartley to Jasper Yeates, June 19, 1789, in Christman, *First Federal Congress,* 271.
19. January 17 and February 22, 1790, *Maclay's Diary,* 184, 207.
20. July 15 and August 16, 1789, ibid., 113, 121; March 8 and 10, 1790, ibid., 214, 216; Maclay to Benjamin Rush, March 27, 1790, Rush Papers, Library of Congress.
21. January 7, 1790, ibid., 179. On the location of the national capital, see Kenneth R. Bowling, *The Creation of Washington, D.C.: The Idea and Location of the American Capital* (Fairfax, Va.: George Mason University Press, 1991), and *Creating the Federal City: Potomac Fever* (Washington, D.C.: Octagon Research Series, 1988).
22. John Armstrong, Jr., to William McPherson, November 26, 1788, McPherson Papers, Historical Society of Pennsylvania. Maclay's elevation to office was also affected by Pennsylvania's ongoing constitutional crisis and the need for an "Agricultural Senator" to balance out the urban, commerce-oriented Robert Morris. Tench Coxe to James Madison, October 22, 1788, *Madison Papers,* 11:312–13; Tinkcom, *Republicans and Federalists in Pennsylvania,* 25; Bernstein, "New Matrix for National Politics," 132.
23. May 5, June 9, and August 26, 1789, *Maclay's Diary,* 24, 72, 135; May 7, 1789, ibid., 25. Cribbed notes were also common in the British Parliament, where members had a similar desire to earn reputation and acclaim. On the theatricality of eighteenth-century oratory, see Fliegelman, *Declaring Independence.*
24. July 16, 1789, *Maclay's Diary,* 115. On Adams's disrespect, see also June 21, 1790, ibid., 299.
25. For a similar account of Congress in the early years of Washington City, see Young, *Washington Community,* 94, 96–97.
26. Fisher Ames to Thomas Dwight, July 25, 1790, *Works of Fisher Ames,* 1:835. Ames was referring here to James Jackson of Georgia, who gave a speech not quite "loud enough for you [Dwight] to hear" in New York. Jackson was notoriously loud; in March 1792, South Carolina

Representative William Loughton Smith noted, "We have got a new orator in the House, [John Francis] Mercer—who is louder than Jackson." Smith to Edward Rutledge, March 24, 1792, in "Letters of William Loughton Smith," 241.

27. March 3, 1791, *Maclay's Diary,* 399–400.
28. March 2, 1790, ibid., 211; March 22, 1790, ibid., 226; John Page to St. George Tucker, February 25, 1790, in Christman, *First Federal Congress,* 305. See also Page to Tucker, February 26 and March 18, 1790, ibid.
29. February 26, 1791, and February 12, 1790, *Maclay's Diary,* 394, 201; June 28 and June 4, 1789, ibid., 91, 67; Robert Morris to Mary Morris, July 2, 1790, Huntington Library, First Federal Congress Project, George Washington University (hereafter FFC). Morris notes that he had been offended the day before by a New Yorker, a probable reference to Rufus King's accusations of illicit bargaining over the location of the capital. King was silenced at least once during his diatribe; even Maclay noted that King railed "Blackguard like." July 1, 1790, *Maclay's Diary,* 309.
30. June 12, 1789, and January 8, 1790, *Maclay's Diary,* 75, 180; April 24, 1789, ibid., 4.
31. February 22 and May 13, 1790, ibid., 207, 267. See also February 19, 1790, ibid., 205.
32. February 21, 1790, ibid., 206. John Page to St. George Tucker, February 25, 1790, Tucker-Coleman Collection, Earl Gregg Swem Library, William and Mary College, FFC; *Maclay's Diary,* 211, note 1. Virginian Arthur Lee likewise considered Madison too proud. Arthur Lee to Thomas Lee Shippen, April 25, 1790, Lee Family Papers, Virginia Historical Society. Page quoted Thomas Tudor Tucker's poem in his letter, which contains a number of other riddles, rhymes, and lampoons that were passed around the House floor.
33. May 13, 1790, *Maclay's Diary,* 266–67. Maclay wanted papers concerning government payments to Revolutionary War general Baron von Steuben; the Senate was debating a resolve to grant him a pension and pay for his services during the war. See ibid., 260, note 8.
34. July 16, 1789, ibid., 114.
35. March 31 and March 10, 1790, ibid., 231, 216.
36. William Loughton Smith to Edward Rutledge, April 2, 1790, "Letters of William Loughton Smith," 111–14. On the Burke-Hamilton dispute and its impact, see John C. Meleney, *The Public Life of Aedanus Burke: Revolutionary Republican in Post-Revolutionary South Carolina* (Columbia: University of South Carolina Press, 1989), 192–207; Alexander Hamilton to Aedanus Burke, April 1 and 7, 1790, Burke to Hamilton, April 1 and 7, 1790, [From Elbridge Gerry, Rufus King, George Mathews, Lambert Cadwalader, James Jackson, and John Henry], April 6, 1790, *Hamilton Papers* 6:333–37, 353–55, 357–58; William Smith to Otho Holland Williams, April 8, 1790, Otho Holland Williams to Dr. Philip Thomas, April 8, 1790, and William Smith to Otho Holland Williams, April 18, 1790, *Calendar of the General Otho Holland Williams Papers in the Maryland Historical Society* (Baltimore: Maryland Historical Records Survey Project, 1940), Documents 573, 574, 577. For the response in Virginia, see Gustavus B. Wallace to James Madison, April 20, 1790, and Adam Stephen to James Madison, April 25, 1790, *Madison Papers,* 13:152, 176–77.
37. Burke to Anthony Walton White, January 3, 1791, in Meleney, *Public Life of Burke,* 206.
38. May 1, 1789, *Maclay's Diary,* 17; Maclay to Rush, May 18, 1789, William Maclay Diary, Library of Congress. (Maclay recorded a handful of letters in his first diary volume; the published edition of his diary does not contain them.) Maclay again tried to placate Adams the next day by engaging him (unsuccessfully) in a friendly chat. Unfortunately, Adams was no better at small talk than Maclay. May 2, 1789, *Maclay's Diary,* 19–20. For Maclay's request for Rush's assistance, see ibid., 17, note 1.
39. December 30, 1790, *Maclay's Diary,* 350. See also January 1, 1790, ibid., 177.
40. June 14 and July 20, 1790, *Maclay's Diary,* 293, 327. Maclay referred to Morris's vote to place the national capital along the Potomac. February 25, 1791, ibid., 390.

41. July 19 and April 1, 1790, ibid., 325. On another occasion, Maclay detected "rather a Coolness of the Citizens towards me." December 31, 1790, ibid., 351. Wynkoop had returned by April 22.
42. Henry Wynkoop to Reading Beatty, August 6, 1790, in Christman, *First Federal Congress,* 189; Robert Morris to Mary Morris, July 2, 1790, Huntington Library, FFC. See also Robert Morris to Mary Morris, June 2, 1790, ibid., FFC. For examples of the cartoons, see Christman, *First Federal Congress,* 190–95.
43. William Eustis to David Cobb, December 4, 6, and 18, 1794, David Cobb Papers, Massachusetts Historical Society.
44. February 7, 1790, and editorial note, *Maclay's Diary,* 199, 406. For copies of those pieces that can be documented as Maclay's work, see ibid., 406–26.
45. June 8 and 18, 1790, *Maclay's Diary,* 287, 297. The piece appeared in the Philadelphia *Federal Gazette* on June 16, 1790. *Maclay's Diary,* 419–20. Maclay occasionally "contrived" to get his essays into New York City newspapers as well. April 28, 1790, *Maclay's Diary,* 255, 418–19. See also Maclay's "sham petition" from Rhode Island, published in the New York *Federal Gazette* on April 3, 1789, suggesting that the state would join the Union if the national capital were placed in Pennsylvania. Maclay to Tench Coxe, March 30, 1789, Tench Coxe Papers; Jacob E. Cooke, *Tench Coxe and the Early Republic,* 141. The petition is not included in the assemblage of newspaper articles in *Maclay's Diary,* 406–26.
46. April 28 and May 1, 1790, *Maclay's Diary,* 255, 257; June 10, 1790, ibid., 288. For the newspaper piece, see ibid., 418.
47. March 14, 1790, ibid., 218. For other attempts to prove public opinion with correspondence, see June 21, 1789, June 14, 1790, ibid., 84–85, 293. For a list of all extant letters written by Maclay during his term of office, see ibid., 428–31.
48. July 17 and July 8, 1789, ibid., 116, 103–4; May 27 and July 3, 1789, ibid., 56, 100. The letters were from Pennsylvania's Chief Justice Thomas McKean, Supreme Court Associate Justice James Wilson, City Council member Miers Fisher, Assembly Speaker Richard Peters, éminence grise Tench Coxe, "and Sundry others."
49. September 24, 1789, and January 5, 1791, ibid., 162–63, 356–57. On public opinion, see also Wood, *Radicalism of the American Revolution,* 363–64.
50. December 8 and 29, 1790, *Maclay's Diary,* 340, 349; Thatcher to Robert Southgate, July 1, 1789, Scarborough MSS, Maine Historical Society, FFC; August 25, 1789, *Maclay's Diary,* 133–34.
51. December 14, 1790, *Maclay's Diary,* 342. On one occasion, Maclay attended the levee in a new suit, worn explicitly for that occasion. December 28, 1790, ibid., 349. During assemblies, George II moved around a circle of visitors, honoring some with a word or two; Pennsylvania socialites Anne and William Bingham saw the same ceremony in the French court. Beattie, *English Court in the Reign of George I,* 14; Alberts, *Golden Voyage: The Life and Times of William Bingham,* 154–55. On the etiquette of Washington's levees, see Scudder, *Men and Manners in America One Hundred Years Ago,* 244–46; Decatur, *Private Affairs of George Washington,* 73–74; and Elkins and McKitrick, *Age of Federalism,* 49–50.
52. Oliver Wolcott, Jr., to Oliver Wolcott, Sr., March 28, 1791, in *Memoirs of the Administrations of Washington and John Adams,* ed. George Gibbs, 2 vols. (New York: William Van Norden, 1846), 1:64; June 5, 1789, *Maclay's Diary,* 70. See also Elias, *Court Society,* 88.
53. David Hume, *Essays Moral, Political, and Literary,* ed. Eugene F. Miller (Indianapolis: Liberty Classics, 1985), Essay XXI, 203–4. For example, Elkins and McKitrick question the importance of this agitation over etiquette. Elkins and McKitrick, *Age of Federalism,* 46. McDonald stresses the comedy of the debate. McDonald, *Presidency of George Washington,* 28–31.
54. Walter Jones to James Madison, September 15, 1789, *Madison Papers,* 12:403.
55. Eléanor-François-Elie, comte de Moustier, to Thomas Jefferson, June 24, 1789, in *The Papers*

of Thomas Jefferson [hereafter *Jefferson Papers*], ed. Julian Boyd, Charles T. Cullen, and John Catanzariti, 27 vols. to date (Princeton: Princeton University Press, 1950–), 15:210–12. My translation. For a strikingly similar self-conscious construction of a republican political culture, see Hunt, *Politics, Culture, and Class in the French Revolution*.

56. On republican ambivalence over traditional props of authority, see Richard Bushman, *The Refinement of America: Persons, Houses, Cities* (New York: Random House, 1992), 181–203.
57. August 25 and 28, 1789, *Maclay's Diary,* 133–34, 138.
58. *The New-York Journal,* April 8, 1790; ibid., May 18, 1790.
59. April 25, May 11 and 14, 1789, *Maclay's Diary,* 6, 33, 37. See also Reverend James Madison to James Madison, August 15, 1789, *Madison Papers,* 12:337–39. For an example of Adams's views, see Adams to Benjamin Rush, June 9, 1789, Adams Family Papers, Massachusetts Historical Society. Also James H. Hutson, "John Adams' Title Campaign," *New England Quarterly* 41 (March 1968): 30–39; John Ferling, *John Adams: A Life* (New York: Henry Holt, 1996), 302–4; and Peter Shaw, *The Character of John Adams* (New York: Norton, 1977), 230–33.
60. James Madison to William Short, April 6, 1790, *Madison Papers,* 13:140. See also March 29, 1790, *Maclay's Diary,* 230. The Senate charge to the House was made months before Madison's comment, but it was part of the same debate over titles of address. May 14, 1789, *Maclay's Diary,* 38. Politicians also fretted about the monarchical implications of such words as *splendor* and the phrase "His Most gracious Speech." May 1 and 7, 1789, ibid., 16, 26. See also Benjamin Rush to John Adams, July 21, 1789, *Rush Papers,* 1:522–25.
61. April 28, 1789, March 9, 1790, *Maclay's Diary,* 8–9, 215–16.
62. Public figures in revolutionary France had a similar sensitivity to the politics of fashion. Hunt, *Politics, Culture, and Class in the French Revolution,* 74–86. On clothing and social authority, see Bushman, *Refinement of America,* chap. 3. For useful overviews of the literature on republicanism, see Robert E. Shalhope, "Towards a Republican Synthesis: The Emergence of an Understanding of Republicanism in American Historiography," *William and Mary Quarterly* 29 (January 1972): 49–80, and "Republicanism and Early American Historiography," *William and Mary Quarterly* 39 (April 1982): 334–56. Also note the newspaper squib declaring that after the celebration of Washington's birthday one onlooker felt "his Republicanism a little wounded." *Boston Gazette,* February 15, 1790.
63. May 4, 1789, *Maclay's Diary,* 21.
64. Washington to Catharine Macaulay Graham, January 9, 1790, *Washington Papers,* 4:551–54; Decatur, *Private Affairs of Washington,* 8–9. See also Washington to John Adams, May 10, 1789, and Washington to John Jay, May 11, 1789, *Washington Papers,* 2:245–50, 270. Washington's suit (as well as the vice president's and those of the entire Connecticut delegation) was made of wool manufactured in Hartford, Connecticut. Christman, *First Federal Congress,* 112. On the symbolism of homespun, see also Jeremiah Wadsworth to Tobias Lear, February 15, 1789, in Decatur, *Private Affairs of Washington,* 10.
65. Douglass Southall Freeman, *George Washington: A Biography,* 7 vols. (New York: Scribner's, 1948–57), 6:180; William Sullivan, *The Public Men of the Revolution,* ed. John T. S. Sullivan (Philadelphia: Carey and Hart, 1847), 119–20; Scudder, *Men and Manners*, 244–46; Decatur, *Private Affairs of Washington*, 67–68. On *President* versus *General* Washington, see *New-York Daily Gazette,* May 28, 1789; Decatur, *Private Affairs of Washington,* 43–44.
66. Decatur, *Private Affairs of Washington,* 67–68.
67. William Loughton Smith, [April 30, 1790], *Journal of William Loughton Smith, 1790–1791,* ed. Albert Matthews (Cambridge: The University Press, 1917), 67.
68. Benjamin Rush, March 17, 1790, "Commonplace Book," *The Autobiography of Benjamin Rush: His 'Travels Through Life' Together with his Commonplace Book for 1789–1813,* ed. George W. Corner (Princeton: Princeton University Press, 1948), 181.
69. May 24, 1790, *Maclay's Diary,* 275; Lord Dorchester to Lord Grenville, September 25, 1790,

Canadian Archives Report of 1890, 146, FFC. See also February 18, 1791, *Maclay's Diary,* 386; [William Loughton Smith], "The Politicks and Views of a Certain Party, Displayed" (Philadelphia, 1792). Sir Augustus Foster made a similar observation about Jefferson's egalitarian etiquette and costume as president. Mary Carolina Crawford, *Romantic Days in the Early Republic* (Boston: Little, Brown, 1912), 175. Lockridge labels Jefferson's brand of democratized gentility "radical chic." Kenneth A. Lockridge, "Colonial Self-Fashioning: Paradoxes and Pathologies in the Construction of Genteel Identity in Eighteenth-Century America," in *Through a Glass Darkly: Reflections of Personal Identity in Early America,* ed. Ronald Hoffman, Mechel Sobel, and Frederika J. Teute (Chapel Hill: University of North Carolina Press, 1997), 330–32.

70. Many noted Washington's "happy mixture of authority and modesty." Otto to Montmorin, January 12, 1790, in O'Dwyer, "French Diplomat's View of Congress," 413; Abigail Adams to Mary Cranch, July 12, 1789, and January 5, 1790, *New Letters of Abigail Adams,* 14–17, 35; Thomas Twining, May 13, 1796, in *Henry Wansey and His American Journal, 1794,* ed. David John Jeremy (Philadelphia: American Philosophical Society, 1970).
71. Freeman, *George Washington,* 6:295; Otto to Montmorin, June 13, 1790, in O'Dwyer, "French Diplomat's View of Congress," 434; also Kenneth and Anna M. Roberts, *Moreau de St. Méry's American Journey: 1793–1798* (Garden City, N.Y.: Doubleday, 1947), 350; July 15, 1789, *Maclay's Diary,* 113 (Oliver Ellsworth of Connecticut was speaking). For a more detailed description of Washington's carriage, see Decatur, *Private Affairs of Washington,* 42, 138, 177. On carriages, see T. H. Breen, "Horses and Gentlemen: The Cultural Significance of Gambling among the Gentry of Virginia," *William and Mary Quarterly* 34 (1977): 239–57; and Michael J. Rozbicki, *The Complete Colonial Gentleman: Cultural Legitimacy in Plantation America* (Charlottesville: University Press of Virginia, 1998), 162–64.
72. Tristram Dalton to Benjamin Goodhue, February 17, 1789, Benjamin Goodhue Papers, New-York Society Library; May 7, 1790, *Maclay's Diary,* 262.
73. *The New-York Journal,* March 4, 1790. Of course, considering that Hamilton's way of processing problems was to talk to himself while walking, it is possible that he *was* occasionally "lost in thought profound." For contemporary descriptions of Hamilton's public manner, see Sullivan, *Public Men of the Revolution,* 260–61; Jacques Pierre Brissot de Warville, *New Travels in the United States of America, 1788* (1797; Cambridge: Belknap, 1964), 147.
74. John Adams to unknown correspondent, March 3, 1792, Adams Family Papers, Massachusetts Historical Society; David Stuart to George Washington, July 14, 1789, *Washington Papers,* 3:198–204; Washington to David Stuart, July 26, 1789, *Washington Papers,* 3:321–27.
75. May 3–5 and 18, 1791, *The Diaries of George Washington, 1748–1799,* ed. John C. Fitzpatrick (1925; New York: Kraus Reprint, 1971), 172–73, 179; Sedgwick to Pamela Sedgwick, January 1, 1791, Theodore Sedgwick Papers, Massachusetts Historical Society; January 13, 1791, *Maclay's Diary,* 361.
76. Walter Jones to James Madison, July 25, 1789, *Madison Papers,* 12:308; Lund Washington to George Washington, ca. April 28, 1790, Mount Vernon Library.
77. Adams to John Trumbull, April 25 and April 2, 1790, Adams Family Papers, Massachusetts Historical Society.
78. February 26, 1791, *Maclay's Diary,* 395. On the "rules" of politics and the prevailing discomfort with personal alliances and political intrigues, see Young, *Washington Community,* chap. 3.
79. July 2 and 15, June 18, and May 20, 1790, *Maclay's Diary,* 310, 320–21, 297, 272.
80. June 14 and 23, 1790, ibid., 293, 302; William Loughton Smith to Edward Rutledge, June 14, 1790, "Letters of William Loughton Smith," 116; "Residence, 2d session" [memorandum], ca. June 30, 1790, Rufus King Papers, New-York Historical Society; *Portland Gazette,* September 26, 1808, in Fischer, *Revolution of American Conservatism,* 161. See also Richard Peters to Timothy Pickering, February 26, 1806, in Fischer, *Revolution of American Conservatism,* 161.

Hamilton's conversation complies with his 1790 dinner deal with Madison. See Bowling, *Creation of Washington, D.C.,* 187. For an alternate view of the 1790 "dinner deal," see Jacob E. Cooke, "Compromise of 1790," *William and Mary Quarterly* 27 (1970): 523–45. See also Bowling (with a rebuttal by Cooke), "Dinner at Jefferson's: A Note on Jacob E. Cooke's 'The Compromise of 1790,'" *William and Mary Quarterly* 28 (October 1971): 629–48; and Norman K. Risjord, "The Compromise of 1790: New Evidence on the Dinner Table Bargain," *William and Mary Quarterly* 33 (April 1976): 309–14.

81. July 10, 1790, *Maclay's Diary,* 317; March 26, 1790, ibid., 229.
82. June 14, 1790, ibid., 292. Morris must have discussed his conversation with the entire Pennsylvania delegation; within three days, Peter Muhlenberg reported to Benjamin Rush that "It is now established *beyond a doubt* that the Secretary of the Treasury guides the movements of the Eastern Phalanx." Peter Muhlenberg to Benjamin Rush, June 17, 1790, Gratz Collection, Historical Society of Pennsylvania, FFC.
83. Comte de Moustier to George Washington, May 1 and 19, 1789, Washington to Moustier, May 25, 1789, *Washington Papers,* 2:183–86, 329–31, 389–91.
84. Pierre Auguste Adet to unknown correspondent, 1795, in Charles H. Sherrill, *French Memories of Eighteenth Century America* (New York: Scribner's, 1915), 254. See also Young, *Washington Community,* 47, though Young overlooks the larger ideological significance of this politicized social realm, attributing it to the close quarters in Washington.
85. January 2 and February 9, 1790, September 6, 1789, January 26, 1791, *Maclay's Diary,* 178, 200, 147, 369. Pickering to William Bingham, December 17, 1795, in Alberts, *Golden Voyage,* 298–99; John Adams to John Trumbull, April 2, 1790, Adams Family Papers. See also Coxe to Jefferson, n.d. [between December 1801 and May 1802], in Cooke, *Tench Coxe and the Early Republic,* 249, note 30.
86. The weekly Pennsylvania dinners began in February 1790. See February 22, May 3, 17, and 24, June 7 and 21, 1790, *Maclay's Diary,* 207, 259, 270, 274–75, 285, 299. On the weekly levees of political wives, see Shields and Teute, "Republican Court and the Historiography of a Woman's Domain."
87. August 27, 1789, and March 4, 1790, *Maclay's Diary,* 136–37, 212–13. Maclay dined with the president on August 27, 1789, January 14, March 4, May 6, July 8, 1790, and January 20, 1790, ibid., 136–37, 182, 212–13, 261, 315, 364–65. Washington played with his silverware on more than one occasion. Jay told an anecdote about "the Duchess of Devonshire leaving no *Stone* unturned, to carry Fox's election"—a story based on the rumor that she gave kisses in exchange for votes (though Jay's pun on the word *stone* suggests something more than kisses). August 27, 1789, *Maclay's Diary,* 137, note 37; Donald R. McAdams, "Electioneering Techniques in Populous Constituencies, 1784–96," *Studies in Burke and His Time* 14 (Fall 1972): 23–53, see 33–34.
88. Abigail Adams to Mary Cranch, September 1, 1789, *New Letters of Abigail Adams: 1788–1801,* ed. Stewart Mitchell (1947; Westport, Conn.: Greenwood, 1973), 24–26. Adams's attacker was Edward Church, who was already upset with Adams for failing to get him a public office. Church's poem appeared in the *Massachusetts Centinel* on August 22, 1789; for an excerpt, see ibid.
89. Alexander White to Mrs. Wood, March 8, 1789, Morristown National Historical Park; Theodore Sedgwick to Pamela Sedgwick, July 10, 1789, Theodore Sedgwick Papers, Massachusetts Historical Society; May 1, 1789, *Maclay's Diary,* 17–18; Abigail Adams to Mary Cranch, July 12 and August 9, 1789, and December 12, 1790, *New Letters of Abigail Adams,* 14–17, 19–20, 66. See also John Page to St. George Tucker, March 26, 1789, Tucker-Coleman Papers, Earl Gregg Swann Library, College of William and Mary, FFC; July 18, 1789, Robert Lewis diary, Mount Vernon Library. On the rituals of visiting, see C. Dallett Hemphill, *Bowing to Necessities: A History of Manners in America, 1620–1860* (New York: Oxford University Press, 1999),

151–54. Hemphill discusses the codification of these rituals in etiquette books of the 1820s, but clearly they were in practice much earlier.

90. The Bréhan scandal took place in the last days of the Confederation government. Madison to Jefferson, December 8, 1788, Madame de Bréhan and Comte de Moustier to Jefferson, December 29, 1788, *Jefferson Papers,* 14:300–304, 399–401. See also John Jay to Jefferson, November 25, 1788; David Humphreys to Jefferson, November 29, 1788, Jefferson to John Jay, February 4, 1789, Jefferson to Angelica Schuyler Church, February 15, 1789, John Trumbull to Jefferson, March 10, 1789, *Jefferson Papers,* 14:291, 339–42, 520–23, 553–54, 634–35. On Moustier's dinner gaffe, see Roberts and Roberts, *Moreau de St. Méry's American Journey,* 275. Also Griswold, *Republican Court,* 92–93.
91. April 28, 1789, *Maclay's Diary,* 8.
92. April 28 and 30, and August 24, 1789, ibid., 8, 13, 132.
93. January 20, 1791, ibid., 364–66.
94. Jefferson, [Memorandum of Conversation between Senator Philemon Dickinson and George Hammond], March 26, 1792, *Jefferson Papers,* 23:344–45. See also Louis Guillaume Otto to Montmorin, December 13 1790, ibid., 18:539 headnote.
95. June 11, 1789, and June 20, 1790, *Maclay's Diary,* 74, 298. On the role of elite women in the national political arena, see Catherine Allgor, *Parlour Politics: In Which the Ladies of Washington Help Build a City and a Government* (Charlottesville: University Press of Virginia, 2000); Susan Branson, "Politics and Gender: The Political Consciousness of Philadelphia Women in the 1790s" (Ph.D. diss., Northern Illinois University, 1992); and Shields and Teute, "Republican Court and the Historiography of a Woman's Domain." See also Paula Baker, "The Domestication of Politics: Women and American Political Society, 1780–1920," *American Historical Review* 89 (1984): 628–32; Linda Kerber, *Women of the Republic: Intellect and Ideology in Revolutionary America* (Chapel Hill: University of North Carolina Press, 1980); and Rosemarie Zagarri, "Gender and the First Party System," in *Federalists Reconsidered,* ed. Doron Ben-Atar and Barbara B. Oberg (Charlottesville: University Press of Virginia, 1998), 118–34.
96. Jefferson to James Madison, February 14, 1783, in James Morton Smith, ed., *The Republic of Letters: The Correspondence Between Thomas Jefferson and James Madison, 1776–1826* (New York: Norton, 1995), 1:223. Madison agreed that "for all *unconfidential services he is a convenient instrument.*" Madison to Jefferson, February 18, 1783, ibid., 1:226–27. Franks later accompanied Jefferson to France as his secretary.
97. Adams to Mary Cranch, April 3, 1790, *New Letters of Abigail Adams,* 44; Lear to George Augustine Washington, May 3, 1789, *Washington Papers,* 2:248–49, note. (Martha had not yet joined her husband in New York.) The office-seeker was Joseph Cranch. Adams eventually spoke with Secretary of War Henry Knox concerning the matter.
98. December 29, 1790, *Maclay's Diary,* 349; December 31, 1790, and March 3, 1791, ibid., 352, 401.
99. December 31, 1790, and February 23, 1791, ibid., 351–52, 387. See also February 26, 1791, ibid., 392.
100. Samuel Barr to George Washington Harris, July 18, 1882, FFC; George Washington Harris, ed., *Sketches of Debate in the First Senate of the United States, in 1789–90–91, by William Maclay, A Senator from Pennsylvania* (Harrisburg: Lane and Hart, Printer, 1880). On the efforts of George Washington Harris to get the diary published, see ibid., xvi–xviii. See also the Epilogue, below. My thanks to Ken Bowling and Charlene Bickford for providing access to their files concerning Harris.
101. The 1890 edition, edited by Edgar S. Maclay (a distant relation), is relatively accurate, by nineteenth-century editorial standards. Edgar S. Maclay, *The Journal of William Maclay, United States Senator from Pennsylvania, 1789–1791* (New York: Appleton, 1890). The chief of

the Library of Congress Manuscript Division thought that the diary was worth only $500 "in view of the great number of other offers of material which would be equally important"—unless the Librarian of Congress was willing to pay for it out of his own "special fund," in which case a price as high as $1,500 would be reasonable. Memorandum from St. George L. Sioussat to Chief Assistant Librarian, February 5, 1941, FFC. A third edition, nearly identical to the second, was published in 1927 by Charles Beard, who added a contextual introduction. *The Journal of William Maclay, United States Senator from Pennsylvania, 1789–1791* (New York: A & C Boni, 1927). The 1988 edition published under the auspices of the Documentary History of the First Federal Congress is the first completely accurate version of Maclay's diary.

2
Slander, Poison, Whispers, and Fame

1. The first advertisement for Marshall's biography appeared in the Georgetown *Washington Federalist* on March 27, 1802. The book was published in five volumes between 1804 and 1807. *Hamilton Papers,* 25:604, note 1. On Marshall's authorship of Washington's *Life,* see Robert K. Faulkner, "John Marshall and the 'False Glare' of Fame," in McNamara, *Noblest Minds,* 163–84.
2. Jefferson to Elbridge Gerry, March 29, 1801, *The Writings of Thomas Jefferson,* ed. Paul L. Ford, 12 vols. (New York: Scribner's, 1905), 9:241.
3. Jefferson to Joel Barlow, October 8, 1809, ibid., 11:121–22; John Marshall, *The Life of George Washington,* 5 vols. (Philadelphia: C. P. Wayne, 1807), 5:33; Thomas Jefferson, undated notes, *The Complete Anas of Thomas Jefferson,* ed. Franklin B. Sawvel (New York: Round Table Press, 1903), 43. For all of Jefferson's corrections, see pp. 41–43.
4. I compared a recently discovered table of contents for the "Anas" with Jefferson's published papers; the table of contents included almost every piece of official correspondence included in the published *Jefferson Papers*. See also Merrill Peterson, *The Jefferson Image in the American Mind* (New York: Oxford University Press, 1960), 33. Jefferson recorded conversations throughout his public career, but only the memoranda from Washington's administration were included in his documentary "history."
5. Jefferson to John Adams, August 10 [11], 1815, *The Adams-Jefferson Letters: The Complete Correspondence Between Thomas Jefferson and Abigail and John Adams,* ed. Lester J. Cappon, 2 vols. (Chapel Hill: University of North Carolina Press, 1959), 2:452.
6. Thomas Jefferson Randolph, ed., *Memoir, Correspondence, and Miscellanies, from the Papers of Thomas Jefferson,* 4 vols. (Charlottesville, Va.: F. Carr, 1829), 4:443; Peterson, *Jefferson Image in the American Mind,* 33; and Malone, *Jefferson and the Rights of Man,* 497. For the most authoritative discussion of the "Anas," see *Jefferson Papers,* 22:33–38. I occasionally refer to Jefferson's compilation as the "Anas" for convenience; as noted above, he himself never used this title. This study relies on Jefferson's published memoranda in the *Jefferson Papers,* his draft table of contents, and Franklin Sawvel's flawed 1903 published edition of the "Anas" which excludes some of Jefferson's revisions, and includes memoranda from long after Jefferson's service as secretary of state, as well as altered spelling and punctuation and misinterpreted abbreviations. On the discovery of the table of contents, see Eugene Sheridan, "Thomas Jefferson and the Giles Resolutions," *William and Mary Quarterly* 49 (1992): 607, note. Long assumed to be an epistolary record, the list appears to be a draft table of contents for Jefferson's "history," compiled over the course of several years. A comparison of Jefferson's table of contents with the *Jefferson Papers* reveals that Jefferson excluded only a few documents from his three volumes, leading to the likely conclusion that the volumes were at most marginally different from his draft table of contents.

7. Though the word *gossip* best describes this political practice, I do not use the word pejoratively; those who gossiped would not have seen their behavior as disreputable.
8. William Seton to Alexander Hamilton, April 9, 1792, *Hamilton Papers,* 11:258; Henry Lee to James Madison, January 8, 1792, *Madison Papers,* 14:183; George Washington to Hamilton, August 26, 1792, *Hamilton Papers,* 12:276 (also Washington to Thomas Jefferson, August 23, 1792, *Jefferson Papers,* 24:315–19); Fisher Ames to John Lowell, December 6, 1792, *Works of Fisher Ames,* 2:956–57. For an evocative sociological study of gossip, see Goodman and Ben-Ze'ev, *Good Gossip.* See also Spacks, *Gossip;* Bonomi, *Lord Cornbury Scandal;* and Wiebe, *Opening of American Society,* 44. For related studies of the art of conversation, see Elias, *Civilizing Process,* 88–93; Burke, *Art of Conversation;* and Shields, *Civil Tongues and Polite Tongues in British America.*
9. On the practical purposes of gossip, see Nicholas Emler, "Gossip, Reputation, and Social Adaptation," in Goodman and Ben-Ze'ev, *Good Gossip,* 134.
10. On the "moral grammar of lies" and genteel status, see Shapin, *Social History of Truth,* esp. chap. 3. On the "lie direct" see generally, John Lyde Wilson, *The Code of Honor, or Rules for the Government of Principals and Seconds in Duelling* (Charleston, S.C., 1838). On slander, libel, and reputation in the early republic, see Rosenberg, *Protecting the Best Men,* chaps. 1–5.
11. William Loughton Smith, "An Address From William Smith, of South-Carolina, to his Constituents" (Philadelphia, 1794), 27; Alexander Hamilton to William Short, February 5, 1793, *Hamilton Papers,* 14:7. Hamilton was concerned about the international reaction to Republican Representative William Branch Giles's hostile congressional resolutions questioning Hamilton's conduct as secretary of the treasury.
12. William Willcocks to Alexander Hamilton, September 5, 1793, *Hamilton Papers,* 15:324; Alexander Hamilton to John Jay, December 18, 1792, ibid., 13:338.
13. Aaron Burr to unknown correspondent, December 30, 1804, Allyn Kellogg Ford Papers, Minnesota Historical Society; Robert R. Livingston to George Washington, May 2, 1789, *Washington Papers,* 2:192–96. Henry Lee made a similar suggestion. Lee to Washington, July 1, 1789, *Washington Papers,* 3:98–100.
14. Beckley to Tench Coxe, October 30, 1800, in Gawalt, *Justifying Jefferson,* 220. Jefferson to Madison, November 22, 1799, *Madison Papers,* 17:277–78.
15. Alexander Hamilton to unknown correspondent, December 17, 1791, *Hamilton Papers,* 10: 389–90. Heading off to meet with James Reynolds, a disgruntled former treasury employee who was blackmailing him, Hamilton informed an unknown correspondent of his destination and his fears about the outcome. For more on the "Reynolds affair," see Broadus Mitchell, *Alexander Hamilton,* 2 vols. (New York: Macmillan, 1962), 399–422; John C. Miller, *Alexander Hamilton: Portrait in Paradox* (New York: Harper and Brothers, 1959), 458–65; and Jacob K. Cogan, "The Reynolds Affair and the Politics of Character," *Journal of the Early Republic* 16, no. 3 (Fall 1996): 389–417. On Hamilton's obvious concern for his fame, see also John Fenno to Joseph Ward, October 10, 1789, Joseph Ward Papers, Chicago Historical Society, FFC; Stourzh, *Hamilton and the Idea of Republican Government,* 95–106; Peter McNamara, "Alexander Hamilton, the Love of Fame, and Modern Democratic Statesmanship," in McNamara, *Noblest Minds,* 141–62. On "fame" as gossip, see for example, Fisher Ames to Thomas Dwight, November 12, 1792: "The men of the south are well trained for Clinton, says fame." *Works of Fisher Ames,* 2:950–51.
16. William Plumer to Jeremiah Smith, December 10, 1791, William Plumer Papers, Library of Congress.
17. A survey of forty-four collections of the papers of national politicians for the years 1792–1793 produced little political gossip but many references to the process of gossiping; politicians often responded to circulating rumors without repeating them (a phenomenon that I dub

"the ouch factor"). Eighteenth-century Americans were particularly attuned to nuances of *manner,* which often said far more than the words themselves. See Fliegelman, *Declaring Independence;* also Ziff, *Writing in the New Nation,* 55–56. This emphasis on external appearance invited fears of deception, a fertile watering ground for a culture of gossip. For an excellent discussion of this "paranoid" mentality, see Gordon Wood, "Conspiracy and the Paranoid Style," *William and Mary Quarterly* 29 (July 1982): 401–41.

18. Robert Troup to Alexander Hamilton, March 19, 1792, *Hamilton Papers,* 11:158; Henry Lee to Alexander Hamilton, May 6, 1793, ibid., 14:416.
19. September 24, 1789, *Maclay's Diary,* 164. The Latin appears on the only known page of Maclay's rough notes, taken on the Senate floor (see fig. 3, above). Jefferson, memorandum, December 17, 1792, *Jefferson Papers,* 24:751. Sawvel's *Anas* includes a badly scrambled version of this memorandum. *Anas,* 100. Muhlenberg, Monroe, and Venable visited Hamilton on December 15. *Hamilton Papers,* 113:15–16, note 1.
20. Gustavus B. Wallace to James Madison, April 20, 1790, Adams Stephen to James Madison, April 25, 1790, *Madison Papers,* 13:152, 176. Madison's letter has not been found. See also Brown, *Knowledge Is Power,* 266, 278; Bonomi, *Lord Cornbury Scandal,* 150–58.
21. Jefferson, introduction, February 4, 1818, *Anas,* 24.
22. Ibid., *Anas,* 36; Jefferson, memorandum, August 13, 1791, *Jefferson Papers,* 22:39.
23. Jefferson, memorandum, July 18, 1793, *Anas,* 146–47. See also June 12, 1793, ibid., 129. The Treasury "clerk" Irvine was actually a federal commissioner at the Department of the Comptroller in the Treasury Department who was in charge of settling state claims against the national government. Beckley befriended him in the course of doing business for Madison, so it is interesting that Jefferson sent Lear—not Beckley, his customary agent—to investigate Irvine's guilt. Berkeley and Berkeley, *John Beckley,* 67; "List of the Several Persons Employed in the Office of the Comptroller of the Treasury of the United States on the 31st. of December 1792, and of the Salaries Per Annum Allowed to Each," January 4, 1793, *Hamilton Papers,* 13:464.
24. Jefferson, memorandum, April 7, 1793, *Jefferson Papers,* 25:517; Alexander Hamilton to George Washington, September 9, 1792, *Hamilton Papers,* 12:348; Thomas Jefferson to George Washington, September 9, 1792, *Jefferson Papers,* 24:352.
25. Jefferson, memorandum, November 11, 1792, *Jefferson Papers,* 24:607. (Sawvel's *Anas* incorrectly dates this memorandum November 21, 1792; *Anas,* 96–97.) Jefferson, memorandum, February 16, 1793, *Jefferson Papers,* 25:208.
26. [Georgetown, Washington, D.C.], *Washington Federalist,* December 19, 1800, in Donald Stewart, *The Opposition Press of the Federalist Period* (Albany: State University of New York Press, 1969), 638. See, for example, William Livingston to George Washington, April 27, 1778: "I have sent Collins a number of letters as if by different hands. . . . This mode of rendering a measure unpopular, I have frequently experienced in my political days to be of surprising efficacy, as the common people collect from it that everybody is against it." In Philip Davidson, *Propaganda and the American Revolution* (Chapel Hill: University of North Carolina Press, 1941), 12. Also Fisher Ames to Timothy Pickering, January 1, 1807, Pickering Papers, Massachusetts Historical Society.
27. Thomas Jefferson to Angelica Church, October 1798, in Cunningham, *Jeffersonian Republicans,* 31. Angelica Church was Alexander Hamilton's sister-in-law. Cunningham (and most other writers who cite this letter) have consistently misdated it 1792.
28. Jefferson had warned Washington about "monarchical federalists" in a May 23, 1792, letter; see *Jefferson Papers,* 23:535–41. He informed Madison of the conversation in a June 10, 1792 letter; see ibid., 24:50.
29. Jefferson, memorandum, October 1, 1792, ibid., 24:435. Washington responded by 1) noting that some self-interest was to be expected in any government; 2) praising Hamilton's funding

system; and 3) stating that "experience was the only criterion of right." Thomas Jefferson, memorandum, October 1, 1792, ibid., 24:435.

30. Thomas Jefferson, introduction, February 4, 1818, *Anas,* 40.

31. Jefferson, memorandum, March 23, 1793, *Jefferson Papers,* 25:432–33; Benjamin Rush, August 27, 1792, "Commonplace Book," in *Autobiography of Benjamin Rush,* 227; Rush to Burr, September 24, 1792, *Political Correspondence and Public Papers of Aaron Burr* [hereafter *Papers of Aaron Burr*], ed. Mary-Jo Kline, 2 vols. (Princeton: Princeton University Press, 1983), 1:317.

32. Abigail Adams to John Adams, January 25, 1801, and [A Conversation at table between Mrs A and Mr J], [January 1801], Adams Family Papers. For an example of Jefferson's views about women and politics, see Jefferson to Anne Willing Bingham, May 11, 1788, in *Jefferson: Writings,* ed. Merrill Peterson (New York: Library of America, 1984), 922–23. See also Lewis, "'Blessings of Domestic Society'"; and Allgor, *Parlour Politics.*

33. See James Sullivan to Elbridge Gerry, August 30, 1789, Sullivan Papers, Massachusetts Historical Society, FFC; Gerry to unknown correspondent, March 22, 1789, Elbridge Gerry Papers, Library of Congress; and Arthur Lee to Thomas Lee Shippen, April 25, 1790, Lee Family Papers, Virginia Historical Society. On unpredictable friendships, see James Madison to Thomas Jefferson, August 27, 1793, *Madison Papers,* 15:75; and Alexander Hamilton to Edward Carrington, May 26, 1792, *Hamilton Papers,* 11:433. On the many meanings of *friendship,* see Wood, *Radicalism,* 224, 178; Taylor, "'Art of Hook and Snivey,'" 1382; Taylor, *William Cooper's Town,* 234–35; J. Mills Thornton III, *Politics and Power in a Slave Society: Alabama, 1800–1860* (Baton Rouge: Louisiana State University Press, 1978), 140–41. For a sociological discussion of gossip as a reinforcement for friendship, see Goodman and Ben-Ze'ev, *Good Gossip,* passim, esp. 3.

34. Troup's letter quotes the Roman senator Marcus Porcius Cato, who ended every speech with the words "Delenda est Carthago"(Carthage must be destroyed). Carthage was one of Rome's greatest political and commercial rivals. Troup implies that for Jefferson and his friends, Hamilton is their Carthage. Robert Troup to Alexander Hamilton, June 15, 1791, *Hamilton Papers,* 8:478. See also Wiebe, *Opening of American Society,* 44.

35. William Heth, diary, August 31, 1792, William Heth Papers, Library of Congress; Beckley to Madison, September 2 and October 17, 1792, *Madison Papers,* 14:354–58; Hamilton to Edward Carrington, May 26, 1792, *Hamilton Papers,* 11:444–45.

36. This understanding complements John Howe's discussion of the Founders' "volatile and crisis-ridden ideology." Men who knew the frailties of republics and found themselves in an unstable, personal political realm could not help but connect these two factors, fueling the crisis mentality of the 1790s. Howe, "Republican Thought and the Political Violence," 165.

37. Jefferson, introduction, February 4, 1818, *Anas,* 24.

38. On the "isolation of the governors from the governed," see Young, *Washington Community,* 32.

39. Henry Van Schaack to Theodore Sedgwick, June 9, 1797, Sedgwick I Correspondence, Massachusetts Historical Society. See also Henry Van Schaack to Theodore Sedgwick, January 15, 1796, ibid.; and Arlette Farge, *Subversive Words: Public Opinion in Eighteenth-Century France* (University Park: Pennsylvania State University Press, 1995), 66–77. Farge discusses the suppression of public opinion in France, making for an interesting comparison with republican America.

40. Jefferson and Washington conversed on July 10 and October 1, 1792, and February 7, 1793. *Jefferson Papers,* 24:210–11, 433–35, 25:153–55. Washington initially planned to have levees on both Tuesday and Friday afternoons, but the Friday event evolved into Martha Washington's weekly evening reception. May 4, 1789, *Maclay's Diary,* 21; Thomas Jefferson, memorandum, October 1, 1792, *Jefferson Papers,* 24:434. In addition to Lear's gleanings, Washington wanted feedback from the South and seemed (to Jefferson) to be soliciting it from him.

41. Jefferson, Memoranda, November 19, 1792, and April 7, 1793, *Jefferson Papers,* 24:638, 25:517; memorandum, June 7, 1793, *Anas,* 125–27.
42. Jefferson, memorandum, June 12, 1793, *Anas,* 128–29; John Beckley to unknown correspondent, June 22, 1793, *Hamilton Papers,* 14:467, editorial note. Hamilton pointed out in a later pamphlet that Fraunces felt comfortable enough with his new "friends" to ask Jefferson for a loan and a "certificate of character" to be used in seeking employment. See Thomas Jefferson to Andrew Fraunces, June 27, 1797, and Jefferson to Fraunces, June 28, 1797, in Alexander Hamilton, "Observations on Certain Documents Contained in No. V & VI of 'The History of the United States for the Year 1796'" (Philadelphia, 1797). Reprinted in *Hamilton Papers,* 21:238–85, letters on 284–85.
43. John Beckley to unknown correspondent, June 22, 1793, *Hamilton Papers,* 14:467, editorial note.
44. John Beckley to unknown correspondent, July 1, 1793, ibid., 14:468–69, editorial note. William Willcocks to Alexander Hamilton, August 25 and September 5, 1793, ibid., 15:277, 324. See also Robert Affleck to Hamilton, September 7, 1793, ibid., 15:326, and Robert Troup to Hamilton, December 25, 1793, ibid., 15:587–89. Fraunces also voiced his charges to Washington, urged action in the House of Representatives, and eventually published a pamphlet containing his accusations. For the House resolution, see Alexander Hamilton, "Observations on Certain Documents . . . ," 21:242. For Fraunces's correspondence with Washington, see Andrew Fraunces, "An Appeal to the Legislature of the United States, and to the Citizens Individually, of the Several States" (Philadelphia, 1793).
45. *The [New York] Diary: or Loudon's Register,* and the *New York Daily Gazette,* October 11, 1793, *Hamilton Papers,* 15:354–55. Fraunces wrote, "If I am a *dispicable calumniator,* I have been unfortunately, for a long time past a pupil of Mr. Hamilton's—and that it remains to be proved whether I do honor to my tutor or not." *The [New York] Diary,* October 12, 1793, *Hamilton Papers,* 15:355.
46. Jefferson, memorandum, March 23, 1793, *Jefferson Papers,* 25:432–33. For the published version of the list, see John Beckley and James Monroe, "An Examination of the Late Proceedings in Congress, Respecting the Official Conduct of the Secretary of the Treasury" (Philadelphia, 1793).
47. Thomas Jefferson to James Madison, June 4, 1792, *Jefferson Papers,* 24:26. Madison sent the list on June 12, 1792; see ibid., 24:69–71, note.
48. Jefferson, memorandum, July 10, 1792, ibid., 24:211.
49. After 1795 Tench Coxe worked close by Beckley's side. See Michael Durey, *Transatlantic Radicals and the Early American Republic* (Lawrence: University Press of Kansas, 1997), 234; and Jacob Cooke, *Tench Coxe and the Early Republic* (Chapel Hill: University of North Carolina Press, 1978). On Beckley, see esp. Jeffrey L. Pasley, "'A Journeyman, Either in Law or Politics': John Beckley and the Social Origins of Political Campaigning," *Journal of the Early Republic* 16 (Winter 1996): 531–69, and "'Artful and Designing Men,'" chaps. 1 and 3. Also Philip M. Marsh, "John Beckley: Mystery Man of the Early Jeffersonians," *Pennsylvania Magazine of History and Biography* 72 (1948): 54–69; Raymond V. Martin, Jr., "Eminent Virginian—A Study of John Beckley," *West Virginia History* 11 (1949–50): 44–61; Noble E. Cunningham, Jr., "John Beckley: An Early American Party Manager," *William and Mary Quarterly,* 3rd ser., 13 (1956): 40–52; Gloria Jahoda, "John Beckley: Jefferson's Campaign Manager," *Bulletin of the New York Public Library* 64 (May 1960): 247–60; Cunningham, *Jeffersonian Republicans,* passim; and Berkeley and Smith Berkeley, *John Beckley*. For a selection of Beckley's correspondence, see Gawalt, *Justifying Jefferson*.
50. James Monroe to James Madison, October 9, 1792, *Madison Papers,* 14:377–81; Monroe and Madison to Melancton Smith and Marinus Willet, October 19, 1792, ibid., 14:387. For an example of Madison filtering a pamphlet, see Thomas Jefferson to Madison, September 1,

1793, ibid., 14:88–91; Jefferson to Madison, September 8, 1793, ibid., 14:104; and Madison to Monroe, September 15, 1793, ibid., 14:111.

51. On Jefferson's political method, see Caldwell, *Administrative Theories of Hamilton and Jefferson;* Cunningham, *Jeffersonian Republicans in Power;* Dumas Malone, *Thomas Jefferson as a Political Leader* (Los Angeles: University of California Press, 1963); White, *The Jeffersonians,* 29–88; and Young, *Washington Community,* 128–31, 163–78.

52. Plumer, December 3, 1804, *William Plumer's Memorandum of Proceedings in the United States Senate, 1803–1807,* ed. Everett Somerville Brown (New York: Macmillan, 1923), 211–12; Young, *Washington Community,* 169.

53. Margaret Bayard Smith quotes Jefferson declaring at one dinner "You see we are alone . . . and *our walls have no ears*." Young, *Washington Community,* 169.

54. 1 U.S. Statutes at Large, 65–67, signed September 2, 1789. On the act itself, see Mitchell, *Alexander Hamilton,* 2:14–21; Charlene Bangs Bickford and Helen E. Veit, eds., *Legislative Histories,* volume 6 of the *Documentary History of the First Federal Congress, 1789–1791* (Baltimore: Johns Hopkins University Press, 1986), 1975–91; and White, *Federalists,* 67–76.

55. Jefferson, [Memorandum on References by Congress to Heads of Departments], [March 10, 1792], *Jefferson Papers,* 24:246–48. On the attack on references to heads of departments, see White, *Federalists,* 68–74.

56. Beckley to Tench Coxe, January 24, 1800, in Gawalt, *Justifying Jefferson*, 164–65 (see also Cooke, *Tench Coxe,* 372, note 3); Jefferson to Washington, May 23, September 9, 1792, and February 7, 1793, and [Notes of a Conversation with George Washington], October 1, 1792, *Jefferson Papers,* 23:537, 24:353 and 435, 25:155; Jefferson to Thomas Mann Randolph, Jr., November 2, 1792, *Jefferson Papers,* 24:556–57. Given the prevailing fears of military despotism attached to the idea of a standing army, Jefferson's military metaphor had particular power. See Gordon Wood, *The Creation of the American Republic, 1776–1787* (Chapel Hill: University of North Carolina Press, 1969), 32–34; Lawrence Delbert Cress, *Citizens in Arms: The Army and Militia in American Society to the War of 1812* (Chapel Hill: University of North Carolina Press, 1982).

57. On Hamilton's political method, see Joanne B. Freeman, "'The Art and Address of Ministerial Management': Alexander Hamilton and Congress," in *Neither Separate Nor Equal: Congress and the Executive Branch in the 1790s,* ed. Kenneth R. Bowling and Donald R. Kennon (Athens: Ohio University Press, 2000); Caldwell, *Administrative Theories of Hamilton and Jefferson;* White, *Federalists*; and Mitchell, *Alexander Hamilton,* 2:24–31.

58. Jefferson, introduction, *Anas,* 33–34. For Jefferson's original account, see Jefferson, [Memorandum], 1792, *Jefferson Papers,* 17:205–7.

59. Hamilton was accusing Jefferson of attacking him indirectly through *National Gazette* editor Philip Freneau, a printer employed as a translator by Jefferson in the State Department. [Hamilton], "Catullus III," [Philadelphia] *Gazette of the United States,* September 29, 1792, 12:504.

60. Hamilton to Robert Morris, November 9, 1790, *Hamilton Papers,* 7:146.

61. Charles Carroll to Alexander Hamilton, October 22, 1792, *Hamilton Papers,* 12:608; Fisher Ames, [Untitled], [1794?], *Works of Fisher Ames,* 2:977; Fisher Ames to George Richards Minot, February 16, 1792, *Works of Fisher Ames,* 2:913. See also John Zvesper, *Political Philosophy and Rhetoric: A Study of the Origins of American Party Politics* (Cambridge: Cambridge University Press, 1977), 30.

62. Alexander Hamilton to James A. Bayard, April 16–21, 1802, *Hamilton Papers,* 25:606; James McHenry to Oliver Wolcott, Jr., July 22, 1800, *Hamilton Papers,* 25:112–15. Hamilton's realization led him to urge the use of newspapers and "Christian Constitutional Societies" to rouse the people against the Republican regime. See Fischer, *Revolution of American Conservatism*.

63. On the Genet Affair, see Harry Ammon, *The Genet Mission* (New York: Norton, 1973); Elkins and McKitrick, *Age of Federalism,* 330–73; and Dumas Malone, *Jefferson and the Ordeal of Liberty,* vol. 3 of *Jefferson and His Time* (Boston: Little, Brown, 1962), chap 6. On Democratic-Republican Societies, see Elkins and McKitrick, *Age of Federalism,* 451–61; Eugene P. Link, *Democratic-Republican Societies, 1790–1800* (New York: Columbia University Press, 1942); Philip S. Foner, *The Democratic-Republican Societies, 1790–1800: A Documentary Sourcebook of Constitutions, Declarations, Addresses, Resolutions, and Toasts* (Westport: Greenwood, 1976); Waldstreicher, *In the Midst of Perpetual Fetes,* 131–33; and Matthew Schoenbachler, "Republicanism in the Age of Democratic Revolution: The Democratic-Republican Societies of the 1790s," *Journal of the Early Republic* 18 (Summer 1998): 237–61. On revolutionary echoes, see Elkins and McKitrick, *Age of Federalism,* 848, note 14; Waldstreicher, *In the Midst of Perpetual Fetes,* 132–33; and Richard Buel, Jr., *Securing the Revolution: Ideology in American Politics, 1789–1815* (Ithaca: Cornell University Press, 1972), 97–101.
64. King to Hamilton, August 3, 1793, *Hamilton Papers,* 15:173.
65. Aaron Burr to John Nicholson, July 16, 1793, Aaron Burr Papers, Library of Congress; William Smith to Otho Williams, July 19, 1793, cited in *Calendar of the General Otho Holland Williams Papers in the Maryland Historical Society* (Baltimore: Maryland Historical Records Survey Project, Baltimore, 1940), 293; Concord, N.H., *Mirrour,* December 16, 1793, in Link, *Democratic-Republican Societies,* 192. Otho Williams, Baltimore's collector of customs, was in frequent communication with his supervisor, Alexander Hamilton.
66. Thomas Jefferson to James Madison, August 11, 1793, *Madison Papers,* 14:57; Hamilton, "No Jacobin No. I," *Dunlap's [Philadelphia] American Daily Advertiser,* July 31, 1793, *Hamilton Papers,* 15:145.
67. Unsigned copy, Rufus King Papers, New-York Historical Society. An identical copy is in the Edmond C. Genet Papers, Library of Congress. The statement was published in the New York *Diary* on August 12, 1793, and reprinted in newspapers around the country. See Ammon, *Genet Mission,* 135; and *Hamilton Papers,* 15:233–39, editorial note.
68. Robert R. Livingston to Edward Livingston, August 19, 1793, Robert R. Livingston Papers, New-York Historical Society.
69. Unsigned letter to John Jay and Rufus King, in Rufus King Papers, New-York Historical Society.
70. See Thomas Jefferson, [Notes on Edmond Genet's threat to appeal from President to people of U.S.], ca. August 20, 1793, Thomas Jefferson Papers, Library of Congress. Rather than notes, this document appears to be a draft of a public statement on the Genet affair that Jefferson never published. In the draft, Jefferson explains that "silence on my part might beget surmises which would not be just." In the document's last paragraph Jefferson tries to justify editing his official report for publication; the many crossed-out words and rewritten sentences reveal Jefferson struggling with the idea of editing "history." See also Ammon, *Genet Mission,* 151
71. Thomas Jefferson to James Madison, September 1, 1793, *Madison Papers,* 14:89; Jefferson, memorandum, July 10, 1793, *Anas,* 138–39; Receipt from Genet to Freneau, September 20, 1793, Edmond Genet Papers, New-York Historical Society. Jefferson's charge that Genet had appealed not to Congress but to the people circulated as gossip as well; Hamilton combated it in "No Jacobin No. VIII." *Hamilton Papers,* 15:281–84.
72. James Monroe to Thomas Jefferson, December 4, 1793, in *The Writings of James Monroe* [hereafter *Monroe Papers*], ed. Stanislaus Murray Hamilton, 7 vols. (New York: Putnam's, 1898–1910), 1:279. In a letter to Hamilton, John Jay foresaw Jefferson's silence: "It is generally understood that you and Mr Jefferson are not perfectly pleased with each other, but surely he has more magnanimity than to be influenced by that consideration to suppress Truth, or

what is the same Thing refusing his Testimony to it. Men may be hostile to each other in politics and yet be incapable of such conduct." Jay to Hamilton, November 26, 1793, *Hamilton Papers,* 15:412–13.

73. Cornelia Clinton to Edmond Genet, January 5, 1794, Edmond Genet Papers, New-York Historical Society; Ammon, *Genet Mission,* 152–53; Fisher Ames to Thomas Dwight, August 1793, *Works of Fisher Ames,* 2:964; Robert Troup to James Duane, August 14, 1793, Robert Troup Papers, New-York Historical Society. Genet eventually demanded that Jay and King face prosecution for libel, but the matter was never acted on.
74. Thomas Jefferson to James Madison, August 3, 1793, *Madison Papers,* 14:50; and Madison to Jefferson, September 2, 1793, ibid., 14:92–93 (in which Madison refers to their solution as an "antidote"); James Monroe to John Brackenridge, August 23, 1793, *Monroe Papers,* 1:272–73; and Madison to Archibald Stuart, September 1, 1793, *Madison Papers,* 14:87–88. For the outline of Madison's plan, see Madison to Jefferson, September 2, 1793, *Madison Papers,* 15: 92–95.
75. James Madison to Thomas Jefferson, September 2, 1793, *Madison Papers,* 14:92–93; Henry Van Schaack to Theodore Sedgwick, January 27, 1798, Sedgwick I Papers, Massachusetts Historical Society; Smith to Hamilton, April 24, 1793, *Hamilton Papers,* 14:338–41. After Edmund Randolph, on a "collecting mission" for Washington, reported that Virginia supported Hamilton's fiscal measures, Madison concluded that Randolph spoke with "tainted sources"—not the true "body of the people." Madison to Jefferson, July 30, 1793, *Madison Papers,* 14:49. See also Morgan, *Inventing the People,* 223–30, on inventing fake petitions containing "public opinion."
76. Rufus King to John Laurance, December 14, 1793, *Hamilton Papers,* 15:587, note 3.
77. John Taylor of Caroline to James Madison, June 20, 1793, *Madison Papers,* 15:35. "Defense pamphlet" and "formal defense" were contemporary terms, as was "vindication." See, for example, Oliver Wolcott, Jr., to Alexander Hamilton, September 3, 1800, *Hamilton Papers,* 25:107; Hamilton to James Monroe, July 22, 1797, *Hamilton Papers,* 21:180–81. The French equivalent was the "mémoire judiciaire," a genre identified by historian Dena Goodman. Goodman, "The Hume-Rousseau Affair: From Private Querelle to Public Procés," *Eighteenth-Century Studies* 25 (1991–92): 171–201.
78. Jefferson to Washington, September 9, 1792, Peterson, *Jefferson: Writings,* 1000–1001. Examples of defense pamphlets include Alexander Hamilton, "Letter From Alexander Hamilton Concerning the Public Conduct and Character of John Adams, Esq." (1800); James Monroe, "A View of the Conduct of the Executive in the Foreign Affairs of the United States Connected with the Mission to the French Republic During the Years 1794, 5 & 6" (1798); Edmund Randolph, "A Vindication of Mr. Randolph's Resignation" (1795); James McHenry, "A letter to the honorable, the Speaker of the House of Representatives of the United States with the acompanying documents read in that Honorable House on the 28th of Dec, 1802" (Baltimore, 1803).
79. Peterson, *Jefferson Image in the American Mind,* 33.
80. Jefferson, introduction, February 4, 1818, *Anas,* 23–24.
81. Jefferson, memorandum, March 2, 1793, *Jefferson Papers,* 25:311. Excluded from the "Anas" are Thomas Jefferson to George Washington, May 23, 1792, September 9, 1792, October 17, 1792. For a comprehensive examination of Jefferson's involvement in the Giles Resolutions, see Sheridan, "Jefferson and the Giles Resolutions."
82. Jefferson, introduction, February 4, 1818, *Anas,* 37.
83. Jefferson, memorandum, June 7, 1793, *Anas,* 125–27. The editors of the Jefferson Papers have studied the ink used in many of the "Anas" memoranda. They have noted scribbled additions, often in a different ink or by a different hand, leading them to believe that Jefferson added them at a later date. It is noteworthy that most of these corrections concern Hamilton. My

thanks to John Catanzariti for this information. The table of contents includes memoranda that do not appear in published versions of the *Anas* or in Jefferson's surviving papers; missing memoranda include "Notes. Hamilton," October 6, 1792; "d[itt]o," October 7, 1792; "history of A. Hamilton," February 2, 1793.

84. Jefferson, introduction, *Anas,* 33; Jefferson, memorandum, [1792?], *Jefferson Papers,* 17: 205–7.
85. Benjamin Rush counseled Adams to leave behind an address to posterity for the same reason; he would appear to have no other purpose than a mere desire to communicate thoughts. Rush to Adams, August 20, 1811, *Spur of Fame,* 189–90.
86. On Jefferson's creative adaptation of history, see Marcus Cunliffe, "Thomas Jefferson and the Dangers of the Past," *Wilson Quarterly* (Winter 1982): 96–107. He also wanted to "correct" David Hume's history of England by editing the text and excising the "heresies." Douglas L. Wilson, "Jefferson and the Republic of Letters," in *Jeffersonian Legacies,* 50–76, quote at 60–61; Wilson, "Jefferson Versus Hume," *William and Mary Quarterly* (1989): 49–70.
87. Theodore Dwight, *The Character of Thomas Jefferson, as Exhibited in His Own Writings* (Boston: Weeks, Jordan, 1839), 217–18, 225. Dwight insightfully notes that repetition of Jefferson's claims—dissemination of Jefferson's gossip—made his accusations seem true to "a large portion of the people, and at the same time established his own claim to the character of the great champion of republicanism." See also "Jefferson's Half Craze," in Cornelis De Witt, *Jefferson and the American Democracy* (London: Longman, Green, Longman, Roberts, and Green, 1862), 408–11; Peterson, *Jefferson Image in the American Mind,* 33–35; and the Epilogue, below.

3
The Art of Paper War

1. James McHenry to Oliver Wolcott, Jr., November 9, 1800, in Gibbs, *Memoirs of the Administrations of Washington and Adams,* 2:445; McHenry to John Adams, May 31, 1800, enclosed in McHenry to Alexander Hamilton, June 2, 1800, *Hamilton Papers,* 24:557. The foremost studies of Adams's character and political career are Peter Shaw, *Character of John Adams;* John Ferling, *John Adams: A Life;* Ellis, *Passionate Sage;* Page Smith, *John Adams.* On Adams's political thought, see Zoltan Haraszti, *John Adams and the Prophets of Progress* (New York: University Library, 1964); Thompson, *Adams and the Spirit of Liberty;* and John Howe, *The Changing Political Thought of John Adams* (Princeton: Princeton University Press, 1966).
2. Adams to Rush, January 25, 1806, in Schutz and Adair, *Spur of Fame,* 48; Adams to Jefferson, July 12, 1813, *Adams-Jefferson Letters,* 354.
3. Hamilton to Oliver Wolcott, Jr., August 3, 1800, *Hamilton Papers,* 25:54–55. For Adams's gossip, see Timothy Phelps to Oliver Wolcott, Jr., July 15, 1800, Wolcott to Chauncey Goodrich, July 20, 1800, George Cabot to Wolcott, July 20, 1800, Benjamin Goodhue to Wolcott, July 30, 1800, Fisher Ames to Wolcott, August 3, 1800, Wolcott to Ames, August 10, 1800, Goodrich to Wolcott, August 26, 1800, in Gibbs, *Memoirs of the Administrations of Washington and Adams,* 2:380, 382, 383, 395, 400–402, 411–12. Adams later denied making any such charge; see Cabot to Wolcott, September 1800, in Gibbs, *Memoirs of the Administrations of Washington and Adams,* 2:423; Adams to William Tudor, November 1, 1800, Tudor-Adams Correspondence, Massachusetts Historical Society. The rapid spread of Adams's charges—from Adams to Noah Webster to Timothy Phelps to Oliver Wolcott, Jr., to Chauncey Goodrich—is a wonderful example of the passage of gossip. Adams's denial passed through similar channels: Adams to Theophilus Parsons to George Cabot to Oliver Wolcott, Jr., in Gibbs, *Memoirs of the Administrations of Washington and Adams,* 2:423.

4. Hamilton, "Letter," *Hamilton Papers,* 25:190–91. Hamilton was defending his reputation against more than Adams's abuse. He was offended by an article in the *Aurora* on July 12, accusing him of using public funds for private profit. Hamilton to Oliver Wolcott, Jr., *Hamilton Papers,* 25:54–56. Hamilton also wrote (but did not circulate) a letter defending himself against a second Republican newspaper attack suggesting that his low birth made him unfit for the presidency. Hamilton to William Jackson, August 26, 1800, *Hamilton Papers,* 25:88–91.
5. C. Bradley Thompson, "John Adams and the Quest for Fame," in McNamara, *Noblest Minds,* 73–96; Thompson, *Adams and the Spirit of Liberty;* Shaw, *Character of Adams*. William Plumer noted in his journal that Adams "never could forgive Hamilton's writing a book agt. him." Plumer, 1804, "Repository—Volume 5," 58, William Plumer Papers, New Hampshire Historical Society.
6. Mercy Otis Warren to John Adams, July 28, 1807, in Ellis, *Passionate Sage,* 72; Adams to John Trumbull, March 9, 1790, Adams Family Papers; *Diary and Autobiography,* III:434–35, 62. On his placement of public papers with the Historical Society and in the newspapers, see John Adams to William Tudor, December 25, 1800, and William Tudor to John Adams, January 9, 1801, Tudor-Adams Correspondence, Massachusetts Historical Society. On his historical defense in general, see Ferling, *John Adams,* 421–23, 428–29; Shaw, *Character of Adams,* 273–99; Ellis, *Passionate Sage,* 57–83. Adams began his autobiography in 1802, put it down in 1805, and resumed it in 1806, but he never finished it. Ferling, *John Adams,* 421–23.
7. Erastus Lyman and Daniel Wright to John Adams, March 3, 1809, in *Boston Patriot,* April 22, 1809.
8. Adams to William Cunningham, February 22 and March 20, 1809, "Correspondence Between the Hon. John Adams, Late President of the United States, and the Late Wm. Cunningham Esq, Beginning in 1803, and Ending in 1812" (hereafter "Adams-Cunningham Correspondence") (Boston, 1823), 93–94, 101–2. For similar sentiments about his negotiations with France, see Adams to James Lloyd, January 1815 and March 31, 1815, Adams Family Papers, Massachusetts Historical Society.
9. Adams to Erastus Lyman and Daniel Wright, *Boston Patriot,* March 24, 1809; Lyman and Wright printed Adams's letter in a broadside in their hometown of Northampton; the letter was reprinted shortly thereafter in Worcester.
10. Cunningham to Adams, March 31, 1809, "Adams-Cunningham Correspondence," 108. Cunningham's grandmother was Adams's aunt. Adams to Cunningham, November 25, 1808, ibid., 54.
11. John Adams to William Cunningham, April 24 and June 7, 1809, "Adams-Cunningham Correspondence," 113–14, 122–24. Also John Adams to Benjamin Rush, August 7, 1809, in Schutz and Adair, *Spur of Fame,* 149–50.
12. See Ellis, *Passionate Sage,* 79; Smith, *John Adams,* 2:1044; Mitchell, *Hamilton: The National Adventure,* 474; Elkins and McKitrick, *Age of Federalism,* 736; and Thompson, *Adams and the Spirit of Liberty,* chap. 2. Peter Shaw sees the link with reputation, fame, and the historical record. Shaw, *Character of John Adams,* 296.
13. Oliver Wolcott, Jr., to Timothy Pickering, December 28, 1800, in Gibbs, *Memoirs of the Administrations of Washington and Adams,* 1:461; Steiner, *Life and Correspondence of McHenry,* 481; Benjamin Stoddert to James McHenry, April 14, 1810, in Steiner, *Life and Correspondence of McHenry,* 557. Pickering was fired; McHenry resigned. Stoddert ultimately wrote a letter of correction to Adams, who returned a "short but polite answer." Pickering to McHenry, February 11, 1811, in Steiner, *Life and Correspondence of McHenry,* 567. Of the abundant scholarship on print culture, works with particular relevance include Richard D. Brown, *Knowledge Is Power;* Richard R. John, *Spreading the News;* and Michael Warner, *Letters of the Republic.*

Robert Wiebe, in *Opening of American Society,* also offers insights into political print culture scattered throughout. On the ground-level use of political print weapons in the 1790s, see the meticulously researched *The Jeffersonian Republicans: The Formation of Party Organization, 1789–1801,* by Noble Cunningham.

14. For example, William Van Ness's brother John scolded him for defending Aaron Burr under his own name, thereby exposing himself "to all that abuse & malignant treatment to which those who come forward with their real names are exposed from anonymous scribblers." John Van Ness to William P. Van Ness, June 9, 1802, William P. Van Ness personal miscellaneous, New-York Historical Society.
15. John Taylor of Caroline to James Madison, June 20, 1793, *Madison Papers,* 15:34–37. See also Taylor to Madison, May 11, 1793, ibid., 13–14. Taylor was discussing "An Enquiry into the Principles and Tendency of Certain Public Measures" (Philadelphia, 1794).
16. On letter writing, see Andrew Burstein, *The Inner Jefferson: Portrait of a Grieving Optimist* (Charlottesville: University of Virginia Press, 1995), 116–31; Keith Stewart, "Towards Defining an Aesthetic for the Familiar Letter in Eighteenth-Century England," *Prose Studies* (September 1982): 179–92; and Decker, *Epistolary Practices*, esp. chaps. 1–2. On the difficulties and expense of letter writing, see John, *Spreading the News,* 42–44, 156–61.
17. Tobias Lear to David Humphreys, April 12, 1791, Rosenbach Foundation, FFC; John Rutledge, Jr., to William Short, March 30, 1791, William Short Papers, Library of Congress; David Humphreys to George Washington, October 31, 1790, in Frank Landon Humphreys, ed., *Life and Times of David Humphreys,* 2 vols. (New York: Putnam's, 1917), 2:52; and Griswold, *Republican Court,* 378. Andriani did not help his case when he declared English women to be superior to American women, and "a french washerwoman . . . infinitely more graceful" than an Englishwoman. Rutledge to William Short, March 30, 1791, William Short Papers, Library of Congress. My thanks to Kenneth R. Bowling of the First Federal Congress project at George Washington University for alerting me to these letters.
18. Henry Van Schaack to Theodore Sedgwick, January 14, 1798, and December 25, 1796, Sedgwick I, Massachusetts Historical Society. Van Schaack had heard that Republicans were taking "unwarrantable sums of money out of the Pennsylvania Bank." See also John Taylor of Caroline to James Madison, May 11, 1793, *Madison Papers,* 15:14; Aaron Burr to William Eustis, December 5, 1800, *Papers of Aaron Burr,* 1:464–66. See also Decker, *Epistolary Practices,* 40.
19. Alexander Hamilton to David Ross, September 26, 1792, *Hamilton Papers,* 12:490–92. On the Walker affair, see Dumas Malone, *Jefferson the President, First Term, 1801–1805* (Boston: Little, Brown, 1970), 216–23; Malone, *Jefferson the Virginian* (Boston: Little, Brown, 1948), 153–55, 447–51; and Charles Royster, *Light-Horse Harry Lee and the Legacy of the American Revolution* (Cambridge: Cambridge University Press, 1981), 208–9. Contemporaries considered it an affair of honor; some charged that Walker even sent Jefferson a challenge. William Plumer, March 14 and November 12, 1804, "Repository—Volume 5," 48, 60, William Plumer Papers, New Hampshire Historical Society.
20. Jefferson to Madison, March 31, 1793, *Madison Papers,* 15:3. For Jefferson's letter—its concluding paragraph full of barely repressed hostility—see Jefferson to Hamilton, March 27, 1793, *Hamilton Papers,* 14:255–57. Jefferson sent a draft to Madison in his letter of March 31, 1793.
21. Adams to Joseph Delaplaine, August 31, 1818, in Cunningham, *Circular Letters,* xxiii. These modest quantities become more significant when compared with the number of voters in a typical district. Although numbers varied greatly, it was not uncommon to have 1,200–4,000 voters per district. Cunningham, *Circular Letters of Congressmen to Their Constituents,* xix–xxi. On circular letters in general, see pp. xv–xlv.
22. John Taylor of Caroline to James Madison, May 11, 1793, *Madison Papers,* 15:14.
23. Jefferson to James Callender, October 6, 1799, Thomas Jefferson Papers; Hamilton to Oliver Wolcott, Jr., and Hamilton to James McHenry, July 1 and August 27, 1800, *Hamilton Papers,*

25:4, 97; Washington to Hamilton, August 10, 1796, *Hamilton Papers,* 20:292–93. Washington later explained that the address "was designed in a more especiall manner for the Yeomanry of this Country." Washington to Hamilton, August 25, 1796, *Hamilton Papers,* 20: 308. On pamphlets, see also Cunningham, *Jeffersonian Republicans,* 198, 225; Bernard Bailyn, *The Ideological Origins of the American Revolution* (Cambridge: Belknap Press, 1992), chap. 1; and Robert A. Ferguson, *The American Enlightenment, 1750–1820* (Cambridge: Harvard University Press, 1997), chap. 4.

24. Thomas Henshaw to Theodore Sedgwick, February 16, 1796, Sedgwick I, Massachusetts Historical Society. Clearly, there were exceptions to this rule, like Thomas Paine's "Common Sense." Pamphlets aimed at unusually broad audiences were often reduced in price for this purpose. For example, Thomas Selfridge reduced the price of his defense pamphlet to reach the "industrious and less opulent classes of society." Thomas O. Selfridge, *A Correct Statement of the Whole Preliminary Controversy between Tho. O. Selfridge and Benj. Austin; Also a Brief Account of the Catastrophe in State Street, Boston, on the 4th August, 1806, With Some Remarks* (Charlestown, 1807), 29, 35. On Beckley's pamphleteering, see John Beckley to James Monroe, April 10, 1793, May 25, 1795, August 26, 1800, and John Beckley to Tench Coxe, September 29, 1800, in Gawalt, *Justifying Jefferson,* 69, 86–89, 191–93.
25. Robert Gamble to John Preston, February 9, March 2, 3, 23, April 7, 9, 1796, Preston Family Papers, Virginia Historical Society.
26. Henry Van Schaack to Theodore Sedgwick, February 1, 1797, Sedgwick I, Massachusetts Historical Society; Jefferson to James Madison, September 1, 1793, Madison to John Taylor of Caroline, September 20, 1793, *Madison Papers,* 15:90–91, 121; Taylor to Madison, September 25, 1793, *Madison Papers,* 15:123. See also Taylor to Madison, June 20, 1793, *Madison Papers,* 15:34–37.
27. [William Van Ness], "Vindix No. III," New York *Morning Chronicle,* August 11, 1804; Adams to Benjamin Rush, August 7, 1809, in Schutz and Adair, *Spur of Fame,* 150. *New-York Post* editor William Coleman's *A Collection of the Facts and Documents, relative to the Death of Major-General Alexander Hamilton* was the Hamiltonian counterpart pamphlet, though it has not been recognized as such. Nor had anyone recognized Van Ness's pamphlet; I found it only because the "rules" of paper war suggested that a pamphlet would be Van Ness's next move.
28. Charles Carroll to James McHenry, November 4, 1800, in Steiner, *Life and Correspondence of McHenry,* 476.
29. Hamilton to Oliver Wolcott, Jr., August 3, 1800, *Hamilton Papers,* 25:54; Cabot to Hamilton, November 29, 1800, ibid., 249; Robert Troup to Rufus King, June 3, 1798, *Correspondence of Rufus King,* 2:330. See also Robert Troup to Rufus King, December 31, 1800, Robert Troup Papers, New-York Historical Society.
30. Thomas Jefferson to Edmund Pendleton, January 29, 1799, in Cunningham, *Jeffersonian Republicans,* 130; Beckley to William Irvine, September 22 and October 4, 1796, in Gawalt, *Justifying Jefferson,* 123–25; Jefferson to Edmund Pendleton, January 29, 1799, in Cunningham, *Jeffersonian Republicans,* 130. For other examples of broadsides, see Peter Van Schaack to Theodore Sedgwick, October 29, 1800, Sedgwick I, Massachusetts Historical Society; and Edmund Pendleton, "An Address of the Honorable Edmund Pendleton of Virginia to the American Citizens" (Boston, 1799).
31. The broadside was republished in 1804. Early American Imprints no. 6314.
32. *Boston Patriot,* September 9, 1809.
33. John Francis Mercer to Alexander Hamilton, October 16[–28], 1792, *Hamilton Papers,* 12:572–76; Hamilton to Mercer, December 6, 1792, ibid., 13:289–91. For more on the controversy, see Hamilton to Mercer, September 26, November 3, and December 1792, Ross to Hamilton, October 5–10 and November 23, 1792, Mercer to Hamilton, December 1792 and January 31, 1793, and editorial note, ibid., 12:481–90, 525–27, 13:13–14, 218–28, 289–91, 390–93, 513–18.

34. Warner, *Letters of the Republic,* 68; Waldstreicher, *In the Midst of Perpetual Fetes,* 10–11 and passim; and John, *Spreading the News,* 30–42; M. l'Abbé Robin, 1782, and Jacques Pierre Brissot de Warville, 1791, in Sherrill, *French Memories,* 248. For more French commentaries on the impact of newspapers in America, see the comments of Pierre Samuel Dupon de Nemours, Comte Guillaume de Deux-Ponts, J. E. Bonnet, Brillat Savarin, and Moreau de St. Méry, in Sherrill, *French Memories,* 248–52. On Federalist complaints about Republican use of newspapers, see John Rutledge to Theodore Sedgwick, September 24, 1801, Sedgwick I, Massachusetts Historical Society; Fisher Ames to Theodore Dwight, March 19, 1801, *Works of Fisher Ames,* 1:293; Cunningham, *Jeffersonian Republicans,* 167–74; Fischer, *Revolution of American Conservatism,* chap. 7; Durey, *Transatlantic Radicals,* 256–57.
35. These are rough estimates. Richard John estimates that by 1800, roughly 1.9 million newspapers per year were transmitted by mail. John, *Spreading the News,* 4, 38. John's figures—and the population estimate—do not include Native Americans and slaves. See also Stewart, *Opposition Press,* 17, 654, note 85.
36. Pickering to Hamilton, March 30, 1797, *Hamilton Papers,* 20:558–59.
37. Thomas Adams to Abigail Adams, October 2? and 3, 1800, and Abigail Adams to Thomas Adams, October 5, 1800, Adams Family Papers, Massachusetts Historical Society.
38. Thomas Jefferson to Walter Jones, January 22, 1814, in Levy, *Jefferson and Civil Liberties,* 67; January 17, 1791, *Maclay's Diary,* 362. For contemporary recognition of the institutional role of the public papers, see *Madison Papers,* 14:57, editorial note. On the political role of newspapers in the public sphere, see Jürgen Habermas, *The Structural Transformation of the Public Sphere: An Inquiry into a Category of Bourgeois Society* (Cambridge, Mass.: MIT Press, 1992).
39. Alexander Hamilton to Oliver Wolcott, Jr., September 26, 1800, *Hamilton Papers,* 25:12–23. See also Hamilton to Wolcott, August 3, 1800, Hamilton to James McHenry, August 27, 1800, ibid., 25:54–56, 97–98.
40. Robert Troup to Rufus King, November 9, 1800, *Correspondence of Rufus King,* 3:330–31. On the leaking of Hamilton's pamphlet, see *Papers of Aaron Burr,* 1:456–57; *Hamilton Papers,* 25: 173–77; Matthew L. Davis, *Memoirs of Aaron Burr* 2 vols. (New York: Harper and Brothers, 1837), 2:65; and John Church Hamilton, *History of the Republic of the United States of America, as Traced in the Writings of Alexander Hamilton and his Contemporaries,* 7 vols. (New York: Appleton, 1860), 7:407–8. Some historians insist that Hamilton wanted his pamphlet to be excerpted in the newspapers. He did make plans in case newspaper editors began publishing his pamphlet in bits and pieces, but his sense of decorum, the prestige of both Hamilton and Adams, the precise instructions that Hamilton issued for his pamphlet's circulation, the highly personal nature of his charges, the heat of his prose, and the fact that he published his work in a pamphlet suggest that he wrote for a select, elite audience.
41. William Vans Murray to John Quincy Adams, December 30, 1800, Rufus King to John Quincy Adams, December 28, 1800, and William Tudor to John Adams, November 5, 1800, Adams Family Papers, Massachusetts Historical Society. For a similar statement, see Samuel Smith to John S. Smith, July 14, 1811, Samuel Smith Papers, Alderman Library, University of Virginia.
42. Adams to Cunningham, April 24, 1809, "Adams-Cunningham Correspondence," 116; Cunningham to Adams, August 9, 1809, ibid., 154. See also Adams to Cunningham, June 7, 1809, ibid., 123.
43. William S. Shaw to Abigail Adams, February 25, 1801, Adams Family Papers, Massachusetts Historical Society; Alexander Hamilton to Oliver Wolcott, Jr., September 26, 1800, *Hamilton Papers,* 25:122; Adams to William Cunningham, November 25, 1808, "Adams-Cunningham Correspondence," 55.
44. John Beckley to James Madison, September 10, 1792, in Gawalt, *Justifying Jefferson,* 43–45;

Adams to Jefferson, August 24, 1815, *Adams-Jefferson Letters,* 455; John Beckley to Tench Coxe, November 24, 1800, in Gawalt, *Justifying Jefferson,* 226; Aaron Burr to William Eustis, December 5, 1800, Letters of Aaron Burr to William Eustis, Massachusetts Historical Society.

45. Thomas Adams to Abigail Adams, October 2? 1800, Adams Family Papers, Massachusetts Historical Society; William Vans Murray to John Quincy Adams, January 7, 1801, ibid. See also Rufus King to John Quincy Adams, [January 7, 1801], ibid.
46. *Boston Patriot,* September 9, 1809; Shapin, *Social History of Truth,* chaps. 2 and 3.
47. Gabriel Duvall to James Madison, October 17, 1800, *Madison Papers,* 17:424–25. Madison sent a copy of the handbill to Jefferson a few weeks later. Madison to Jefferson, November 11, 1800, ibid., 17:437.
48. Ward and Gould to DeWitt Clinton, December 12, 1803, December 7, 1804, and May 5, 1805, DeWitt Clinton Papers, Columbia University; Brockholst Livingston to Thomas Tillotson, December 18, 1803, Thomas Tillotson Papers, New York Public Library. See also Pasley, "'Artful and Designing Men,'" 464, 478; and Pasley, *"Tyranny of Printers."*
49. Jefferson to Madison, July 7, 1793, *Madison Papers,* 15:43. Jeffrey Pasley notes that lower-level politicians felt constrained to fight their battles in print because their personal influence was negligible. Pasley, "'Artful and Designing Men,'" 98.
50. James Monroe to James Madison, August 1, 1796, *Madison Papers,* 16:383–90. See also Monroe to Madison, December 7, 1798, and Madison to Edmund Randolph, September 13, 1792, ibid., 17:182–83; Benjamin Rush to Abigail Adams, October 13, 1800, Adams Family Papers, Massachusetts Historical Society; Richard Bland Lee to unknown correspondent, December 13, 1794, in Cunningham, *Jeffersonian Republicans,* 74; Thomas Jefferson to Edmund Randolph, September 17, 1792, *Jefferson Papers,* 24:387.
51. Davis, *Memoirs of Aaron Burr,* 2:98–99.
52. Adams to Cunningham, April 24 and June 7, 1809, "Adams-Cunningham Correspondence," 114–15, 123.
53. *Boston Patriot,* June 24, 1809.
54. Adams to Cunningham, April 24, 1809, "Adams-Cunningham Correspondence," 114. Philip Freneau edited the *National Gazette;* Peter Markoe was a poet and dramatist; Edward Church attacked Adams in a newspaper satire after Adams didn't bow to him at a levee; see p. 53, above. Andrew Brown edited the Philadelphia *Federal Gazette;* Thomas Paine was a renowned pamphleteer; James T. Callender edited the *Richmond Examiner;* William Cobbett edited *Porcupine's Gazette;* and John Ward Fenno edited the *Gazette of the United States*. John Adams to Skelton Jones, March 11, 1809, Adams Family Papers, Massachusetts Historical Society. For a similar response to an 1808 journalistic assault, see Adams to Cunningham, September 27, 1808, "Adams-Cunningham Correspondence," 25.
55. William Vans Murray to John Quincy Adams, December 30, 1800, and January 3, 1801, Adams Family Papers, Massachusetts Historical Society; Jefferson to Madison, July 7, 1793, *Madison Papers,* 15:43. See also John Beckley to James Monroe, September 23, 1795, in Gawalt, *Justifying Jefferson,* 99–100.
56. Adams to Jefferson, April 19, 1817, *Adams-Jefferson Letters,* 508; Timothy Pickering to Rebecca Pickering, June 19, 1809, Timothy Pickering Papers, Massachusetts Historical Society.
57. Joseph Ward to Theodore Sedgwick, March 8, 1798, Sedgwick I, Massachusetts Historical Society; Adams to Mercy Otis Warren, August 19, 1807, Adams Family Papers. See also General H. Dearborn to James Bowdoin, April 10, 1802, Winthrop Papers (in Bowdoin and Temple Papers), Massachusetts Historical Society; Jefferson to Madison, July 7, 1793, *Madison Papers,* 15:43. Jefferson was responding to charges of being "clossetted" with incendiary Republican newspaper editor Benjamin Franklin Bache. Thomas Jefferson to Samuel Smith, August 22, 1798, Thomas Jefferson Papers. His letter defense against an attack on his *Notes*

on the State of Virginia took the same form. John Page to Jefferson, June 21, 1798, Thomas Jefferson Papers. See also Jefferson to John Adams, Jefferson to Messrs. Ritchie and Gooch, Jefferson to James Monroe, and Jefferson to Uriah McGregory, May 13 and June 1, 1822, January 12 and August 13, 1800, ibid.

58. Ames to Thomas Dwight, February 24, 1795, *Works of Fisher Ames,* 2:1105–6; Orville Carpenter to Philenia Carpenter, April 21, 1814, Allyn Kellogg Ford Papers, Minnesota Historical Society. For a similar strategy, see also Henry Van Schaack to Theodore Sedgwick, May 14, 1797, Sedgwick I, Massachusetts Historical Society.

59. James McHenry to Timothy Pickering, February 23, 1811, in Steiner, *Life and Correspondence of McHenry,* 568–69; Cunningham to Adams, June 30, 1809, "Adams-Cunningham Correspondence," 138. See also "Adams-Cunningham Correspondence," August 9 and 18, November 22, 1809, 151–54, 160–62, 190–92.

60. John Adams to Uriah Forrest, June 20, 1797, Adams, *Works,* 6:546–47; Adams to Cunningham, January 16, 1810, "Adams-Cunningham Correspondence," 216–17. See also James Bridge to John Quincy Adams, May 24, 1802, Adams Family Papers. Steven Stowe notes that many stylistic rules for letter writing were intended to discourage honor disputes. Stowe, *Intimacy and Power in the Old South,* 24–30.

61. See, for example, Rufus King to John Quincy Adams, December 28, 1800, William Vans Murray to John Quincy Adams, December 30, 1800, and John Adams to Thomas Pinckney, October 29, 1800, Adams Family Papers, Massachusetts Historical Society. Adams was responding to the publication of a letter attacking Pinckney.

62. Cunningham to Adams, January 15, 1810, "Adams-Cunningham Correspondence," 214–16. See also Cunningham to Adams, December 29, 1809, ibid., 200; and Spacks, *Gossip,* 74.

63. Abigail Adams to Thomas Adams (repeating advice she intended for John), October 10, 1800, Adams Family Papers.

64. Kenneth S. Greenberg, "The Nose, the Lie, and the Duel," in Greenberg, *Honor and Slavery,* 14.

65. John Adams to Abigail Adams, January 3, 1797, Adams Family Papers. "They carefully conceal them from me," he complained.

66. John Adams to John Binns, November 26, 1812, Morristown National Historical Park; Cunningham to Adams, August 18, 1809, "Adams-Cunningham Correspondence," 159. The pamphlet was William Cobbett's, "A Letter to a Friend in England" (Philadelphia, 1800; 1812 reprint).

67. Charles Peale Polk to James Madison, June 20, 1800, *Madison Papers,* 17:394–96; Adams to Cunningham, October 15, 1808, "Adams-Cunningham Correspondence," 40 (see also *Boston Patriot,* June 24, 1809); Cunningham to Adams, January 14, 1809, "Adams-Cunningham Correspondence," 78; Adams to Jefferson, June 25, 1813, *Adams-Jefferson Letters,* 333.

68. William Eustis to David Cobb, December 1, 1794, David Cobb Papers, Massachusetts Historical Society. See also Eustis to Cobb, December 4, 1794, ibid.; Jonathan Mason, Jr., to Harrison Gray Otis, March 30, 1798, Harrison Gray Otis Papers, Massachusetts Historical Society; Thomas B. Wait to George Thatcher, July 2, 1809, Thomas B. Wait Letters to George Thatcher, Massachusetts Historical Society.

69. Adams to Jefferson, November 10, 1823, *Adams-Jefferson Letters,* 602.

70. Franklin to Robert R. Livingston, July 22, 1783, *Hamilton Papers,* 25:3, note 5 (Hamilton attempted to paraphrase Franklin's comment in a July 1, 1800, letter to Charles Carroll of Carrollton, ibid., 25:2); John Adams to Benjamin Rush, July 23, 1806, in Schutz and Adair, *Spur of Fame,* 61.

71. John Adams, [Birthday address], October 30, 1802, Adams Family Papers, Massachusetts Historical Society.

72. Cunningham to Adams, August 18 and September 9, 1809, "Adams-Cunningham Correspondence," 162, 164. For a sense of the contents of Adams's letters, see these two letters to Adams in full. Ibid., 156–64. Also Cunningham to Adams, January 15, 1810, ibid., 206.
73. Adams to Cunningham, November 25, 1808, ibid., 54.
74. William Cunningham to John Adams, May 6 and June 14, 1809, ibid., 122, 126–27.
75. Fisher Ames to Josiah Quincy, January 20, 1806, *Works of Fisher Ames,* 2:1493–95; Henry Langdon to William Eustis, November 29, 1803, William Eustis Papers, Massachusetts Historical Society. For other such pleas for information, see Thomas Tillotson to DeWitt Clinton, April 14, 1802, DeWitt Clinton Papers, Columbia University; Joseph G. Chambers to Albert Gallatin, December 18, 1798, Albert Gallatin Papers, New-York Historical Society; Richard Bland Lee to James Madison, April 17, 1791, and Hubbard Taylor to James Madison, January 3, 1792, *Madison Papers,* 14:6–7.
76. Cunningham to Adams, January 10, 1804, "Adams-Cunningham Correspondence," 6–7.
77. Hugh Henry Brackinridge to Thomas Jefferson, January 30, 1801, and John Odgen to Thomas Jefferson, February 7, 1799, Thomas Jefferson Papers. The mere fact that a political letter came from the "seat of government" gave it "seeming status of authenticity." Timothy Pickering to Samuel Putnam, November 8, 1804, Samuel Putnam Papers, Massachusetts Historical Society.
78. Peter Van Schaack to Theodore Sedgwick, April 20, 1798, Sedgwick I, Massachusetts Historical Society. See also Grasso, *Speaking Aristocracy,* 456–57; and Benjamin [Rossiter?] to Theodore Sedgwick, February 10, 1798, Sedgwick I, Massachusetts Historical Society.
79. Henry Van Schaack to Theodore Sedgwick, January 24, February 19, and March 18, 1798, Sedgwick I, Massachusetts Historical Society; Joseph G. Chambers to Albert Gallatin, December 18, 1798, Albert Gallatin Papers, New-York Historical Society. On letters as political bonds, see also Taylor, "'Art of Hook and Snivey,'" 1382–83.
80. Henry Van Schaack to Theodore Sedgwick, January 8, 1798, Sedgwick I, Massachusetts Historical Society; Van Schaack to Loring Andrews, August 1[?], 1798, Henry Van Schaack Papers, Massachusetts Historical Society. For examples of the extensive Sedgwick-Van Schaack-Williams-Andrews correspondence, see Sedgwick III and Henry Van Schaack Papers, Massachusetts Historical Society. National politicians also sent newspapers to constituents because they were sure to reach their destination under cover of a congressional frank. John, *Spreading the News,* 32.
81. Joseph Jones to James Madison, February 5, 1797, *Madison Papers,* 16:485–86. As an indication of the speed of the mails, it took roughly four weeks for news to travel from the Philadelphia *Aurora* to a Connecticut newspaper, three weeks for John Adams's inaugural address to be printed in New Hampshire; and two weeks for readers in Kinderhook, New York, to receive William Cobbett's Philadelphia *Censor.* Cunningham, *Jeffersonian Republicans,* 201; Walt Brown, *John Adams and the American Press: Politics and Journalism at the Birth of the Republic* (Jefferson, N.C.: McFarland, 1995), 45; Henry Van Schaack to Theodore Sedgwick, May 28, 1797, Sedgwick I, Massachusetts Historical Society. For the definitive work on the American postal system and its institutional influence on national governance, see John, *Spreading the News.*
82. William Vans Murray to James McHenry, October 9, 1796, in Steiner, *Life and Correspondence of McHenry,* 199. See also Hugh Williamson to James McHenry, October 20, 1796, ibid., 200.
83. James Sullivan to Thomas Jefferson, June 3, 1807, James Sullivan transcripts, Massachusetts Historical Society; Robert Goodloe Harper to Alexander Hamilton, June 5, 1800, *Hamilton Papers,* 24:568–70. See also Alexander Dallas to Albert Gallatin, February 21, 1801, Albert Gallatin Papers.
84. Edmund Quincy, *Life of Josiah Quincy of Massachusetts* (Boston, 1867), in Cunningham, *Circu-*

lar Letters, xix; George Cabot to Alexander Hamilton, October 11, 1800, *Hamilton Papers,* 25:148–50.

85. John Daly Burk, New York *Time Piece,* July 11, 1798, in Smith, *Freedom's Fetters,* 213; Theodore Sedgwick, Jr., to Theodore Sedgwick, December 19, 1800, Theodore Sedgwick III, Massachusetts Historical Society; George Washington to James McHenry, June 4, 1796, in Steiner, *Life and Correspondence of McHenry,* 185, note 1. The relative scarcity of letters also encouraged people to treat them like commodities. John, *Spreading the News,* 156–61.

86. See, for example, Benjamin Rossiter to Theodore Sedgwick, February 10, 1798, and Peter Van Schaack to Theodore Sedgwick, April 20, 1798, Sedgwick I, Massachusetts Historical Society; Theodore Sedgwick, Jr., to Theodore Sedgwick, December 19, 1800, Sedgwick Papers, Massachusetts Historical Society; Prince, *New Jersey Republicans,* 45; and John, *Spreading the News,* 154–56, 161–67.

87. Peter Van Schaack to Theodore Sedgwick, April 20, 1798, Sedgwick I, Massachusetts Historical Society; Harrison Gray Otis to Sally Foster Otis, February 29, 1816, Harrison Gray Otis Papers, Massachusetts Historical Society. My thanks to Catherine Allgor for bringing this letter to my attention.

88. Peter Van Schaack to Theodore Sedgwick, April 20 and March 20, 1798, Sedgwick I, Massachusetts Historical Society. See also Henry Van Schaack to Theodore Sedgwick, December 27, 1796, January 2, May 24 and 28, June 1, and December 10, 1797, and January 25, 1798, ibid.

89. Peter Van Schaack to Theodore Sedgwick, April 20, 1798, and June 1, 1797, ibid. For the post office anxieties of other politicians, see Peregrine Foster to Dwight Foster, June 23, 1797, and February 10, 1801, Dwight Foster Papers, Massachusetts Historical Society; Thomas Jefferson to James Monroe, January 23, 1799, Thomas Jefferson Papers, Library of Congress; Jefferson to John Taylor of Caroline, November 26, 1799, in Cunningham, *Jeffersonian Republicans,* 139; Uriah Tracy to James McHenry, January 11, 1800, in Steiner, *Life and Correspondence of McHenry,* 517–18; John Trumbull, Jr., to Jeremiah Wadsworth, February 7, 1796, John Trumbull, Jr., Collection, Connecticut Historical Society.

90. Henry Van Schaack to Theodore Sedgwick, February 5, 1798, Sedgwick I, Massachusetts Historical Society.

91. James Madison to Joseph Jones, Mann Page, Jr., and Charles Simms, August [post 23], 1791, *Madison Papers,* 14:71–73. Jefferson told Thomas Bell that if he convinced fifteen men to subscribe to the *National Gazette,* he would get his own subscription free. Jefferson to Thomas Bell, March 16, 1792, Jefferson to Philip Freneau, March 13, 1792, and Jefferson to Thomas Mann Randolph, January 22, 1792, *Jefferson Papers,* 25:52–53. See also Henry Van Schaack to Theodore Sedgwick, May 28, June 1 and 9, 1797, January 9, 21, and 29, and March 18, 1798, and John Hopkins to Sedgwick, December 18, 1797, Sedgwick I, Massachusetts Historical Society. Daniel Carroll did the same for Madison in Maryland, as did Henry Lee and Madison's father in Virginia; Van Schaack peddled *Porcupine's Gazette* in Massachusetts.

92. Thomas Jefferson to Tunis Wortman, August 15, 1813, in Levy, *Jefferson and Civil Liberties,* 197, note 29. Washington, Jefferson, and Monroe kept their names off certain subscription lists. Philip Freneau to Tench Coxe, November 22, 1796, Tench Coxe Papers, Historical Society of Pennsylvania; James Monroe to Jefferson, January 4, 1800, Thomas Jefferson Papers, Library of Congress.

93. John Adams, [subscription request], September 17, 1802, Adams Family Papers, Massachusetts Historical Society; James Callender to Thomas Jefferson, August 10, 1799, Thomas Jefferson Papers; Tunis Wortman to Albert Gallatin, December 24, 1799, Albert Gallatin Papers, New-York Historical Society.

94. Henry Van Schaack to Theodore Sedgwick, June 9, 1797, and January 9 and 21, 1798, Sedgwick I, Massachusetts Historical Society.

95. See John C. Williams to Theodore Sedgwick, March 13, 1798, Francis Silvester to Sedgwick, March 15, 1798, Henry Van Schaack to Sedgwick, March 16, 1798, and Benjamin Rossiter to Sedgwick, March 30, 1798, Sedgwick I, Massachusetts Historical Society. See also Daniel Dewey to Sedgwick, December 8, 1800, ibid.
96. Rutledge to Theodore Sedgwick, September 24, 1801, Sedgwick I, Massachusetts Historical Society; Thomas Jefferson, memorandum, August 10, 1800, Jefferson Papers; John Page, "An Address to the Citizens of the District of York in Virginia, by their Representative, John Page, of Rosewell, dated June 20, 1794," in Cunningham, *Circular Letters,* xxvi. Rutledge subscribed to the Boston *Palladium* for several friends in South Carolina; see also Michael Kern to Albert Gallatin, February 14, 1799, Albert Gallatin Papers. The national government funded subscriptions to three daily newspapers per congressman, to be forwarded to men of influence back home. Cunningham, *Circular Letters,* xxx–xxxi.
97. Cunningham to Adams, December 29, 1809, "Adams-Cunningham Correspondence," 200.
98. *Boston Patriot,* May 20, 24, 27, 31, June 3, 7, 10, 14, 17, 21, 24, 1809; Cunningham to Adams, June 14 and 30, 1809, "Adams-Cunningham Correspondence," 128–29, 142.
99. Cunningham to Adams, June 14 and 30, 1809, "Adams-Cunningham Correspondence," 128, 144–46.
100. Hamilton to Adams, August 1, 1800, *Hamilton Papers,* 51; Cunningham to Adams, June 30, 1809, "Adams-Cunningham Correspondence," 147–48. In a pamphlet defending Burr's conduct in his duel with Hamilton, the author compares Burr's behavior in 1804 with that of Hamilton in 1800 when he demanded an explanation for Adams's insults. ["Lysander"], "A Correct Statement of the Late Melancholy Affair of Honor, Between General Hamilton and Col. Burr, in which the Former Unfortunately Fell, July 11, 1804 . . . To which is added, A Candid Examination of the Whole affair In a Letter to a Friend" (New York, 1804); see also [William Van Ness], "Vindix No. II," New York *Morning Chronicle,* August 8, 1804.
101. Adams to Cunningham, November 7, 1808, "Adams-Cunningham Correspondence," 42–50. See also Adams to Cunningham, October 15 and November 25, 1808, ibid., 34–40, 54–58.
102. *Boston Patriot,* September 9, 1809; Timothy Pickering to James McHenry, June 4, 1809, in Steiner, *Life and Correspondence of McHenry,* 552–53. Pickering appears to have been considering a self-defense ("a defence of my character") even before Adams's essays, stemming back to the dishonor of being fired from Adams's cabinet. Pickering to McHenry, April 8, 1808, and Pickering to Jacob Wagner, January 19, 1809, ibid., 547, 550–52; Pickering to Rebecca Pickering, January 18, 1809, and John Jay to Timothy Pickering, March 24, 1809, Timothy Pickering Papers, Massachusetts Historical Society.
103. John Adams, "Mr. Hamilton's Letter," 37, 46; *Boston Patriot,* June 7, 1809. For other passages from Adams's 1801 draft that made their way into the *Patriot* essays, see "Mr. Hamilton's Letter," p. 23, 27, 76, 87, Adams Family Papers, Massachusetts Historical Society.
104. Almost every essay from May and June 1809 begins with a reference to "Mr. Hamilton" and his "famous pamphlet."
105. John Adams to William Cunningham, July 31, 1809 and Cunningham to Adams, August 9, 1809, "Adams-Cunningham Correspondence," 150–52.
106. William Cunningham to John Adams, June 14 and August 9, 1809, ibid., 130, 153.
107. Cunningham to Adams, January 15, 1810, ibid., 206–10.
108. Adams to Rush, December 19, 1808, in Schutz and Adair, *Spur of Fame,* 123–24. Also Adams to Rush, January 25, 1806, Sol Feinstone Collection, David Library of the American Revolution.
109. Cunningham to Adams, October 17, 1809, "Adams-Cunningham Correspondence," 169.
110. Cunningham to Adams, December 9, 1809, and January 15, 1810, ibid., 195–96, 214.
111. Cunningham to Adams, December 29, 1809, "Adams-Cunningham Correspondence," 201.
112. Adams to Cunningham, January 16, 1810, and Cunningham to Adams, January 28, 1810, January 21, 1812, ibid., 216–18; introduction, ibid., ix–x. See also William Cunningham, Jr., to

William Shaw, July 13, 1811, Miscellaneous Bound Manuscripts, 1809–1818, Massachusetts Historical Society. The editor of the Adams-Jefferson letters notes that several people who funded the pamphlet's publication were later made postmasters or custom collectors by President Andrew Jackson. *Adams-Jefferson Letters,* 601, note 78.

113. Introduction, "Adams-Cunningham Correspondence," vi.
114. Thomas Jefferson to John Adams, October 12, 1823, and Adams to Jefferson, November 10, 1823, *Adams-Jefferson Letters,* 599–602; Malone, *Sage of Monticello,* 434–35.
115. James McHenry to Timothy Pickering, June 16, 1809, in Steiner, *Life and Correspondence of McHenry,* 553.
116. For Pickering's initial letter-by-letter response, see miscellaneous notes, [1811?] and [Queries suggested by John Adams's Letters], [1809], Timothy Pickering Papers, Massachusetts Historical Society; and Clarfield, *Pickering and the American Republic,* 266.
117. Timothy Pickering, "A Review of the Correspondence Between the Hon. John Adams, Late President of the United States, and the Late Wm. Cunningham, Esq." (Salem, 1824), 3–5.
118. Malone, *Sage of Monticello,* 434–35. Timothy Pickering showed Adams's *Patriot* letters to John Marshall, who had not yet seen them. Pickering to James McHenry, March 12, 1811, in Steiner, *Life and Correspondence of McHenry,* 571.
119. Gibbs, *Memoirs of the Administrations of Washington and Adams,* 1:452–56, 462–73, 2:427, 465–66, 498. Gibbs in fact compared the "Anas" and Adams's essays throughout his work; he used Pickering's "Review" as well. Ibid., 1:468.

4
Dueling as Politics

1. Alexander Hamilton, [Statement on Impending Duel with Aaron Burr], [June 28–July 10, 1804], *Hamilton Papers,* 26:278. Internal evidence suggests that Hamilton wrote this statement on July 10, for it explains his decision to withhold his fire, a decision finalized with his second the night before the duel. Further evidence is contained within Hamilton's July 10 letter to his wife, explaining that he would withhold his fire owing to "the Scruples of a Christian," words that echo both his July 10 remarks to his second and the introductory passage of his apologia. [Nathaniel Pendleton's Amendments to the Joint Statement Made by William P. Van Ness and Him on the Duel Between Alexander Hamilton and Aaron Burr], [July 19, 1804] and Hamilton to Elizabeth Hamilton, [July 10, 1804], ibid., 26:337–39, 308; Charles King to Rufus King, April 7, 1819, and Rufus King to Matthew Clarkson, August 24, 1804, in King, *Correspondence of Rufus King,* 4:396, 400–401. Burr seems to have dated Hamilton's statement July 10 as well; see text at note 77.
2. The best Hamilton biographies are by Forrest McDonald, John C. Miller, and Nathan Schachner. The encyclopedia of Hamilton is Broadus Mitchell's *Alexander Hamilton;* an abridged version is also available: Mitchell, *Alexander Hamilton: A Concise Biography.*
3. Alexander Hamilton to John Rutledge, Jr., January 4, 1801, Hamilton to James Bayard, April 6, 1802, Hamilton, [Speech at a Meeting of Federalists in Albany], [February 10, 1804], and Hamilton to Rufus King, February 24, 1804, *Hamilton Papers,* 25:293–98, 587–89; 26:187–90, 194–96.
4. Biddle, *Autobiography,* 305; New York *American Citizen,* January 6, 1804. See also Aaron Burr to Theodosia Burr Alston, March 8, 1802, Aaron Burr Papers, New-York Historical Society; Thomas Jefferson, [Memorandum of a conversation with Burr], January 26, [1804], *Papers of Aaron Burr,* 2:820. Cheetham, not Hamilton, wrote the pamphlets. Mitchell, *Alexander Hamilton,* 2:526. Burr's supporters blamed the duel on Cheetham's newspaper diatribes. [Van Ness], *Correct Statement,* 63–64.

5. Charles D. Cooper to Philip Schuyler, [April 23, 1804], *Hamilton Papers,* 26:246; *Albany Register,* April 24, 1804. For firsthand accounts of the duel's proceedings, see William Coleman, *A Collection of the Facts and Documents, relative to the Death of Major-General Alexander Hamilton* (New York, 1804); Syrett and Cooke, *Interview in Weehawken;* [William P. Van Ness], *A Correct Statement of the Late Melancholy Affair of Honor, Between General Hamilton and Col. Burr* (New York, 1804); *Hamilton Papers,* 26:235–349. Also see Mitchell, *Alexander Hamilton,* 2:527–38; W. J. Rorabaugh, "The Political Duel in the Early Republic: Burr v. Hamilton," *Journal of the Early Republic* 15 (1995), 1–23.
6. *Hamilton Papers,* 26:240, headnote; Cooke, *Alexander Hamilton,* 240–43; Milton Lomask, *Aaron Burr,* 2 vols. (New York: Farrar, Straus and Giroux, 1979), 1:344; McDonald, *Alexander Hamilton,* 360; and Mitchell, *Alexander Hamilton,* 2:527, 542. Mary-Jo Kline confesses herself "baffled." *Papers of Aaron Burr,* 2:881. On honor and dueling in America see Ayers, *Vengeance and Justice;* Bruce, *Violence and Culture in the Antebellum South;* Gorn, "'Gouge and Bite, Pull Hair and Scratch'"; Greenberg, *Masters and Statesmen,* and "The Nose, the Lie, and the Duel in the Antebellum South"; Stowe, *Intimacy and Power in the Old South;* and Wyatt-Brown, *Southern Honor,* and "Andrew Jackson's Honor."
7. Alexander Hamilton to unknown recipient, September 21, 1792, *Hamilton Papers,* 12:408. Hamilton, [Statement on Impending Duel], [June 28–July 10, 1804], ibid., 26:279; Charles King to Rufus King, April 7, 1819, and Rufus King to Matthew Clarkson, August 24, 1804, in King, *Correspondence of Rufus King,* 4:396, 400–401; [Nathaniel Pendleton's Amendments], [July 19, 1804], *Hamilton Papers,* 26:338.
8. [Nathaniel Pendleton's Amendments], [July 19, 1804], *Hamilton Papers,* 26:338. Hamilton's 1804 apologia is extreme but not unique. Burr wrote a (somewhat utilitarian) parting statement the night before the duel, as had Hamilton before his anticipated duel with James Nicholson nine years earlier. The three statements reveal shared concerns—debts, family, friends—but they also display significant differences in tone and content, a reminder of the importance of considerations of temperament, self-conception, and circumstance to an understanding of the duel. Aaron Burr to Joseph Alston, July 10, 1804, in Davis, *Memoirs of Aaron Burr,* 2:324–26; Alexander Hamilton to Robert Troup, July 25, 1795, *Hamilton Papers,* 26: 503–7.
9. Alexander Hamilton, [Statement on Impending Duel with Aaron Burr], [June 28–July 10, 1804], *Hamilton Papers,* 26:278–81. All quotations within the next four paragraphs are from this statement, as are all subheads.
10. On incompatible value systems see Douglass Adair and Marvin Harvey, "Was Alexander Hamilton a Christian Statesman?" *William and Mary Quarterly,* 3d Ser., 12 (1955), 308–29; Steinmetz, *Romance of Duelling in all Times and Countries,* 1:5–6; and Stourzh, *Hamilton and the Idea of Republican Government,* 94.
11. Stourzh argues that during Hamilton's public career, "'selfishness' and public service merged in a single passion"—the love of fame—a reminder that even self-interest can be multidimensional. A public servant could desire fame or power without necessarily being conscious of the difference. Stourzh, *Hamilton and the Idea of Republican Government,* 105–6. See also Adair, "Fame and the Founding Fathers"; and Adam Smith, *The Theory of Moral Sentiments,* ed. D. D. Raphael and A. L. Macfie (1759; Indianapolis: Liberty Press, 1982), 126–27.
12. One recent account of the Burr-Hamilton duel summarizes three weeks of meticulously reasoned correspondence in two sentences. Rorabaugh, "Political Duel in the Early Republic," 9. On the importance of negotiations see Stowe, *Intimacy and Power in the Old South,* 30; Bruce, *Violence and Culture,* 32; and Greenberg, "The Nose, the Lie, and the Duel," 57, and *Honor and Slavery,* xii. On dueling rules and rituals see Sabine, *Notes on Duels and Duelling;* Steinmetz, *Romance of Duelling;* and Wilson, *Code of Honor.*
13. Hamilton was a principal in eleven affairs of honor: Reverend William Gordon (1779), Aeda-

nus Burke (1790), John Francis Mercer (1792–93), James Nicholson (1795), Maturin Livingston (1795 and 1796), James Monroe (1797), John Adams (1800), Ebenezer Purdy/George Clinton (1804), and Aaron Burr (1804). He claimed to have had one additional honor dispute with Burr; Burr thought that there were *two* previous incidents. Nathaniel Pendleton to William P. Van Ness, June 26, 1804, *Hamilton Papers,* 26:270; Burr to Charles Biddle, July 18, 1804, *Papers of Aaron Burr,* 2:887. He also "posted" Andrew Fraunces, a man he deemed too base to challenge (1793), and hovered on the edge of an honor dispute with John De Ponthieu Wilkes (1785). He played a role in three other duels: as a second to John Laurens in his duel with General Charles Lee (1779), as a second to legal client John Auldjo in his duel with fellow Federal Convention delegate William Pierce (1787), and as an unofficial adviser to his son Philip before his duel with George Eacker (1801). Also not counted among Hamilton's disputes is Major John Eustace's failed attempt to provoke a duel with him in defense of General Charles Lee's honor (1779); see Eustace to Lee, August 24 and November 28, 1779, "The Lee Papers (1778–1782)," *Collections of the New-York Historical Society for the Year 1873* (New York, 1874), 362–63, 393–94.

14. The duel's political function was so widely recognized that anti-dueling tracts regularly suggested ending the practice by "withholding your suffrages from every man whose hands are stained with blood." Lyman Beecher, "The Remedy for Duelling. A Sermon" (New York, 1809), 4. See also Samuel Spring, "The Sixth Commandment Friendly to Virtue, Honor and Politeness" (n.p., 1804), 24–25. This study is grounded on the analysis of sixteen interrelated political duels in New York City between 1795 and 1807. My list is not comprehensive. Because dueling was illegal, politicians often destroyed their correspondence once an affair was resolved. In addition, less controversial duels sometimes received little or no newspaper coverage. For the purposes of this study, the precise number of duels is less important than the persistence of dueling as a form of political combat. Similarly, 1807 does not mark the demise of dueling in New York City; on the contrary, I have discovered additional disputes brewing for years thereafter.
15. J. M. Mason to William Coleman, July 18, 1804, in Coleman, *Collection of the Facts and Documents,* 53. See also James Nicholson to Albert Gallatin, May 6, 1800, Albert Gallatin Papers.
16. David Denniston and James Cheetham to Robert R. Livingston, March 23, 1802, Robert R. Livingston Papers, New-York Historical Society. On public opinion, see also Wyatt-Brown, *Southern Honor,* 14. A common eighteenth-century conceit depicted public opinion as a "mirror" enabling men to see themselves. See, for example, Smith, *Theory of Moral Sentiments,* 110–11; David Hume, *A Treatise of Human Nature,* ed. L. A. Selby-Bigge (1739–40; Oxford: Liberty, 1960), 365.
17. Joseph L. Buckminster to James Sullivan, April 3, 1806, Miscellaneous Bound Manuscripts, Massachusetts Historical Society. See also James Sullivan to Joseph L. Buckminster, April 2, 1806, ibid; Argument of James Sullivan, *Trial of Thomas O. Selfridge, Attorney at Law, Before the Hon. Isaac Parker, Esquire. For Killing Charles Austin, on the Public Exchange, in Boston, August 4th,* 1806 (Boston, 1806), 140–55.
18. Christopher Gore to William Eustis, September 1, 1803, William Eustis Papers, Massachusetts Historical Society; John H. Farnham to Mary B. Farnham, March 29–30, 1810, Farnham Family Papers, Massachusetts Historical Society. See also Gore to Eustis, July 3, and August 8, 1803, William Eustis Papers, Massachusetts Historical Society; Theodore Sedgwick, Jr., to Theodore Sedgwick, November 26, 1801, Theodore Sedgwick Papers, Massachusetts Historical Society. Bertram Wyatt-Brown discusses the same ambivalence in the South. Wyatt-Brown, *Southern Honor,* 353.
19. John Gardner to Harrison Gray Otis, March 24, 1798, Harrison Gray Otis Papers, Massachusetts Historical Society; *Albany Centinel,* July 4, 1797. On violence within the U.S. Congress during the late 1790s, see Kurtz, *Presidency of John Adams,* 51–53.

20. For example, a duel resulted from John Swartwout's assertion that Senator DeWitt Clinton was "governed by unworthy motives." DeWitt Clinton to John Swartwout, July 26, 1802, *New-York Evening Post,* August 2, 1802. Similarly, Clinton and fellow Senator Jonathan Dayton almost dueled after Dayton said that Clinton "was in the habit of impeaching in debate the motives of Members." Robert Wright and Samuel Smith, [Statement of facts in an affair of honor between DeWitt Clinton and Jonathan Dayton], November 20, 1803, DeWitt Clinton Papers, Columbia University Rare Book and Manuscript Library. As Connecticut representative Samuel Dana said after the Griswold-Lyon dispute, "What could be a more serious charge than to be told, "You have betrayed your trust?" February 12, 1798, *Annals of Congress,* Fifth Congress, Second Session, 1007.
21. For a similar phenomenon among newly promoted Revolutionary War officers, see Royster, *Revolutionary People at War,* 88–95, 207–11. See also Wyatt-Brown, *Southern Honor,* 357.
22. Aaron Burr to Alexander Hamilton, June 21, 1804, *Hamilton Papers,* 26:250; Robert Goodloe Harper, *Annals of Congress,* February 8, 1798, Fifth Congress, Second Session, 980; Wyatt-Brown, *Southern Honor,* 61; Kiernan, *Duel in European History,* 97.
23. William Plumer, December 20, 1803, and February 14, 1804, "Repository—Volume 5," 24–27, 38–40, William Plumer Papers, New Hampshire Historical Society.
24. New York *The People's Friend & Daily Advertiser,* January 24, 1807. The quotation concerns an account of a political duel near Washington, D.C. On using honor to assert one's membership in an elite group, see also Wyatt-Brown, *Southern Honor,* 331.
25. Smith, *Theory of Moral Sentiments,* sect. 3, passim; Stowe, *Intimacy and Power,* 11–12.
26. George Thatcher to Sarah Thatcher, February 17, 1798, Thatcher Family Papers. Thatcher was witnessing the resolution of the Griswold-Lyon dispute; see below.
27. Matthew Davis to Albert Gallatin, May 9, 1798, Albert Gallatin Papers; New York *Commercial Advertiser,* May 11 and 14, 1798. See also Greenberg, "The Nose, the Lie, and the Duel." Alan Taylor describes another nose-twisting episode in *William Cooper's Town,* 248.
28. William Plumer, January 23, 1808, "The Register of Opinions & events . . . From May 7, 1807 to April 2, 1836," Papers of William Plumer, Library of Congress.
29. *Annals of Congress,* Fifth Congress, Second Session, 955–1068, passim; Aedanus Burke, quoted in *Greenleaf's New York Journal & Patriotic Register,* April 15, 1790, *Hamilton Papers,* 6:335, note 2; William Maclay, March 31, 1790, *Maclay's Diary,* 231; William Loughton Smith to Edward Rutledge, April 2, 1790, *Letters of William Loughton Smith,* 111–14. The *Oxford English Dictionary* defines a *rascal* as "a low, mean, unprincipled or dishonest fellow . . . a person of the lowest class." A *scoundrel* was a "mean rascal," a man lacking moral principles. A *puppy* was a fop or coxcomb; corresponding to the French *poupée,* the word charges a man with being little more than a woman's plaything or pet. In writing of the southern duel, Greenberg adds *abolitionist* to the list of words that demand a challenge. Greenberg, *Masters and Statesmen,* 38.
30. James Madison to Thomas Jefferson, [ca. February 18, 1798], *Madison Papers,* 17:82. Modern-day accounts of the Griswold-Lyon dispute often overlook its conformance with the honor code; rather than a spontaneous brawl, the tussle on the House floor was a ritualistic caning. For accounts of the dispute, see George Thatcher to Sarah Thatcher, February 17, 1798, Thatcher Family Papers, Massachusetts Historical Society; Austin, *Matthew Lyon: "New Man" of the Democratic Revolution,* 96–102; and Samuel Eliot Morison, *Harrison Gray Otis, 1765–1848: The Urbane Federalist* (Boston: Houghton Mifflin, 1969), 110–11. Many New Englanders wanted Griswold to cane Lyon. See, for example, Theodore Sedgwick to Ephraim Williams, February 1 and 2, 1798, Benjamin Rossiter to Sedgwick, February 10, 1798, and Henry Van Schaack to Sedgwick, February 19 and 25 and March 7, 1798, Sedgwick I, Massachusetts Historical Society; Jonathan Mason, Jr., to Harrison Gray Otis, February 19, 1798, Harrison Gray Otis Papers, Massachusetts Historical Society.
31. J. Hamilton Moore, *The Young Gentleman and Lady's Monitor, and English Teacher's Assistant*

(Wilmington, Del., 1797), 213. Chesterfield's letters comprise most of the body of this popular eighteenth-century schoolbook (that went through at least thirty-seven editions); one essayist blamed it for the rise of the duel in America. "Anti-Duellist," "On the Increasing Prevalence of Duelling. No. II" (misnumbered "No. III"), [Hudson, New York] *The Balance, and Columbian Repository,* January 18, 1803; Hemphill, *Bowing to Necessities,* 72. On Chesterfield in eighteenth-century America, see Bushman, *Refinement of America,* 30, 36–37, 84–86, and passim.

32. [David Gelston's Account of an Interview between Alexander Hamilton and James Monroe], July 11, 1797, *Hamilton Papers,* 21:160–61.
33. John De Ponthieu Wilkes to Hamilton, November 8, 1785, and Hamilton to Wilkes, November 8, 1785, *Hamilton Papers,* 3:628–31.
34. Hamilton to Nicholson, July 20, 1795, Nicholson to Hamilton, July 20, 1795, Hamilton to Nicholson, July 20, 1795, and Nicholson to Hamilton, July 21, 1795, *Hamilton Papers,* 18:471–73.
35. Hamilton to Monroe, [July 10, 1797], ibid., 21:157.
36. David Hosack to John Church Hamilton, January 1, 1833, *Hamilton Papers,* 25:437, note 1.
37. Spring, "Sixth Commandment," 15; Rufus King to E. King, February 12, 1819, in King, *Correspondence of Rufus King,* 6:214–15. Though Spring differentiated "polite" from "malicious" duelists, he condemned them both as murderers—polite duelists were guilty of self-murder. King was discussing an 1819 duel fought at four paces with muskets, in which (not surprisingly) one man was killed. See also Frevert, "Bourgeois honour," 268.
38. For example, see Federalist charges against New York Republican Brockholst Livingston after he killed Federalist James Jones in a duel. Lewis Morgan to Robert R. Livingston, May 15, 1798, Robert R. Livingston Papers, New-York Historical Society; New York *Commercial Advertiser,* May 11 and 14, 1798.
39. [Petition for the discontinuance of charges against Burr], November 4, 1804, in *Autobiography of Charles Biddle,* ed. James S. Biddle (Philadelphia: E. Claxton, 1883), 306–8. Of New York City's four fatal political duels between 1795 and 1807, only the Burr-Hamilton duel resulted in murder charges, though Robert Swartwout and District Attorney Richard Riker were charged with dueling two years after their duel—probably an attempt to dispel accusations that the charges against Burr were exceptional and thereby partisan. New York *Spectator,* January 12, 1805. After the 1798 Livingston-Jones duel, a police officer refused to arrest Livingston when urged by Jones's friends, responding that if he did, "seconds & surgeons should be arrested likewise." There were no arrests. James Nicholson to Albert Gallatin, May 14, 1798, Albert Gallatin Papers, New-York Historical Society. In 1804, the chief justice of the district court in Washington, D.C., was informed about a duel between two congressmen; he issued a warrant and brought before him the participants, who were "recognized to keep the peace." Talk of a duel persisted nonetheless. William Plumer, February 14, 1804, "Repository—Volume 5," 38–40, William Plumer Papers, New Hampshire Historical Society.
40. James Nicholson to Albert Gallatin, May 14, 1798, Albert Gallatin Papers, New-York Historical Society; New York *Morning Chronicle,* January 5, 1804. On the infrequency of deaths and injuries see Greenberg, *Masters and Statesmen,* 31–32; Steinmetz, *Romance of Duelling,* 1:12, 89–92.
41. [David Gelston's Account of an Interview], July 11, 1797, *Hamilton Papers,* 21:161. The two men continued to warn each other that they were "ready" to fight for more than five months, each signaling his defiance in the hope that the other would take responsibility for issuing a challenge. Hamilton eventually drafted—but did not send—an acceptance of Monroe's challenge. See James Monroe to Alexander Hamilton, July 25 and 31; Hamilton to Monroe, August 4; Monroe to Hamilton August 6; Monroe to Hamilton, December 2; Hamilton to Monroe, [January 1798]; ibid., 21:184, 193, 200, 204–5, 316–20, 346.

42. *New-York Evening Post,* August 6, 1802.
43. William P. Van Ness vs. the People, [January 1805], Duel papers, William P. Van Ness Papers, New-York Historical Society. This detailed transcript of Van Ness's trial contains invaluable eyewitness accounts of the duel. Quotes in this account are from this transcript.
44. Rufus King to Matthew Clarkson, August 24, 1804, in King, *Correspondence of Rufus King,* 4:400; Timothy Pickering to William Coleman, July 1, 1825, in Mitchell, *Alexander Hamilton,* 2:762, note 41; Lomask, *Aaron Burr,* 1:353; James Parton, *The Life and Times of Aaron Burr* (New York: Mason Brothers, 1864), 352.
45. The two men advised Monroe during his dispute with Hamilton. James Monroe to Thomas Jefferson, July 12, 1797, *Hamilton Papers,* 21:136–37, headnote; James Monroe to James Madison, October 15, 1797, and James Madison to James Monroe, October 19, 1797, *Madison Papers,* 17:50–51, 53–54. They also advised Monroe during his later dispute with John Adams; see introduction, above.
46. Robert Troup to Rufus King, August 24, 1802, Robert Troup Papers, New-York Historical Society.
47. Aaron Hill to William Eustis, February 20, 1803, and Jacob Eustis to William Eustis, February 10, 1803, William Eustis Papers, Library of Congress; Robert Troup to Rufus King, October 1 and December 31, 1800, Robert Troup Papers, New-York Historical Society; Aaron Burr to Joseph Alston, July 3, 1802, Aaron Burr Papers, New-York Historical Society. The familial nature of many political alliances demonstrates the small scale and intimacy of the early republic's political community. For example, John and William P. Van Ness, and John, Robert, and Samuel Swartwout were Burrites. Clintonians included a mass of relatives by marriage. See also Fischer, *Revolution of American Conservatism,* 220–21. On the link between family and honor, see Wyatt-Brown, *Southern Honor,* passim.
48. Robert R. Livingston to DeWitt Clinton, February 4, 1803, DeWitt Clinton papers, Columbia University Rare Book and Manuscript Library; Aaron Burr to Joseph Alston, July 19, 1802, Aaron Burr Papers, New-York Historical Society.
49. Matthew L. Davis to William P. Van Ness, August 15, 1805, Matthew L. Davis Papers, New-York Historical Society.
50. "A Clintonian Memorandum for Nine Hours," New York *Morning Chronicle,* January 26, 1807; New York *American Citizen,* March 30, 1804; Morgan, *Inventing the People,* 304–5.
51. Robert Wright and Samuel Smith, [Statement of facts in an affair of honor between DeWitt Clinton and Jonathan Dayton], November 20, 1803, W. C. Nicholas to Clinton, October 27, 1803, and Pierce Butler to Clinton, October 30, 1803, DeWitt Clinton Papers, Columbia University Rare Book and Manuscript Library; *New-York Evening Post,* November 8 and 10, 1803; Clinton to unnamed correspondent, October 25, 1803, DeWitt Clinton Papers, New York Public Library; John Van Ness to William P. Van Ness, November 11, 1803, personal misc. William P. Van Ness, New York Public Library. Van Ness suggests that Dayton's attack was also intended to defeat a pending bill that Clinton supported.
52. *New-York Evening Post,* August 9, 1802. Burrites responded to Clinton's challenge with their own snide challenge, published in the *Post* the next day. Viewed in this light, duels between contending factions were a type of feud—a dispute between subgroups of a "politically organized whole" that involved intermittent instances of violence over a prolonged period and usually occurred in a delicately balanced society experiencing an unsettling controversy. Leopold Pospisil, "Feud," *International Encyclopedia of the Social Sciences,* 5:389–93; Harold D. Lasswell, "Feuds," *Encyclopedia of the Social Sciences,* 6:220–21. On the link between elections and honor, see Wyatt-Brown, *Southern Honor,* 184–86.
53. *New-York Evening Post,* August 11, 1802; "Anti-Duellist," "On the Increasing Prevalence of Duelling, No. III," Hudson, N.Y., *The Balance, and Columbian Repository,* January 18 and 25, 1803.

54. See, for example, Brockholst Livingston vs. James Jones, New York *Commercial Advertiser,* May 14, 1798; George Eacker vs. Philip Hamilton, *New-York Evening Post,* November 28, 1801; John Swartwout vs. DeWitt Clinton, *New-York Evening Post,* August 2, 1802, and New York *American Citizen,* August 9, 1802.
55. "An Old Soldier," New York *American Citizen,* August 27, 1802; "A Young Soldier," *New-York Evening Post,* August 30, 1802; William S. Smith, [untitled article], ibid., August 6, 1802.
56. Charles D. Cooper to Philip Schuyler, April 23, 1804, *Hamilton Papers,* 26:243–46. For the details of this print controversy, see ibid., 26:243–44, notes 3 and 4; *Papers of Aaron Burr,* 2:876–77, headnote.
57. [Van Ness], "A Candid Examination of the Whole affair In a Letter to a Friend. By Lysander," in *Correct Statement,* 51. As Burr later explained, Hamilton "had a peculiar habit of saying things improper & offensive in such a Manner as could not well be taken hold of." Aaron Burr to Charles Biddle, July 18, 1804, *Papers of Aaron Burr,* 2:887.
58. *Papers of Aaron Burr,* 2:881; John Adams to William Tudor, January 20, 1801, Tudor-Adams Correspondence, Massachusetts Historical Society; Aaron Burr to Charles Biddle, July 18, 1804, *Papers of Aaron Burr,* 2:887; [Van Ness], "Candid Examination," 52.
59. Aaron Burr to Charles Biddle, July 18, 1804, *Papers of Aaron Burr,* 2:887; [Van Ness], "Candid Examination," 62–63. During Monroe's 1797 dispute with Hamilton, Burr assured him that Hamilton "woud not fight." John Dawson to James Monroe, December 24, 1797, *Hamilton Papers,* 21:319, note 1.
60. [Nathaniel Pendleton's First Account of Alexander Hamilton's Conversation at John Tayler's House], June 25, 1804, *Hamilton Papers,* 26:260–61; William P. Van Ness to Nathaniel Pendleton, [June 26, 1804], *Hamilton Papers,* 26:268.
61. Alexander Hamilton to Aaron Burr, June 20, 1804, ibid., 26:247–49. See also Stourzh, *Hamilton and the Idea of Republican Government,* 94. For examples of Burr's outrage at Hamilton's "defiance," see Burr to Hamilton, June 22, 1804, [Aaron Burr's Instructions to William P. Van Ness], [June 22–23, 1804], and Burr to Van Ness, [June 26, 1804], *Hamilton Papers,* 26: 255–56, 256–57, 266–67, as well as Van Ness's narrative of events as cited in notes throughout the duel correspondence in *Hamilton Papers.*
62. [Van Ness], "Candid Examination," 68; Alexander Hamilton to Elizabeth Hamilton, [July 10, 1804], *Hamilton Papers,* 26:308; Aaron Burr to Joseph Alston, July 10, 1804, in Davis, *Memoirs of Aaron Burr,* 2:324–26.
63. J. M. Mason to William Coleman, July 18, 1804, in Coleman, *Collection,* 51. Unless otherwise noted, the account in this paragraph is taken from Parton, *Life and Times of Aaron Burr,* 356–57.
64. Gouverneur Morris, [diary entry], July 13–14, 1804, *The Diary and Letters of Gouverneur Morris,* ed. Anne Carry Morris, 2 vols. (New York, 1888), 2:456–58.
65. See [Joint Statement by William P. Van Ness and Nathaniel Pendleton], [July 17, 1804]; [Pendleton's Amendments], [July 19, 1804]; [William P. Van Ness's Amendments], [July 21, 1804], *Hamilton Papers,* 26:333–36, 337–39, 340–41. Also see correspondence between Van Ness and Pendleton between July 11 and 16, 1804, ibid., 26:311–12, 329–32. In a public statement, attending physician David Hosack noted that Hamilton, after regaining consciousness, did not remember discharging his pistol. David Hosack to William Coleman, August 17, 1804, ibid., 26:345 (first published in Coleman's *Collection,* 18–22).
66. For examples of Cheetham's charges, see New York *American Citizen,* July 23, July 26, August 7, August 16, 1804. For dueling offenses, see Sabine, *Notes on Duels and Duelling,* 37; Steinmetz, *Romance of Duelling,* vol. 1. Burr allegedly laughed when he came across the following verse on a wax museum's re-creation of the duel: "O Burr, O Burr, what hast thou done?/ Thou has shooted dead great Hamilton. / You hid behind a bunch of thistle, / And shooted him dead with a great hoss pistol." Parton, *Life and Times of Aaron Burr,* 616.

67. Aaron Burr to Joseph Alston, July 13, 1804, Aaron Burr Papers, New-York Historical Society; Burr to Charles Biddle, July 18, 1804, *Papers of Aaron Burr,* 2:887. Albert Gallatin agreed. Gallatin to James Nicholson, July 19, 1804, Albert Gallatin Papers.
68. [William P. Van Ness], "Vindix No. I," New York *Morning Chronicle,* August 6, 1804. Also see "Vindix No. II" and "Vindix No. III," ibid., August 8 and August 11, 1804.
69. [Van Ness], "Vindix No. III," ibid., August 11, 1804. Van Ness's pamphlet bears careful comparison with his original autograph manuscripts detailing the events of the duel; with the account he published in the newspapers; and most important, with the Hamiltonian version of the duel as detailed by Pendleton in the newspapers and restated by Coleman in his defense pamphlet.
70. Coleman, *Collection,* 14–16; [Van Ness], "Correct Statement," 22.
71. [Van Ness], "Candid Examination," 47–48.
72. Ibid., 52, 48, 49.
73. Nathaniel Pendleton, [unsigned draft], [ca. July 1804], Nathaniel Pendleton papers, "Duel Material," New-York Historical Society; "The Warning III," February 21, 1797, *Hamilton Papers,* 20:517–20.
74. Gouverneur Morris, diary entry, July 14, 1804, *Letters of Gouverneur Morris,* 2:458–59.
75. Aaron Burr to Charles Biddle, July 18, 1804, *Papers of Aaron Burr,* 2:887. In yet another instance of Hamilton's tortured logic, he decided that he might shoot at Burr if they exchanged a second round of fire. This explains his response to Pendleton's query about setting his pistol's hair trigger: "Not this time." Alexander Hamilton, [Statement on Impending Duel], [June 28–July 10, 1804], and [Nathaniel Pendleton's Amendments], [July 19, 1804], *Hamilton Papers,* 26:280, 338.
76. [Aaron Burr's Instructions to William P. Van Ness], [June 22–23, 1804], *Hamilton Papers,* 26:257; Burr to Charles Biddle, July 18, 1804, *Papers of Aaron Burr,* 2:887. On Burr's self-conception as a man of honor, also see Burr to Joseph Alston, July 10, 1804, *Memoirs of Aaron Burr,* 2:324–26. On his deathbed, Hamilton told Reverend J. M. Mason, "I used every expedient to avoid the interview; but I have found, for some time past, that my life *must* be exposed to that man." Hamilton felt compelled to oppose Burr, a man he considered a threat to the republic, and in doing so, he recognized that he ran a continual risk of inviting a challenge. J. M. Mason to William Coleman, July 18, 1804, Coleman, *Collection,* 53.
77. Aaron Burr to Charles Biddle, July 18, 1804, *Papers of Aaron Burr,* 2:887–88.
78. Parton, *Life and Times of Aaron Burr,* 615. Burrite Matthew Davis's *Memoirs of Aaron Burr,* published thirty years earlier, was largely an annotated assemblage of Burr's correspondence, compiled with Burr's assistance. For the long-term impact of the Burr-Hamilton duel (which did *not* end dueling in the North), see Wayne C. Minnick, "A Case Study in Persuasive Effect: Lyman Beecher on Duelling," *Speech Monographs* 38 (November 1971): 262–76.

5
An Honor Dispute of Grand Proportions

1. James Bayard to Aaron Burr, March 8, 1830, Burr to Bayard, March 10, 1830, Burr to Matthew L. Davis, March 15, 1830, and Davis to Burr, March 18, 1830, *Papers of Aaron Burr,* 2:1197–1202. On Davis and his views of Jefferson (and Jefferson's memoranda) see Pasley, "'Artful and Designing Men,'" chap. 2.
2. In addition to Bayard, Adams, Burr, Smith, and Jefferson, complainants included Timothy Green, Abraham Bishop, John Swartwout, David A. Ogden, and Edward Livingston—all accused of assisting Burr in his intrigues for the presidency. Though they did not defend themselves publicly, New York Republican Pierpont Edwards (Burr's uncle) and Connecticut

Republican Gideon Granger were also attacked. See Davis, *Memoirs of Aaron Burr,* 2:91–98; Pancake, *Samuel Smith and the Politics of Business,* 55; Richard Bayard, "Documents Relating to the Presidential Election in the Year 1801: Containing a Refutation of Two Passages in the Writings of Thomas Jefferson, Aspersing the Character of the Late James A. Bayard, of Delaware" (Philadelphia, 1831). Merrill Peterson tracks the controversy until 1855, but Bayard's great-grandson republished the 1855 defense in 1907 when a Delaware newspaper published an excerpt from the 'Anas.' Thomas F. Bayard, "Remarks in the Senate of the United States, January 31, 1855, Vindicating the Late James A. Bayard, of Delaware, and Refuting the Groundless Charges Contained in the 'Anas' of Thomas Jefferson, Aspersing His Character" (n.p., 1907). Peterson, *Jefferson Image in the American Mind,* 34.

3. Smith refused Jefferson's offer, though he agreed to serve as acting secretary until a replacement could be found. Pancake, *Samuel Smith and the Politics of Business,* 61–62; Cassell, *Merchant Congressman in the Young Republic,* 105–9; Thomas Jefferson, April 15, 1806, *Anas.*
4. Accounts that stress the modern aspects of the contest include Cunningham, *Jeffersonian Republicans;* Elkins and McKitrick, *Age of Federalism,* 691–754; Sisson, *Revolution of 1800.* For a more sectional reading of the election—though it remains focused on warring "protoparties"—see Sharp, *American Politics in the Early Republic.* Peter S. Onuf offers a provocative account of the election as a nationalizing—*and* boundary-setting—event for the Republicans. Onuf, *Jefferson's Empire,* chap. 3. For more general accounts of the election, see Malone, *Jefferson and the Ordeal of Liberty,* 484–506; Kurtz, *Presidency of John Adams;* and Dauer, *Adams Federalists.*
5. Peterson, *Jefferson Image in the American Mind.*
6. Davis, *Memoirs of Aaron Burr,* 1:iii.
7. Peterson, *Jefferson Image in the American Mind,* 463–64.
8. The two standard biographies of Burr are Lomask, *Aaron Burr;* and Schachner, *Aaron Burr.* See also Nolan, *Burr and the American Literary Imagination.* On Davis, see Mushkat, "Davis and the Political Legacy of Aaron Burr"; and Pasley, "'Artful and Designing Men,'" chap. 2.
9. Davis, *Memoirs of Aaron Burr,* 1:44–45, 328. See also 2:15.
10. Aaron Burr to Joseph Alston, October 16, 1825, in ibid., 2:432–34.
11. Davis, *Memoirs of Aaron Burr,* 2:387; Aaron Burr to Alexander Hamilton, June 21, 1804, *Hamilton Papers,* 26:250.
12. Thomas Jefferson to James Madison, January 16, 1799, *Madison Papers,* 17:208–11.
13. See Elkins and McKitrick, *Age of Federalism,* 701, 740; for a corrective of this view, see Ben-Atar and Oberg, *Federalists Reconsidered.*
14. Lomask, *Aaron Burr,* 244; Aaron Burr to Aaron Ward, January 14, 1832, *Papers of Aaron Burr,* 2:1210–11. South Carolina Republican Charles Pinckney made a similar confession.
15. Theodore Sedgwick to Alexander Hamilton, January 10, 1801, and Hamilton to James Bayard, January 16, 1801, *Hamilton Papers,* 25:311, 320–21. See also the insightful essay by Gordon S. Wood, "The Real Treason of Aaron Burr," *Proceedings of the American Philosophical Society* 143 (June 1999).
16. During the election of 1800, Hamilton recalled a conversation in which Burr blamed him for not taking advantage of his command of the army to "change the Government." When Hamilton responded that "this could not have been done without guilt," Burr replied, "Les grand ames se soucient peu de petits morceaux" (Great souls care little about small matters). Alexander Hamilton to James A. Bayard, January 16, 1801, *Hamilton Papers,* 25:319–24.
17. Alexander Hamilton, [Speech at a Meeting of Federalists in Albany], [February 10, 1804], *Hamilton Papers,* 26:188. Hamilton notes that the "mass of the people" admire Burr "as the Grandson of President Edwards, and the son of President Burr."
18. Davis, *Memoirs of Aaron Burr,* 1:182, 2:56. For Burr's admiration of Chesterfield, see Theodosia Burr to Aaron Burr, February 12, 1781, in Davis, *Memoirs of Aaron Burr,* 1:224–25; Parton,

Life and Times of Aaron Burr, 1:63, 373. On Burr's assumptions about aristocratic license, see Davis, *Memoirs of Aaron Burr,* 1:27, 40, 91, 181–82; and Parton, *Life and Times of Aaron Burr,* 2:276.

19. Davis, *Memoirs of Aaron Burr,* 2:56.
20. Hannah Nicholson Gallatin to Albert Gallatin, May 7, 1800, and James Nicholson to Albert Gallatin, May 7, 1800, Albert Gallatin Papers; Burr to Joseph Alston, November 15, 1815, *Papers of Aaron Burr,* 2:1165–69. On mass confusion over political loyalties, also see also Oliver Wolcott, Jr., to James McHenry, August 26, 1800, in Gibbs, *Memoirs of the Administrations of Washington and Adams,* 2:409.
21. Jonathan Dayton to Oliver Wolcott, Jr., September 15, 1796, in Gibbs, *Memoirs of the Administrations of Washington and Adams,* 1:383–84.
22. For accounts of the presidential election of 1796, see Cunningham, *Jeffersonian Republicans,* 89–115; Dauer, *Adams Federalists,* 92–119; Elkins and McKitrick, *Age of Federalism,* 518–28; Kuroda, *Origins of the Twelfth Amendment*, 63–72; Kurtz, *Presidency of John Adams,* 78–238; Malone, *Jefferson and the Ordeal of Liberty,* 273–94; Scherr, "'Republican Experiment' and the Election of 1796 in Virginia"; Smith, "The 1796 Election: A World Without Washington," in *Crisis, Unity, and Partisanship;* Smith, *John Adams,* 2:878–917; and "Election of 1796," in *History of American Presidential Elections, 1789–1968,* ed. Arthur M. Schlesinger, Jr. (New York: Chelsea House, 1971), 59–80.
23. See also Kuroda, *Origins of the Twelfth Amendment;* Kurtz, *Presidency of John Adams,* 145–76; and Slonim, "Electoral College at Philadelphia."
24. Chauncey Goodrich to Oliver Wolcott, Sr., December 17, 1796, in Gibbs, *Memoirs of the Administrations of Washington and Adams,* 1:411–13.
25. William Vans Murray to James McHenry, November 2, 1796, in Steiner, *Life and Correspondence of McHenry,* 200. For examples of such party labels, see George Thatcher to the Town of Wells, May 11, 1796, Thatcher Family papers, Massachusetts Historical Society; John Beckley to William Irvine, September 22 and October 17, 1796, in Gawalt, *Justifying Jefferson,* 123, 128–29; Fisher Ames to Oliver Wolcott, Jr., September 26, 1796, in Gibbs, *Memoirs of the Administrations of Washington and Adams,* 1:384–85; Robert Troup to Rufus King, November 16, 1796, *Correspondence of Rufus King,* 2:110; David Ross to Alexander Hamilton, November 16, 1796, *Hamilton Papers,* 20:395–97; Charles Carroll to James McHenry, December 5, 1796, in Steiner, *Life and Correspondence of McHenry,* 204–5; John Adams to Abigail Adams, December 16, 1796, Adams Family Papers, Massachusetts Historical Society; Joseph Jones to James Madison, [January] 1797, *Madison Papers,* 16:448–49.
26. William Loughton Smith to Rufus King, July 23, 1796, *Correspondence of Rufus King,* 2:65–66; William Vans Murray to James McHenry, November 2, 1796, and undated, in Steiner, *Life and Correspondence of McHenry,* 201–2; Dauer, *Adams Federalists,* 93–97; John Adams, diary, August 11, 1796, and John Adams to John Quincy Adams, October 28, 1796, Adams Family Papers, Massachusetts Historical Society.
27. William Loughton Smith to Ralph Izard, November 8, 1796, "South Carolina Federalist Correspondence, 1789–1797," *American Historical Review* 14 (July 1909): 784–85. See also William Loughton Smith to Ralph Izard, May 18, 1796, ibid., 780–81; Christopher Gore to John Quincy Adams, July 5, 1796, Adams Family Papers, Massachusetts Historical Society; Oliver Wolcott, Jr., to Jonathan Dayton, September 7, 1796, in Gibbs, *Memoirs of the Administrations of Washington and Adams,* 1:381; Jonathan Dayton to Oliver Wolcott, Jr., September 15, 1796, ibid., 1:383–84; William Vans Murray to James McHenry, October 2, 1796, in Steiner, *Life and Correspondence of McHenry,* 198; Rufus King to John Quincy Adams, November 10, 1796, *Correspondence of Rufus King,* 2:103–4. For Republican confusion about Burr and the vice presidency, see John Beckley to James Madison, June 20 and October 15, 1796, 119–21, 127–28, and Madison to Monroe, February 26, 1796, *Madison Papers,* 16:232–34.

28. For example, see James Madison to Henry Tazewell, October 18, 1796, *Madison Papers,* 16: 410–11. See also Kuroda, *Twelfth Amendment,* 65; and Smith, *Crisis, Unity, and Partisanship.*
29. Fisher Ames to Josiah Quincy, February 1, 1806, *Works of Fisher Ames,* 2:1504–5; William Vans Murray to James McHenry, October 9, 1796, in Steiner, *Life and Correspondence of McHenry,* 199. See also Hugh Williamson to McHenry, October 20, 1796, ibid., 200. On newspaper coverage of the election of 1796, see Smith, "Election of 1796." See also Cunningham, *Circular Letters,* xv–xlv; Brown, *Knowledge Is Power;* Fischer, *Revolution of American Conservatism;* and Warner, *Letters of the Republic.*
30. Tinkcom, *Republicans and Federalists in Pennsylvania,* 174; Abigail Adams to John Adams, December 23, 1796, Adams Family Papers, Massachusetts Historical Society. See also John Adams to Abigail Adams, January 3, 1797, ibid. The shopkeeper responded by reminding the man that Adams was a lawyer, asking, "Can you believe that a lawyer can't talk?"
31. It is worth noting that well over thirty thousand people voted in Pennsylvania's gubernatorial elections. John Beckley to James Madison, October 15, 1796, Beckley to William Irvine, September 15 and 22, October 4 and 17, 1796, in Gawalt, *Justifying Jefferson,* 122–23, 124–25, 127, 128–29; and Cooke, *Tench Coxe,* 285. For detailed accounts of Beckley's efforts, see Elkins and McKitrick, *Age of Federalism,* 519–23; Cunningham, *Jeffersonian Republicans,* 101–7; Berkeley and Berkeley, *John Beckley;* and Pasley, "'Artful and Designing Men,'" 104–30. See also Tinkcom, *Republicans and Federalists in Pennsylvania,* 162–74.
32. See Jonathan Dayton to Theodore Sedgwick, November 12 and 13, 1796, and Sedgwick to Dayton, November 19, 1796, enclosed in Sedgwick to Alexander Hamilton, November 19, 1796, *Hamilton Papers,* 20:402–7.
33. Theodore Sedgwick to Jonathan Dayton, November 19, 1796, enclosed in Sedgwick to Alexander Hamilton, November 13, 1796, ibid., 404–6.
34. For example, a cursory examination of New Jersey in the late eighteenth and early nineteenth centuries reveals that five electors went on to become U.S. senators, sometimes at the next election: Franklin Davenport, Theodore Frelinghuysen, Aaron Ogden, James Parker, and Richard Stockton. On undeclared presidential electors, see Scherr, "'Republican Experiment,'" 96–98; Gilpatrick, *Jeffersonian Democracy of North Carolina,* 74–75; Cunningham, *Jeffersonian Republicans,* 94–98; Joseph Bloomfield to Tench Coxe, November 20, 1796, Tench Coxe Papers, Historical Society of Pennsylvania; George Cabot to Oliver Wolcott, Jr., November 30, 1796, in Gibbs, *Memoirs of the Administrations of Washington and Adams,* 1:404.
35. Samuel Andrew Law to Tench Coxe, December 12, 1796, Tench Coxe Papers, Historical Society of Pennsylvania; Moore Furman to Tench Coxe, November 28, 1796, ibid.
36. Aaron Burr to William Eustis, November 30, 1796, *Papers of Aaron Burr,* 1:277–78. On Burr's electioneering, see Abigail Adams to John Quincy Adams, November 25, 1796, Adams Family Papers; Ebenezer Foote to Peter Van Gaasbeek, February 14, 1796, in Alfred F. Young, *Democratic Republicans of New York,* 548; [John Gardner], "A Brief Consideration of the Important Services and Distinguished Virtues and Talents, which Recommend Mr. Adams for the Presidency of the United States" (Boston, 1796), 29; and Peter Van Gaasbeek to Burr, November 25, 1796, State House Museum, Kingston, N.Y.
37. Aaron Burr to Elbridge Gerry, November 30, 1796, *Papers of Aaron Burr,* 1:278–79; John Adams to Abigail Adams, December 18, 1796, Adams Family Papers, Massachusetts Historical Society; Stephen Higginson to Alexander Hamilton, December 9, 1796, *Hamilton Papers,* 20:437–38. On Burr, see also Gerry to Abigail Adams, December 28, 1796, Adams Family Papers, Massachusetts Historical Society.
38. George Clinton to Michael Leib, November 19, 1796, in Kuroda, *Origins of the Twelfth Amendment,* 69; William Loughton Smith to Ralph Izard, November 3, 1796, "South Carolina Federalist Correspondence," 781–82; Moore Furman to Tench Coxe, November 28, 1796, Tench Coxe Papers; William Vans Murray to James McHenry, October 9, 1796, in Steiner, *Life and*

Correspondence of McHenry, 199; Stephen Higginson to Alexander Hamilton, December 9, 1796, *Hamilton Papers,* 20:437–38.

39. For information about electoral votes, see *Congressional Quarterly's Guide to U.S. Elections* (Washington, D.C.: Congressional Quarterly, 1994), 361; Kurtz, *Presidency of John Adams,* 412–14. See also Elkins and McKitrick, *Age of Federalism,* 514.

40. Philip Freneau to Tench Coxe, November 22, 1796, Tench Coxe Papers, Historical Society of Pennsylvania; Henry Tazewell to James Madison, October 3, 1796, *Madison Papers,* 16: 405–8; Thomas Jefferson to James Monroe, March 2 and July 10, 1796, Thomas Jefferson Papers, Library of Congress; William Wirt Henry, *Patrick Henry: Life, Correspondence and Speeches,* 2:568–75; Rufus King to Alexander Hamilton, May 2, 1796, Hamilton to King, May 4, 1796, and John Marshall to King, May 24, 1796, *Hamilton Papers,* 20:151–53,158–59.

41. George Cabot to Oliver Wolcott, Jr., April 13, 1797, in Gibbs, *Memoirs of the Administrations of Washington and Adams,* 1:491–93; John Beckley to James Madison, June 20, 1796, and Beckley to William Irvine, October 4, 1796, in Gawalt, *Justifying Jefferson,* 119–21, 124–25. In these three letters, John Browne Cutting and John Brown declare that Hamilton urged Jefferson on them personally, a claim that could indict them as liars if proven untrue; far more typical would be an assertion that they "had heard it said that" Hamilton supported Jefferson. The willingness of both men to risk their reputations on such a comment, joined with a close reading of Hamilton's supposed words, suggests that he may indeed have endorsed Jefferson, though in an extremely hypothetical manner. Brown asked Hamilton whether "there may be a state of things in which it would be desirable that Mr. J. should be elected." Hamilton's agreement that in case of war with France, Jefferson might be the only man able to save the Union is not quite an endorsement of Jefferson's candidacy, though it could be creatively interpreted as such.

42. George Clinton to DeWitt Clinton, December 13, 1803, in Kaminski, *George Clinton: Yeoman Politician of the New Republic,* 251–52.

43. Theodore Sedgwick to Ephraim Williams, January 9, 1797, Sedgwick III, Massachusetts Historical Society. See also Chauncey Goodrich to Oliver Wolcott, Sr., December 17, 1796, in Gibbs, *Memoirs of the Administrations of Washington and Adams,* 1:411–13; Fisher Ames to Thomas Dwight, January 5, 1797, *Works of Fisher Ames,* 2:1211–12; Robert Troup to Rufus King, January 28, 1796, Theodore Sedgwick to King, March 12, 1797, and William Smith to King, April 3, 1797, *Correspondence of Rufus King,* 2:135, 156, 164–67; Hamilton to King, February 15, 1797, *Hamilton Papers,* 20:551–56.

44. Thomas Jefferson to Archibald Stuart, January 4, 1797, Thomas Jefferson Papers, Library of Congress; Joseph Jones to James Madison, January 29, 1797, *Madison Papers,* 16:477–79. See also Jones to Madison, February 5, 1797, *Madison Papers,* 16:485–86.

45. Thomas Jefferson to John Adams, December 28, 1796, Thomas Jefferson Papers; Smith, "Election of 1796," in *History of American Presidential Elections,* 73. On Jefferson's letter to Adams, see *Adams-Jefferson Letters,* 1:243, 262–63; Smith, *John Adams,* 2:909; Elkins and McKitrick, *Age of Federalism,* 539–49; Malone, *Jefferson and the Ordeal of Liberty,* 293–94; and Ellis, *Passionate Sage,* 29–30.

46. James Madison to Thomas Jefferson, January 15, 1797, *Madison Papers,* 16:455–57; Jefferson to Madison, December 17, 1796, and January 30, 1797, ibid., 16:431–32, 479–80; John Adams to Abigail Adams, January 1, 1797, Adams Family Papers, Massachusetts Historical Society; Jefferson to John Langdon, January 27, 1797, Thomas Jefferson Papers; Jefferson to Madison, January 22, 1797, *Madison Papers,* 16:473–74. See also Jefferson to Thomas Mann Randolph, January 22, 1797, Thomas Jefferson Papers.

47. Charles Carroll to James McHenry, November 28, 1796, in Steiner, *Life and Correspondence of McHenry,* 202–3; Joseph Jones to James Madison, December 9, 1796, *Madison Papers,* 16:

423–24; Thomas Jefferson to Archibald Stuart, January 4, 1797, Thomas Jefferson Papers; Jefferson, memorandum, March 2, 1797, *Anas,* 184–85.

48. On the "cease-fire," see Theodore Sedgwick to Rufus King, March 12, 1797, *Correspondence of Rufus King,* 2:156–59; and Tagg, *Benjamin Franklin Bache and the Philadelphia Aurora,* 295–300. See also Alexander Hamilton to Rufus King, February 15, 1797, *Hamilton Papers,* 20: 515–16; James Madison to Thomas Jefferson, January 29 and February 5, 1797, *Madison Papers,* 16:476, 483–84.
49. Roll-call congressional votes or petition signing could serve the same purpose, forcing people to commit their name to a cause—and politicians often used them in this way. John Beckley to DeWitt Clinton, July 24, 1795, DeWitt Clinton Papers, Columbia University; Hamilton to Rufus King, February 21, 1795, and Hamilton to Theodore Sedgwick, February 18, 1795, *Hamilton Papers,* 17:277–81.
50. Memo of James Nicholson, December 26, 1803, *American Historical Review* 8 (April 1903): 511–13; Aaron Burr to John Taylor of Caroline, October 22, 1800, *Papers of Aaron Burr,* 1: 451–52.
51. On sectional identity and its interconnectedness with nationalism, see Onuf, *Statehood and Union;* and Ayers, Limerick, Nissenbaum, and Onuf, *All over the Map.* The foremost proponent of the sectional view of partisan politics is Sharp, *American Politics in the Early Republic.* Note also Jefferson's 1795 letter in which he wrote "Southern" and then crossed it out and replaced it with "Republican." Jefferson to Madison, April 27, 1795, *Madison Papers,* 16:1–2. Sharp discusses this letter in "Unraveling the Mystery of Jefferson's Letter of April 17, 1795," *Journal of the Early Republic* 6 (1986): 411–18.
52. Hamilton to John Jay, May 7, 1800, *Hamilton Papers,* 24:464–67; Gideon Granger to Thomas Jefferson, October 18, 1800, Thomas Jefferson Papers; see Wood, *Radicalism of the American Revolution,* 296–98.
53. Matthew Davis to Albert Gallatin, May 5, 1800, Albert Gallatin Papers; John Adams to Abigail Adams, November 15, 1800, Adams Family Papers; Philadelphia *Aurora,* May 7, 1800. For preelection jitters, see also Abigail Adams to Thomas Adams, October 12, 1800, and William Tudor to John Adams, November 5, 1800, Adams Family Papers; Gideon Granger to Thomas Jefferson, October 18, 1800, Thomas Jefferson Papers.
54. Several historians consider the 1798 Virginia and Kentucky resolutions the opening salvo of the 1800 campaign, and at least one contemporary saw Burr's ardent support of the resolutions in the New York Senate as evidence of a link between New York and Virginia in the impending presidential contest. Burr began conferring with Jefferson as early as January 1800. *Papers of Aaron Burr,* 1:393–95 and note 1; Theodore Sedgwick to Peter Van Schaack, February 10, 1799, Sedgwick III, Massachusetts Historical Society. On preparation among "professional" politicians, see Pasley, "'Artful and Designing Men,'" 144–60.
55. Thomas Jefferson to Tench Coxe, May 21, 1799, Thomas Jefferson Papers; Jefferson to Madison, November 22, 1799, and Monroe to Madison, November 22, 1799, *Madison Papers,* 17: 277–78, 278–79. Monroe suggested an alternate plan, noting that "there wod. be nothing extr[aordinar]y" in a visit by Madison and his wife to his new house—where Jefferson might just happen to be present.
56. Thomas Jefferson to James Monroe, March 26 and April 16, 1800, and Monroe to Jefferson, [May 1800], Thomas Jefferson Papers, Library of Congress.
57. Davis, *Memoirs of Aaron Burr,* 1:434–35, 2:54–55, 60; Matthew Davis to Albert Gallatin, May 1, 1800, Albert Gallatin Papers. As evidence of the electoral importance of New York, Davis cites a letter of March 4, 1800, from Thomas Jefferson to James Madison, *Madison Papers,* 367–71.
58. Davis, *Memoirs of Aaron Burr,* 1:434–35, 2:54–55, 60; Davis to Gallatin, May 1, 1800, Albert

Gallatin Papers; *Daily Advertiser,* April 2, 1800; *General Advertiser,* April 3, 1800, in Lomask, *Aaron Burr,* 244, note 39; Robert Troup to Peter Van Schaack, May 2, 1800, in Cunningham, *Jeffersonian Republicans,* 183; Hamilton, *History of the Republic of the United States of America,* 375–76. The story may be apocryphal. John Church Hamilton reports that his father was on horseback because he was on his way to his country home; he then offers a questionable anecdote about how his father swayed the "rabble" after being forced from his horse.

59. Charles Pinckney to James Madison, September 30, 1799, *Madison Papers,* 17:272–74; Charles Carroll to Alexander Hamilton, August 27, 1800, *Hamilton Papers,* 25:93–95; circular letter from Massachusetts Delegates in Congress, January 31, 1800, in Cunningham, *Jeffersonian Republicans,* 146. See also Pinckney to Madison, May 16, 1799, ibid., 17:250–51; John Dawson to Madison, November 28, 1799, *Madison Papers,* 17:281–82; Stevens Thomas Mason to Madison, January 16, 1800, *Madison Papers,* 17:357–58; Charles Peale Polk to Madison, June 20, 1800, *Madison Papers,* 17:384–86. For a detailed discussion of such electoral reform in 1800, see Cunningham, *Jeffersonian Republicans,* 144–47.
60. Alexander Hamilton to John Jay, May 7, 1800, *Hamilton Papers,* 24:464–67. See Gabriel Duvall to James Madison, June 6, 1800, Charles Peale Polk to Madison, June 20, 1800, and John Dawson to Madison, July 28, 1800, *Madison Papers,* 17:392, 395, 399.
61. Alexander Hamilton to Charles Carroll, July 1, 1800, and Hamilton to James A. Bayard, August 6, 1800, *Hamilton Papers,* 25:1–3, 56–58; Robert Goodloe Harper to Hamilton, June 5, 1800, ibid., 24:568–70; Cunningham, *Jeffersonian Republicans,* 129–31.
62. Thomas Jefferson to James Madison, February 7, 1799, *Madison Papers,* 17:225–27; Jefferson to Tench Coxe, May 21, 1799, Thomas Jefferson Papers; Samuel Harrison Smith to Madison, August 17, 1800, *Madison Papers,* 17:405–6; Fisher Ames to Thomas Dwight, March 19, 1801, and Ames to John Rutledge, July 30, 1801, *Writings of Fisher Ames,* 2:1409–12, 1414–17. On Federalist and Republican use of newspapers, see also Pasley, "'Artful and Designing Men,'" 416–31, 445–57.
63. Matthew L. Davis, notebook, May 30, 1830, Rufus King Papers, New-York Historical Society. See also George Clinton to DeWitt Clinton, December 13, 1803, in Kaminski, *George Clinton,* 251–52; Davis, *Memoirs,* 2:58–59 (in which Davis claims to be quoting from the notes quoted above).
64. Gabriel Duvall to James Madison, October 17, 1800, *Madison Papers,* 17:424–25; Theodore Sedgwick to Rufus King, May 24, 1801, *Correspondence of Rufus King,* 3:454–57.
65. James Bayard to John Rutledge, Jr., June 8, 1800, *Hamilton Papers,* 25:36–38, note; Aaron Burr to Robert R. Livingston, September 24, 1800, Robert R. Livingston Papers, New-York Historical Society (see also Robert R. Livingston to Edward Livingston, February 20, 1801, ibid.); Thomas Adams to Abigail Adams, October 19, 1800, Adams Family Papers, Massachusetts Historical Society; George Cabot to Alexander Hamilton, August 23, 1800, *Hamilton Papers,* 25:77–79. For more Federalist suspicions, see Hamilton to James McHenry, June 6, 1800, Charles Cotesworth Pinckney to Hamilton, July 17, 1800, John Rutledge, Jr., to Hamilton, July 17, 1800, Timothy Phelps to Oliver Wolcott, July 15, 1800, *Hamilton Papers,* 25:573, 27–29, 30–38, 52, note 2, and 24:484–86, note 3; Pinckney to McHenry, June 10 and 19, 1800, in Steiner, *Life and Correspondence of McHenry,* 459–61; Timothy Pickering to Rufus King, June 26, 1800, Fisher Ames to King, July 15, August 19, August 26, and September 24, 1800, *Correspondence of Rufus King,* 3:261–63, 273–74, 293–97, 303–7; Benjamin Stoddart to John Adams, October 27, 1811, Adams Family Papers, Massachusetts Historical Society; Trenton, N.J., *The Federalist,* June 2, 1800. Hamilton hints at this possibility in his notorious 1800 "Letter to John Adams." *Hamilton Papers,* 25:169–234.
66. John Taylor of Caroline to Thomas Jefferson, June 25, 1798, Thomas Jefferson Papers.
67. See, for example, James Monroe to James Madison, October 21, 1800, George Jackson to Madison, *Madison Papers,* 17:426, 460–61, Charles Cotesworth Pinckney to James McHenry,

June 10, 1800, in Steiner, *Life and Correspondence of McHenry,* 459–60; Robert Troup to Rufus King, December 4, 1800, Fisher Ames to Rufus King, August 26, 1800, in King, *Correspondence of Rufus King,* 3:295–97, 340–41; John Adams to Abigail Adams, December 16, 1796, Adams Family Papers, Massachusetts Historical Society; John Rutledge, Jr., to Alexander Hamilton, July 17, 1800, *Hamilton Papers,* 25:30–38; David Gelston to Madison, October 8 and November 21, 1800, *Madison Papers,* 17:418–19, 438; George Cabot to Hamilton, August 21, 1800, *Hamilton Papers,* 25:74–75.

68. Thomas Adams to John Adams, January 22, 1801, Adams Family Papers, Massachusetts Historical Society; John Francis Mercer to James Madison, January 5, 1801, *Madison Papers,* 17: 452–53.
69. George Cabot to Alexander Hamilton, August 21, 1800, *Hamilton Papers,* 25:74–75.
70. John Rutledge, Jr., to Alexander Hamilton, July 17, 1800, ibid., 25:30–38. See also Hamilton to Theodore Sedgwick, May 8 and 10, 1800, ibid., 25:24; Sedgwick to Peter Van Schaack, May 9, 1800, Theodore Sedgwick III, Massachusetts Historical Society; Charles Cotesworth Pinckney to James McHenry, June 10 and 19, 1800, in Steiner, *Life and Correspondence of McHenry,* 459–61; Fisher Ames to Rufus King, August 26, 1800, *Correspondence of Rufus King,* 3:295–97.
71. Robert Goodloe Harper to Harrison Gray Otis, August 28, 1800, *Hamilton Papers,* 25:59, note 9; Bushrod Washington to Oliver Wolcott, Jr., November 11, 1800, ibid., 25:249–50, note 7.
72. George Cabot to Alexander Hamilton, ibid., 25:247–49; Charles Cotesworth Pinckney to James McHenry, June 10, 1800, in Steiner, *Life and Correspondence of McHenry,* 459–60; James A. Bayard to Hamilton, August 18, 1800, *Hamilton Papers,* 25:68–71.
73. David Gelston to James Madison, October 8 and November 21, 1800, *Madison Papers,* 17:418–19, 438; Madison to Thomas Jefferson, October 21, 1800, ibid., 17:425–26 (see also Madison to James Monroe, [ca. October 21, 1800], Madison to David Gelston, October 24, 1800, ibid., 17:426); Jefferson, memorandum, January 26, 1804, *Anas,* 224–28.
74. Timothy Green to David Denniston and James Cheetham, October 11, 1802, John Swartwout to Denniston and Cheetham, October 13, 1802, in Davis, *Memoirs of Aaron Burr,* 2:91–93. Green's defense appeared in the New York *American Citizen,* October 11, 1802. Though Green explicitly denied it, he did, indeed, report to Burr about South Carolina politics at least twice; see Aaron Burr to William Eustis, December 9 and 16, 1800, *Papers of Aaron Burr,* 1:466–67, 470. He likewise reported to Burr on Rhode Island politics during a trip there; see Burr to John Taylor of Caroline, December 18, 1800, *Papers of Aaron Burr,* 1:472–73.
75. Davis, *Memoirs of Aaron Burr,* 2:99, 139.
76. Uriah Tracy to James McHenry, December 30, 1800, in Steiner, *Life and Correspondence of McHenry,* 483–84. See also John Francis Mercer to James Madison, January 5, 1801, *Madison Papers,* 17:452–53. Studies that stress party loyalty include Elkins and McKitrick, *Age of Federalism,* 744; Cunningham, *Jeffersonian Republicans,* 239; Sharp, *American Politics in the Early Republic,* 249. Sharp sees northern Federalists fighting southern Republicans but does not examine sectionalism within the parties themselves.
77. Hugh Henry Brackenridge to Thomas Jefferson, January 19, 1801, Thomas Jefferson Papers. See also Thomas Mann Randolph to James Monroe, February 14, 1801, in Hamilton, *History of the Republic,* 7:432–33.
78. James Gunn to Alexander Hamilton, January 9, 1801, *Hamilton Papers,* 25:303–4. For more Federalist fears, see William Tudor to John Adams, November 5, 1800, Abigail Adams to Thomas Adams, October 12, 1800, John Adams to Abigail Adams, November 15, 1800, Elbridge Gerry to John Adams, January 16, 1801, Adams Family Papers, Massachusetts Historical Society; James Bayard to Allen McLane, February 17, 1801, Thomas Jefferson Papers.
79. Edward Livingston to Robert R. Livingston, January 29, 1801, Robert R. Livingston Papers,

New-York Historical Society. Thomas Jefferson to James Monroe, February 15, 1801, in Cunningham, *Jeffersonian Republicans,* 246; Jefferson to James Madison, February 18, 1801, *Madison Papers,* 17:467–68. Jefferson denied the "idea of force" a few weeks later, claiming that a constitutional convention "would have been on the ground in 8. weeks," and "repaired the Constitution." Jefferson to Dr. Joseph Priestley, March 21, 1801, Thomas Jefferson Papers.

80. See, for example, Albert Gallatin to Hannah Nicholson Gallatin, January 5, 7, and 29, 1801, Aaron Burr to Albert Gallatin, January 16, 1801, William Eustis to Gallatin, March 6, 1801, John Beckley to Gallatin, February 15, 1801, Albert Gallatin Papers; Thomas Jefferson to Andrew Ellicott, December 18, 1800, Caesar Rodney to Jefferson, December 28, 1800, Jefferson to Tench Coxe, December 31, 1800, Monroe to Jefferson, January 6, 1801, Thomas McKean to Jefferson, January 10, 1801, Horatio Gates to Jefferson, February 9, 1801, Thomas Jefferson Papers; Jefferson to Madison, December 19 and 26, 1800, *Madison Papers,* 17:444–46, 448; James Bayard to Alexander Hamilton, March 8, 1801, Gouverneur Morris to Hamilton, December 19, 1800, *Hamilton Papers,* 25:266–69, 322–46. Hamilton declared usurpation of the government a "most dangerous and unbecoming policy." Hamilton to Morris, January 9, 1801, *Hamilton Papers,* 304–5.
81. James Monroe to Thomas Jefferson, December 30, 1800, and January 6, 1801, Thomas Jefferson Papers; James Madison to Monroe, [ca. November 10, 1800], *Madison Papers,* 17:435. See also Jefferson to Thomas Mann Randolph, January 9, 1801, Thomas McKean to Jefferson, January 10, 1801, Horatio Gates to Jefferson, February 9, 1801, and Caesar Rodney to Jefferson, December 28, 1800, Thomas Jefferson Papers; and Madison to Jefferson, December 20, 1800, *Madison Papers,* 17:446–48.
82. See Onuf, *Statehood and Union,* esp. chaps. 1 and 7; and Ayers, Limerick, Nissenbaum, and Onuf, *All over the Map,* 11–37.
83. Samuel Smith to Aaron Burr, January 11, 1801, Samuel Smith Papers, Alderman Library, University of Virginia. Ogden denied any connection with Burr, Bishop dismissed the accusations as lies, and Livingston stated only that he had never heard Burr say anything to suggest that he would seek the presidency over Jefferson. On Ogden, see [Deposition of James Bayard], 1805, Peter Irving to Ogden, November 24, 1802, and Ogden to Irving, November 24, 1802; *Memoirs of Aaron Burr,* 2:95–97, 124–26; Samuel Smith to Burr, January 11, 1801, Samuel Smith Papers, Alderman Library, University of Virginia; Burr to Smith, January 16, 1801, *Correspondence of Aaron Burr,* 1:493, 489–90, note 1. On Livingston, see [Statement regarding Aaron Burr], ca. 1802, and [Deposition of James Bayard], Davis, *Memoirs of Aaron Burr,* 2:97, 125; Alexander Hamilton to Gouverneur Morris, January 9, 1801, *Hamilton Papers,* 25:304–5; Burr to Albert Gallatin, January 16, 1801, *Papers of Aaron Burr,* 1:492–93 and note 3. On Bishop, see *Papers of Aaron Burr,* 2:728–29, note 2; Burr to Tench Coxe, October 25, 1800, and Burr to Pierpont Edwards, November 18, 1800, *Papers of Aaron Burr,* 1:452–53, 459.
84. See George Jackson to James Madison, February 5, 1801, *Madison Papers,* 17:460–61.
85. Davis, *Memoirs of Aaron Burr,* 2:116, 130, 126, 115–16, 130.
86. James Bayard to John Adams, February 19, 1801, "Papers of James A. Bayard, 1796–1815," *Annual Report of the American Historical Association* 2 (1913): 129–30. See also [Deposition of Samuel Smith], 1802; [Deposition of James Bayard], 1805, in Davis, *Memoirs of Aaron Burr,* 2:108, 127; Bayard to Hamilton, March 8, 1801, *Hamilton Papers,* 25:344–46.
87. James Bayard to Alexander Hamilton, January 7, 1801, *Hamilton Papers,* 25:199–303. On Bayard's decision, see Morton Borden, *The Federalism of James A. Bayard* (New York: Columbia University Press, 1995).
88. James Bayard to Samuel Bayard, February 22, 1801, *Annual Report of the American Historical Association,* 131–32.

89. [Deposition of James Bayard], 1805, in Davis, *Memoirs of Aaron Burr,* 2:122–28.
90. Davis, *Memoirs of Aaron Burr,* 1:181–82. See also ibid., 1:27, 40, 90–92.
91. Shapin, *Social History of Truth,* 83–85.
92. Aaron Burr to Samuel Smith, December 16, 1800, *Papers of Aaron Burr,* 1:471.
93. Burr to William Eustis, January 16, 1801, ibid., 1:490–91.
94. Burr to Smith, December 24 and 29, 1800, ibid., 1:475–76, 478–79.
95. James Madison to John Dawson, January 3, 1801, *Madison Papers,* 17:451–52; James Gunn to Alexander Hamilton, January 9, 1801, *Hamilton Papers,* 25:303; Robert Troup to Rufus King, February 12, 1801, *Correspondence of Rufus King,* 3:391; Gabriel Christie to Samuel Smith, December 19, 1802, *Papers of Aaron Burr,* 1:484, editorial note. See also Benjamin Hichborn to Thomas Jefferson, January 5, 1801, Thomas Jefferson Papers; and Jefferson, memorandum, January 2, 1804, *Anas,* 223. For Smith's role in the electoral tie, see Pancake, *Smith and the Politics of Business;* and Cassell, *Merchant Congressman in the Young Republic.*
96. Burr to Joseph Alston, November 15, 1815, *Papers of Aaron Burr,* 2:1165–69.
97. See Sharp, *American Politics in the Early Republic,* 27–33; Malone, *Jefferson and the Ordeal of Liberty;* and Elkins and McKitrick, *Age of Federalism.* Malone wrestles with this issue in *Jefferson the President, First Term,* 12–15, 487–93.
98. [Deposition of James Bayard], April 3, 1806, in Davis, *Memoirs of Aaron Burr,* 2:129–33.
99. [Deposition of Samuel Smith], April 15, 1806, in Davis, *Memoirs of Aaron Burr,* 2:133–37.
100. Jefferson, memorandum, April 15, 1806, *Anas,* 238.
101. January 12, 1831, *Memoirs of John Quincy Adams,* 8:272–73. Adams was reading Jefferson's "Anas" at the time. Bayard told Adams about Jefferson's deal "more than once." February 11 and March 6, 1830, ibid., 8:188, 200.
102. Joseph Bloomfield to Aaron Burr, September 17, 1802, and Burr to Bloomfield, September 21, 1802, in *New-York Evening Post,* September 29, 1802, reprinted from the *Trenton True American,* Aaron Burr Papers, New-York Historical Society; Hamilton, *History of the Republic,* 7:760–61. Editor Peter Irving of the Burrite *Morning Chronicle* also solicited a statement of innocence from David Ogden, one of Burr's supposed "agents."
103. Aaron Burr to Charles Biddle, July 18, 1804, *Papers of Aaron Burr,* 2:887; *New-York Evening Post,* October 13, 1802, in Hamilton, *History of the Republic,* 7:760–61.
104. [Speech of James A. Bayard on the Judiciary Act,] February 20, 1802, in Hamilton, *History of the Republic,* 7:467–68; Bayard to Hamilton, April 12, 1802, *Hamilton Papers,* 25:600–601; "Address of Ajax, to James A. Bayard, Esq.," March 25, 1802. Jefferson owned a copy. E. Millicent Sowerby, comp., *Catalogue of the Library of Thomas Jefferson* (Charlottesville: University Press of Virginia, 1983), 3:337, no. 3293.
105. Jefferson, memorandum, January 26, 1804, *Anas,* 224–28.
106. [Deposition of Samuel Smith], Samuel Smith Papers, Alderman Library, University of Virginia. Burr's suit against Cheetham was filed in 1804 and again in 1805; Bayard and Smith deposed on both occasions. Additional deponents included Robert Goodloe Harper of South Carolina, and James Ross of Pennsylvania. Burr notes that Jonathan Dayton of Maryland, Samuel Dana of Pennsylvania, and Roger Griswold of Connecticut likewise offered depositions, but they have not been found. Burr to Robert Goodloe Harper, May 29, 1804, and Harper to Burr, June 28, 1804, *Papers of Aaron Burr,* 2:870–76, 962–68. Jefferson claimed that the libel suit was nothing more than an attempt to calumniate him, and accused Bayard of "pretending" to have negotiated with him. Jefferson, memorandum, April 15, 1806, *Anas,* 237–41.
107. Gales and Seaton's *Debates and Proceedings of the Congress,* 1830, 6:43–45, 54–55, 92–95. Also February 11, 1830, *Memoirs of John Quincy Adams,* 8:187, 199–200. Also Peterson, *Jefferson Image in the American Mind,* 34. The issue was discussed in the Senate a *second* time in 1855.

108. Richard and James Bayard, "Documents Relating to the Presidential Election of the Year 1801" (Philadelphia, 1831). Madison's defense is mentioned in Peterson, *Jefferson Image in the American Mind,* 34; March 1, 1831, *Memoirs of John Quincy Adams,* 8:331.
109. James Hamilton, *Reminiscences,* 20–21.

Epilogue

1. On William Plumer, see Peabody, *Life of William Plumer;* and Turner, *Plumer of New Hampshire*.
2. *William Plumer's Memorandum of Proceedings in the United States Senate, 1803–1807* [hereafter *Memoranda*], ed. Everett Somerville Brown (New York: Macmillan, 1923), May 2, 1805, 321. See also ibid., November 8, 1804, 186.
3. Ibid., December 23, 1806, 537–39.
4. Ibid.; Turner, *William Plumer of New Hampshire,* 99–100, 174.
5. On this historical impulse in general, see Cohen, *Revolutionary Histories;* McCoy, *Last of the Fathers;* Peterson, *Jefferson Image in the American Mind;* and Casper, *Constructing American Lives*. On early nineteenth-century visions of the Revolution, see Kammen, *Season of Youth,* 37–58.
6. Plumer, *Memoranda,* November 8, 1804, 186; Plumer, "Autobiography," page 108, William Plumer Papers, Library of Congress.
7. The published edition of Plumer's memoranda omits "a few" entries (such as those between March 7 and April 21, 1807) as well as Plumer's appendixes, in the former case because the editor deemed them purely "personal" and in the latter because the included documents are readily available in print. For a full understanding of Plumer's view of national politics, the memoranda should be studied in their original form. For a detailed description of Plumer's papers, see Turner, *William Plumer,* 349–51.
8. Plumer *Memoranda,* November 15, 1804, 195. Young offers a lively treatment of life in early Washington in *Washington Community,* but makes no use of Plumer's memoranda. Noble E. Cunningham, Jr., is an exception: see *Process of Government Under Jefferson* and *Jeffersonian Republicans in Power.*
9. Plumer, *Memoranda,* November 28, 1804, 209. The *Oxford English Dictionary* describes a memorandum as "'a note to help the memory'; by extension, a record of events or of observations made on a particular subject, esp. when intended for the writer's future consideration or use."
10. Plumer, *Memoranda,* November 17 and December 3, 1804, and March 12, 1806, 200, 211, 449. See also Turner, *Plumer of New Hampshire,* 169.
11. "Repository—Volume 5," title page, William Plumer Papers, New Hampshire State Library. Plumer's only modern biographer does not seem to have had access to this "Repository" volume, for it does not appear in his detailed note on sources, nor is it mentioned by the editor of Plumer's *Memoranda*. It is the fifth in a series of at least nine "Repository" volumes of varied contents. Lumped in with these collections of data, it has never been linked with Plumer's *Memoranda,* though it dates to his Senate term, covering the same year included in his least anecdotal first volume of memoranda. On character, see Casper, *Constructing American Lives,* 6.
12. "President Jefferson," "Aaron Burr VP," and "My design," March 1, 1804, December 7, 1803, and undated, "Repository—Volume 5," 43, 4[?], 77, William Plumer Papers, New Hampshire Historical Society.
13. The *OED* defines a register as a book or volume in which regular entry is made of particulars or details of any kind. A repository is a receptacle in which things are placed, deposited, or stored.

14. Plumer, *Memoranda,* July 22, 1806, 508.
15. Ibid., 507–12. On Plumer's decision to write a history, see Plumer to Jeremiah Mason, January 4, 1807, William Plumer Papers, Library of Congress; Plumer, *Life of William Plumer,* 357–60.
16. Plumer, *Memoranda,* June 25, 1806, 506; [Notes for Writing the History of North America], undated, and March 1, 1807, William Plumer Papers, Library of Congress. See also Plumer, *Memoranda,* February 4, 1807, 601. On Plumer's shifting politics, see also Turner, *William Plumer,* 164–67.
17. Plumer, *Memoranda,* February 4, 1807, 600–602.
18. Ibid., February 9, 1807, 605–7. Plumer must have been struck by Adams's words, because twenty-three years later, he repeated them back to Adams in a discussion of Jefferson's historical reputation. Plumer to John Quincy Adams, October 13, 1830, William Plumer Papers, Library of Congress.
19. Plumer, *Memoranda,* February 11, 1807, 607; June 5, 1829, *Memoirs of John Quincy Adams,* 8:153. Adams was discussing the possibility of writing a history of his father's life; he also pondered withholding the history until after his own death. Ibid. Madison echoed these sentiments. Madison to Samuel H. Smith, February 2, 1827, in McCoy, *Last of the Fathers,* 163. Charles Thomson, longtime secretary of Congress, mused along similar lines; Benjamin Rush to John Adams, February 12, 1812, in Schutz and Adair, *Spur of Fame,* 210.
20. Plumer to John Quincy Adams, February 13, 1829, William Plumer Papers, Library of Congress; Turner, *William Plumer,* 200–201, 320.
21. Plumer filled at least a dozen notebooks with more than 2,000 biographical sketches. "The Register of Opinions & events—his readings &c. of William Plumer, From May 7, *1807* to April 2, *1836,*" William Plumer Papers, Library of Congress. On the popularity of this genre, see Casper, *Constructing American Lives,* 21–22.
22. Plumer, "Register of Opinions & events . . . ," April 22, 29, and May 7, 1808, William Plumer Papers, Library of Congress. Readers criticized Marshall's work for its broad focus and inattention to details of Washington's life and character. Casper, *Constructing American Lives,* 29, 35. In addition to Marshall, Plumer read Aaron Bancroft, *Essay on the Life of George Washington, commander in chief of the American Army, through the Revolutionary War; and the first President of the United States* (Worcester, Mass.: Thomas and Sturtevant, 1807); and David Ramsay, *The Life of George Washington* (New York: Hopkins and Seymour, 1807). He considered Ramsay the best.
23. Sawvel, *Anas,* 24–25; Plumer to John Quincy Adams, September 1, 1830, William Plumer Papers, Library of Congress; Henry Lee, Jr., *Observations on the Writings of Thomas Jefferson, With Particular Reference to the Attack They Contain on the Memory of the Late Gen. Henry Lee* (Philadelphia: J. Dobson; Cowperthwait; Carey and Hart, 1839), 86. See also pp. xii–xiii.
24. Pickering, "Review of the Correspondence Between the Hon. John Adams . . . and the Late Wm. Cunningham," 6; Nicholas P. Trist to Martin Van Buren, May 31, 1857, MSS no. 38-414-b, Alderman Library, University of Virginia. Madison himself wrote a brief autobiography (in the third person!) in 1831. Douglass Adair, ed., "James Madison's Autobiography," *William and Mary Quarterly* 2 (April 1945): 191–209. See also Casper, *Constructing American Lives,* 56–57.
25. Samuel Bell to Plumer, January 30, 1830, William Plumer Papers, Library of Congress. Many others denigrated Jefferson's publication of "tattle." See, for example, Sullivan, *Public Men of the Revolution,* 183.
26. William Sullivan, "Introduction by the Author," April 20, 1834, in Sullivan, *Public Men of the Revolution,* 14. See also Bayard, "Documents Relating to the Presidential Election in the Year 1801." On the response to Jefferson's *Memoirs,* see Peterson, *Jefferson Image in the American Mind,* 32–36, 130–35.
27. Hamilton, *History of the Republic of the United States of America,* 1:2; ibid., 7:836; Hamilton,

Reminiscences, preface. Hamilton addressed the same theme in a second work, entitled "Martin Van Buren's Calumnies Repudiated, Hamilton's Conduct as Secretary of the Treasury Vindicated" (New York, 1870).

28. See, for example, William Jay's *Life of John Jay* (1833); Charles Francis Adams's *Letters of John Adams to his Wife* (1841); Henry C. Van Schaack's *Life of Peter Van Schaack* (1842); William B. Reed's *Life and Correspondence of Joseph Reed* (1847). Kammen, *Season of Youth,* 50. James Hamilton told John Quincy Adams that he was worried about a publication by his brother Alexander, because the outcome might suggest that James didn't have "equal zeal for the reputation of his father." April 27, 1829, *Memoirs of John Quincy Adams,* 8:145.
29. Hamilton, *Reminiscences,* 40–41; King, *Correspondence of Rufus King,* 6:612–21. See also Hamilton, *Reminiscences,* 24–34; John Church Hamilton to John Wickham, May 23, 1834, Wickham Family Papers, Virginia Historical Society. John Church demanded access to papers that King had been given in 1810 by Hamilton's second, Nathaniel Pendleton, with the injunction that King keep them away from Hamilton's sons—an attempt to protect Washington's reputation by preventing the Hamiltons from proving their father's authorship of the address; King ultimately burned some of these papers rather than hand them over to the Hamiltons. Debate over its authorship continued for years thereafter. For a detailed treatment of the controversy, see Paltsits, *Washington's Farewell Address,* 75–94. For Daniel Webster's take on the controversy, see John Davis to Eliza Davis, March 23, 1832, John Davis Papers, Family Correspondence, American Antiquarian Society.
30. Hamilton, *Reminiscences,* 55–57. Parton discusses the incident as well in *Life of Aaron Burr,* 265.
31. Casper, *Constructing American Lives,* 381, note 38.
32. Pickering, "Review of the Correspondence . . . ," 2, 5, 4–6.
33. Turner, *William Plumer,* 336, note 9; Joseph Gales, Jr., and William Seaton to Simon Cameron, January 7, 1859, George Washington Harris to James Hamilton, May 13, 1861, and George Washington Harris receipt to Shippen B. Coxe, November 1863, FFC. See also Samuel Barr to Harris, July 18, 1882, John Mitchell to Harris, July 18, 1882; Simon Cameron to Harris, May 29, 1876, A. R. Spofford to Harris, April 9, 1866, and Spofford to Harris, May 12, 1866, ibid. My great thanks to Charlene Bickford and Ken Bowling of the Documentary History of the First Federal Congress for giving me access to these papers.
34. Plumer to John Quincy Adams, March 27, 1829, William Plumer Papers, Library of Congress; Concord *New Hampshire Patriot,* March 9, 1829, in Turner, *William Plumer,* 331, note 82. Also Plumer, *Life of William Plumer,* 293–312. The detritus from this literary shouting match formed the core of Henry Adams's *Documents Relating to New England Federalism, 1800–1815* (Boston: Little, Brown, 1877). On Plumer and the secession plot, see Turner, *Plumer of New Hampshire,* chap. 8.
35. Plumer to Alexander Hamilton, Jr., March 27 and April 11, 1829, and Plumer to John Quincy Adams, March 27, 1829, William Plumer Papers, Library of Congress. James Hamilton also questioned Plumer and John Quincy Adams in person about this issue. Plumer, *Life of William Plumer,* 304–5; diary entry, March 11, 1829, *Memoirs of John Quincy Adams,* 8:110.
36. Gibbs, *Memoirs of the Administrations of Washington and Adams,* 1:ix; Clarfield, *Pickering and the American Republic,* 269; Plumer, *Life of William Plumer,* 529–30. In a diary entry of December 28, 1848, William Plumer, Jr., described his father's conversation at a moment when his death seemed imminent; he rallied unexpectedly a week later and lived for another two years.
37. Parton, *Life and Times of Burr,* 2:326–27. Burr added, "If they persist in saying that I was a bad man . . . they shall at least admit that I was a good soldier." See also ibid., 2:275–76.
38. Plumer, "Autobiography," 217–18, William Plumer Papers, Library of Congress. This explanation of Jefferson's reaction does not appear in Plumer's original February 4, 1807, memorandum.

39. For details of the rise and fall of the reputations of Hamilton and Jefferson, see Peterson, *Jefferson Image in the American Mind,* and John S. Pancake, *Thomas Jefferson and Alexander Hamilton* (Woodbury, N.Y.: Barron's Educational Series, 1974), 371–409.
40. Richard Brookhiser, *Alexander Hamilton: American* (New York: Free Press, 1999); Karl-Friedrich Walling, *Republican Empire: Alexander Hamilton on War and Free Government* (Lawrence: University Press of Kansas, 1999); Mitchell, *Alexander Hamilton: A Concise Biography;* and Peter McNamara, "Alexander Hamilton, the Love of Fame, and Modern Democratic Statesmanship," in his *Noblest Minds,* 141–62. There has also been a spurt of children's books: John M. Rosenburg, *Alexander Hamilton: America's Bold Lion* (Breckenridge, Colo.: Twenty-First Century Books, 2000); Veda Boyd Jones, *Alexander Hamilton: First U.S. Secretary of the Treasury* (New York: Chelsea House, 2000); and Stuart A. Kallen, *Alexander Hamilton* (Edina, Minn: Abdo and Daughters, 2000).
41. Roger G. Kennedy, *Burr, Hamilton, and Jefferson: A Study in Character* (New York: Oxford University Press, 2000); Arnold A. Rogow, *A Fatal Friendship: Alexander Hamilton and Aaron Burr* (New York: Hill and Wang, 1998). Somewhat less Burr-centric is Thomas Fleming, *Duel: Alexander Hamilton, Aaron Burr, and the Future of America* (New York: Basic, 1999).
42. See, for example, Gail Collins, *Scorpion Tongues: The Irresistible History of Gossip in American Politics—Updated with the Latest Scandals and Innuendo* (New York: Harvest, 1999).
43. Matthew L. Davis to William Van Ness, August [7?], 1809, Miscellaneous manuscripts, Matthew Livingston Davis, New-York Historical Society.
44. See Bonomi, *Lord Cornbury Scandal.*

A Note on Method

1. Following similar lines are Reddy, *Invisible Code,* 2–4; Rakove, *Beginnings of National Politics,* 217; Young, *Washington Community,* 61; and Elias, *Court Society,* 211–13.

Bibliography

Manuscript Collections

American Antiquarian Society

John Davis Papers

Chicago Historical Society

Joseph Ward Papers

College of William and Mary

Tucker-Coleman Papers

Columbia University Rare Book and Manuscript Library

DeWitt Clinton Papers
John Jay Papers

David Library of the American Revolution

Sol Feinstone Collection

Historical Society of Pennsylvania

Tench Coxe Papers

Library of Congress

John Adams Papers
Beckley Family Papers
Aaron Burr Papers
Tench Coxe Papers
Alexander Dallas Papers
William Eustis Papers
John Fenno Papers
Edmond C. Genet Papers
Elbridge Gerry Papers
William Heth Papers
Harry Innes Papers
Ralph Izard Papers
Thomas Jefferson Papers
Tobias Lear Papers
William Maclay Papers
James McHenry Papers
James Monroe Papers
Gouverneur Morris Papers
Robert Morris Papers
W. C. Nicholas Papers
John Nicholson Papers
Timothy Pickering Papers
Pinckney Family Papers
William Plumer Papers
Benjamin Rush Papers
T. L. Shippen Papers
William Short Papers
Oliver Wolcott Papers

Massachusetts Historical Society

Adams Family Papers
Jeremy Belknap Papers
Jacob Bigelow Papers
Bowdoin and Temple Papers
Aaron Burr Letters to William Eustis
David Cobb Papers
Christopher P. Cranch Papers
William Cushing Papers
De Windt Collection
Dwight-Howard Papers
William Eustis Papers
Farnham Family Papers
Dwight Foster Papers
Charles Pelham Greenough Papers

David S. Greenough Papers
Benjamin Lincoln Papers
Jacob Norton Papers
Norton Family Papers
Harrison Gray Otis Papers
Phillips Family Papers
Timothy Pickering Papers
Samuel Putnam Papers
Theodore Sedgwick Papers
James Sullivan Transcripts
Thatcher Family Papers
Tudor-Adams Correspondence
Henry Van Schaack Papers
Peter Van Schaack Papers
Thomas B. Wait Letters to George Thatcher
Mercy Otis Warren Papers
Winthrop Papers

Morristown National Historical Park

Miscellaneous manuscripts

Mount Vernon Library

Tobias Lear diary
Robert Lewis diary
Miscellaneous manuscripts

New-York Historical Society

Aaron Burr Papers
DeWitt Clinton Correspondence
George Clinton Papers
Matthew Livingston Davis Papers
James Duane Papers
Albert Gallatin Papers
Edmond Genet Papers
Rufus King Papers
Robert R. Livingston Papers
Nicholas Low Papers
Gouverneur Morris Papers
Nathaniel Pendleton Papers
Thomas Tillotson Papers
Robert Troup Papers
John Trumbull Papers
William P. Van Ness Papers
Jeremiah Wadsworth Papers
Miscellaneous manuscripts filed under: DeWitt Clinton, Matthew L. Davis, Herman Ely, David Hosack, Nathaniel Pendleton, Thomas Tillotson, William P. Van Ness

New York Public Library

DeWitt Clinton Papers
Thomas Addis Emmet Collection
Theodorus Bailey Myers Collection
Thomas Tillotson Papers
Miscellaneous manuscripts, filed under: William Coleman, Charles Holt, Thomas Tillotson, John P. Van Ness, William P. Van Ness

New-York Society Library

Benjamin Goodhue Papers

Princeton University Library

Stimson Boudinot Collection

State House Museum, Kingston, N.Y.

Peter Van Gaasbeek Papers

University of Virginia

Samuel Smith Papers
Archibald Stuart Papers
Stuart-Baldwin Papers
Creed Taylor Papers
Miscellaneous manuscripts filed under Nicholas P. Trist
Papers relating to the presidential election of 1800

Virginia Historical Society

Preston Family Papers
Wickham Family Papers

Pamphlets

Adams, John. "Correspondence of the Late President Adams. Originally Published in the Boston Patriot. In a Series of Letters." Boston: Everett and Monroe, 1809.

[Bayard, Richard]. "Documents Relating to the Presidential Election in the Year 1801: Containing a Refutation of Two Passages in the Writings of Thomas Jefferson, Aspersing the Character of the Late James A. Bayard, of Delaware." Philadelphia: Mifflin and Parry, printers, 1831.

Bayard, Thomas F. "Remarks in the Senate of the United States, January 31, 1855, Vindicating the Late James A. Bayard, of Delaware, and Refuting the Groundless Charges Contained in the 'Anas' of Thomas Jefferson, Aspersing His Character." N.p., 1907.

[Beckley, John J.]. "Address to the People of the United States with an Epitome and Vindication of the Public Life and Character of Thomas Jefferson." Philadelphia: James Carey, 1800.

[Beckley, John J., and James Monroe]. "An Examination of the Late Proceedings in Congress, respecting the Official Conduct of the Secretary of the Treasury." Philadelphia, 1793.

Beecher, Lyman. "The Remedy for Duelling. A Sermon." New York: J. Seymour, printer, 1809.

[Cheetham, James]. "The American Annual Register, or, Historical Memoirs of the United States for . . . 1796." Philadelphia: Bioren and Madran, 1797.

[———]. "An Answer to Alexander Hamilton's Letter, concerning the Public Conduct and Character of . . . Adams. By a Citizen of New-York." New York: Johnson and Stryker, 1800.

[———]. "The History of the United States for 1796." Philadelphia: Snowden and McCorkle, 1797.

[———]. "A Narrative of the Suppression by Col. Burr, of the History of the Administration of John Adams." New York: Denniston and Cheetham, 1803.

[———]. "Nine Letters on the Subject of Aaron Burr's Political Defection . . ." New York: Denniston and Cheetham, 1803.

[———]. "A View of the Political Conduct of Aaron Burr." New York: Denniston and Cheetham, 1802.

Coleman, William. "A Collection of the Facts and Documents, relative to the Death of Major-General Alexander Hamilton." New York, 1804.

Cunningham, E. M., ed. "Correspondence Between the Hon. John Adams, Late President of the United States, and the Late William Cunningham, Esq. Beginning in 1803, and Ending in 1812." Boston: True and Greene, Printers, 1823.

Eacker, George I. "An Oration delivered at the request of the officers of the brigade of the City and County of New-York . . . , Fourth of July, 1801." New York, 1801.

Fraunces, Andrew. "An Appeal to the Legislature of the United States, and to the Citizens Individually, of the Several States." Philadelphia: For the author, 1793.
[Gardner, John]. "A Brief Consideration of the Important Services and Distinguished Virtues and Talents, which Recommend Mr. Adams for the Presidency of the United States." Boston: Manning and Loring, 1796.
Hamilton, Alexander. "Letter From Alexander Hamilton Concerning the Public Conduct and Character of John Adams, Esq." New York: Printed for John Lang by George F. Hopkins, 1800.
———. "Observations on Certain Documents Contained in No. V & VI of 'The History of the United States for the Year 1796'. . . Written by himself." Philadelphia: Printed by John Bioren for John Fenno, 1797.
Pickering, Timothy. "A Review of the Correspondence between the Hon. John Adams, Late President of the United States, and the Late Wm. Cunningham, Esq. Beginning in 1803, and Ending in 1812." Salem, Mass.: Published by Cushing and Appleton. Printed by Joshua and J. D. Cushing, 1824.
Smith, William Loughton. "An Address From William Smith, of South-Carolina, to his Constituents." Philadelphia, 1794.
[———]. "The Politicks and Views of a Certain Party, Displayed." Philadelphia: 1792.
[———]. "The Pretensions of Thomas Jefferson to the Presidency, examined, and the Charges against John Adams, refuted." Philadelphia, October, 1796.
Spring, Samuel. "The Sixth Commandment Friendly to Virtue, Honor and Politeness." N.p., 1804.
Taylor, John. "A Definition of Parties." Philadelphia: F. Bailey, 1794.
[Van Ness, William P.]. "A Correct Statement of the Late Melancholy Affair of Honor, Between General Hamilton and Col. Burr." New York, 1804.
[———]. "An Examination of the Various Charges Exhibited Against Aaron Burr, Esq. Vice President of the United States; and a Development of the Characters and Views of his Political Opponents. By Aristides." New York: Ward and Gould, 1803.
Wood, John. "The Suppressed History of the Administration of John Adams." Philadelphia, 1802.

Newspapers

Connecticut

Bee (New London)
Connecticut Courant (Hartford)

Maryland

Niles' Weekly Register (Baltimore)
Washington Federalist (Georgetown)

Massachusetts

Boston Gazette
Boston Patriot
Columbian Centinel (Boston)
Independent Chronicle (Boston)
Mirrour (Concord)
New England Palladium (Boston)
The Repertory (Boston)

New York

Albany Register
American Citizen (New York City)
The Argus, or Greenleaf's New Daily Advertiser (New York City)
The Balance, and Columbian Repository (Hudson)
Commercial Advertiser (New York City)
The Diary: or Loudon's Register (New York City)
Gazette of the United States (New York City)
Greenleaf's New York Journal & Patriotic Register
Morning Chronicle (New York City)
The New-York Daily Gazette
New-York Evening Post
New York Journal
New York Weekly Museum
The People's Friend & Daily Advertiser (New York City)
Spectator (New York City)
Time Piece (New York City)

New Jersey

Jersey Chronicle (Mount Pleasant)

Pennsylvania

Aurora and General Advertiser (Philadelphia)
Dunlap's American Daily Advertiser (Philadelphia)
Gazette of the United States (Philadelphia)
General Advertiser (Philadelphia)
National Gazette (Philadelphia)
Porcupine's Gazette (Philadelphia)

Virginia

Virginia Argus (Richmond)

Printed Primary Sources

Adams, Charles Frances, ed. *Letters of Mrs. Adams, the Wife of John Adams*. Boston: Little, Brown, 1840.

———. *The Works of John Adams, Second President of the United States*. 10 vols. Boston: Little, Brown, 1854.

Allen, W. B., ed. *Works of Fisher Ames, as Published by Seth Ames*. 2 vols. Indianapolis: Liberty Fund, 1983.

Amory, Thomas C. *Life of James Sullivan with Selections from His Writings*. Boston: Phillips, Sampson, 1859.

Bayard, James. "Papers of James A. Bayard, 1796–1815." *Annual Report of the American Historical Association* 2 (1913).

Biddle, James S., ed. *Autobiography of Charles Biddle, Vice-President of the Supreme Executive Council of Pennsylvania, 1745–1821*. Philadelphia: E. Claxton, 1883.

Bowling, Kenneth R., and Helen E. Veit, eds. *The Diary of William Maclay and Other Notes on Senate Debates*. Baltimore: Johns Hopkins University Press, 1988.

Boyd, Julian, Charles T. Cullen, and John Catanzariti, eds. *The Papers of Thomas Jefferson*. 27 vols. to date. Princeton: Princeton University Press, 1950–.

Brown, Everett Somerville, ed. *William Plumer's Memorandum of Proceedings in the United States Senate, 1803–1807*. New York: Macmillan, 1923.

Butterfield, L. H., ed. *Letters of Benjamin Rush*. Princeton: Princeton University Press, 1951.

Calendar of the General Otho Holland Williams Papers in the Maryland Historical Society. Baltimore: Maryland Historical Records Survey Project, 1940.

Cappon, Lester J., ed. *The Adams-Jefferson Letters: The Complete Correspondence Between Thomas Jefferson and Abigail and John Adams*. Chapel Hill: University of North Carolina Press, 1987.

Cole, G. D. H. *Letters from William Cobbett to Edward Thornton Written in the Years 1797 to 1800*. London: Oxford University Press, 1937.

Corner, George W., ed. *The Autobiography of Benjamin Rush: His 'Travels Through Life' Together with His Commonplace Book for 1789–1813*. Princeton: Princeton University Press, 1948.

Cunningham, Noble, Jr., ed. *Circular Letters of Congressmen to Their Constituents, 1789–1829*. 3 vols. Chapel Hill: University of North Carolina Press, 1978.

Davis, John. *Travels of Four Years and a Half in the United States of America During 1798, 1799, 1800, 1801, and 1802*. New York: Henry Holt, 1909.

Davis, Matthew L. *Memoirs of Aaron Burr*. 2 vols. New York: Harper and Brothers, 1837.

Decatur, Stephen, Jr. *Private Affairs of George Washington: From the Records and Accounts of Tobias Lear, Esquire, His Secretary*. Boston: Houghton Mifflin, 1933.

De Warville, Brissot. *New Travels in the United States of America, 1788*. Cambridge: Belknap, 1964.

De Witt, Cornelis. *Jefferson and the American Democracy*. London: Longman, Green, Longman, Roberts, and Green, 1862.

Dwight, Theodore. *The Character of Thomas Jefferson, as Exhibited in His Own Writings*. Boston: Weeks, Jordan, 1839.

Fields, Joseph E., ed. *"Worthy Partner": The Papers of Martha Washington*. Westport, Conn.: Greenwood, 1994.

Fitzpatrick, John C., ed. *The Autobiography of Martin Van Buren*. Rpt.; New York: Chelsea House, 1983.

———. *The Diaries of George Washington, 1748–1799*. 1925. New York: Kraus Reprint, 1971.

Ford, Paul L., ed. *The Writings of Thomas Jefferson*. 12 vols. New York: Putnam's, 1905.

Gales, Joseph, Sr., William Seaton, et al., eds. *The Debates and Proceedings of the Congress of the United States*. 42 vols. Washington, D.C.: Gales and Seaton, 1834–56.

Gawalt, Gerard. *Justifying Jefferson: The Political Writings of John James Beckley*. Washington, D.C.: Library of Congress, 1995.

Gibbs, George, ed. *Memoirs of the Administrations of Washington and John Adams*. 2 vols. New York: William Van Norden, 1846.

Hamilton, James A. *Reminiscences of James A. Hamilton, or Men and Events at Home and Abroad*. New York: Scribner's, 1869.

Hamilton, John C. *History of the Republic of the United States of America, as Traced in the Writings of Alexander Hamilton and of His Contemporaries*. 7 vols. New York: Appleton, 1860.

Hamilton, Stanislaus Murray, ed. *The Writings of James Monroe*. 7 vols. New York: Putnam's, 1898–1910.

Hume, David. *A Treatise of Human Nature*. Ed. L. A. Selby-Bigge. 1739–40. Oxford: Liberty, 1960.

Humphreys, Frank Landon, ed. *Life and Times of David Humphreys*. 2 vols. New York: Putnam's, 1917.

Jeremy, David John, ed. *Henry Wansey and His American Journal, 1794*. Philadelphia: American Philosophical Society, 1970.

King, Charles R., ed. *The Life and Correspondence of Rufus King*. 6 vols. New York: Putnam's, 1897.

Kline, Mary-Jo, ed. *Political Correspondence and Public Papers of Aaron Burr*. 2 vols. Princeton: Princeton University Press, 1983.

Lee, Charles. "The Lee Papers (1778–1782)." *Collections of the New-York Historical Society for the Year 1873*. New York, 1874.

Lee, Henry. *Observations on the Writings of Thomas Jefferson, with Particular Reference to the Attack They Contain on the Memory of the Late Gen. Henry Lee*. Philadelphia: J. Dobson; Cowperthwait; Carey and Hart, 1839.

Letters and Recollections of George Washington. New York: Doubleday, Page, 1906.

"Letters of Noah Webster, 1786–1840." *Massachusetts Historical Society Proceedings* 43 (October 1909–June 1910).

Marshall, John. *The Life of George Washington*. 5 vols. Philadelphia: C. P. Wayne, 1807.

Matthews, Albert, ed. *Journal of William Loughton Smith: 1790–1791*. Cambridge, Mass.: The University Press, 1917.

Mitchell, Stewart, ed. *New Letters of Abigail Adams: 1788–1801*. Rpt. Westport, Conn.: Greenwood, 1973.

Moore, J. Hamilton. *The Young Gentleman and Lady's Monitor, and English Teacher's Assistant*. Wilmington, Del., 1797.

Morris, Anne Carry, ed. *The Diary and Letters of Gouverneur Morris,* 2 vols. New York, 1888.

Nicholls, James C. "Lady Henrietta Liston's Journal of Washington's 'Resignation,' Retirement, and Death." *Pennsylvania Magazine of History and Biography* 95 (October 1971): 511–20.

Nicholson, James. "Memo of James Nicholson." *American Historical Review* 8 (April 1903): 511–13.

Niemcewicz, Julian Ursyn. *Under Their Vine and Fig Tree: Travels Through America in 1797–1799, 1805, with Some Further Account of Life in New Jersey*. Ed. J. E. B. Metchie. Elizabeth, N.J.: Grassman, 1965.

Norton, Lucy, ed. *Historical Memoirs of the Duc de Saint-Simon: A Shortened Version*. 2 vols. Rpt. New York: McGraw-Hill, 1967.

O'Dwyer, Margaret M. "A French Diplomat's View of Congress, 1790." *William and Mary Quarterly* (July 1964): 408–44.

Parton, James. *The Life and Times of Aaron Burr*. New York, 1864.

Perkins, Bradford. "A Diplomat's Wife in Philadelphia: Letters of Henrietta Liston, 1796–1800." *William and Mary Quarterly* 11 (1954).

Phillips, Ulrich B., ed. "South Carolina Federalist Correspondence, 1789–1797." *American Historical Review* 14 (July 1909).

Randolph, Thomas Jefferson, ed. *Memoir, Correspondence, and Miscellanies, from the Papers of Thomas Jefferson*. 4 vols. Charlottesville, Va.: F. Carr, 1829.

Roberts, Kenneth, and Anna M. Roberts. *Moreau de St. Méry's American Journey: 1793–1798*. Garden City, N.Y.: Doubleday, 1947.

Rogers, George C., Jr. "The Letters of William Loughton Smith to Edward Rutledge, June 8, 1789–April 28, 1794," *South Carolina Historical Magazine* 70 (January 1969).

Rutland, Robert, and J. C. A. Stagg, eds. *The Papers of James Madison*. 17 vols. to date. Charlottesville: University Press of Virginia, 1962–.

Sawvel, Franklin B., ed. *The Complete Anas of Thomas Jefferson*. New York: Round Table Press, 1903.

Schutz, John A., and Douglass Adair, eds. *The Spur of Fame: Dialogues of John Adams and Benjamin Rush, 1805–1813*. San Marino, Calif.: Huntington Library, 1966.

Sherrill, Charles H. *French Memories of Eighteenth-Century America*. New York: Scribner's, 1915.

Smith, Adam. *The Theory of Moral Sentiments*. Ed. D. D. Raphael and A. L. Macfie. 1759. Indianapolis: Liberty, 1982.
Smith, James Morton, ed. *The Republic of Letters: The Correspondence Between Thomas Jefferson and James Madison, 1776–1826*. New York: Norton, 1995.
Stanhope, Philip Dormer, earl of Chesterfield. *Letters Written by the Late Right Honourable Philip Dormer Stanhope, Earl of Chesterfield, to His Son*. Ed. Eugenia Stanhope. London, 1792.
Steiner, Bernard C. *The Life and Correspondence of James McHenry*. Cleveland: Burrows Brothers, 1907.
Sullivan, John T. S. *The Public Men of the Revolution, Including Events from the Peace of 1783 to the Peace of 1815, in a Series of Letters by the Late Hon. Wm. Sullivan, LL.D.* Philadelphia: Carey and Hart, 1847.
Syrett, Harold C., ed. *The Papers of Alexander Hamilton*. 27 vols. New York: 1961–1987.
Syrett, Harold C., and Jean G. Cooke, eds. *Interview in Weehawken: The Burr-Hamilton Duel as Told in the Original Documents*. Middletown, Conn.: Wesleyan University Press, 1960.
Twohig, Dorothy, ed. *The Papers of George Washington: Presidential Series*. Charlottesville: University Press of Virginia, 1987–.
Wagstaff, H. M., ed. *The Papers of John Steele*. Raleigh, N.C.: Edwards and Broughton, 1924.
Wilson, John Lyde. *The Code of Honor, or Rules for the Government of Principals and Seconds in Duelling*. Charleston, S.C., 1838.

Secondary Sources

Adair, Douglass. *Fame and the Founding Fathers*. Ed. Trevor Colbourn. New York: Norton, 1974.
Adair, Douglass, and Marvin Harvey. "Was Alexander Hamilton a Christian Statesman?" *William and Mary Quarterly* 12 (1955): 308–29.
Alberts, Robert C. *The Golden Voyage: The Life and Times of William Bingham, 1752–1804*. Boston: Houghton Mifflin, 1969.
Allgor, Catherine. *Parlour Politics: In Which the Ladies of Washington Help Build a City and a Government*. Charlottesville: University Press of Virginia, 2000.
Ammon, Harry. "The Formation of the Republican Party in Virginia, 1789–1796." *Journal of Southern History* 19 (August 1953): 283–310.
———. *The Genet Mission*. New York: Norton, 1973.
Andrew, Donna T. "The Code of Honour and Its Critics: The Opposition to Duelling in England, 1700–1850." *Social History* 5 (October 1980): 409–34.
Appleby, Joyce. *Inheriting the Revolution: The First Generation of Americans*. Cambridge: Harvard University Press, 2000.
Argersinger, Peter H. "Electoral Processes." In *Encyclopedia of American Political History*, gen. ed. Jack P. Greene. 3 vols. New York: Scribner's, 1984.
Atkinson, John A. *Duelling Pistols and Some of the Affairs They Settled*. Harrisburg, Pa., 1966.
Austin, Aleine. *Matthew Lyon: "New Man" of the Democratic Revolution, 1749–1822*. University Park: Pennsylvania State University Press, 1981.
Ayers, Edward L. *Vengeance and Justice: Crime and Punishment in the Nineteenth-Century American South*. New York: Oxford University Press, 1984.
Ayers, Edward L., Patricia Nelson Limerick, Stephen Nissenbaum, and Peter S. Onuf, eds. *All over the Map: Rethinking American Regions*. Baltimore: Johns Hopkins University Press, 1996.
Baker, Jean H. *Affairs of Party: The Political Culture of Northern Democrats in the Mid-Nineteenth Century*. Ithaca: Cornell University Press, 1983.

Bane, Steven Kirk. " 'A Group of Foreign Liars': Republican Propagandists and the Campaign Against the Federalists, 1789–1801." Ph.D. Diss., Texas A & M University, 1993.

Banning, Lance. *The Jeffersonian Persuasion*. Ithaca: Cornell University Press, 1978.

Beattie, John M. *The English Court in the Reign of George I*. Cambridge: Cambridge University Press, 1967.

Beeman, Richard R., Stephen Botein, and Edward C. Carter II, eds. *Beyond Confederation: Dimensions of the Constitution and American National Identity*. Chapel Hill: University of North Carolina Press, 1987.

Bemis, Samuel Flagg. *Pinckney's Treaty: America's Advantage from Europe's Distress, 1783–1800*. New Haven: Yale University Press, 1960.

Ben-Atar, Doron, and Barbara B. Oberg, eds. *Federalists Reconsidered*. Charlottesville: University Press of Virginia, 1998.

Berkeley, Edmund, and Dorothy Smith Berkeley. *John Beckley: Zealous Partisan in a Nation Divided*. Philadelphia: American Philosophical Society, 1973.

Bernstein, R. B. "A New Matrix for National Politics: The First Federal Elections, 1788–1790." In *Inventing Congress: Origins and Establishment of the First Federal Congress*, ed. Kenneth R. Bowling and Donald R. Kennon. Athens: Ohio University Press, 1999.

Bernstein, R. B., with Kym S. Rice. *Are We to Be a Nation? The Making of the Constitution*. Cambridge: Harvard University Press, 1987.

Bond, Donovan H., and W. Reynolds McLeod, eds. *Newsletters to Newspapers: Eighteenth-Century Journalism*. Morgantown: West Virginia University Press, 1977.

Bonomi, Patricia U. *The Lord Cornbury Scandal: The Politics of Reputation in British America*. Chapel Hill: University of North Carolina Press, 1998.

Borden, Morton. *The Federalism of James A. Bayard*. New York: Columbia University Press, 1954.

Bowling, Kenneth R. *Creating the Federal City: Potomac Fever*. Washington, D.C.: Octagon Research Series, 1988.

———. *The Creation of Washington, D.C.: The Idea and Location of the American Capital*. Fairfax, Va.: George Mason University Press, 1991.

———. "Dinner at Jefferson's: A Note on Jacob E. Cooke's 'The Compromise of 1790,'" *William and Mary Quarterly* 28 (October 1971): 629–48.

Branson, Susan. "Politics and Gender: The Political Consciousness of Philadelphia Women in the 1790s." Ph.D. diss., Northern Illinois University, 1992.

Breen, T. H. "Horses and Gentlemen: The Cultural Significance of Gambling Among the Gentry of Virginia," *William and Mary Quarterly* 34 (1977): 239–57.

Brown, Richard D. *Knowledge Is Power: The Diffusion of Information in Early America, 1700–1865*. New York: Oxford University Press, 1989.

———. *The Strength of a People: The Idea of an Informed Citizenry in America, 1640–1850*. Chapel Hill: University of North Carolina Press, 1996.

Brown, Walt. *John Adams and the American Press: Politics and Journalism at the Birth of the Republic*. Jefferson, N.C.: McFarland, 1995.

Bruce, Dickson D., Jr. *Violence and Culture in the Antebellum South*. Austin: University of Texas Press, 1979.

Buel, Richard, Jr. *Securing the Revolution: Ideology in American Politics, 1789–1815*. Ithaca: Cornell University Press, 1972.

Burke, Peter. *The Art of Conversation*. Ithaca: Cornell University Press, 1993.

Burnett, Edmund Cody. *The Continental Congress: A Definitive History of the Continental Congress from Its Inception in 1774 to March 1789*. New York: Norton, 1964.

Burstein, Andrew. *The Inner Jefferson: Portrait of a Grieving Optimist*. Charlottesville: University Press of Virginia, 1995.

Bushman, Richard L. *The Refinement of America: Persons, Houses, Cities*. New York: Vintage, 1993.

Caldwell, Lynton K. *The Administrative Theories of Hamilton and Jefferson: Their Contribution to Thought on Public Administration*. New York: Holmes and Meier, 1988.

Casper, Scott. *Constructing American Lives: Biography and Culture in Nineteenth-Century America*. Chapel Hill: University of North Carolina Press, 1999.

Cassell, Frank A. *Samuel Smith: Merchant Congressman in the Young Republic*. Madison: University of Wisconsin Press, 1971.

Chambers, Sarah C. *From Subjects to Citizens: Honor, Gender, and Politics in Arequipa, Peru, 1780–1854*. University Park: Pennsylvania State University Press, 1999.

Chambers, William Nisbet. *Political Parties in a New Nation: The American Experience, 1776–1809*. New York: Oxford University Press, 1963.

Charles, Joseph. "Adams and Jefferson: The Origins of the American Party System." *William and Mary Quarterly* 12 (July 1955): 410–46.

———. *The Origins of the American Party System*. New York: Harper and Row, 1961.

Christie, Ian R. *"Myth and Reality in Late-Eighteenth-Century British Politics" and Other Papers*. Berkeley: University of California Press, 1970.

Christman, Margaret C. S. *The First Federal Congress, 1789–1791*. Washington, D.C.: Smithsonian Institution Press, 1989.

Clarfield, Gerard H. *Timothy Pickering and the American Republic*. Pittsburgh: University of Pittsburgh Press, 1980.

Cmiel, Kenneth. *Democratic Eloquence: The Fight over Popular Speech in Nineteenth-Century America*. Berkeley: University of California Press, 1990.

Cochran, Hamilton. *Noted American Duels and Hostile Encounters*. Philadelphia: Chitton, 1963.

Cogan, Jacob K. "The Reynolds Affair and the Politics of Character," *Journal of the Early Republic* 16, no. 3 (Fall 1996): 389–417.

Cohen, Lester H. *The Revolutionary Histories: Contemporary Narratives of the American Revolution*. Ithaca: Cornell University Press, 1980.

Congressional Quarterly's Guide to U.S. Elections. Washington, D.C.: Congressional Quarterly, 1994.

Cooke, Jacob E. *Alexander Hamilton*. New York: Scribner's, 1982.

———. "Compromise of 1790," *William and Mary Quarterly* 27 (1970): 523–45.

———. *Tench Coxe and the Early Republic*. Chapel Hill: University of North Carolina Press, 1978.

Cooke, Jacob E., ed. *The Federalist*. Hanover, N.H.: Wesleyan University Press, 1961.

Cress, Lawrence Delbert. *Citizens in Arms: The Army and Militia in American Society to the War of 1812*. Chapel Hill: University of North Carolina Press, 1982.

Cunningham, Noble E., Jr. *The Jeffersonian Republicans: The Formation of Party Organization, 1789–1801*. Chapel Hill: University of North Carolina Press, 1957.

———. *The Jeffersonian Republicans in Power: Party Operations, 1801–1809*. Chapel Hill: University of North Carolina Press, 1963.

———. "John Beckley: An Early American Party Manager." *William and Mary Quarterly* 13 (1956): 40–52.

———. *The Process of Government Under Jefferson*. Princeton: Princeton University Press, 1978.

Dabney, Virginius. *Pistols and Pointed Pens: The Dueling Editors of Old Virginia*. Chapel Hill: University of North Carolina Press, 1987.

Dauer, Manning. *The Adams Federalists*. Baltimore: Johns Hopkins University Press, 1953.

Davidson, Philip. *Propaganda and the American Revolution*. Chapel Hill: University of North Carolina Press, 1941.

Decker, William Merrill. *Epistolary Practices: Letter Writing in America Before Telecommunications*. Chapel Hill: University of North Carolina Press, 1998.
Durey, Michael. *Transatlantic Radicals and the Early American Republic*. Lawrence: University Press of Kansas, 1997.
Elazar, Daniel J., and Ellis Katz, eds. *American Models of Revolutionary Leadership: George Washington and Other Founders*. Boston: University Press of America, 1992.
Elias, Norbert. *The Civilizing Process: The History of Manners and State Formation and Civilization*. Trans. Edmund Jephcott. 1939; Oxford: Basil Blackwell, 1994.
———. *The Court Society*. Trans. Edmund Jephcott. 1969; Oxford: Basil Blackwell, 1983.
Elkins, Stanley, and Eric McKitrick. *The Age of Federalism*. New York: Oxford University Press, 1993.
Ellet, Elizabeth F. L. *The Court Circles of the Republic*. 1869; New York: Arno, 1975.
Ellis, Joseph J. *Passionate Sage: The Character and Legacy of John Adams*. New York: Norton, 1993.
Ferguson, Robert A. *The American Enlightenment, 1750–1820*. Cambridge: Harvard University Press, 1997.
Ferling, John. *John Adams: A Life*. New York: Henry Holt, 1996.
Fischer, David Hackett. *Albion's Seed: British Folkways in America*. New York: Oxford University Press, 1989.
———. *The Revolution of American Conservatism: The Federalist Party in the Era of Jeffersonian Republicanism*. New York: Harper and Row, 1965.
Fliegelman, Jay. *Declaring Independence: Jefferson, Natural Language, and the Culture of Performance*. Stanford: Stanford University Press, 1993.
Foner, Philip S. *The Democratic-Republican Societies, 1790–1800: A Documentary Sourcebook of Constitutions, Declarations, Addresses, Resolutions, and Toasts*. Westport, Conn.: Greenwood, 1976.
Formisano, Ronald P. *The Birth of Mass Political Parties*. Princeton: Princeton University Press, 1971.
———. "Deferential-Participant Politics: The Early Republic's Political Culture, 1789–1840," *American Political Science Review* 68 (1974): 473–87.
———. "Federalists and Republicans: Parties, Yes—System, No." In *The Evolution of American Electoral Systems,* ed. Paul Kleppner et al. Westport, Conn.: Greenwood, 1981.
———. *The Transformation of Political Culture: Massachusetts Parties, 1790s–1840s*. New York: Oxford University Press, 1983.
Freeman, Douglas Southall. *George Washington: A Biography*. 7 vols. New York: Scribner's, 1948–57.
Freeman, Joanne B. "Aristocratic Murder and Democratic Fury: Honor and Violence in Early National New England." Paper delivered at the annual meeting of the American Historical Association, New York City, January 1997.
Frevert, Ute. "Bourgeois Honour: Middle-Class Duellists in Germany from the Late Eighteenth to the Early Twentieth Century." In *The German Bourgeoisie: Essays on the Social History of the German Middle Class from the Late Eighteenth to the Early Twentieth Century,* ed. David Blackbourn and Richard J. Evans. London: Routledge, 1991.
———. *Men of Honor: A Social and Cultural History of the Duel*. Trans. Anthony Williams. Cambridge: Polity, 1995.
Gearhart, Heber G. "The Life of William Maclay," *Proceedings of the Northumberland County Historical Society* 2 (May 1930): 46–73.
Gilpatrick, Delbert Harold. *Jeffersonian Democracy of North Carolina, 1789–1816*. New York: Columbia University Press, 1931.
Gluckman, Max. "Gossip and Scandal." *Current Anthropology* 4 (June 1963): 307–16.

Goodman, Dena. "The Hume-Rousseau Affair: From Private Querelle to Public Procès." *Eighteenth-Century Studies* 25 (1991–92): 171–201.

Goodman, Robert F., and Aaron Ben-Ze'ev. *Good Gossip*. Lawrence: University Press of Kansas, 1994.

Gordon, Daniel. " 'Public Opinion' and the Civilizing Process in France: The Example of Morellet." *Eighteenth-Century Studies* 22 (Spring 1989): 302–28.

Gorn, Elliott J. " 'Gouge and Bite, Pull Hair and Scratch': The Social Significance of Fighting in the Southern Backcountry." *American Historical Review* 90 (1985): 18–43.

Grasso, Christopher. *A Speaking Aristocracy: Transforming Public Discourse in Eighteenth-Century Connecticut*. Chapel Hill: University of North Carolina Press, 1999.

Greenberg, Kenneth S. *Honor and Slavery*. Princeton: Princeton University Press, 1996.

———. *Masters and Statesmen: The Political Culture of American Slavery*. Baltimore: Johns Hopkins University Press, 1985.

———. "The Nose, the Lie, and the Duel in the Antebellum South." *American Historical Review* 95 (1990): 57–74.

Greene, Evarts B. "The Code of Honor in Colonial and Revolutionary Times, with Special Reference to New England." *Publications of the Colonial Society of Massachusetts* 26 (1927): 367–88.

Griswold, Rufus Wilmot. *The Republican Court, or American Society in the Days of Washington*. 1867; New York: Haskell House, 1971.

Habermas, Jürgen. *The Structural Transformation of the Public Sphere: An Inquiry into a Category of Bourgeois Society*. Cambridge, Mass.: MIT Press, 1992.

Hamilton, Allan McLane. *The Intimate Life of Alexander Hamilton*. New York: Scribner's, 1911.

Hammond, Jabez D. *The History of Political Parties in the State of New-York, from the Ratification of the Federal Constitution to December 1840*. Albany: C. Van Benthuysen, 1842.

Harlow, Ralph V. *The History of Legislative Methods in the Period Before 1824*. New Haven: Yale University Press, 1917.

Hemphill, C. Dallett. *Bowing to Necessities: A History of Manners in America, 1620–1860*. New York: Oxford University Press, 1999.

Henry, William Wirt. *Patrick Henry: Life, Correspondence and Speeches*. 2 vols. 1891; Harrisonburg, Va.: Sprinkle, 1982.

Hofstadter, Richard. *The Idea of a Party System: The Rise of Legitimate Opposition in the United States, 1780–1840*. Berkeley: University of California Press, 1969.

Howe, John. "Republican Thought and the Political Violence of the 1790s." *American Quarterly* 19 (1967): 147–65.

Hunt, Lynn. "The French Revolution in Culture: New Approaches and Perspectives." *Eighteenth-Century Studies* 22 (Spring 1989): 293–301.

———. *Politics, Culture, and Class in the French Revolution*. Berkeley: University of California Press, 1984.

Hutson, James H. "John Adams' Title Campaign." *New England Quarterly* 41 (March 1968): 30–39.

Imbarrato, Susan Clair. *Declarations of Independency in Eighteenth-Century American Autobiography*. Knoxville: University of Tennessee Press, 1998.

John, Richard R. *Spreading the News: The American Postal System from Franklin to Morse*. Cambridge: Harvard University Press, 1995.

Kaminski, John P. *George Clinton: Yeoman Politician of the New Republic*. Madison, Wis.: Madison House, 1993.

Kammen, Michael. *A Season of Youth: The American Revolution and the Historical Imagination*. New York: Knopf, 1978.

Kann, Mark E. *A Republic of Men: The American Founders, Gendered Language, and Patriarchal Politics*. New York: New York University Press, 1998.
Kerber, Linda K. *Federalists in Dissent: Imagery and Ideology in Jeffersonian America*. Ithaca: Cornell University Press, 1980.
Ketcham, Ralph. *Presidents Above Party: The First American Presidency, 1789–1829*. Chapel Hill: University of North Carolina Press, 1984.
Kiernan, V. G. *The Duel in European History: Honour and the Reign of Aristocracy*. Oxford: Oxford University Press, 1986.
Kollman, Nancy Shields. *By Honor Bound: State and Society in Early Modern Russia*. Ithaca: Cornell University Press, 1999.
Kuroda, Tadahisa. *The Origins of the Twelfth Amendment: The Electoral College in the Early Republic, 1787–1804*. Westport, Conn.: Greenwood, 1994.
Kurtz, Stephen. *The Presidency of John Adams: The Collapse of Federalism, 1795–1800*. Philadelphia: University of Pennsylvania Press, 1957.
Lasswell, Harold D. "Feuds." In *Encyclopedia of the Social Sciences,* vol. 6. 15 vols. New York: Macmillan, 1930–34.
Lendon, J. E. *Empire of Honor: The Art of Government in the Roman World*. Oxford: Clarendon, 1997.
Levy, Leonard W. *Emergence of a Free Press*. New York: Oxford University Press, 1985.
———. *Jefferson and Civil Liberties: The Darker Side*. Chicago: Elephant, 1963.
Lewis, Jan. "'The Blessings of Domestic Society': Thomas Jefferson's Family and the Transformation of American Politics." In *Jeffersonian Legacies,* ed. Peter S. Onuf. Charlottesville: University Press of Virginia, 1993.
Link, Eugene Perry. *Democratic-Republican Societies, 1790–1800*. New York: Columbia University Press, 1942.
Lockridge, Kenneth A. "Colonial Self-Fashioning: Paradoxes and Pathologies in the Construction of Genteel Identity in Eighteenth-Century America." In *Through a Glass Darkly: Reflections of Personal Identity in Early America,* ed. Ronald Hoffman, Mechel Sobel, and Fredrika J. Teute. Chapel Hill: University of North Carolina Press, 1997.
Lomask, Milton. *Aaron Burr*. 2 vols. New York: Farrar, Straus and Giroux, 1979.
McAdams, Donald R. "Electioneering Techniques in Populous Constituencies 1784–96," *Studies in Burke and His Time* 14 (Fall 1972): 25–53.
McCormick, Richard P. *The Presidential Game: The Origins of American Presidential Politics*. New York: Oxford University Press, 1982.
McCoy, Drew. *The Last of the Fathers: James Madison and the Republican Legacy*. Cambridge: Cambridge University Press, 1989.
McDonald, Forrest. *Alexander Hamilton: A Biography*. New York: Norton, 1979.
———. *The Presidency of George Washington*. Lawrence: University Press of Kansas, 1974.
McGerr, Michael E. *The Decline of Popular Politics: The American North, 1865–1928*. New York: Oxford University Press, 1986.
McNamara, Peter, ed. *The Noblest Minds: Fame, Honor, and the American Founding*. Lanham, Md.: Rowman and Littlefield, 1999.
Malone, Dumas. *Jefferson and the Ordeal of Liberty*. Boston: Little, Brown, 1962.
———. *Jefferson and the Rights of Man*. Boston: Little, Brown, 1951.
———. *Jefferson the President, First Term, 1801–1805*. Boston: Little Brown, 1970.
———. *Jefferson the Virginian*. Boston: Little Brown, 1948.
———. *The Sage of Monticello*. Boston: Little, Brown, 1977.
Marsh, Philip M. "John Beckley: Mystery Man of the Early Jeffersonians." *Pennsylvania Magazine of History and Biography* 72 (1948): 54–69.

Martin, Raymond V., Jr. "Eminent Virginian—A Study of John Beckley." *West Virginia History* 11 (1949–50): 44–61.
Meleney, John C. *The Public Life of Aedanus Burke: Revolutionary Republican in Post-Revolutionary South Carolina*. Columbia: University of South Carolina Press, 1989.
Miller, John C. *Alexander Hamilton: Portrait in Paradox*. New York: Harper and Brothers, 1959.
———. *The Federalist Era*. New York: Harper and Brothers, 1960.
Minnick, Wayne C. "A Case Study in Persuasive Effect: Lyman Beecher on Duelling," *Speech Monographs* 38 (November 1971): 262–76.
Mitchell, Broadus. *Alexander Hamilton*. 2 vols. New York: Macmillan, 1962.
———. *Alexander Hamilton: A Concise Biography*. New York: Barnes and Noble Books, 1999.
Morgan, Edmund S. *Inventing the People: The Rise of Popular Sovereignty in England and America*. New York: Norton, 1998.
Mott, Frank L. *Jefferson and the Press*. Baton Rouge: Louisiana State University Press, 1943.
Morison, Samuel Eliot. *Harrison Gray Otis, 1765–1848: The Urbane Federalist*. Boston: Houghton Mifflin, 1969.
Morris, Richard B. *Seven Who Shaped Our Destiny*. New York: Harper, 1973.
Mushkat, Jerome. "Matthew Livingston Davis and the Political Legacy of Aaron Burr." *New-York Historical Society Quarterly* 59 (April 1975): 123–48.
Newman, Simon P. *Parades and the Politics of the Street: Festive Culture in the Early American Republic*. Philadelphia: University of Pennsylvania Press, 1997.
Nolan, Charles J., Jr. *Aaron Burr and the American Literary Imagination*. Westport, Conn.: Greenwood, 1980.
Nye, Robert A. *Masculinity and Male Codes of Honor in Modern France*. New York: Oxford University Press, 1993.
Onuf, Peter S. *Jefferson's Empire: The Language of American Nationhood*. Charlottesville: University Press of Virginia, 2000.
———. *Statehood and Union: A History of the Northwest Ordinance*. Bloomington: Indiana University Press, 1987.
Onuf, Peter S., ed. *Jeffersonian Legacies*. Charlottesville: University Press of Virginia, 1993.
Paine, Robert. "What Is Gossip About? An Alternative Hypothesis." *Man: The Journal of the Royal Anthropological Institute* 2 (June 1967): 265–78.
Paltsits, Victor Hugo. *Washington's Farewell Address*. 1935; New York: Arno, 1971.
Pancake, John S. *Samuel Smith and the Politics of Business, 1752–1839*. Tuscaloosa: University of Alabama Press, 1972.
———. *Thomas Jefferson and Alexander Hamilton*. Woodbury, N.Y.: Barron's Educational Series, 1974.
Pasler, Rudolph J., and Margaret C. Pasler. *The New Jersey Federalists*. Rutherford, N.J.: Fairleigh Dickinson University Press, 1975.
Pasley, Jeffrey L. "'Artful and Designing Men': Political Professionalism in the Early American Republic, 1775–1820." Ph.D. Diss., Harvard University, 1993.
———. "'A Journeyman, Either in Law or Politics': John Beckley and the Social Origins of Political Campaigning." *Journal of the Early Republic* 16 (Winter 1996): 531–69.
———. *"The Tyranny of Printers": Newspaper Politics in the Early Republic*. Charlottesville: University Press of Virginia, 2001.
Peabody, A. P., ed. *Life of William Plumer, by His Son, William Plumer, Junior*. Boston: Phillips, Sampson, 1856.
Peterson, Merrill. *The Jefferson Image in the American Mind*. Oxford: Oxford University Press, 1960.

Pitt-Rivers, Julian. "Honor." *International Encyclopedia of the Social Sciences,* 6:503–10. 18 vols. New York: Macmillan, 1968–79.

———. "Honour and Social Status." In *Honour and Shame: The Values of Mediterranean Society,* ed. J. G. Peristiany. London: Nicholson, 1966.

Pomerantz, Sidney I. *New York: An American City, 1783–1803: A Study of Urban Life*. New York: Columbia University Press, 1938.

Pospisil, Leopold. "Feud." *International Encyclopedia of the Social Sciences,* 5:389–91. 18 vols. New York: Macmillan, 1968–79.

Prince, Carl E. *The Federalists and the Origins of the U.S. Civil Service*. New York: New York University Press, 1977.

———. *New Jersey's Jeffersonian Republicans: The Genesis of an Early Party Machine, 1789–1817*. Chapel Hill: University of North Carolina Press, 1967.

Rakove, Jack, N. *The Beginnings of National Politics: An Interpretive History of the Continental Congress*. New York: Knopf, 1979.

Reddy, William M. *The Invisible Code: Honor and Sentiment in Postrevolutionary France, 1814–1848*. Berkeley: University of California Press, 1997.

Renzulli, L. Marx, Jr. *Maryland: The Federalist Years*. Rutherford, N.J.: Fairleigh Dickinson University Press, 1972.

Risjord, Norman K. "The Compromise of 1790: New Evidence on the Dinner Table Bargain," *William and Mary Quarterly* 33 (April 1976): 309–14.

Rogers, George C., Jr. *Evolution of a Federalist: William Loughton Smith of Charleston (1758–1812)*. Columbia: University of South Carolina Press, 1962.

Rorabaugh, W. J. "The Political Duel in the Early Republic: Burr v. Hamilton." *Journal of the Early Republic* 15 (1995): 1–23.

Rose, Lisle A. *Prologue to Democracy: The Federalists in the South, 1789–1800*. Lexington: University of Kentucky Press, 1968.

Rosenberg, Norman L. *Protecting the Best Men: An Interpretive History of the Law of Libel*. Chapel Hill: University of North Carolina Press, 1986.

Royster, Charles. *Light-Horse Harry Lee and the Legacy of the American Revolution*. Cambridge: Cambridge University Press, 1981.

———. *A Revolutionary People at War*. New York: Norton, 1981.

Rozbicki, Michael J. *The Complete Colonial Gentleman: Cultural Legitimacy in Plantation America*. Charlottesville: University Press of Virginia, 1998.

Sabine, Lorenzo. *Notes on Duels and Duelling, Alphabetically Arranged, with a Preliminary Historical Essay*. Boston: Crosby, Nichols, 1859.

Sabini, John, and Maury Silver. *Moralities of Everyday Life*. Oxford: Oxford University Press, 1982.

Schachner, Nathan. *Aaron Burr*. Rpt. New York: Perpetua, 1961.

Scherr, Arthur. "The 'Republican Experiment' and the Election of 1796 in Virginia." *West Virginia History* 37 (January 1976): 89–108.

Schlesinger, Arthur M., Jr. *History of American Presidential Elections, 1789–1968*. New York: Chelsea House, 1971.

Schlesinger, Joseph A. *Political Parties and the Winning of Office*. Ann Arbor: University of Michigan Press, 1991.

Scudder, H. F., ed. *Men and Manners in America One Hundred Years Ago*. N.Y.: Scribner's, 1887.

Seitz, Don C. *Famous American Duels*. New York: Crowell, 1929.

Shalhope, Robert E. "Republicanism and Early American Historiography." *William and Mary Quarterly* 39 (1982): 334–56.

———. "Toward a Republican Synthesis: The Emergence of an Understanding of Republicanism in American Historiography." *William and Mary Quarterly* 29 (1972): 49–80.

Shapin, Steven. *A Social History of Truth: Civility and Science in Seventeenth-Century England*. Chicago: University of Chicago Press, 1994.

Sharp, James Roger. *American Politics in the Early Republic: The New Nation in Crisis*. New Haven: Yale University Press, 1993.

Shaw, Peter. *The Character of John Adams*. New York: Norton, 1976.

Sheridan, Eugene. "Thomas Jefferson and the Giles Resolutions." *William and Mary Quarterly* (1992): 589–608.

Sherrill, Charles H. *French Memories of Eighteenth-Century America*. New York: Scribner's, 1915.

Shields, David. *Civil Tongues and Polite Tongues in British America*. Chapel Hill: University of North Carolina Press, 1997.

Shields, David S., and Fredrika J. Teute. "The Republican Court and the Historiography of a Women's Domain in the Public Sphere." Paper delivered at the annual meeting of the Society for Historians of the Early American Republic, Boston, Massachusetts, July 16, 1994.

Sisson, Daniel. *The American Revolution of 1800*. New York: Knopf, 1974.

Slonim, Shlomo. "The Electoral College at Philadelphia: The Evolution of an Ad Hoc Congress for the Selection of a President." *Journal of American History* 73 (June 1986): 35–58.

Smelser, Marshall. "The Federalist Period as an Age of Passion." *American Quarterly* 10 (1958): 391–419.

Smith, James Morton. *Freedom's Fetters: The Alien and Sedition Laws and Civil Liberties*. Ithaca: Cornell University Press, 1956.

Smith, Jay M. "No More Language Games: Words, Beliefs, and the Political Culture of Early Modern France," *American Historical Review* (December 1997): 1413–40.

Smith, Jeffery A. *Franklin and Bache: Envisioning the Enlightened Republic*. New York: Oxford University Press, 1990.

Smith, Mark A. "Crisis, Unity, and Partisanship: The Partisan Press and Political Culture in the Early Republic." Ph.D. Diss., University of Virginia, 1997.

Smith, Page. *John Adams*. 2 vols. Westport, Conn.: Greenwood, 1963.

Smith, T. V. "Honor." *Encyclopedia of the Social Sciences,* 7:456–58. 15 vols. New York: Macmillan, 1930–34.

Sowerby, Millicent, comp. *Catalogue of the Library of Thomas Jefferson*. Charlottesville: University Press of Virginia, 1983.

Spacks, Patricia Meyer. *Gossip*. New York: Knopf, 1985.

Spierenburg, Pieter, ed. *Men and Violence: Gender, Honor, and Rituals in Modern Europe and America*. Athens: Ohio State University Press, 1982.

Stamps, Norman L. "Political Parties in Connecticut, 1789–1819." Ph.D. Diss., Yale University, 1950.

Steinmetz, Andrew. *The Romance of Duelling in all Times and Countries*. 2 vols. 1868; Richmond, England: Richmond, 1971.

Stewart, Donald. *The Opposition Press of the Federalist Period*. Albany: State University of New York Press, 1969.

Stewart, Frank Henderson. *Honor*. Chicago: University of Chicago Press, 1994.

Stewart, Keith. "Towards Defining an Aesthetic for the Familiar Letter in Eighteenth-Century England." *Prose Studies* (September 1982): 179–92.

Stourzh, Gerald. *Alexander Hamilton and the Idea of Republican Government*. Stanford: Stanford University Press, 1970.

Stowe, Steven M. *Intimacy and Power in the Old South: Ritual in the Lives of the Planters*. Baltimore: Johns Hopkins University Press, 1987.
Sydnor, Charles S. *Gentleman Freeholders: Political Practices in Washington's Virginia*. Chapel Hill: University of North Carolina Press, 1952.
Tagg, James. *Benjamin Franklin Bache and the Philadelphia Aurora*. Philadelphia: University of Pennsylvania Press, 1991.
Taylor, Alan. "'The Art of Hook and Snivey': Political Culture in Upstate New York During the 1790s." *Journal of American History* 79 (1993): 1371–96.
———. *Liberty Men and Great Proprietors: The Revolutionary Settlement on the Maine Frontier, 1760–1820*. Chapel Hill: University of North Carolina Press, 1990.
———. *William Cooper's Town: Power and Persuasion on the Frontier of the Early American Republic*. New York: Knopf, 1995.
Thomas, Edmund B., Jr. "Politics in the Land of Steady Habits: Connecticut's First Political Party System, 1789–1820." Ph.D. Diss., Clark University, 1972.
Thompson, C. Bradley. *John Adams and the Spirit of Liberty*. Lawrence: University Press of Kansas, 1998.
Thornton, J. Mills III. *Politics and Power in a Slave Society: Alabama, 1800–1860*. Baton Rouge: Louisiana State University Press, 1978.
Tinkcom, Harry Maarlin. *The Republicans and Federalists in Pennsylvania, 1790–1801: A Study in National Stimulus and Local Response*. Harrisburg: Pennsylvania Historical and Museum Commission, 1950.
Travers, Len. *Celebrating the Fourth: Independence Day and the Rites of Nationalism in the Early Republic*. Amherst: University of Massachusetts Press, 1997.
Truman, Ben C. *Duelling in America*. Ed. Stephen Randolph Wood. N.d. [Nineteenth century]; San Diego, Calif.: Josiah Tabler Books, 1992.
Turner, Lynn W. *William Plumer of New Hampshire, 1759–1850*. Chapel Hill: University of North Carolina Press, 1962.
Waldstreicher, David. *In the Midst of Perpetual Fetes: The Making of American Nationalism, 1776–1820*. Chapel Hill: University of North Carolina Press, 1997.
Warner, Michael. *The Letters of the Republic: Publication and the Public Sphere in Eighteenth-Century America*. Cambridge: Harvard University Press, 1990.
Wharton, Anne Hollingsworth. *Martha Washington*. Scribner's, 1898.
———. *Salons Colonial and Republican*. Philadelphia: Lippincott, 1900.
———. *Social Life in the Early Republic*. Philadelphia: Lippincott, 1902.
———. *Through Colonial Doorways*. Philadelphia: Lippincott, 1893.
White, Leonard D. *The Federalists: A Study in Administrative History*. New York: Macmillan, 1948.
———. *The Jeffersonians: A Study in Administrative History, 1801–1829*. New York: Macmillan, 1951.
Whitman, James Q. "Enforcing Civility and Respect: Three Societies." *Yale Law Journal* 109 (April 2000): 1279–1398.
Wiebe, Robert H. *The Opening of American Society: From the Adoption of the Constitution to the Eve of Disunion*. New York: Knopf, 1984.
Williams, Wilson Carey. "Honor in Contemporary American Politics." Paper presented to John Olin Carter Conference on Democratic Honor, Chicago, May 20, 1999.
Wills, Garry. *Cincinnatus: George Washington and the Enlightenment*. New York: Doubleday, 1984.
Wilson, Douglas L. "Jefferson and the Republic of Letters." In *Jeffersonian Legacies*, ed. Peter S. Onuf. Charlottesville: University Press of Virginia, 1993.

———. "Jefferson versus Hume." *William and Mary Quarterly* 46 (1984): 49–70.

Wood, Gordon. "Conspiracy and the Paranoid Style: Causality and Deceit in the Eighteenth Century." *William and Mary Quarterly* 39 (July 1982): 401–41.

———. *The Radicalism of the American Revolution*. New York: Knopf, 1992.

———. "The Real Treason of Aaron Burr." *Proceedings of the American Philosophical Society* 143 (June 1999).

Wyatt-Brown, Bertram. "Andrew Jackson's Honor." *Journal of the Early Republic* 17 (Spring 1997): 1–36.

———. "Honour and American Republicanism: A Neglected Corollary." In *Ideology and the Historians,* ed. Ciaran Brady. Dublin: Lilliput, 1991.

———. *Southern Honor: Ethics and Behavior in the Old South*. New York: Oxford University Press, 1982.

Young, Alfred F. *The Democratic Republicans of New York: The Origins, 1763–1797*. Chapel Hill: University of North Carolina Press, 1967.

Young, James Sterling. *The Washington Community*. New York: Harcourt Brace Jovanovich, 1966.

Zagarri, Rosemarie. *A Woman's Dilemma: Mercy Otis Warren and the American Revolution*. Wheeling, Ill.: Harlan Davidson, 1995.

Ziff, Larzer. *Writing in the New Nation: Prose, Print, and Politics in the Early United States*. New Haven: Yale University Press, 1991.

Zvesper, John. *Political Philosophy and Rhetoric: A Study of the Origins of American Party Politics*. Cambridge: Cambridge University Press, 1977.

Index

Page numbers in *italics* indicate illustrations.